Camden After the Fall

POLITICS AND CULTURE IN MODERN AMERICA

Series Editors
Michael Kazin
Glenda Gilmore
Thomas J. Sugrue

A complete list of books in the series is available from the publisher.

Camden After the Fall

Decline and Renewal in a
Post-Industrial City

Howard Gillette, Jr.

PENN

University of Pennsylvania Press
Philadelphia

Publication of this book was assisted by a grant from the Ford Foundation

10   9   8   7   6   5   4   3   2   1

First paperback edition published 2006

Published by
University of Pennsylvania Press
Philadelphia, Pennsylvania 19104-4112

Library of Congress Cataloging-in-Publication Data

Gillette, Howard.
    Main Title: Camden after the fall : decline and renewal in a post-industrial city / Howard
Gillette, Jr.
        p.   cm. — (Politics and culture in Modern America)
    Includes bibliographical references and index.
    ISBN-10: 0-8122-1968-6 (pbk. : alk. paper)
    ISBN-13: 978-0-8122-1968-5 (pbk. : alk. paper)
    1. Urban renewal—New Jersey—Camden—History.   2. Camden (N.J.)—History.
3. Camden (N.J.)—Politics and government.   4. Camden (N.J.)—Economic conditions.
I. Title.   II.
F144.C2 G55   2005
974.9′87—dc22   2005047160

When it is dark enough, you can see the stars
—Posting, billboard of Hatch Middle School,
Camden, May 1998

For Margaret

Contents

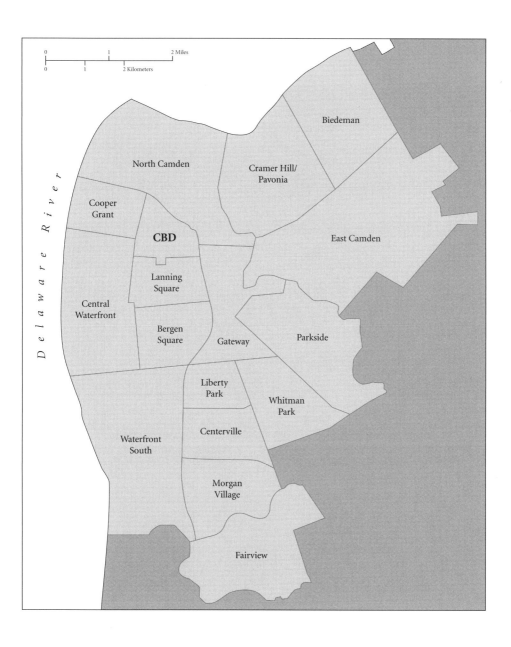

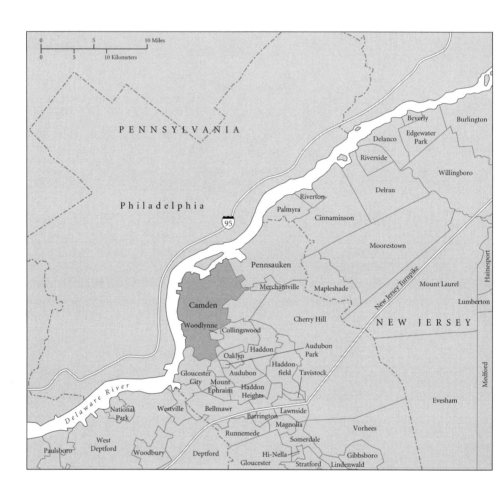

Preface

There is a scene in William Dean Howells's *Hazzard of New Fortunes* in which Mr. and Mrs. Basil March, new to New York City and intoxicated with its vitality even as they are frightened by its unknown qualities, take a ride on the newly constructed elevated line. As they are whisked high above the city, they become captivated by the scenes they view through the windows of the tenement buildings that crowd the tracks. "What suggestion! What drama! What infinite interest!" Howells writes to represent the Marches' reaction to these glimpses of working people who would otherwise remain invisible to their genteel lives. That excitement is tempered, however, by the realization of the costs the tracks had extracted from the streets below in order to make their guilty pleasures possible. "They kill the streets and the avenues," Basil March remarks, "but at least they partially hide them, and that is some comfort."[1]

A century later, generations of proper suburbanites can replicate daily the Marches' experience: seeing the city, glimpsing the energy lying behind its foreign nature, and yet still keeping their distance. In the area around Camden, New Jersey, commuters traveling between southern New Jersey's suburbs and Philadelphia on the PATCO Speedline may catch similar views of the urban scene. As they do, they literally look down on the losses of an entire generation. Amid the occasional towering church spire signaling the aspirations of an earlier era lie the debris of disinvestment: abandoned factories and buildings, empty lots piled with old tires or garbage, even overgrown cemeteries neglected and unattended. As trains approach the waterfront and passengers look south, quite another image appears: the lush green of a new baseball diamond, the regal dome of an aquarium, and beyond, a battleship docked to receive tourists anxious to relive past glories. But turning to the other side of the tracks, to North Camden, observers take in another view, more consistent with the city as a whole. There, the premier waterfront residence is reserved for prisoners of the state. Nearby streets retain all the marks of decline and decay.

A drive through Camden from the south offers a similar perspective.

As one travels the few miles on the I-676 Connector, it is hard to miss the spire of Saint Joseph's Polish church. The new towers of an incinerator, a cement plant, and a cogeneration factory dominate the skyline, however. Cars passing through won't be bothered by the smoke emitted from the stacks. Their drivers won't contemplate the homes displaced or the neighborhoods disrupted to make their commutes easier. Like the Marches, they may be stimulated by what they see, but they remain safely distant. What they know—or think they know—of this city assures them that it is best to keep that distance. Far more than the Marches, they have learned through repeated media accounts that the city is not just poor and badly run. It is a dangerous and inhospitable place marked by crime as well as corruption.

Like so many others, my first impression of Camden after living for some years in Washington, D.C., came from a distance. My interest was not captured fully until I responded to a challenge in the form of an advertisement promising the best wine in the Delaware Valley. The claim appeared in a circular irreverently titled "Corkscrewed," with the intriguing subhead, "No one finds us by accident." So it was that I gathered a group to visit Triangle Liquor at what had once been the heart of Camden's commercial sector, Broadway and Kaighn Avenue. There we found, in a cellar below the typical ghetto trade of cheap wines, pints, and big bottles of malt liquor, a stunning collection, as promised, of vintage wines at reasonable prices. Over time, as I returned, I got to know the owner, Stanley Brown. He had bought the property in the early 1980s on the presumption that Camden had no place to go but up. A decade and a half later, when I met him, he readily admitted his mistake. The streets outside confirmed his error. While a few old businesses survived from an earlier generation—Penn Fish across the street and Gold Star Shoe Repair down the street, both run by the college-educated relatives of the original owners—most everything that had once made the area a magnet for shopping and recreation had changed. A movie theater down the street—one of eighteen that had once operated in the city—was now a storefront church. In fact, no movie theaters remained in the city. Across the street was an abandoned building known for sales of crack cocaine. On the other side of Broadway, prostitutes openly traded their services, often for liquor or drugs if money was not available. Brown acknowledged that his business was good at the start of the month, when welfare checks were issued. The last days of the month, the main floor of the store could be pretty empty. Regardless, there were almost always men sitting on the stoop around the corner, drinking away their idle hours. They took pleasure one day when Stan's partner, John McNulty, called out my name as I headed back to my car to give me a revised bill. At this I was greeted with a not unfriendly chorus from the men on the stoop, "Have a good day, Howard."

In the seven years I worked on this book Camden had a number of good days. More than I even imagined when I launched my research, the city became the object of high level care and attention. In the first years of the project, the city was one of only a handful around the county to be named a beneficiary, in partnership with Philadelphia, of an urban empowerment grant. Major foundations took an interest in the city and committed significant funds, Annie E. Casey and Ford among them. Practically every year a new program was announced by state authorities, Republican as well as Democrat, promising funds to address Camden's ills. In 2002 the state finally authorized a $175 million recovery package that proved to be the start of the city's physical reconstruction. More of those who had simply passed through Camden for years began to venture into the city, some of them even to invest in businesses and to make the city their home. In a single month, as I was completing the manuscript, both local papers ran special sections on the city, one headlined "City Craves its Comeback," the other "Dramatic Era of Rebirth Energizes Hope-Filled City."[2] The same papers that for years had detailed the horrors of poverty, crime, and political dysfunction now struggled to find a dark lining in the silver cloud of recovery.

The story of urban decay and efforts to reverse it are, of course, much more complicated than daily observations would make them, whether registered over the long or the short term. Much of what shapes that struggle is virtually invisible: the structures that shape housing markets, determine the flow of public revenue, and even determine who might be empowered to make tough decisions about limited resources. Much too of what transpires is embedded in elusive historical circumstances, which dictated a reversal of fortunes to make once booming cities the outcasts of a new era. It does not help that such information is not retained, let alone valued. In Camden, the condition of public records, like much of the rest of the city's infrastructure, is extremely poor. There are no public deposits of any former mayor's papers. There are no public files of city departments. Records of public works are stashed in impossible environmental conditions in attic space above facility headquarters, without an index or any conscious effort to organize them. In 2001, Paul Schopp, then director of the Camden County Historical Society, and I attempted to review and assess back records of the Camden Housing Authority. What we found, in the sub-basement of a unit of the Westfield Acres housing complex, appalled us.

Although some older records had miraculously survived in file cabinets much as they had been arranged as many as fifty years earlier, many had been stolen or destroyed. Blueprints of the historic Westfield structure, by then scheduled to be demolished to make way for a HOPE VI reconstruction project, lay scattered on the floor, many damaged beyond repair as they soaked in pools of water traced with rat feces. From the moment I first came to City Hall, I found piles of department records sitting in hallways waiting to be destroyed. The records of City Council, meticulously maintained for the city by Rose Giuffre for some sixty years, are the only ones to detail official acts of government.

So it has been out of the weave of daily observations that I have necessarily drawn much of my own account of Camden's fall from power and productivity, from newspapers and from several hundred interviews. Any such approach carries risks, two of which I have attempted to balance. The first was suggested in a conversation I had with a parishioner between services at the historically black St. Bartholomew's Roman Catholic church in Camden early in my research. "You'll never be able to tell the real story of Camden," she asserted, "because you don't live here. You can't *feel* what it is like." Of course I bridled initially at such a suggestion, but she was perfectly right to recognize me as an outsider. I was a white suburban commuter like many others who worked in the city. I was not there as a participant-observer either, a time-honored approach in anthropology and sociology, however many meetings I attended, however many lives I attempted to follow. That being said, I had the equal challenge of *keeping enough distance* to remain objective. It was undeniably hard in this effort not to sympathize with the struggles so many people endured to make their city work. Moreover, that commitment undeniably extended beyond the point at which most people would have given up. That a number of people remained active and committed to reversing the city's fortunes over a quarter century and more could not help but be impressive. Such longevity, of course, helps to sustain a historical narrative, but it is also admirable in itself. So I can only ask my readers to bear with me as I navigate the shoals between sympathizing with the passion for justice that emerged in so many conversations with Camden natives and recounting the more academic story of the structural elements that compromised the city's many attempts at recovery.

Due to the availability of significant new public as well as private resources, Camden will be structurally reorganized in the near future. Physical decay will recede from the areas outsiders can see as they pass through.

For those who have borne the burden of decline for so long, the prospects are not so clear. My hope in writing this book is that their passions and commitment will be recognized and respected as a crucial and not just incidental element of the first and most prominently featured urban recovery effort of the twenty-first century. Their fortunes under such conditions will say much about the prospects for effectively addressing the needs of many other post-industrial cities and their beleaguered residents in the years to come.

Introduction

Few aspects of life are as important as the places where we live. To a considerable degree they determine the resources we have available to educate and socialize our children, to shelter our families and keep them secure, and to find employment within a reasonable distance from our homes. For the first half of the twentieth century America's largest industrial cities affirmed through their growth the reputation that they offered the richest share of those opportunities. Generations of immigrants flowed to these areas and formed attachments to them. Changes in the second half of the century radically altered the allocation of local amenities, however, and fully tested those attachments. The flight of human and monetary capital, from city to suburb and from the industrial Northeast and Middle West to the South and West, marked a considerable shift in fortunes. For those arriving too late to capitalize on urban material resources, most notably the African Americans who migrated to take advantage of new opportunities during and after World War II, the industrial city became a hollow prize. As decline set in, the legacy for those unable or unwilling to leave the city for new opportunities was deteriorating homes, shrinking employment opportunities, and inferior services.

To be sure, the nation did not accept such changes passively, at least not initially. In the early 1960s, private foundations as well as some government agencies began to grapple with the ill effects of rising urban unemployment and associated antisocial behavior, especially among juveniles who found it difficult to secure decent entry-level jobs. These early efforts laid the foundation for Lyndon Johnson's War on Poverty. As bold as this effort was in confronting urban poverty in particular, it had neither enough time nor enough money to achieve its lofty goals.[1] Instead, rising incidents of civil disorder brought to the fore a widely acknowledged "urban crisis." The body named to address its causes, the U.S. Commission on Civil Disorders (known as the Kerner Commission for its chair, Illinois Governor Otto Kerner) concluded starkly in its 1968 report, "The nation is moving towards two societies, one black, one white—separate and unequal. . . . Discrimination and segregation have long permeated much of American life; they now threaten the future of every American."[2]

A generation later, with the advent of a new century, no such crisis generates national attention. If the War on Poverty failed, as many supporters acknowledge, civil rights legislation passed in the aftermath of 1960s disorders, including measures designed to eliminate housing discrimination and open employment opportunities through affirmative action, appears to have improved the overall situation of African Americans. A growing number of critics have even begun to tout the recovery of America's most beleaguered cities.[3] Such optimistic pronouncements are difficult to sustain, however. The most comprehensive assessment of metropolitan social patterns, Douglas Massey and Nancy Denton's aptly titled 1993 study, *American Apartheid*, concludes every bit as pessimistically as the Kerner Commission, "No group in the history of the United States has ever experienced the sustained high level of residential segregation that has been imposed on blacks in large American cities for the past fifty years."[4] A decade later, as the nation reviewed the progress of desegregation that resulted from the landmark *Brown v. Board of Education* Supreme Court case, the assessment was equally bleak. "Racial segregation is still pervasive, and class segregation seems to be an accepted norm," writes Georgetown Law professor Sheryll Cashin. "Choosing a neighborhood that separates oneself and one's family from 'worse elements farther down the economic scale' has become the critical gateway to upward mobility."[5] A close look at even the most highly regarded "comeback cities"—Baltimore, Cleveland, and Chicago, for instance—reveals a striking unevenness in patterns of investment and opportunities for residents. While the number of cities succumbing to extreme fiscal distress was small in the new century—Pittsburgh and Buffalo being the most prominent—a host of once vital areas struggle even to approach a self-sustaining condition. Typically these were once important industrial centers of now highly suburbanized states: Detroit and Flint, Michigan; Gary, Indiana; Dayton, Youngstown, and Cleveland, Ohio; Holyoke, Lawrence, and Lowell, Massachusetts; Hartford, New Haven, and Bridgeport, Connecticut; Chicago and East St. Louis, Illinois; and Newark, Patterson, Trenton, and Camden, New Jersey, to name a few. In 1993 urban commentator and former mayor of Albuquerque David Rusk described these cities as "past the point of no return." For Rusk, the chief criteria for the ongoing urban crisis were sharp discrepancies between a city's wealth and that of its surrounding suburbs (the concentration of metropolitan poverty), loss of population, and disproportionately high percentages of African American and Hispanic residents. Rusk's subsequent evaluation, following the 2000 census, showed that only a few of these cities were materially improving their status.[6]

By any criteria, the persistent concentration of poor residents in older cities and suburbs, isolated from the opportunities that could improve their life chances, constitutes a major national problem, and yet the general public remains largely indifferent. This is no accident. Since the height of commitment to cities in the late 1960s, a host of politicians and social commentators have stirred a virulent backlash to the policy changes as well as to the turmoil stemming from the era. Even as the value of public assistance and minimum wages fell in real monetary terms over the following generation, thus depriving the working poor of any means of security, critics of 1960s liberalism launched an assault against its central premise, that the poor were deserving of government support. Ronald Reagan was only the most prominent of those who caricatured the "welfare queen" for her extravagant lifestyle at government expense.[7] The very term "underclass," as it came into use in the late 1970s and early 1980s, suggested a permanence to poverty that defied public intervention, at least in the form of additional funds. In adopting behavioral norms that ran counter to productive employment, the argument ran, poor people sealed their own fates and those of their offspring. By the mid-1990s, sociologist Norman Fainstein could report, "For whites, the physical ghettoization of nearly all blacks, along with the media focus on the 'worst' black neighborhoods and the most socially deviant elements in them has reinforced a stereotyped image of black people. By blurring or eliminating class differences among blacks, and by equating blacks with criminals and welfare mothers, whites are freed from guilt or even sympathy."[8] Pointing to the ability of their own ancestors to cope with the vicissitudes of the marketplace, the descendants of earlier migrants to the city looked critically at those who relied on modern welfare provisions to sustain themselves.[9] The Manhattan Institute's Fred Siegel added a late embellishment to this theme by arguing in his 1998 book that black politicians in particular assured the maintenance of the status quo by encouraging policies that fostered dependency among constituents, even as they milked the public till in the process.[10]Bolstered by such negative commentary, first federal and then state governments backed away from expenditures directly related to rebalancing the unequal resources flowing to cities and their older suburbs. Across the board, programs for assistance to the poor—for housing, for employment training, and for education—were sharply reduced or eliminated. The radical shift in federal welfare policy institutionalized in 1996 represented the culmination of this campaign, though efforts continue to scale back or eliminate other associated programs, most notably affirmative action and certain housing subsidies.

Advocates for the poor have scored some successes over the past quarter century. The federal Community Reinvestment Act, adopted in 1977, directed banks, which had for a generation refused loans to applicants in declining urban areas, to reserve a portion of their funds specifically for those areas. Congressional supporters of the effort won enough votes to beat back an effort to block reauthorization of the program in the last years of the Clinton administration.[11] Courts, which played such a critical role in overturning discriminatory laws in the era of the civil rights movement, provided further victories in challenging more subtle discriminatory effects: of zoning on home prices, of funding formulas on public education, and of environmentally detrimental decisions that affected poor communities disproportionately. Such efforts had their limits, however, as political bodies at all levels found ways to sidestep or blunt the effect of decisions that did not find favor with the majority of their constituents. For all the "progress" the nation made in the last half of the twentieth century in addressing the big domestic issues of the era—most notably racism and publicly sanctioned poverty—those issues had not disappeared in the early twenty-first century. Rather, they were minimized as problems that should concern political majorities. Again, this was no accident.

As Thomas Sugrue, among others, has demonstrated so pointedly, the New Deal ties forged between disparate constituencies around entitlements to decent wages and a secure home came unraveled in the postwar years.[12] Not only did the number of well-paying union jobs decline as industries migrated away from older urban areas, housing support to those in greatest need declined too, even as subsidies increased for those who already had significant resources to buy homes in preferred locations. Both policy elements assumed stark spatial dimensions. As jobs decentralized and as federally financed loans underwrote the rapid growth of the suburbs, what publicly assisted housing was available was directed at older cities, causing both controversy and, eventually, inadequate housing options for the African Americans and other minority populations whose mobility remained strictly limited by racial or economic discrimination.

By the time Congress instituted open housing legislation in 1968 and court decisions such as the *Mount Laurel* cases described in Chapter 7 in this book overturned exclusionary zoning, suburban areas had already assumed their own special sense of entitlement. Despite the promise that all

Americans could become full participants in a post-World War II "consumer republic," as Lizabeth Cohen coined the term, the distribution of benefits in a robust market economy was extremely uneven.[13] For those who made it to the suburbs, housing value came to be considered the key to security, and any changes that threatened to undercut that investment had to be resisted, including economic and racial diversity, environmental nuisances, or additional strains on social services that might raise property taxes. As Yale law professor Peter Schuck puts it, "Housing is among Americans' most important sources of enjoyment, security, and emotional well-being. . . . Once a home is acquired, real or perceived threats to its value can create genuine financial and psychological risks to the family that owns it."[14] Such communities of privilege—dubbed "metamarkets" by Rutgers-Newark law professor David Dante Troutt—relied on land use law and public finance to set themselves apart from undesirable inner city areas—what he calls "antimarkets." The notion that this could be due to chance, or even the result of global economic factors beyond any group's control, Troutt asserts, is untenable. "African American ghetto poverty remains the quintessential form of inner-city or 'underclass' poverty," he writes, "because exclusion of, and discrimination against, African Americans have been the most essential means to sustaining middle-class metamarkets."[15]

Such scholarship begins to undermine significantly the contemporary popular impulse to blame the urban poor for their own problems. Politically sustained social and economic structures, not individual or group character, have the greatest impact in shaping the kind of antisocial behavior critics associate with urban ghettoes. After reviewing the "tangle of pathology" brought on by deviant behavioral norms believed to be sustaining such inner city areas, Paul Jargowsky concludes in his definitive study, *Poverty and Place*, "the pathologies are a symptom of the problem, not its cause." The root causes of concentrated poverty in older inner city areas, he asserts, "are the changing opportunity structure faced by the minority community and, to a lesser degree, the changing spatial organization of the metropolis." Neighborhood poverty, he adds, rises and falls in response to local labor market conditions. "Although such a conclusion seems obvious, it challenges the popular view that ghettos and barrios are the product of the personal failings of the people who live in them."[16] Massey and Denton agree with his assessment, arguing that

residential segregation has been instrumental in creating a structural niche within which a deleterious set of attitudes and behaviors—a culture of segregation—has arisen and flourished. Segregation created the structural conditions for the emergence of an oppositional culture that devalues work, schooling, and marriage and that stresses attitudes and behaviors that are antithetical and often hostile to success in the larger economy. . . . Residential segregation is the institutional apparatus that supports other racially discriminatory processes and binds them together into a coherent and uniquely effective system of racial subordination. Until the black ghetto is dismantled as a basic institution of American urban life, progress ameliorating racial inequality in other arenas will be slow, fitful, and incomplete.[17]

Politicians and the general public may blame inner city problems on bad individual choices and a lack of money. According to the University of Minnesota's Myron Orfield, however, research shows "that the concentration of poverty destroys the lives of children in poor schools by depriving them of opportunity, intensifies health risks and crime, and destroys the urban fabric and the fiscal base of cities."[18] To be sure, the process of concentrating poverty has not been neat or uniform. Over the past two decades the migration of African Americans from city to suburbs has accelerated. By 2000 that number reached 12 million people, more than one third of the nation's black population. Such diversity as has resulted, however, has failed to reverse the spatial segregation that has lain at the heart of metropolitan change over the past half century.[19]

Jargowsky and Orfield write in the spirit of what has become identified as the "new regionalism."[20] These critics argue that metropolitan regions are the most important economic units in the new global economy, and that the health of the region's interdependent parts largely determines the economic success of the whole area. The corrosive effects of inner city poverty dampen regional performance. Conversely, reductions in concentrated poverty boost overall performance, benefitting suburbanites as well as city dwellers.[21] Such conclusions call for new approaches to addressing poverty, most notably approaches which connect efforts aimed at improving inner city physical and social conditions to the larger metropolitan opportunity structure. In the volume *Regions That Work*, Manuel Pastor and three colleagues describe this connection as linking efforts to forge strong bonds within particular neighborhoods to a bridging strategy "that can connect the poor and their advocates to new sources of employment and arenas of decision-making." Citing Joan Walsh's book, *Stories of Renewal*, they report that

Community builders know inner city neighborhoods cannot rebuild themselves alone, when race and class discrimination and decades of disinvestment have done so much to fray the social fabric of urban communities. Thus these initiatives seek to build relationships between the poor and the powerful, to develop a sense of mutual obligation and reciprocity, a new social contract that keeps the urban poor from simply being discards of a volatile, changing economy.[22]

Such an approach, Pastor and his colleagues argue, should not just embrace efficiency and a better environment, through combating suburban sprawl, for instance. It should also strive for greater social equity through regional cooperation to deconcentrate poverty, promote a broader tax base, and provide for more equitable distribution of resources for schools and other services. To illustrate their argument, they provide examples of high performing metropolitan areas: greater Boston; San Jose, California; and Charlotte, North Carolina. Although each area exploited different strengths in outperforming competitors, each built upon the three central goals of a successful regional approach. "We cannot go back and rewrite a past characterized by metropolitan sprawl, environmental indifference, and widening economic and racial disparities," they conclude. "But we can adopt a new approach that creatively links regional and community development."[23]

As promising as the new regionalist approach might appear, its work to date suffers two problems. First, it underestimates the difficulty of overcoming past patterns, whether the result of conscious policy or the cumulative effect of individual and group decisions. As widespread as the concept of "smart growth" has become, instituting its goal of redirecting resources and, ultimately, population flows back to older cities and suburbs is a difficult task as long as open land continues to appeal so strongly to so many individuals. Moreover, evidence supporting the complementary approach of deconcentrating the poor by increasing opportunities for them to live in the suburbs is mixed. While a review of the Department of Housing and Urban Development's move-to-opportunity program reports statistically significant improvements for children in educational performance and mental and physical well-being for adults, expected improvements in family income have been less pronounced.[24]

By their own accounts at this point, the new regionalists remain chiefly publicists for a good cause. They have yet to affect urban policy at the federal level. Ultimately, they recognize that their case depends on the political process, and here they reveal a second and related weakness: few examples stand to advance their case fully. As representatives of places that remain highly fragmented by jurisdiction as well as by race and income, politicians rarely pursue metropolitanwide strategies, despite the presumed benefits re-gionalists claim might follow. Even Al Gore, who indicated early in his 2000 presidential campaign that he would be a strong advocate for metropolitan solutions to the nation's most pressing domestic issues, sacrificed that em-phasis to stress less divisive and more easily understood issues.[25]

The one regionalist who has managed to implement his ideas is Myron Orfield, former Minnesota state senator and author of several landmark ini-tiatives to advance regional equity through alliances between older cities and their nearby older suburbs. Through two books, a national consulting firm, and, most recently, a faculty position at the University of Minnesota, Orfield has been the chief publicist of the growing diversity of American's suburbs and the alliances they could and should be making, as their indices of poverty and racial diversity increase, with inner cities. In the Minnesota legislature he forged alliances between cities and what he called inner ring suburbs to secure regional tax sharing, which discouraged continued growth at the periphery and redirected revenues back to areas with the greatest social needs.[26] As he extended his argument nationally as a consul-tant, Orfield developed a sophisticated methodology to show converging points of policy agreement between core cities, at-risk suburbs, and even affluent bedroom-developing communities. Urging what he calls a new "metropolitics," he argues that all metropolitan communities benefit from policies that embrace tax equity, comprehensive land-use planning, and shared metropolitan governance.[27] An independent assessment of the effort to deconcentrate poverty in the Twin Cities, argues, however, that even Or-field has had difficulty achieving his goals. A Liveable Communities Act passed in 1995 as a compromise to Orfield's more aggressive affordable housing strategy, actually reduced the number of low-income units re-quired of each community.[28]

Camden, New Jersey, might seem to be the last place to test the philos-ophy of the new regionalists. Listed as one of David Rusk's twenty-four "cities past the point of no return," Camden could legitimately be described as one the toughest challenges to urban revitalization in the country. With an overall poverty rate of 44 percent in 1995—the highest rate in the coun-try—the lowest wealth index in relation to its suburbs, and a concentration of nonwhite residents at close to 90 percent, the city stood sharply apart from surrounding jurisdictions.[29] Through a congruence of factors, how-ever, Camden emerged as a primary target for reconstitution at the turn of the new century. Its reputation for extreme poverty drew its own audience, including Rusk, who keynoted a 1999 summit on the future of the South

Jersey region. Addressing a large audience in Camden, Rusk argued for a number of measures to advance Camden's revitalization as part of a regional strategy, including an affordable housing policy that would help deconcentrate Camden's extremely high level of poverty.[30] A subsequent conference, like the first sponsored as part of a commitment to community-oriented journalism by the South Jersey newspaper, the *Courier-Post*, focused on the other side of regional imbalance, suburban sprawl. Held in adjacent Gloucester County's most rapidly growing community, the conference featured former Camden mayor Randy Primas, who, like Rusk, pressed a regional approach that could simultaneously deal with overheated suburban growth and continued inner city decline.[31] Three years later Primas found himself the state-appointed chief operating officer of Camden, backed by unprecedented political as well as economic resources. The Ford Foundation, with the strong encouragement of Orfield, joined the effort to reconstitute Camden by backing a series of activities intended to promote Camden's recovery as part of a larger campaign to achieve regional equity.

This book is not an effort to evaluate that effort. It is too early to judge end results fully. Rather, by putting the contemporary challenge to Camden's revitalization in historical perspective, I intend to illuminate both the depths from which the city—and cities like it—must recover and the hurdles, political as well as social, to making revitalization a process that will address issues of concentrated poverty with the same vigor with which it seeks to enhance municipal revenues. For it is not too early in Camden's recovery process to show that recent history has sharply narrowed the policy options likely to be used in instituting changes that advance social equity as well as efficiency and improved municipal revenues. It did not take long to reveal, for instance, that tax breaks for corporations were easier to come by than similar measures for residents, or that upgrading whole neighborhoods for newcomers took precedence over improving the options of people already living in the city. This was no simple repeat of the unhappy experience of the urban renewal efforts of the 1960s that caused lasting controversy and division. Yet such lessons as had been derived from earlier experience were hard to live by because the political landscape had changed to further isolate the poor and their advocates. As one of the more influential participants in Camden's recovery, The Reinvestment Fund's Jeremy Nowak put it in a rather dispirited tone, "We have to pursue recovery within the options open to us, don't we?"[32] And those options, at a time when the public sector had been weakened in any effort to form partnerships with private interests and in which suburban privilege remained entrenched, limited the reach of "recovery" from the start. Neither commitments to neighborhood needs nor those to regional solutions to concentrated poverty assured a fair result. Rather, recovery came to mean, as it has elsewhere in the county, an investment in physical structures over a commitment to people in need. Reversing that pattern, institutionalized over a half century of accumulated disinvestment and urban decline, remains a primary challenge to the next generation of policymakers.

In examining the consequences of spatial patterns of social inequity, I build on the emerging work of a group of largely younger historians who have helped illuminate the nature of modern metropolitan transformation in the United States. Thomas Sugrue set the stage for this tremendously important reassessment of recent urban history in his landmark book, *The Origins of the Urban Crisis: Race and Inequality in Postwar Detroit.*[33] Sugrue demonstrated that Detroit's precipitous decline derived as much from the reactions, heightened by deep-seated social and racial prejudice, of individuals and groups to declining resources as from the disinvestment process unleashed by footloose automobile manufacturers. Human actions, conditioned but not entirely determined by economic changes, brought a great city virtually to its knees. Sugrue's study offered a powerful rebuttal to contemporary critics who blame the victims of poverty for their own misfortune. Wendell Pritchett's subsequent examination of the Brownsville section of Brooklyn further explored the changing sociospatial relationships of different generations of largely poor people—immigrants as well as African Americans—within a larger city's shifting structures of opportunity.[34] Robert Self's *Babylon Revisited* examined what he calls the "spatial dynamics of industrial restructuring." In extraordinary and powerfully focused detail, Self revealed the ways in which white privilege first contested emergent black empowerment efforts in Oakland, then institutionalized its power in greater San Francisco's East Bay area.[35] His searing indictment of regional inequity in the post-industrial era provides a sharp edge to Lizabeth Cohen's equally critical assessment of the unequal rewards derived from the promise of a consumer's republic.

Whether pursued through the case study or a wider lens, as in Cohen's book, historical examinations of the shifting fortunes in metropolitan areas tend not to include contemporary practice. Similarly, modern assessments lack much in the way of historical perspective. It may be that "poster cities" for decline (like Detroit, Cleveland, Oakland, or even Newark and Gary) are too large, their stories of decline and attempted rebirth too complex to tell in a single volume. I have tried to illuminate contemporary practice through an historical account. No doubt the decision to choose a smaller, less visible city in order to encompass both past and present carries risks. Any case study raises issues of representativeness. But I would argue that Camden's modern history offers full value as the locus for evaluating trends both in their particularity and in general.

Camden has been, in the first count, the source of landmark "fair share housing" and environmental justice litigation that carries implications well beyond the city and state. It was the recipient of one of the largest per capita public housing investments in the country in the 1930s and 1940s, a major urban renewal program in the 1960s, an Empowerment Zone in the 1990s, and extensive foundation as well as public support for community development corporations. Every urban policy initiative of the past fifty years has been tried and tested in Camden. More broadly, Camden's changing function in its metropolitan area has been very much like that of every city forced to undergo the transition to a post-industrial economy. It was once one of the most productive industrial centers in the nation, its neighborhoods perfect examples of the classic ethnic villages so much written about by sociologists. Camden's loss of status to its adjacent suburbs represents an equally classic example of the consequences of social as well as economic restructuring. At the same time, as a city of only some 80,000, Camden offers the special advantage of not being so large as to escape comprehension or thorough examination. Nearly universally impoverished, it offers a case study of how an entire political unit, not just some of its constituent elements, operates within a climate of crushing austerity, thus bringing to the fore the central role of public power in dealing with urban poverty. At the same time its strategic location directly between a similarly beleaguered big city, Philadelphia, and a largely prosperous suburban hinterland raises tough questions about the future of regional solutions to localized poverty. In short, while Camden offers a small stage, all the major issues associated with the descent of the classic blue-collar city appear on it in recognizable form and in comprehensible fashion.

Camden's recent history is animated by the stories of some extraordinary individuals. Stirred from a sleazy life of shooting pool and running numbers, Charles "Poppy" Sharp transformed his life and that of many of his followers by forming the Black People's Unity Movement and pushing for fundamental changes in how African Americans were treated by both the public and private sectors. Peter O'Connor, who during the tumultuous 1960s used to talk strategy with Sharp while shooting baskets, carried his campaign against discrimination to the courts well after it was fashionable to do so. Tom Knoche gave up a career as a professional planner in Baltimore to live, work, and organize in North Camden's tough streets. Described twenty years after his arrival in Camden in the early 1980s as too rigid in his ideology, it could just as well be said that he was consistent in his principles. At a time when critics bemoaned the decline in civic engagement, followers of Camden's struggle for sustainability had to be impressed with the host of residents—many of them elderly—who gave their time to form block patrols, to challenge drug dealers on their streets, and to join a host of organizations aimed at improving some aspect of the city. Just one of many dedicated people was Elmer Winston. Following his retirement from a career as a television salesman and later a high school instructor of electronic technology, he headed the citywide Camden Neighborhood Renaissance organization, devoted to reducing crime in the city, and served as an elected member of the Camden Board of Education. He also played an active role in his own neighborhood's revitalization effort. Yolanda Aguilar DeNeely, after cochairing another critical citywide residents' organization, Camden Churches Organized for People, assumed responsibility for activating a community development corporation near her church even though she had lost her job and faced the loss of her home. Exceptional as these people, among others, in Camden are, I suspect they have their counterparts in other cities living with the legacy of disinvestment.

More broadly, Camden's story can be considered central to the three major elements in the recent history of the economy of older American cities: how working-class residents were sustained while industry flourished; how African Americans and Hispanics secured political power, even as they witnessed the loss of economic resources; and how different place-based strategies have attempted to overcome the effects of disinvestment. The first topic, which I refer to as Old Camden, is taken up in Chapter 1. While I in no way suggest that the opportunities open to African Americans or Hispanics were equal to those of whites, I detail a number of significant parallels across communities that suggest that every ethnic group with roots in Camden has a common usable past upon which to draw and build.[36] Chapter 2 details how the older way of life was completely overturned in an approximately thirty-year period between 1950 and 1980. It is in this period that the patterns of social pathology so often criticized in the popular press emerged as real elements of everyday life. But as Jargowsky and other academics have suggested, such actions followed from unprecedented shifts in the way opportunities were restructured and poverty was contained within the city. If such behavior remained confined to a relatively small element in the "New Camden," it was nonetheless the fate of a predominantly black, Hispanic, and poor clientele to deal with the residual effects of precipitous economic decline. These chapters set the stage for Camden's primary story here, "after the fall." In Chapters 3 and 4 I detail the associated shift in power that accompanied the flight of human and monetary resources out of the city. Localized as these arrangements were, they owed much to changing national policies, away from commitments to eliminating urban poverty, as well as to the rise in suburban influence over cities.

Despite their disproportionate share of hardships, Camden residents and policymakers did not accept their fate passively. Their actions in downtown waterfront development, as well as neighborhood redevelopment, were impressive by any standard, forming the potential basis for lifting the city onto the list of other "comeback" cities. Moreover, public interest lawyers, building on an impressive history of civil rights litigation, advanced the cause of equal justice in dealing both with environmental and housing discrimination. As Chapters 5 through 7 demonstrate, however, none of these approaches were sufficient in themselves to reverse Camden's continuing decline. The cumulative weight of human and monetary losses to the city were simply too great to allow recovery, whatever new programs or policies were instituted. It is in Chapters 8 and 9 that the possibilities for a more comprehensive approach emerge. Though a highly contested process, the state of New Jersey finally approved in 2002 a $175 million stimulus package for Camden with associated legislation that offered some hope of making Camden's recovery part of a regional success story. New Jersey's bold actions attracted new interest from the philanthropic as well as the private sector. From the interaction of engaged parties emerged a new contest to control the vision for Camden's future, thus providing a window into American urban policy, with all its complexities and contradictions, in the early twenty-first century. This most recent chapter in the city's history does not so much suggest how far government has come in addressing the effects of disinvestment as it confirms how far the nation has yet to go to overcome the legacy of remaining two societies, one poor, one wealthy, separate and unequal. Camden and the great majority of its citizens remain, after the fall, strivers for that illusive urban renewal that invests as much in human lives as it does in monetary return.

PART I

Shifting Fortunes

Chapter 1
A City That Worked

Chief among the reasons why Camden is a desirable and prosperous place of residence, may be mentioned the fact that its people govern it. They have not surrendered their own sovereignty to an unscrupulous, corrupt ring of professional politicians. . . . The old-fashioned notion that a "public office is a public trust" is still adhered to and practiced in Camden with the result that capital and new residents are attracted instead of being repelled. . . . It has no slum sections in which human beings are packed like sardines in a box, as they are in some portions of the city across the river, nor need it ever have, if the city continues to be as wisely and liberally governed as at present.

—*Camden Chamber of Commerce*, Camden, New Jersey: The City's Rise and Growth

Ask a former Camden resident, one who has been out of the city for years, what the city was once like, and the answer is always the same: it was a wonderful place to live and work. When the same people are asked about its present state, Camden is described only in negative terms. The foundations that once made the city one of the most economically productive in the nation came unraveled in the life of a single generation. Collective memory of that experience has coalesced into the judgment that "old Camden" is dead. Neither its once diverse economic nor its rich social opportunities remain. Such sharply etched distinctions between the city's past and present make that conclusion appear special to the place. In fact, the experience is common to many cities that have undergone post-industrial transformations. In Camden, as in Alan Ehrenhalt's "Lost City" of Chicago, old neighborhood-based urban communities appear to have broken down, victims as much to changing social mores as to the shift in fortunes.[1] No doubt a strong element of nostalgia drives the articulation of widespread regrets about these places, yet objective evidence suggests they once served the vital function of providing two ingredients essential for surviving the vicissitudes of the marketplace: work and social assistance. Such sites offered access to both monetary and social capital, what Robert Putnam describes as networks of civic engagement and norms of trust and reciprocity.[2] Camden's rich history before World War II demonstrated the accumulation of both elements.

The Camden Chamber of Commerce's 1904 claims touch on these elements. Yet they are neither an accurate snapshot of the contemporary city nor simply another example of urban boosterism. Within the Chamber's pious homilies lies the central assumption of every aspiring twentieth-century city: that success is measured by growth, that growth requires adequate opportunities for work and decent places to live, along with proper governance. If there is a fault here, it may be in the overemphasis on the formal aspects of government. For the many who aspired to employ the urban opportunity structure, informal networks of power were as important as those vested in elected offices.[3] Either way, even with all its limitations, old Camden was a city that worked.

*   *   *

Camden originally developed largely as an extension of Philadelphia, which during the colonial period was the leading city on the North American continent. Camden's incorporation in 1828 did not remove it from the larger city's sphere; Philadelphians across the Delaware River continued to exercise influence by using Camden to pursue their own business or personal interests. The city began to acquire standing on its own in 1834, when the Camden and Amboy Railroad, then the longest line in the country, made Camden its terminus. In testimony to its growing importance, the town became the county seat in 1844. Although it remained very much in Philadelphia's shadow through the Civil War Era, with peace Camden attracted both the immigrant work force and the capital to establish its own industrial base. It was home to plants that produced carriages, woolen goods, and lumber, and to Richard Esterbrook's steel pen company. In 1891 the modest canning business Joseph Campbell had started in 1869 incorporated as Campbell Soup. Eight years later the New York Ship Company opened yards, which soon employed as many as 5,000 workers. In 1901 Eldridge Johnson, who had begun work on a "talking machine" two years earlier, formed the Victor Talking Machine Company. Other smaller but important manufacturing firms joined these three emerging giants to produce everything from fountain pens to cigars. By 1909 Camden's board of trade could

Figure 1. Opening day on what came to be known as the Benjamin Franklin Bridge, July 4, 1926. Courtesy Camden County Historical Society.

assert that "the city has within these ten bright and busy years thrown off the shackles inspired by a fear of being so near to a metropolitan city." A 1917 report listed 365 industries employing 51,000 people.[4]

By 1920 Camden's population exceeded 100,000 for the first time, ranking the city fifty-eighth nationally, just behind New Bedford, Trenton, and Nashville and ahead of Lowell, Wilmington, and Fort Worth.[5] On July 4, 1926, the city proclaimed a new standing for itself with the opening of an imposing new bridge connecting it to Philadelphia. The largest single span suspension bridge in the world at the time, the new $40 million structure, which would be named after Benjamin Franklin in 1954, extended two miles in length and rose 385 feet above the high tide mark. More than a simple convenience in supplementing ferry traffic between the two cities, the bridge, supporters claimed, would determine an even brighter future for Camden. Anticipating the opening two years hence, the Chamber of Commerce journal *Camden First* proclaimed on its cover, "Camden is a growing metropolitan city. No longer a satellite city, she stands on her own feet, her eyes to the stars. She sees great development ahead, she is all but ready." An advertisement in the same journal saw Camden as a "second Brooklyn," and the Van Sciver furniture store, located on the Camden waterfront, called the new structure a "Bridge of Confidence across which tens of thousands of customers have come to buy in ever increasing numbers from Pennsylvania and adjoining states." William Leonard Hurley, head of a Camden department store and an original supporter of the bridge, asked rhetorically, "how many of us, in the light of our experience as a city within the past few days, ever realized the fact that the actual opening of the bridge has made of Camden a metropolis over night?"[6] Although many would subsequently blame the bridge's approach for hurting Camden by dividing northern from southern neighborhoods, Camden natives still continue to recount proudly how family members took the opportunity to cross the bridge the day it opened.[7]

Charles Leavitt, recruited from New York to provide a plan equal to the hopes for this aspiring city, asked his new clients, "Is not the daily contact with carelessly planned, poorly kept streets, inadequate buildings, and other makeshifts an influence highly detrimental and to be avoided? Do not dignified and beautiful public buildings, well-ordered, well-placed and easily fetched, properly equipped and surrounded by equally fine structures for other purposes, instill in the people a respect similar to that inculcated in the younger generation by proper home surroundings administered by wholesome parents?" He envisioned creation of a "Greater Camden" that would dominate all of South Jersey. The foundation would be a complex web of highways connecting city and suburbs, crowned by an elaborately landscaped boulevard parkway to the bridge. "New boulevards," Leavitt claimed "create new values and new centers of activity, and rehabilitate old values and old centers."[8] New downtown structures sprang up to confirm and extend that vision of Camden's increased regional importance: the expansive Walt Whitman Hotel in 1925, the $1 million Stanley movie theater in 1926, the imposing, classically garbed Sears Department Store in 1927, at what was intended to be the gateway on the bridge boulevard to a new civic center, and the 1931 opening of the new twenty-two story $10 million city hall, court house annex, and civic plaza. By 1935 the *Philadelphia Evening Bulletin* was forced to admit that Camden had created its own tributaries and was the beneficiary of "a very considerable amount of trade which does not cross the river."[9]

But by then Camden was a victim of the nation's deep depression. By the mid-1930s, times were so difficult that the city had to pay its workers in scrip. Nonetheless, a directory of Camden enterprises in 1937 fully suggested the strength of the city's underlying industrial foundation. The city's big three manufacturers continued to employ large numbers of residents: Campbell Soup (5,600), New York Shipbuilding Corporation (5,522), and RCA Victor (13,030). Other well-known industries as well as smaller companies ranging from metalwork to shipbuilding, textiles, and soap-making complemented the giants. Edna Martin recalls that "with so many factories ringing the city, most people walked to work and downtown. Every morning there would be crowds on the streets. Children walking to school, workers hurrying to their respective places of employment. I could tell time by the factory whistles. Different starting times meant different bursts of sound."[10]

Not all these companies improved their position or even survived the war years. The implication of the first industrial directory published with peace, in 1946, however, was increased production overall, especially in the larger industries which adopted defense operations (Table 1). Camden Forge, for instance, witnessed a sharp increase in employment as it manufactured the camshafts and propeller shafts that drove the engines for new ships being built at nearby New York Ship. Campbell tomato juice was considered so important to troops abroad that Fort Dix joined other area institutions in commandeering extra workers in 1943, when it appeared there might not be enough manpower to process the whole summer crop.[11] Work remained plentiful for those arriving in Camden into the early 1950s. Jose Vasquez made this point about his arrival in 1951. He had only settled in a North Camden apartment at Third and Linden a single day before he walked out to the street where contractors sought workers, and he was employed for years thereafter.[12]

In addition to the larger manufacturing companies, Camden's vital entrepreneurial activity was manifest in a series of commercial corridors, most notably along Broadway, Kaighn, Haddon, and Westfield. There, movie theaters, real estate operations, doctors, dentists, and lawyers mixed with a host of commercial and retail services. In addition, neighborhood commercial corridors emerged to serve specific ethnic constituencies. On Mt. Ephraim Avenue, one could buy homemade kielbasa at Jaskolski's or pick up fresh made Polish bread at the Morton Bakery.[13] One former resident remembers the atmosphere as "that of an actual Polish city. The men grouped together on corners and talked in Polish all day."[14] In the Italian section around Mount Carmel parish, South Third Street became a focus.

TABLE 1. MAJOR CAMDEN EMPLOYERS, 1937, 1946

Company	Product	1937 jobs	1946 jobs
Campbell Soup		5,600	
New York Ship		5,522	
RCA Victor		13,030	
Abbott's Dairy		74	
Allied Kid	leather	155	114
Armstrong Cork	cork insulation	277	330
Camden Forge	iron & steel forging	235	1,110
Camden Pottery	plumbers sanitary earthenware	111	
Congress Cigar		1,100	
Continental Can	tin cans	455	
Courier-Post	newspaper publishing	350	
Di Paola & Co.	sackcoats	152	259
Eavenson & Levering	scouring, carbonizing wool	485	279
Eskin & Sons	ladies coats & suits	180	204
Esterbrook Steel Pen Mfg Co	fountain pens	325	395
Freihofer Baking Co	baked goods	287	
Graboskey Brothers	cigars	131	
Haddon Press	printing books, magazines	496	
Himmelein & Bailey Co	tanners	96	77
R.M. Hollingshead	auto, household chemical products	500	1,000
Howland, Croft	yarns	498	446
Hunt Pen	pens, pencil sharpeners	250	229
Samuel Langston	paper working machinery	168	207
Levering-Riebel	printers, lithographers	100	125
John Mathis & Co.	Shipbuilding	130	270
McAndrews & Forbes	licorice extract, paperboard	562	530
Parkway Baking	bakery products	106	
Radio Condenser Co.	radio parts	1,400	1,000
Wm. S. Scull Co.	roasters, packers of coffee	180	290
Louis Seitchik	women & children's coats	180	175
Standard Tank and Seat	toilet seats	125	150
Supplee-Wills Jones	dairy products	207	80
J.B. Van Sciver Co.	furniture	503	345

Source: Industrial Directories of New Jersey. Figures for big three manufacturers not available for 1946.

TABLE 2. COMMERCIAL PROPERTIES, SOUTH THIRD STREET, CAMDEN, 1931, 1947

Address	1931	1947
523	Union & Brothers, hose	Flamini jewelry
525	Michael Ruccolo, shoes	Same
528	Nicholas Tota, hardware	Sondo Presti, grocery
530	Frank DelGozza, confectioner	Same, meats
534	Luigi Stippoli, confectioner	Arges Flamini
535	Henry Tambo, grocer	Attilio Tamburri
539	Antonio Rossi, fish dealer	Same, produce
542	James Roselli, barber	Adam Colalillo, Alex's Candy
544	Lalli Bros., tailor	Same, dry goods
548	Vito Meloni, grocer	Same
550	Mary Tedeschi, confectioner	John Tedeschi, confectioner
556	Pasquale DiRenzo, grocer	Same
600	Joseph Grippo, soft drinks	Roma Cafe
617	Stefano Greco, barber	Same
618	Charles Rifici physician	James Marchisello
622	Anthony Malatesta real estate	Same
626	Max Wingrad, grocer	Same

Source: Camden city directories, 1931, 1947.

As city directories indicate, activities to serve local needs remained remarkably stable. In sixteen tumultuous years encompassing not just a depression but a world war, more than half the properties remained in the same hands. Where businesses changed, they remained similar in kind, mainly family operations serving the local community (see Table 2). A former resident, if called away from the city in those years, would have had no problem knowing where he or she was on returning to South Camden or any other part of the city. It had survived the most difficult of times and emerged virtually intact.

Such continuities should not be overemphasized, however. In an era where jobs carried no tenure and few public forms of insurance existed to counter the vicissitudes of either the marketplace or the life course, working people had to rely on others in times of difficulty. For the most part, that meant turning to those of the same ethnicity. Germans, Irish, Poles, Eastern European Jews, Lithuanians, and Italians may have worked in different establishments, but they clustered together in homes located close to churches or synagogues where services often were conducted in their native language. They formed their own associations to provide for emergencies.

Such ties were reinforced through elaborate social structures that reinforced their sense of belonging both to a particular neighborhood and to a larger ethnic group. Among the city's large Catholic population there was always the local parish, most often with its own school; mutual aid associations to cover insurance and other needs; the building association to make home-ownership possible; and, most important, the network of associates who were always ready to point the way to a job opportunity when it was needed. Here were the evidences of social capital that facilitated and sustained the primary goal of building monetary capital.

Such communities formed out of the early experience of immigration and the often difficult first encounters in American cities, and most relied on key facilitators. Among Camden's Italians, Tony Mecca played that role. Mecca was so central to the community in the 1920s and 1930s that area residents taking the citizenship exam consistently identified the White House as "Tony Mec's funeral home at Fourth and Division." Mecca's business just across from Our Lady of Mount Carmel Parish, performed a central social as well as economic role in community formation. Mecca was born in Italy in 1873, and he arrived in Camden in 1890 after picking berries in nearby Hammonton for a year. He spent years establishing a good business reputation before building his stately funeral home in 1909. Mecca was likely to touch each neighborhood family in some way in the course of their lives as well as their deaths. Out of his South Fourth Street office, Mecca served as a navigator for those many immigrants who spoke no English. He operated a sub-post office to assist residents in sending money home and was a notary pubic. He was an organizer (and president from 1907) of the Camden Italian and American Building and Loan Association. Later he became president of the first Italian Republican League, popularly known as the Tony Mecca Club, conveniently located nearby on South Fourth Street, where older Italian men gathered to socialize nightly. When needed, he interpreted for his fellow Italians in Camden courts, and at a time when Camden was solidly Republican he was one of the party's staunchest supporters as 5th ward district leader. An active supporter of the local Roman Catholic church, he found employment for residents, helped neighbors get citizenship papers, and waived fees for funerals if families could not pay them. When he died in 1952, the *Courier-Post* took the unusual step of running his extensive obituary on the front page.[15]

Mecca was a man of his times, the lynchpin in a dynamic community-building process that created tight-knit and stable, if poor, ethnic neighborhoods throughout Camden. Similar figures appeared in the city's other eth-

Figure 2. Left: Dominick Argenteiri outside his home in the 300 block of Division, the Mecca Funeral home over his left shoulder. Right: Maria Argenteiri, his wife, with her friend Angelena DiMarco. Both photos, c. 1940. Courtesy of Carmela Argenteiri.

nic neighborhoods, but even with such leaders the sustenance of social well-being was a collective effort. Typically central to Camden's Italian community was Our Lady of Mount Carmel Church. It kept families closely tied to it through a host of service organizations, including the Blessed Virgin Soldaria for women and the Mother of Sorrento Association to provide social activities for young people. Beyond Mecca's First Italian Republican League, there was the Young Men's Catholic Club, appropriately hosted in Mecca's garage initially, for the younger generation, as well as the Catholic Knights of St. George. Each club ultimately moved into a large structure a short distance from the church, also on Fourth Street, and formed its own ladies auxiliary. Immediately next to the church was the mutual aid association building, which Mecca's nephew Fiore Troncone remembered was used extensively for social gatherings as well. There was interplay among such organizations. Troncone's father, Richard, was a member of the Knights of St. George, the Young Men's Catholic Club, Loggia Vitorio Veneto, the Societa Unloone Forca, Loggia Dante Aligheri, and Sant' Antonio

Di Padova.[16] Inez Balestra Pontillo described her father, Frank's role in another men's organization, the Union of Brotherly Love:

Most of the members of this club were from the Italian Immigrant Community. They would show movies on Saturday night. Pop would run the projector. Sometimes, Pop would invite non-professional singers to sing an opera. Of course, everyone volunteered their services so he had a band (not an orchestra) which played for the opera singers. The volunteer band (known as Valeriani's band) was so loud that, many times, it was impossible to hear the opera singers.[17]

At its height, Our Lady of Mount Carmel counted three thousand parishioners, offering two masses in Italian every Sunday. Many of the older parishioners spoke dialects and came from different parts of Italy. Although parishioners quickly formed at least ten regional organizations, the church made a point of melding the whole community by recognizing all the special feast days of Italy's different regions.[18] On any one of these special occasions, parishioners from different parts of Italy joined in a parade through the neighborhood in public display of their solidarity to church, neighborhood, and ethnicity. Bands, which served the additional function of social clubs, such as the A. M. Mucci Veterans Post, led the processions.[19]

Because parishioners were poor and could only offer nickels or dimes at services, the church pursued further fundraising by offering big band concerts featuring name entertainment every year. These efforts would bring the church as much as $5,000. An annual festival in July lasting two weeks netted another $18,000. Still, the parish was poor enough during the Depression that pastor Joseph Monaco denied a request from older residents to build a bell tower, saying the church debt had to be retired first. Two years after Monaco's death, however, the new pastor, Michael Argullo, received the bishop's blessing to raise $75,000 for the tower. This was done in three months. Once completed, the bells tolled not just for mass but throughout celebratory processions.[20]

Such efforts could not entirely transcend Old World differences. According to Louise Gentile Schemanski, the Falco funeral home would not bury someone who was not a *paese*, or fellow townsman. A few Italians chose also to keep their distance from the working people who congregated at Mount Carmel, instead attending the more established Cathedral of St. Peter and St. Paul on the other side of Broadway. Such divisions were rare, however. Italians relied on each other for mutual support, calling on fellow countrymen when they needed help. One need Tony Mecca could not provide was medicine, and for this many South Camden Italians called on Ro-

Figure 3. Procession for the Feast of Our Lady of Mount Carmel, July 23, 1951. Members of Our Lady of Mount Carmel Church, at Fourth and Division, carry her statue as three thousand residents watch. Courtesy *Courier-Post*.

berto Principato, who lived near the church on the 400 block of Walnut Street. Known as a three-dollar man, Dr. Principato, like Mecca, would waive his fee if a patient lacked the funds.[21]

The Polish community in Camden organized itself in similar fashion, around its ethnic parish, St. Joseph's, in the Whitman Park neighborhood. Established initially in South Camden in 1892 after a period in which a Polish priest administered to Polish residents at St. Peter and St. Paul, a grander and more permanent structure was begun in 1913 at Tenth and Mechanic Streets in Whitman Park. What local church historians came to call the "Forward Years" began with the arrival of Monsignor Arthur Strenski in 1934 from Trenton. By 1946, the church boasted as many as twelve thousand members, an estimated 90 percent of whom were homeowners,[22] and it ran a parochial school and cemetery. At its height, the parish had seven priests and fifty nuns. Each Sunday children would report to their grammar school classrooms and march together to church. There were no excused absences. At Easter, John Lack recalls, children would bring baskets of holiday foods, including hard-boiled eggs, kielbasa, and butter shaped like a lamb to St. Joseph's to be blessed. "As you walked to the church, you'd be joined by more and more kids. On the way back we were all eating out of the baskets. Lent was over!" His generation, Lack commented, "can never leave behind the shadow of the spire of St. Joseph's."[23] As at Mount Carmel, parishioners would march through the community on feast days. Residents also participated in the annual Pulaski Day parade, which, according to one participant, concluded with a big black fire engine. She described this as a mixed blessing for children, as "it would set off loud, scary explosions, but the people on board would sometimes throw candy to the crowd."[24] Residents also had a choice of numerous parish, mutual aid, and social societies.[25]

By the 1920s, Camden Jews had organized four synagogues. Three were orthodox: B'nai Abraham (Lichtenstein Shul), in Whitman Park; Sons of Israel at Eighth and Sycamore Streets (known as "Eighth Street Shul," even after it moved to the Parkside neighborhood); and Ahav Zedek on Benson Street. As early as 1912, Jews had begun to move into newly built Parkside, but the real influx started in 1916, and by 1920 several hundred Jewish families were living there. That concentration drew the energies for a new, conservative congregation, Beth El, in Parkside, which was completed in 1924. From that congregation flowed a rich tapestry of social organizations: an annual Chanukah Ball, starting in 1922; a religious school, which opened in 1924; a Hebrew Free Loan Society; a Hebrew ladies charity committee in charge of needy cases and lodging and board for strangers; and many others.[26]

Many first generation Jewish immigrants entered small businesses, often living above their stores. Eventually, many such families purchased their own homes, initially in Parkside and later out Baird Boulevard into East Camden. But even when they were scattered in several different neighborhoods, Camden's Jews were nonetheless strongly communal, answering many calls to support community needs, not the least for Hebrew schooling and recreational activities for youth. These were initially located in Talmud Torah on Kaighn Avenue. In addition to hosting the school, Talmud Torah offered supervised dances on weekends and, like some Catholic parishes, sponsored its own football team. Less formally, children played in the empty lot next door, sometimes gathering paper into a ball for an improvised game of football.[27] During the 1930s it became the headquarters as well of the Ladies Garment Workers Union.[28] Ruth Bogutz, whose father, Henry Schreibstein, operated a plumbing supply store on Kaighn Avenue and who moved to Baird Boulevard in the 1930s, remembers attending religious school two afternoons a week and attending Shabbat services as a school requirement. Sororities and fraternities met on Tuesday nights in individual homes and at Congregation Beth El. When meetings were over, everyone headed for Jane's Soda Shop at Haddon and Kaighn. So regular was attendance there, one could expect standing room only, with the overflow socializing outside. Next door was Lemerman's variety store, where kids knew they could go if they ever needed friendly advice from a sympathetic adult.[29]

Camden's older white ethnic community, as established before World War II, quite perfectly conformed to the "lost communities" described by Alan Ehrenhalt as well as the sociologists at the University of Chicago who pioneered the examination of such ethnic neighborhoods early in the twentieth century.[30] Participants in these worlds remained primarily parochial and isolated from other communities. Each unit of the larger urban fabric thus held strongly unto itself, recognizing other units but keeping a distance. Natalie Shisler, one of the few former residents whose parents insisted that her family live in a "mixed" residential area, could not help but identify the different sectors—"colored town," "dago town"—when she walked home from Campbell Soup's waterfront plant to her South Camden home at Eighth and Line.[31] Had she continued her walk, she would undoubtedly have identified "Polaktown" in Whitman Park, "Irishtown" in North Camden, and "Germantown" in Cramer Hill. Virtually absent in Ehrenhalt's recounting of the "lost city" are the newer ethnic groups which have come to dominate the inner city, African Americans and Puerto Ricans. And yet in Camden there were surprising parallels in these quite distinct sectors as well.

The equivalent of Tony Mecca in Camden's Puerto Rican community was Mario Rodriguez, who was born in Cuba but grew up in Puerto Rico. He arrived in the mainland United States during World War I, settled in New York City, and made his way to Camden by way of Philadelphia through employment at the Consolidated Cigar Company. He settled in Haddon Avenue's mixed residential and commercial sector, at 911, sending his children to Camden Catholic High School. Mario translated for his neighbors and oversaw the many social clubs that formed, like the Spanish Civic Society Club and the Mexican Club.[32] Raymond Mana, a Mexican who worked for the city, played a similar role. Not every realtor would sell a house to a Hispanic customer. If Hispanics wanted to buy a house or make some official transaction, such as getting a driver's license, they went to Mana. He made the arrangements and, as one resident put it, "you threw a little money at him."[33]

In the early years of Puerto Rican migration, newcomers found few familiar structures to help them on their arrival. Louis Rodriguez remembered going into a local store to buy salt, but because he could not pronounce it correctly the grocer did not know what he wanted until he pretended to be pouring salt on food. Eventually, however, neighborhood services caught up with migration. MaMa's Place in North Camden sold foodstuffs identified in Spanish and offered a place for men to gather and drink beer. Tricoche served Spanish food and fried fish, had a juke box, and offered beer on the side. It was frequently raided by the police, but the owner would pay a fine and then go back to work again.[34] And by 1953 Father Roque Longo, an associate of Our Lady of Mount Carmel who had previously ministered to a parish in Argentina, had secured space for a new church on the second floor of a commercial building near the Campbell Soup plant. Mario Rodriguez's wife Carmen was among those who immediately became active in forming the appropriate associated organizations: the Holy Name Society and the Daughters of Maria. When Carmen and Mario died as the result of an automobile accident in 1973, local papers paid them unusual tribute for their role in community-building.[35]

The African American presence in Camden stretched back to the 1830s. The South Camden neighborhood of Fettersville was home to the first black churches, Macedonia AME (1832) and Union AME (1855), along with the West Jersey Orphanage for Colored Children and the John Greenleaf Whittier Colored School for Girls and Boys.[36] As black migration to the city increased before and during World War II, an additional community formed in the Centerville section of the city between Whitman Park and South Camden. There, in addition to several prominent black churches, an expansive swimming pool drew African Americans from around the region as well as from the immediate residential area.

Although ostensibly part of an integrated North, Camden was nearly as segregated as if the city had been located below the Mason-Dixon line. Segregation started early in any black child's life. Even though he lived close to the Starr school for girls and the Liberty school for boys in South Camden, James Troutman walked five additional blocks to the all-black Whittier.[37] Randy Primas, who became Camden's first black mayor, attended Veterans' Junior High School rather than the all-white Cramer Hill school that was closer to his home.[38] Blacks customarily traveled on the back of the bus. When they had the chance to see a performance at the Stanley Theater

Figure 4. In the swim in Centerville. This pool, pictured in the mid-1930s, drew children from outside Camden as well as from the immediate neighborhood. Courtesy *Courier-Post.*

downtown, they were required to sit together in the upper balcony. Charles Ashley recalled that "the only restaurant where you could go and be sure you'd be served was Horn & Hardart," located at the once bustling commercial center at Broadway and Kaighn.[39] One resident recalled that the nearby American Restaurant would grant requests for a drink of water, but would destroy the glass afterward.[40] The downtown "Y" offered admission to whites only; a separate "Y," known as the Hutton Branch, in South Camden accommodated African Americans.[41] Although Campbell Soup had a good record of employing blacks, the company designated separate rest rooms by race in its new 1941 plant.[42] Like other black communities that were forced to turn inward due to external discrimination, Camden developed its own array of specialized services: doctors, lawyers, barbers, funeral homes, and real estate services.

Although there was no single Tony Mecca or Mario Rodriguez among African Americans, individuals provided similar kinds of sacrifices for their neighbors out of a sense of shared heritage. Ulysses Wiggins's importance as a doctor in the African American community enabled him to build the local NAACP, an organization he headed for a quarter century until his death in 1966. As a later president of the organization, Kelly Francis, put it, "You didn't make an office visit without being encouraged to fill out a membership application."[43] It was Wiggins's personal intervention with RCA chief David Sarnoff that finally opened that company's ranks to black employees above the level of custodian.[44] Auto mechanic James Gland built his connections less formally. He knew everyone, high and low, and was frequently called upon to settle disputes. Not everyone could pay for his services, so they bartered. People would ultimately uphold the bargain, whether it was social or financial, because, as his daughter pointed out, what he fixed he could unfix.[45]

Although strict segregation began to break down with integrated classes in middle school, the color line was still quite clear. Ruth Bogutz recalled that the Jews, blacks, Poles, and Italians at her school "were friendly during the day, but we didn't cross at night."[46] Odessa Polk-Jones recounted a telling story of growing up on Eighth Street in Centerville. As teenagers she and some of her neighbors decided to attend a Halloween party in Whitman Park. Everything went well until all those present were asked to take off their masks. As Polk-Jones put it, "we ran for our lives" rather than confront the hostile reception they were about to get from their Polish hosts.[47] Memories of Donza Harmon's decision to "cross Chelton Avenue" in search of candy still brought her to tears years later. The store owner in the then-white Morgan Village section did serve the five-year-old, but his pointed questions about why she was there at all provided an early and defining lesson in racism.[48]

Former white residents claim consistently that there were no significant racial tensions in the old Camden. Eugene Weiser lived and operated a dry cleaner in predominantly black Centerville. Neighbors, his son recalls, often called on him to vouch for their activity to Camden police. After one customer was arrested for participating in a Saturday night poker game, Weiser told police the men were having a prayer meeting.[49] Such memories cannot erase the unequal standing of the separate black community, yet there were a number of striking similarities among communities that transcended racial and ethnic divisions. One ritual frequently cited of white ethnic neighborhoods was the nearly obsessive washing and cleaning that went into the facade of each property. "Every Saturday, the women would come out of their houses and scrub—on their hands and knees, no less—the marble steps of the houses and then use the rest of the water to sweep the brick sidewalks and gutters," Edna Martin remembered of her North Camden neighborhood. "There was a sort of competition, or community pride, I don't know which, that somehow made all of the neighborhoods try to outdo the others."⁵⁰ No one, it is claimed, would disgrace themselves by neglecting to keep this public face to the world in the most pristine quality. The practice, however, was not confined to any one ethnic group, but extended into both the African American and Puerto Rican communities.⁵¹ It was as though Camden residents as a group had internalized the message Charles Leavitt had articulated in the mid-1920s. Because both public and private structures were a reflection on the city, all members of the civic compact were bound to uphold the highest standards of cleanliness and beauty.

Another common theme across racial and ethnic lines was the generosity and trust extended between owners of Camden's many commercial neighborhood-based establishments and their clients. Edna Martin remembers her mother sending her to the corner store to ask for a bone for their dog during the Depression. "And leave some meat on it," she said following her mother's instructions. To her embarrassment, the butcher retorted, "You don't have a dog." He gave her a beef knuckle with a bit of meat on it anyway. "God bless that man—he kept many people from starving to death," she recalled. "Those were lean years."⁵² Frank Harrington recalled that as a young man he could not afford the cost of a new faucet for his home. Because he caddied for plumbing supply store owner Henry Schreibstein, he was able to pay off the cost over time at a rate of twenty-five cents a week. Years later, Harrington told Scheibstein's daughter that when he made the final payment, her father extracted all the quarters he had stored in a box and returned them to him.⁵³ What happened repeatedly among white ethnics also extended to African Americans patronizing the corner stores that dotted their neighborhoods. Rosemary Jackson's family were Seventh Day Adventist, so they did not eat meat and thus patronized a number of Jewish businesses in the area. They shopped at Jacob Foos and Young grocers, popularly known as Foosies, and at Lundy's Meat Market in South Camden. The family were poor and thus relied on these stores to extend credit. Jackson's mother kept a pink account book which she gave her daughter when she was sent to purchase food for the family. When others were in need, she passed the book along, so they too could take advantage of that arrangement.⁵⁴

It could be said, then, that all segments of Camden had access to considerable social capital. Such resources were critical, for jobs were rarely se-

Figure 5. Inside game/outside game. Top: white women work the assembly line at Campbell Soup, August 1, 1949; bottom: temporary black help line up for employment outside the plant, August 8, 1949. Courtesy *Courier-Post*.

cure, and government programs, even under the New Deal, could rarely be relied on to get people through hard times. Campbell Soup was widely considered a good employer, but it fought unionization through the war years. Employment, then, had to be accepted within certain limits. Many young and marginally employed African Americans could count only on summer employment, when lines of trucks bringing tomatoes from the South Jersey fields would fill the streets leading up to the factory. Crowds of African Americans formed for selection for the extra work. Even those with regular jobs could lose them easily enough if they got out of line. Natalie Shisler, for instance, worked on and off at Campbell for a number of years, the last time in 1960. She did a number of different jobs, working with chicken, peeling potatoes and onions, working the soup line, and grading tomatoes. She was frequently laid off at slow times. One time she thought she saw mold in the tomatoes. The line shut down, and Shisler lost her job.[55]

Industrial work for African Americans was especially difficult to obtain on a sustained basis and was subject to a number of perils. One black Camden family, the Rileys, had several members who worked at New York Ship as welders and pipefitters, but only on a seasonal basis. Although RCA did not hire many black workers, both David Riley's mother-in-law and an aunt worked there as assemblers, the latter for close to thirty years. His aunt had been there nearly the twenty-five years she needed to be eligible for a pension when the company laid her off. In response to her request to be reinstated, this small woman, at just under five feet, was told she could return only if she would agree to a position dumping garbage cans. She took the job and finally gained her pension. It was not unusual, however, for black workers to lose their positions just short of their eligibility for retirement benefits. Those lucky enough to hold long-term positions found themselves at the bottom of the scale, in terms of both pay and desirability. A 1956 edition of *Campbell's People*, the company's monthly publication, provided a cheerful commentary about the Riley family: George, who had been employed in night cleaning since 1940, his wife Victoria, who helped out with the third floor packing operation, brother-in-law Lucius Williams, who worked a year in the third floor packing operation, and brother Charles, who held a position on the third floor from 1942 until 1947.[56] In fact, David Riley reported, his father George's health suffered from dangerous work conditions, and he died from a heart attack shortly after his retirement. Because his mother Victoria had a heart condition herself, her work at Campbell was limited. Her primary means of supporting her family was as part of a larger underground economy, by selling dinners to patrons of nearby bars on Friday and Saturday nights. David Riley witnessed Campbell's dangers himself as a summer employee. He once saw steaming water combined with caustic soda break through jury-rigged pipes in the V-8 cocktail juice processing rooms, scalding workers and sending them running half-naked through the corridors as they tore off infected clothing.[57]

Immigrant families embraced the middle-class ideal of a single male breadwinner. Pay for Camden's blue collar jobs was not generous, however, and many women and children worked. A steady stream of women in white uniforms walked to work at Campbell Soup every day.[58] Before World War II, women responsible for the wiring, crimping, and soldering on radio sets made up approximately 75 percent of RCA's workers.[59] Many Polish women worked in one of the numerous cigar factories that dotted the city. This could be especially dirty and arduous work.[60] Many Italian women worked as seamstresses, either full-time in factories or doing piecework at home where they could enlist their children to help. While Dominick Argentieri, a laborer, found some work through the Works Progress Administration, his wife Maria sewed neck and arm portions of coats at home for A. DiPaolo & Co. in South Camden, receiving five cents for each finished piece. After the Depression, she worked at the factory full-time for a number of years.[61] Nettie Odorisio did not work until her husband Joseph died, leaving her to support small children. She also joined DiPaolo after his death. As the number of Italian women employees at DiPaolo fell off after the war, the number of Puerto Rican women employees increased. African American women assumed a range of domestic employment.

Mount Carmel, like other parishes, formed its own parochial school, but it added a special touch by creating a commercial school to train its young women parishioners for employment in the city's clerical sector. Girls used their ethnic contacts to find jobs after completing school, often skirting rules that prohibited children under sixteen from employment.[62] Wartime opened up some traditionally male jobs for women, notably at New York Ship. "When they first came, they had to work (in plain sight) on the top deck because [management] were worried about the men taking advantage of them," one former supervisor recalled. Although relations between the sexes appeared cordial, these women lost their positions with peace.[63]

Some families put their homes to work for them. Stanley Wojtkowiak operated a coal and ice business out of his home on Thurmond Street in Whitman Park from the 1920s into the 1960s. He hired a number of family members to support the business, establishing an accounting area in the enclosed front porch and filling the basement with desks.[64] When Adam Colalillo, an RCA worker, moved to 542 South Third Street in the 1930s, he installed a penny candy machine in a front room and a sign announcing Alex's Candy in front of the house. With this family business, he managed to make enough money to put his son Alex through college.[65]

Even with many family members gainfully employed, low wages prompted residents to find other ways to secure cash. Numbers operations flourished in the city through the 1930s into the 1950s, helping sustain small businesses when volumes in sales were barely enough to get by. While Italians dominated business in South Camden, such operations extended throughout the city. Charles "Poppy" Sharp, who would become the agent of Camden's most forceful civil rights effort in the 1960s, got a boost financially as a young man, collecting scores in South Camden. In his community, he said, everyone played the numbers, and during Prohibition families would designate one house each Saturday night where they would drink.[66] At Trioche's, Jorge Rodriguez recalled, winners were expected to buy a round for everyone as well as to tip the runner so that he, too, would spend money at the bar. Zoe Mazzoni Rodriguez's family lived behind another place in South Camden, Jacobina's, where the owner, who was frequently raided, would throw a bag of money over the fence into her parents' yard so that police would never find any incriminating evidence.[67]

While some of the gambling that went on—the craps in the streets, the billiards in pool halls—remained independent activity, the numbers business ultimately came under the control of organized crime. Sherman's Bar at fourth and Royden in South Camden was widely recognized as the headquarters for this activity, under the watch of Marco Reginelli. Looking back, few former residents could complain. Reginelli and his associates were considered generous to the community, providing gifts of coal or toys at Christmas and keeping drugs and prostitution out of the area. One former resident remembers receiving a basket of good cheese and wine at his family's back door every Christmas.[68] Reginelli maintained order, while at the same time keeping money flowing in the community. His "business under a cloud," as sociologists Cayton and Drake referred to similar kinds of widely sanctioned illegal business in Chicago's South Side ghetto at roughly the same time, was seen as an important stabilizing influence.[69]

In a broader sense, former residents note the ways personal intervention helped mediate the strict interpretation of the law. Fiore Troncone recalls how his grandfather used his position in the police department to serve the role of peacemaker. When a neighbor arrived in trouble, the senior Fiore Troncone would send the family to the back of the house, pull the folding doors to secure privacy, and work out a solution to the problem.[70] Sometimes the exact nature of mutual exchange could only be guessed at, but it was there. Zoe Mazzoni Rodriguez recalls a time when her father was picked up for driving intoxicated on the bridge to Philadelphia. Mrs. Mazzoni had no money to bail him out, so her landlord, Sabba Verdiglione, sent her to Tadeschi's, one of the many commercial establishments on South Third Street. The owner, after hearing her story, handed her a bag full of change, which she took to the station to secure her husband's release. A short time later Mr. Mazzoni was asked to fix the air conditioning unit at Verdiglione's suburban Haddonfield home. It went without saying that no cash changed hands.[71]

Old Camden, as it is often referred to, was never wealthy despite its considerable productivity. Its residents were overwhelmingly working people with limited access to wealth, but with considerable social capital on which to draw, enough to sustain them through difficult times. Camden was a divided city, between different ethnic and racial groups, but its social and political institutions were sufficiently resilient to accommodate change and to assure stability. It was all the more remarkable, then, that these well established patterns and practices could unravel in the course of only a few decades.

Chapter 2
Camden Transformed

We grew up in an era when it was a different place, when the feeling for community, home, family, parents, work . . . well, it was different. . . . You don't have to revere your country, you don't have to revere where you live, but you have to know you have *them, you have to know that you are part of them.*

—*Philip Roth,* American Pastoral

We're going to inherit this whole city in ten years. Because we'll be the only ones left; we're the only ones who can't run away.

—*Robert Moore, Executive Director, Camden Council on Economic Opportunity, 1970*

At 5 A.M. on August 21, 1971, Marie Sheffield's sleep was shattered by the harsh ring of the telephone in her otherwise peaceful suburban home. The news was devastating. Riots had broken out in Camden, some six miles away. The neighborhood where her parents, Andrew and Josephine Graziani, had bought a home for $3,900 cash in 1944 was in flames. Her mother was safe enough traveling in her native Italy, but her father was alone and vulnerable. Sheffield routed her husband out from bed. Together they sped westward toward Camden. As the sun rose behind them, they were shocked to see thick smoke billowing above the city. They made their way through the raucous crowds that filled the narrow streets to her father's home on the 500 block of State Street. Onlookers watched without attempting to intervene as flames consumed the structure. The second floor had already burned, and the heat was so intense it had melted the glass door knob. Mr. Graziani was nowhere to be seen. After attempting unsuccessfully to enter the house, Sheffield pleaded with onlookers for news, hoping against hope that her father had escaped. Finally, a neighbor she recognized directed her to the Holy Name sanctuary around the corner. There she found her father, so dazed he scarcely recognized her. Together they fled to her suburban home. When Mrs. Sheffield's mother returned to the area days later, the family withheld the news of the loss from her as long as they could. As they tarried over supper in the Sheffield home, Mrs. Graziani kept asking to go to her own home. Finally, her daughter had to tell her the news that there was no home to go back to. Neither parent returned to live in Camden again.[1]

The Grazianis, like their daughter and so many other neighbors before them, settled in Camden's suburbs. They were not the only ones to leave as a result of the 1971 riots. For three nights fires and vandalism consumed much of the city. Although no one was killed, at least forty people were injured. Rows of establishments along the Broadway commercial spine were either looted or burned. The area looked, in the words of one observer, "like bombed-out Germany." Camden's future, the *Courier-Post* proffered, never looked darker. For sale signs went up across the city in residential as well as commercial areas. According to Alfredo Alvarado, who operated a grocery store in South Camden for twenty-four years, "You should have seen the people flying out of here . . . there were moving trucks all over the place."[2]

The departure of the Grazianis and other white Camden residents in 1971 extended what already had been a long and building tide. As Table 3 indicates, however, the pace of white departures accelerated considerably in the 1970s, to the point that Camden shifted over the decade to a majority black city. Factors besides civil disturbances contributed to the pattern of white outmigration, not the least the loss of industrial jobs. In fact, the close association between those losses and racial turmoil had a lasting impact, one that contributed greatly to sustaining public memory in the belief that African Americans were somehow responsible for the destruction of work-ing-class communities built up over decades.

In Camden, such beliefs found expression in the readings of a play, *Last Rites*, as it circulated through the city in the early years of the twenty-first century. The story focused on author Joseph Paprzycki's grandparents, Walter and Susanna Evannk, once owners of a neighborhood tavern located near the New York Ship Yard in South Camden. In the play, Walt and Sue lend sympathetic ears to their customers, who first fear and then experience unemployment with the closing of the yard in 1967. As their customers begin to drift away, Sue urges Walt to close the business. He doggedly insists on keeping it going until the full impact of the yard's closing finally reaches him. Even as he makes the decision to close down, two intruders enter the

Figure 6. Camden's industrial waterfront, January 15, 1957, still active and thriving. Courtesy *Courier-Post.*

bar, intending to rob it. A struggle ensues, a shot is fired, and Walt falls to the floor mortally wounded. When asked what he intended in his work, Paprzycki affirmed what many in the audience had already concluded: "He died as the city did, suddenly and without cause."[3]

Paprzycki took liberties with the facts. Walt's bar closed before New York Ship did. His death occurred later, of natural causes. Still, the powerful image of not just a single life but a whole way of life destroyed overnight remains strong in public memory, whether the site is Camden or a host of similar communities. Like Paprzycki's characters Pete and Whitey, workers were forced to move to find new employment or left to drown their sorrows. And while the play's intruders were not specifically identified as black, their dialect and their identification as coming from "the projects" left little doubt that they were.[4] So too, Paprzycki captured a central strand in the modern story of urban transformation: the loss not just of economic but personal security and its association among whites with an unwelcome intrusion of African Americans.

Like any story that seeks to be representative, Paprzycki's account con-

TABLE 3. JOBS AND POPULATION, CAMDEN, 1940–1982

Year	Total jobs	Manufacturing jobs	Operatives	Total population	White	African American
1940				117,536	104,842	11,340
1948	57,955	38,900				
1950	59,489	43,267	23,124	124,555	97,900	17,434
1954	62,564	39,500				
1958	57,581	37,500				
1960	58,883	39,722	18,838	117,159	89,287	27,463
1967	46,222	27,800				
1970	41,588	20,671	10,324	102,305	61,303	40,132
1972	36,388	15,700				
1980	27,926		5,983	84,910	26,003	45,009
1982	26,144	10,200				

Source: U.S. Census reports.

tains an element of truth. It is the historian's job, however, to place such stories in context and to unpack the tangle of social, economic, and cultural elements that contributed to such dramatic change. Which came first, social or economic change? How were they related? And how did they affect the particular epicenter of change, the historic industrial city? The first suggestions for answers emerge from information drawn from U.S. census data for Camden summarized in Table 3.

Several convergent patterns stand out. First, black and white settlement patterns between 1940 and 1970 mirror each other. That is, approximately as many whites left the city in each decade as African Americans arrived. That pattern shifted sharply in the 1970s, when five times the number of whites left as African Americans arrived, offering sure confirmation of the importance of the riots and associated social turmoil in accelerating a process of white migration out of the city. Secondly, we can see that manufacturing losses relate to white departures but do not appear to have driven the process. Most striking, in fact, is how well manufacturing employment held up during the immediate postwar period through 1960. Camden listed slightly more industrial jobs in 1960 than in 1948, paralleling total employment growth in the city. It might be tempting to equate the loss of 5,000 unskilled laborers, or operatives as they were identified in the census, with the departure of some 8,000 whites in the period. Most likely a number of these workers were young women who had worked in high volume and low-cost mass production facilities at RCA, and whose jobs had been moved to other locations as the company sought to reduce costs brought on by successful unionizing efforts.[5] During the period a number of them could have left the work force through marriage and thus not have precipitated a family decision to leave the city. Although it is impossible to tell precisely who did move, given the guarded nature of employment records, information from Camden directories through the last volume published in 1947 suggests it was white collar clerks, managers, and a few skilled workers—a number of them single women—who initiated the outward migration.[6] Through 1960, at least, it would appear that the pull of the suburbs had a greater effect on Camden's changing demography than the push of either shifting employment or social conflict.

Over the next decade, the pace of both job losses and white departures accelerated. Between 1960 and 1967 industrial employment fell sharply, by 12,000 jobs. The city lost another 7,000 industrial positions in the following three years alone, the result in part of New York Ship's closure. In a single decade, Camden's manufacturing base declined by 48 percent. By way of comparison, Philadelphia lost 40 percent of its manufacturing jobs between 1967 and 1977; Chicago, Boston, and Pittsburgh each lost more than a third. In fact, the 1970s marked the onset of what Barry Bluestone and Bennett Harrison publicized in their classic 1981 study as "the deindustrialization of America."[7] Skilled positions represented over half the loss in jobs in Camden, and it would not have been surprising, given both the more cosmopolitan ties of these workers and the shift in employment by RCA, in particular, to the suburbs to see this group add to the stream of white outmigration.[8] African Americans, whose presence was always limited in heavy industry, were less affected, but as their number continued to grow, they competed with whites for housing. Workers congregating in older and thus more affordable housing located near the city's industrial core had reason enough to leave when they lost jobs. Pressures to sell their homes gave them one more excuse to leave, however attached they might have been to their old neighborhood. During the 1960s another 28,000 whites left Camden. Now, clearly, economic change was contributing to the metropolitan area's demographic shift, even before the civil disturbances of 1971.

Industrial employment continued to decline in the 1970s, though not as rapidly as white flight rose. By the end of the decade, two features stood out: Camden could no longer be considered a manufacturing center, nor was it a predominantly white working-class city. For the first time, whites no longer constituted a majority of Camden but just over 30 percent. In this light, Camden's civil disturbances assumed particular importance as a convenient trope, giving power and specificity to Camden's transformation. To the degree that racial and economic change were conflated in the public mind, subsequent reports of rising crime and social disorder, or what the Manhattan Institute's Fred Siegel calls "rolling riots," sealed the city's reputation as an undesirable place. From there, it was not difficult to denigrate the people left behind and burdened with the legacy of disinvestment as the cause of their own misfortune. It is worth examining the process that lead to the crystallization of such conclusions about the post-industrial city.

*   *   *

The suburbanization that mushroomed in every metropolitan area in the country after World War II was so pervasive it has since assumed the aura of inevitability. The G.I. bill, government-guaranteed mortgages, and the availability of new homes on the periphery of central cities provided huge inducements to families to locate outside city limits. Yet these opportunities were neither available immediately after the war nor necessarily embraced by those whose emotional as well as financial attachment had been to cities. As veterans returned from the fighting, to find housing they frequently moved in with their in-laws or parents in the city. One couple who embraced this option was Chester Mattyjaskik and Philomena Plucinski. They chose to reside at her parents' home after the war, just several blocks from where his family resided, so closely attached were both newlyweds to Camden's Whitman Park neighborhood. Described as an area "nurtured by community spirit," Whitman Park, according to a contemporary real estate broker, was a place where fifty houses might sell should that number of dwellings be available. "There's no denying there are some sections of our city that are substandard," he admitted. "We need many things including more good department stores to increase our shopping facilities. But I believe that as our new highway improvement program becomes a reality, that conditions will improve generally. I believe we have a great future as an automobile parking business center."[9] Wedding announcements appearing in the mid-1940s frequently added the word "temporary" to such arrangements, but that experience could stretch out as housing alternatives to the already overcrowded city housing stock were slow to become available. In Camden, demand remained robust as the war wound down. In June 1945 the head of the city's Federal Housing Agency office reported that demand for housing had risen to the point that buyers were being required to put 20 percent down. A year later, the new president of the Home Builders

League of South Jersey, seeking relaxation in government price controls, declared that Camden County needed 3,000 new homes to meet its housing shortage.[10]

Some found homes in the relatively undeveloped portions of East Camden and Cramer Hill. One such couple was John and Maria Zizzamia, who moved to East Camden in order to acquire more space for themselves. Immediately after the war, they had lived in a South Camden household with seven children, a grandmother, and an uncle.[11] In East Camden, advertisements promised, amenities were available according to emerging expectations: a home with modern plumbing facilities, a yard, and a garage. A June 1946 advertisement for an East Camden property selling for $12,500 offered, for instance, a "detached dwelling on large, beautifully landscaped 160 x 200 lot. Two-story stucco on cement block with slate roof. Flagstone terraces face pool and fountain in back yard. Hot water heat. Oil. Two-car garage."[12] Although garages were becoming standard in such locations, a number of sellers, aware that many Camden residents had never owned automobiles, stressed access to good public transportation. One might find comparable homes advertised in the nearby suburbs, but they were far from employment opportunities and other necessities. City apartment living remained very much in demand into the 1950s for those not yet ready to purchase a home. The 1950 census showed Camden's postwar baby-boom population up to a record 125,000. Growth continued over the next four years, accompanied by a rise in consumer spending.[13]

Other factors revealed why the suburban boom was slow to take off. During the war, and immediately thereafter, such a high premium was placed on public transportation that only towns adjacent to the city, notably Pennsauken and Collingswood, showed much in the way of growth. Each of these towns contained a major transportation artery in and out of Camden, and development moved naturally up those routes. A 1946 advertisement for a new home in Collingswood, for instance, made a point of noting that the location was only several blocks from Haddon Avenue, the central route back into Camden. A bit further out, Delaware Township remained dotted with farms. As late as 1949, its predominantly rural character could be seen in an advertisement for a home near Route 38, described as good for poultry raising.[14] Inevitably, new development spurred growth there. But as Marc Shuster, whose family moved to the Woodcrest section from Philadelphia in 1957, later pointed out, such locations lacked even the basic amenities of grocery stores within walking distance. To attract customers, developers offered bus trips to the older and more established suburb of Haddonfield so residents could use the Acme supermarket. To make the new locations attractive, they added other amenities, such as community swimming facilities.[15] As late as 1961, an advertisement for a nearby property in an area dubbed Wilderness Acres may have emphasized the home as "the retreat you have always dreamed of," but it also made a point of stating that Haddonfield was only eight minutes away.[16] Children living in the Erlton section of Delaware Township attended Haddonfield High School. Even mayor Christian Weber's daughter attended the school.[17]

As happened in so many other urban communities, Camden's Jews were among the first to suburbanize. Even so, there was controversy over building a new community center outside the city. When Bernard Dubin arrived in Camden from New York in 1947 to take charge of the Jewish Federation, he bought a house on Baird Boulevard in East Camden, close to the older predominantly Jewish Parkside neighborhood. Because the recreational facilities at Talmud Torah in South Camden appeared inadequate to the needs of the growing Jewish community, in 1949 the Federation bought property for a new community center in East Camden, not far from Dubin's home. An estimated six hundred Jews lived in East Camden then, with another six hundred in Parkside. The property was in an area attractive enough to attract another bid very quickly. The offer of $46,000 in 1951 far exceeded the $15,000 the Federation had paid two years earlier, and it generated considerable interest. The East Camden lot was only 1.5 acres and could offer little off-street parking. Additionally, some worried about the construction of a new public housing project, McGuire Gardens, nearby. The proposal to move to a suburban site, however, generated intense opposition, especially from East Camden, where, Dubin believed, members of an underfinanced synagogue hoped the new community center would boost their ability to compete with Beth El in Parkside. But opposition was deeper than that. Many of the Orthodox Jews of the city who walked to shul in East Camden were appalled at the prospect of getting their children to Hebrew School or attending other functions far from their homes.[18]

A committee formed to guide the decision quickly focused on a nine-acre site along the old Marlton Pike, or Route 70 as it had come to be known, on the western border of Delaware Township closest to Camden. In order to provide the aura of objectivity, the committee drew up a list of criteria, with scores from one to eight for each element. The vote came out heavily in favor of the Delaware Township site. With the benefit of hindsight, one of the committee members, Louis Skulnick, could describe the decision to move to a suburban location as "the progressive thing to do," even though he maintained his jewelry business in Camden until the mid-1990s.[19] A preliminary meeting to unveil the committee's judgment drew heated opposition, however, from some eighty East Camden residents attending. To further voice their cause, opponents secured the support of a Newark Jewish newspaper, which issued special Camden editions highly critical of the Federation. The Federation's decision nonetheless prevailed. It paid $64,000 for the new, much larger site. The new facility opened in 1955 and strained the community's finances in the first years, but it proved in location only a bit ahead of its time. By 1972, only about three hundred Jews remained in Camden. Bernard Dubin himself moved to suburban Haddonfield in 1955.[20]

The Jewish out-migration turned out to be but the first wave of change that dramatically altered Camden's social landscape in the 1950s. During that decade, the nation's housing stock increased by a full quarter, most of it in the suburbs, and the Camden area was no exception.[21] Clearly, by the mid-1950s the locus as well as the look of real estate transaction was changing. As the Camden Realty Company reported in 1954, "The fields and woodlands along all of the main arteries leading into Camden from every direction are being developed into thriving communities at an ever accelerating pace." As a sign of its own suburban business, the company reported that of the twelve hundred homes it had sold in the previous year, over half could be characterized as three bedroom ranches.[22] A late 1950s advertisement could still promote suburban-style living in Camden, at an affordable price under $10,000, complete with Federal Housing Administration financing. The accompanying image of the house, when compared to the suburban residence advertised adjacent to it, told volumes, however.[23] The Camden home had as many rooms as the suburban residence, but its traditional attached row format compared unfavorably with the modern and spacious design of the suburban property. While its price was only half that of the suburban property, by the late 1950s its appeal to a new generation of buyers had sharply declined. A 1961 advertisement for a Pennsauken property priced at $12,500 stated well the new requirements of an age of suburban domesticity:

Want to be happily married? Move into this attractive neatly kept home in this real friendly neighborhood. Some of the nicest people in town live here. There is a wide screened in porch, the coolest place you can find on a hot summer night. Full basement. Huge living room, science kitchen. Full dining room, tile bath. 3 large airy sunlit bedrooms. A full size den plus a powder room. . . . On almost 100 x 100 neatly landscaped lot.[24]

Figure 7. Choice of homes: Delaware Township or Camden? March 20, 1959.
Courtesy *Courier-Post*.

As Robert Scarborough, the president of the Home Builders League of South Jersey and a leading developer of Delaware Township, put it, "Suburban living has been clearly established as the new American way of life."[25]

Population figures clearly support this statement. Delaware Township's population increased from 10,538 in 1950 to 31,522 a decade later. Even greater growth followed in the next decade, as population reached 64,390, well beyond the 45,000 to 56,000 planners had predicted for the township.[26] A central factor in the area's conversion from country to suburb was the opening of the Cherry Hill Mall in October 1961. The new development was anchored by the Philadelphia-based Strawbridge and Clothier department store which maintained its established practice to follow, not lead its customers in location. The mall caused a sensation when it opened. There were traffic jams for weeks, and soon busloads of tourists were arriving daily, not just to shop but to gawk at the vast array of shops and services. Developer James Rouse spoke hopefully of providing the central gathering spot that the otherwise diffuse and decentered area lacked. So successful was the new facility in attaining that role, that many believed Delaware Township's decision to change its name to Cherry Hill the same year followed from the mall's success. In fact, both the shopping facility and the township derived their names from a local landmark. The mall's economic impact, however, was tremendous. By 1965, Cherry Hill's assessed property value, up from $9.5 million in 1950 to $156.2 million, exceeded that of Camden for the first time, making it the richest community in South Jersey.[27] Much of the shift in retail activity came at Camden's expense, as businesses shut down or changed hands during the 1960s along the city's historically dominant commercial corridors.

Yet even as the pace of movement from city to suburb accelerated, employment opportunities remained concentrated in the city. Some of the many shipbuilding industries located along the waterfront began to close after the war. The number of jobs lost, however, was relatively small. Potentially more significant was the demise of Camden Forge, an industry that had swelled to employ over one thousand workers during the war as it hastened production to fit ships with steel forgings. Once the nation's big steel companies made their own forgings, the company could not compete.[28] The *Courier-Post* reported the relocation of several businesses out of Camden in the late 1950s. In each instance, however, the reasons cited pointed to too much business concentration in the city, not the eclipse of industry itself. When Guadio Brothers frozen food distributors announced it was moving to Philadelphia, it complained about congestion at its South Camden location. Two years later, when the Acme Staple Company reported that it would be relocating to Franklin, New Hampshire, it blamed pollution, noting "Camden is becoming like Pittsburgh before that city's redevelopment."[29] Indeed, even as these businesses were departing, others were aggressively expanding, including Universal Rundle Corporation, with two manufacturing plants for bathroom fixtures in Camden. In 1957, the company demolished the New Newton Friends Meeting House, constructed in 1801, to make way for a warehouse to accommodate a nearby plant.[30]

Both Campbell Soup and RCA diversified in the 1950s, expanding their presence outside Camden. Nonetheless their Camden plants continued to function. A combination of shifting national policy away from private contractors and its own internal problems cut New York Ship's funding back, well before it closed in 1967. Still, little commentary at the time suggested that the city's industrial base was in jeopardy. In 1962 the city's big three employers constituted 70 percent of the city's employment base. Generally, prospects for the city remained optimistic, as illustrated in a column from the mid-1950s written by Tom Kenny, Jr., vice president of the popular Kenny's Restaurant, across from City Hall. Listing as major additions to the downtown in recent years offices for Dow Chemical, Reynolds, Travelers Insurance, and General Motors Acceptance Corporation, among others, he stated confidently, "We know more business firms will be coming to Camden."[31] Indeed, the early 1950s witnessed the construction of a major new hospital, Our Lady of Lourdes, the opening of a branch of the Philadelphia-based Lit Brothers Department Store, and a multi-tiered garage facility nearby. By consolidating the South Jersey School of Law and the College of South Jersey, Rutgers established a new Camden campus. As late as 1960, as part of a series of highly optimistic economic forecasts for the Delaware Valley, the *Philadelphia Inquirer* could proclaim, "General growth—a combined reflection of increased population, industry, housing, and bank deposits—of southern New Jersey has about doubled in the past ten years. It is expected to triple in the next ten years. . . . In New Jersey's Industrial Elbow, which borders the Delaware River from Camden to Trenton, a major and palpable industrial miracle has taken place. Probably nowhere else in the United States has so much change been accomplished so swiftly. Here in the past few years, hundreds of acres of farm fields and meadows have been transformed into industrial sites and new homes."[32] An advertisement directed to "Mr. Industrialist," appearing in the *Courier-Post* in 1965, proclaimed all the usual assets for investment in Camden proper, including skilled labor, industrial sites, and major banks located in the city and staffed with industrial-oriented personnel and facilities.[33]

The historic pattern of urban industrial concentration came under pressure, however, as new employment opportunities began to emerge in the suburbs. Esterbrook Pen relocated from Camden to Cherry Hill in 1964, though it did not remain in the area for long. More significant was a new RCA research facility, described effusively in the 1956 annual *Inquirer* supplement touting the prospects of the Delaware Valley:

Wander through the new industrial wonderland of southern New Jersey. Watch the steel girders moving steadily up to fret the sky at Cherry Hill. A few years ago there was no Cherry Hill in a business sense. Just meadows; just opportunity. Now a $2 million inn, which soon will be enlarged, sits beside the 58-acre landscaped site of RCA's new glass and steel air-conditioned office and laboratory building. Nearby, a $160 million apartment development is well underway. A housing development is growing just beyond that. And across Rte 38 is the site of what will be one of the largest shopping centers in the Nation.[34]

Pointing to $47 million in new industrial and commercial investment, the chairman of the Cherry Hill Advisory Industrial Board described such growth as logical "because industry and commerce like to go where people like to live. Industry and commerce need people to provide both a labor force and a consumer market."[35] Opportunities such as those offered by RCA in Cherry Hill and in nearby Moorestown in Burlington County drew new residents to the area from New York and other parts of the country. To Bernard Dubin, who described engineering as becoming a Jewish profession, it was little surprise to see the old Camden synagogues move out to the suburbs.

Cherry Hill was not the only suburban area to seek business investment. In 1946 the sprawling suburb of Pennsauken north and east of Camden listed only one plant of any size: Rundle Sanitary Enamelware. When it merged with Universal, sending two hundred employees to Camden, the loss was more than made up for with new postwar arrivals. A host of companies, generally mid-size employers of between twenty and forty people and subsidiaries of other companies, located in new industrial parks set along the Delaware River. Significantly, many of these firms made products once associated with Camden: metals, tools, paperboard and fibers, and electrical components.[36] These plants, however, were modern, and, like RCA's new facilities, located near growing residential areas. Between 1958 and 1970 the number of manufacturing jobs in Camden County outside the city increased from 6,184 to 21,316, a number on a par with that in Camden itself. Even as Camden City lost 48 percent of its manufacturing base in the 1960s, the county's suburban area manufacturing employment increased at a rate of 95 percent.[37]

Growth was important to suburban leaders, but so were controls to assure that the suburbs would remain physically distinct from older cities like Camden. As early as 1942, Pennsauken determined that it would employ land-use regulation to maintain an identity separate from its Camden neighbor. The township committee limited home construction within the municipality to single-family detached homes. When Camden realtors, including one who had planned to build some six hundred houses on a sixty-acre tract along Browning Road, challenged the new zoning ordinance at a hearing, the lawyer for the Pennsauken Community Association replied that the township was "primarily intended as a suburban district and a number of us are trying to keep it as such."[38] Other nearby suburbs soon followed Pennsauken's lead.[39]

Delaware Township was sufficiently removed from the city to escape pressure for growth during World War II; as a result, it had to scramble to establish zoning regulations in the early 1950s. The township formed a planning board, consisting of the mayor and six other unpaid appointments made by him, in 1954 and revised its zoning ordinance, dating back to 1947, the next year. Mayor Christian Weber and his colleagues increased the size of lots and homes by eliminating the zoning category that authorized small homes. Weber thus made it clear that "there will be no row houses, twin houses or prefabricated homes in the township. Only qualified builders will be allowed to operate in the township, and if an individual builds a home, he must live in it and not offer it for sale, in accordance with state laws."[40] Such requirements, geared at setting an acceptable threshold for quality of construction by putting "a clamp on any 'fly-by-night' contractors,"[41] were meant to assure an ideal living environment, one utterly unlike that in Camden. It would not be long before costs would rise dramatically and building regulations would be relied on specifically to contain the spread of blight associated with Camden. In a 1966 campaign promoting a strong property maintenance code in Collingswood, the weekly *Suburban* journal warned, "Suburban blight can be but a step behind urban blight, the cancer now infecting Camden City and causing so many difficulties there." In placing strict controls on garden apartments, Collingswood took a stand, joined by other suburban communities, that it would remain separate and apart from the city many of its residents had left behind. In the context of growing social change and the racial turmoil mounting in Camden, references to containing physical blight increasingly suggested the will to contain the outward migration of Camden's poorer residents as well.[42] Indeed, by the mid-1960s Camden's suburban neighbors had drawn spatial distinctions with the city comparable to those described by Robert Self in California's East Bay area, underwritten by federally subsidized housing markets and low property taxes made possible by the location of new industry and sustained by racial exclusivity that encouraged white families to "accept as natural the conflation of whiteness and property ownership with upward social mobility."[43]

*   *   *

If the 1950s marked the emergence of modern suburbs, the decade also signaled the social transformation of the city of Camden. Although the black population of the city increased in the 1940s, established residential patterns remained much as they had been historically. African Americans concentrated in a belt near the historic downtown in South Camden. As their numbers grew, they spread outward to adjacent blocks. Coming up against strong rooted ethnic neighborhoods centered around churches and other associated institutions, however, blacks crowded into fewer homes initially rather than spreading into adjoining neighborhoods. The heavily Italian census tract that contained Mount Carmel Church in South Camden, for instance, showed a 12 percent black presence in 1950, but African Americans were isolated in self-contained pockets—a one-block area along Cherry Street, for instance.

Elsewhere, white neighborhoods bordered by predominantly black areas strictly held the color line. In North Camden, just above the Benjamin Franklin Bridge, each of the three census tracts recorded just one African American in 1950. The five city tracts farthest south all recorded African American counts of less than one percent. The historic village of Fairview's count was merely ten, or one tenth of one percent. The newer residential areas to the east—Parkside, East Camden, and Cramer Hill—all registered minuscule black populations, ranking from Parkside's 0.9 percent to the Rosedale neighborhood's 5.6 percent in East Camden. Segregation did not mean, however, that African Americans were shut out of the housing market. Edward Burt's grandfather, though educated only at a third-grade level and confined to day labor, managed to buy a home with $1,700 in cash. He settled in the 1940s on the 800 block of Pine Street, where his black neighbors also owned their homes despite their limited incomes.[44] The number as well as the range of opportunities for blacks to buy remained limited, however. Camden real estate practice in the 1940s and 1950s sanctioned the designation of homes especially for "colored" buyers in its advertising. While not all properties available to blacks appear to have been so designated, the relative lack of such advertising into the 1950s suggests how limited the market might have been. Location appears to have been tightly prescribed to areas where African Americans already resided. Few properties fell outside those areas before 1950. But as the pace of white departure increased in the 1950s, African Americans were quick to seek their places. As the African American population rose by 58.6 percent, from 17,586 to 27,892 during the decade, its numbers approximated that of foreign-born residents for the first time, at just under 25 percent. With that increase, demand finally began to overcome existing restrictive real estate practices.

One could see the transition most dramatically in Parkside. In 1950, the area was predominantly Jewish, with a number of equally upwardly mobile Italians and Germans. A few white ethnics continued to move into the neighborhood into the 1960s, but by about 1958 there was a distinct lack of identifiably Southern European names among new buyers. The new owners—Davis, Brown, Williams, Walker, among others—were African Americans. Initially, the change was subtle: a black professional family bought a home at prevailing market prices to become the first of its race to reside on the block. Among these was Dr. Howard Brown, principal of all-black Whittier School, and Walter L. Gordon, principal of Sumner School, also designated for African American students. In the 1930s, a Whittier teacher, Susan Carroll, purchased a home on Bradley, but she was apparently uncomfortable about living in an all-white neighborhood, so she rented it out to whites.[45] With such incremental changes, the neighborhood remained a stable and a desirable place to live. When his family moved to Parkside in 1951, Washington Hill, one of two brothers who subsequently became prominent black physicians, found the residential quarter was well tended, and there were many vibrant commercial properties located along nearby Haddon Avenue.[46] By 1960, Parkside was changing, as the black population rose to almost 33 percent, compared to the less than 1 percent in the previous census. Realtors now advertised specifically for colored buyers, and whole blocks changed as sellers announced easy terms and low down payments.[47] Delbert and Doris Nelson were among those to take advantage of the new opportunities. Married in 1950, they lived for a while in the Branch Village public housing complex in Centerville, later moving in with her mother when their finances became precarious. They were anxious to find a place of their own and decided to follow up an advertisement for a Parkside home, more as a wishful experience than with an expectation to buy. "We didn't have two nickels to rub together at the time," Doris later recalled. "I'm not sure we had bus fare to return," her husband added. But the owner was so anxious to sell, she covered the closing costs and provided the Nelsons with her own lawyer. With $500 provided by Doris's grandmother as a down payment, the Nelsons became one of the first black families on their block.[48] By 1970 Parkside was 87.9 percent African American.

The transition in Parkside was uncontested and quick, not the least because the Jewish population was already well launched to the suburbs. Changes underway in Camden's manufacturing sector had little impact on their decisions, either individually or collectively. Whether their occupational base was commercial or professional, the combination of desirable housing and new opportunities for sales to families whose income was rising made the lure of the suburbs inescapable. In Camden's working-class neighborhoods, the situation was different. There, at the start of the decade, manual employment remained for the moment close at hand, and residents

resisted pressures created by increases in the black and Puerto Rican population to sell their homes. North Camden offered a case in point.

The area was never ethnically homogeneous. Many families were of
Irish descent, but there was a good mix of Germans and Italians as well. No
single church dominated; Holy Name parish was predominantly Irish, but
it was joined in the area by Presbyterian and Lutheran congregations. Local
rituals helped draw the different strands of the community together.
"Everyone prepared for the Fourth of July parade and picnic in Pyne Poynt
Park," one resident recalled. "We made floats, we joined the games,
watched the fireworks, and walked home by the hundreds."[49] Still, the area
lacked an emotive core. The arrival in the late 1950s and early 1960s of outsiders even to these traditions was unsettling to say the least.

By 1960, the North Camden census tracts that had been virtually all-
white a decade earlier each recorded between 300 and 560 African Americans. The tract with the largest black concentration also recorded 484
Puerto Ricans. Property values, which had held well through the early 1950s,
had now fallen noticeably. The *Courier-Post* tried to remain upbeat about
the area, pointing to construction of the new luxury Northgate apartment
complex and improvements at nearby Rutgers University. "Camden is just
a diamond in the rough. We haven't begun to dig out the gems and make
the city what it could be," the paper quoted one banker as saying, adding,
rather implausibly, that there were increasing reports that suburbanites
were waiting to move back into the city if only adequate housing could be
found.[50] Peter and Helen McHugh, who lived in North Camden nearly fifty
years before moving out in 1996, saw the first changes come with the location of a new middle school in Pyne Poynt in 1967. Reflecting the city's
growing diversity with its black and Puerto Rican students, the school
spawned growing social tensions, which often spilled over into the neighborhood in the form of ethnically charged battles for turf. Added to this
volatile social mix was the arrival of other victims of displacement from the
city's first urban renewal effort at the head of Kaighn Avenue described in
the next chapter. The McHughs urged their pastor at Holy Name parish to
help stabilize the area, but they felt the church failed to respond effectively.[51] Panic set in, and the neighborhood changed dramatically as whites,
many of whom were also losing their jobs, left in a hurry. By 1965, the assistant pastor of Holy Name complained that the neighborhood was becoming
a "neighborhood of transients." From a peak of 900 to 1000 families, his
parish had dwindled to some 250 permanent and many transient members.[52]

By the mid-1960s the area around Our Lady of Mount Carmel in South Camden was changing too, as black and Hispanic residents moved in. For Puerto Ricans, Camden's reputation as a good place to find employment, following Campbell Soup's decision to recruit workers from Puerto Rico during World War II, provided a strong pull. During the 1950s, the city's Hispanic population increased from only 125 to 6,000. While North Camden proved a staging ground, where families stayed until they could find a better and more permanent residence, the area around Our Lady of Fatima parish in South Camden became a concentration of early home-owners. The presence of Hispanics might not have been expected to be as disconcerting to whites as that of African Americans, yet the reaction of the established community was still hostile. Yolanda Aguilar DeNeely, whose Mexican-born parents brought her to Camden from San Antonio in 1957, became one of two Hispanics in the Mount Carmel school. There, she and a Puerto Rican girl were singled out by the other children, who pulled their hair and called them Spics.[53] Carmen Martinez's children complained that they were called similar names in school. After she and her husband managed to buy a home in South Camden in 1957, her Italian neighbors took to calling her family Gypsies. She learned this one day when she accompanied her son to the local barber shop, where several customers started discussing "that Gypsy family" that had just moved in, not knowing that they were referring to the Martinezes.[54] By 1974 Italians had so emptied out the area that Our Lady of Mount Carmel had to consolidate with Fatima just to keep going. Both DeNeely and Martinez quickly took leadership roles in what became, overnight, a predominantly Puerto Rican parish.[55]

As in the Mount Carmel area, residents of Polish Whitman Park rallied around their parish. When realtors started to pressure owners to sell, St. Joseph's priest Joseph Strinsky attempted to intervene. While advertisements as early as 1962 adopted the rhetoric of panic,[56] properties continued to sell at good prices through most of the decade. By the end of the 1960s, however, the buyers were no long predominantly Polish, as white families accelerated the pace of their departure from the neighborhood. Linda Delengowski, who was teaching at Sacred Hart school at the time, remembered especially the negative impact on the neighborhood of a 1970 robbery at the home of Camden City Councilman Daniel Ciechanowski. The *Courier-Post*'s report featured a picture of Mrs. Ciechanowski, posed with the handgun she had wielded to hold the intruder until police arrived. "I knew my husband wasn't around and that it was my duty to do all I could to save our sons from harm," the paper recorded her as saying. Showing her three children carefully posed behind her, the story sent a chilling message of in-security to the neighborhood.[57] Indeed, review of sales in the area following the incident show a quickened pace, with eleven properties selling in 1970 along a three-block area of Morton Street alone. While a few of the buyers on adjacent streets had Polish surnames, the great predominance of buyers were either African American or Hispanic.[58]

In at least a few instances, newcomers worked to speed up the transi-tion. Jorge Rodriguez described a ploy orchestrated in North Camden to secure more homes for Puerto Rican families. A light skinned member of the community who had very little or no accent would buy a home. Once in, the new owner would play loud Latin music and host late-night parties, a strategy that worked well to accelerate the transition that was already being observed. As Rodriguez put it, "As we arrived, others moved." At first newcomers rationalized their practice by saying that older residents were moving out anyway, but it became increasingly clear that this became a way for some people to make money "without having to work." Rodriguez de-scribed these as New York dandies who knew how to make the system work for them.[59] How widespread this practice was is impossible to say, but even one instance provides an idea of how house-hungry these newcomers were.

Some in Camden worked hard to counter scare tactics employed by realtors. The president of an East Camden civic association, whose pro-fessed goal was integration, stated that "some of the finest families in the area are Negroes." His wife added, however, the ultimate goal: "We are striving to halt an invasion of the type of person, black or white, who would turn East Camden into a ghetto." As a sure sign of the growing flight, real estate ads featured special inducements, including sellers offering to pay all settlement costs.[60] When Rosa Ramirez settled in the area in 1967, the white neighbor on one side immediately posted a for sale sign. While the woman of Japanese ancestry on the other side stayed, a white exodus began shortly after she arrived.[61] By the mid-1970s, a *Courier-Post* headline conveyed the increasingly dominant view of the area: "East Camden: From Dream to Nightmare." High levels of defaults and the absence of new mortgage money were adding to abandonment and to the shift from homeownership to rental properties and from white to minority occupancy.[62]

With the traditional base of employment beginning to crumble in the 1960s, manual workers and their families did not always need another ex-cuse to move elsewhere. Heightening racial tension, however, often pro-vided that additional push. Relatively few violent actions accompanied the shift in neighborhood composition, unlike similar shifts in such big cities as Detroit and Chicago.[63] A few incidents were reported in East Camden and in Cramer Hill in the 1960s and, later, in Fairview, which remained virtually all-white into the early 1990s. Stories told by whites who left appear particularly charged, however, often quick to blame those left behind. Responding to an account in the *Courier-Post* about my plan to do this study, Edna Martin recalled vividly the trauma attached to her experience in North Camden. One day her son was playing in their yard when something steel fell a few inches in front of his face with such force that it broke the courtyard brick. The origin of the missile, she discovered, was a group of men and women drinking heavily on a balcony next door. When she went to confront them, she found children placed in a bathtub to contain them. They had wet their clothes while unattended. Not long afterward a friend came to visit, only to be hit on the head by a whiskey bottle tossed from a nearby window by members of another drunken party. This was not a black and white issue, she wrote, "it was a sudden deterioration of our neighborhoods by masses of people being imported from God knows where." Her plaint continued in graphic detail:

Our first hint of the coming of the end was when a neighbor around the corner begged my mother to see what she had to live next to. We all went. Next to this woman was a house with all of the windows open, paper curtains flying out into the wind, a radio blaring music on the window sill—facing the street, no less—front door wide open with the babble of voices coming out of the house. The house had been painted purple. We went into my neighbor's tidy house and she showed us how the fence between the properties had been torn down. Dirty kids were everywhere. Then standing in the dining room window facing my neighbor, was a laughing, naked man making obscene gestures as he yelled, "If you don't like us, move."

That was the beginning. Then the plumber, four doors up from me, died. His house was taken over by a black family. The first thing I heard was the crashing of storm windows that were being removed and thrown into the yard. Then the fence behind and between the houses was torn down to make a bonfire in the yard. Next, two women sat on the open second floor window, dangling their feet, and watched as two men threw a rope over the tree out front and began to dismantle a car that had been driven up onto the sidewalk. The limb of the tree broke but the car and litter remained there for a week until someone called the police. Nothing was done.

Our turn came when a group of women, of all colors, moved in next door. It was a house of prostitution, we soon learned. The woman, who we met and complained to, owned three such houses and took in only welfare recipients "to give them a place to live." There was such loud music all night long that none of us could sleep—the walls shook. One night we heard screaming in the alley in the back of our house. We went out and there was a young black woman who lived in the house. I told the victim that she didn't have to put up with that and that she could come into our house while I called the police. We were told to mind our own business. The woman was dragged back into the house. The police came but left in a few minutes. The noise and the screaming continued.

On Saturday evenings during the hot weather, we always washed, dressed and sat on the front steps. It was a neighborhood custom. The kids would play Red Rover. Women would gather gossip while the men talked of the national problems. Well, this one evening three of the new neighbors paced up and down in front of our house. One of the women had the same leather belt wrapped around her knuckles. She was laughing loudly with her companions and making comments like, "Hey, white bitch, we want your house." This experience turned my blood to ice.[64]

Such experiences prompted Martin to move to suburban Voorhees in 1963. So many of her neighbors also moved, she remembers the corner grocer crying at the realization that soon he would be left without his customers.[65]

Martin's experience was not unique. Growing up in Whitman Park, Justin Bartkeveus found he could no longer leave his bike or other toys on the front porch, for fear of theft. By the early 1970s his family had moved to East Camden, where social conflict again emerged to the point that the family moved out of Camden altogether.[66] Marion and Paul Baratz grew increasingly concerned about turmoil at Camden High School in the 1960s. Their son Brian escaped serious incident as student protests increased by locking himself in the office where he supervised the editing of the yearbook. The family chose to move from East Camden to Cherry Hill, rather than send their last child to the school. Although Brian Baratz describes growing up in East Camden as idyllic, noting that he is still in touch with black friends from his childhood, he also recounts that by high school they no longer socialized together after school. A black family bought the Baratz home, and within a few years whites had largely left the area.[67]

Significantly, a few neighborhoods maintained their racial composition, at least initially, by making social change virtually impossible. As late as 1970, when the black population of Camden had reached 39 percent, Fairview's African American population had risen to only 2.4 percent. Advertisements for homes in the area frequently appeared under the suburban heading of the *Courier-Post*. It was little wonder that the city's first African American mayor, Randy Primas, indicated his surprise to learn that Fairview was part of the city when he first visited there to play in a Little League baseball game about 1960.[68] Still, racial change affected that area as well. In 1967 the city required Fairview public school students to attend the new Morgan Village middle school in an area that had once been white but was rapidly trending black. Some Fairview families moved their children instead to the Joan of Arc parish school. Wendy Strang Rooney's parents decided she should make the transition at the new school, with what she later described as disastrous results. She recalls that she suffered daily beatings from children at school, fearing even to use the bathroom where black girls would stick pins into her arm and pare down their brushes to a sharp point to use as weapons. Although her parents insisted she continue at the school and try to make friends there, nothing she could do helped. Finally, she refused to go to school and remained at home for several months until her parents could find her a suburban alternative.[69]

Such stories recounting the pain whites associate with social as compared to economic displacement have been recounted elsewhere and cannot be dismissed as simple aberrations.[70] It should be noted, however, that such accounts told years after the fact either proceed without knowledge of the larger social context that produced black anger at the time or suppress knowledge of those conditions that might have been apparent then. No less a challenger to entrenched white privilege than the leader of Camden's black power movement, Charles "Poppy" Sharp, confirmed toward the end of his life the difficulties he had in containing the rising tide of anger among young African Americans in particular in the early 1960s. Sharp helped many people find needed housing but found it difficult to convince them to act responsibly as tenants and neighbors. He nonetheless remained sympathetic, because he understood the larger circumstances. Many of the newcomers to the city had come to visit as youngsters from more rural areas of the state, such as Bridgeton or Salem. For them, Camden in the late 1940s and 1950s represented the height of opportunity. Arriving in adulthood with hopes of finding employment and a decent place to live, they were deeply disappointed by the lack of opportunities. Sharp likened the situation to that of a first-time visitor to New York City, who arrives only to find that the Empire State Building has been removed. It was no wonder, he felt, that newcomers to Camden in the 1960s felt anger and resentment.[71]

More of the reasons for that anger will be revealed in Chapter 3. For the moment, however, it is fair to say that the riots of 1971 deepened and confirmed Camden's reputation among whites as a dangerous and undesirable location. Stories told and retold in Camden's suburbs even today associate Camden's transformation with racial change, whether tied directly to the riots or, more subtly, to such changes as transpired at Walt's Bar and other like places. Towards the end of Paprzycki's play the local parish priest voices his frustration about the changes taking place in Camden:

Is it their fault the city is turning into a sewer in front of their eyes? Is it their fault that kids, teenagers are shooting each other for dollar bills? Good families are moving out house by house and block by block because they want to be safe. Here, they're not. They'll never be safe. Hell, they probably never were.[72]

That branding of the city was hardly unique to Camden, as Philip Roth's statement about Newark at the beginning of this chapter suggests. Looking nationally, Robert Beauregard reports, "When we discuss urban decline or read how others perceive it, we engage with highly charged stories built up of layers of subjective impressions, not emotionally flat renditions of objectively specified conditions. Decline involves personal and collective loss and that loss constitutes a symbolic alienation from the city." In the traumatic period of transition in the 1960s and 1970s, he notes, a few critics, attempted to resist blaming inner-city minorities for the ensuing social and fiscal problems. "Separating race from poverty and white flight in this way," he asserts, "was an heroic but futile act, however. Race was increasingly the glue that bound together all of the perceived problems of the declining cities."[73]

So it was for Paprzycki, not a social scientist but an artist, recapturing memories as they came down to him from his youth. What he describes, however, sounds strikingly like Fred Siegel's commentary: "The call to 'bring the war home'—seemingly possible during the most overheated moments of the sixties—was never heeded as such, but the riots themselves never fully ended. Instead, they were followed by a 'rolling riot,' an explosion in crime that has only now begun to subside in some cities."[74] As the suburbs continued to grow and maintain their distance from the city, a reversal of fortunes was completed. Camden like other cities whose industrial and population base had departed, was remembered fondly for what it had been and looked down upon for what it had become, thus sustaining selective memories as well as the arguments of policy analysts and politicians who continued to insist that those left behind had manufactured their own problems. This is the lens through which much of Camden's history has been interpreted over the past quarter century. It remains to be shown more exactly what actions as well as what conditions conspired to seal Camden's dire situation. As the next two chapters will show, this was not a fate brought on by those left behind.

PART II

Shifting Power

Chapter 3
To Save Our City

Camden today stands at the crossroads.
Which turn will it take?
Will its people elect to office a group of candidates qualified to guide the
*   reborn city to maturity of industrial and civic growth?*
Or will lack of foresight blind the people to the importance competent gov-
*   ernment has for the city's future?*
A wrong choice can mean a Camden going downhill.
It can mean a Camden blighted by slums, plagued by unemployment,
*   doomed to the role of an ugly shadow to the large city across the*
*   river. . . .*
Streets once again in disrepair, water never entirely free from rust, rising
*   taxes for lack of new ratables-these could be symptoms of the mor-*
*   dant condition of the Camden of the future.*

—Courier-Post, *1963*

Like so many in his generation, Alfred Pierce eagerly enlisted for combat during World War II. A star athlete at Camden High School and an extrovert widely known as the "flaming redhead" for his high exuberance, Pierce had a religious vision while flying his fighter aircraft over Germany. Should he survive this test, he discerned, it was his destiny to save his native city.[1]

Al Pierce had a chance to realize that dream. Imbued with the era's positivist view that, with triumphs over depression and world war, anything was possible, he turned his attention to reconstructing Camden. Public opinion was ripe for such an effort, and federal housing and highway legislation provided generous funding for physical renewal. Cities still held sway as the primary engines of wealth and culture in the nation. That they had aged, and seemed with new patterns of development increasingly out of date, required attention. Emerging suburban competition for valuable resources made the challenge all the more pressing. By committing himself to

Camden's reconstruction and renewal, Pierce joined a generation of activists committed to restoring cities to positions of regional primacy.[2]

As in other older industrial cities, such reformist efforts coincided with social changes that complicated the simple concept of physical reconstruction. Drawn to the opportunities they represented for employment as well as freedoms denied elsewhere, especially during the war years, African Americans flooded cities like Camden. That they encountered discrimination at every level of existence prompted new exertions to assure their share of the wealth at hand. Despite established patterns of acquiescence, they challenged the status quo, forming first a nascent civil rights movement, then activating more militant protests. The struggle to "save Camden" thus acquired multiple meanings. For Pierce and his business backers, success meant an economically viable city, one that generated enough revenue in taxes to sustain the city's immediate needs for goods and services. For African Americans, the goals were closely related but more personal. They wanted access to employment as well as the benefits that were assumed to follow: decent homes in stable neighborhoods. Full success hung, therefore, on the ability to blend the two purposes. Unfortunately, timing and process conspired to assure a result that fell well short of either party's hopes and expectations.

*   *   *

When Al Pierce returned to Camden in 1945 there seemed no immediate demand for his services as savior. Plants that increased production rapidly during the war cut back, it was true. A number of his friends, finding few opportunities to buy a family home in the city, headed to the suburbs. But Camden seemed to be returning to business as ususal. So Pierce settled down himself, returning to live in the East Camden neighborhood he grew up in and to practice law. He offered his assistance to the Democratic party, for which he was awarded an appointed position on the school board.[3] It would be fourteen years before he would have the chance to act on his wartime revelation.

In 1959 Pierce announced that he would run for city commission, Camden's governing body. Prompted by Mayor George Brunner's decision to retire, he put together his own "Save Our City" slate for the nonpartisan election of at-large commissioner positions—five in all. Pierce pointed to the loss of jobs and the decline in the city's economic base, which he blamed on the ill effects of machine politics. Speaking for the ticket, Isadore

Bornstein described how he had bought the dilapidated Eagles Lodge building on Broadway at a city tax sale twenty years earlier. Having rehabilitated it, he ran an electrical appliance business downstairs and rented space on the upper floors. As residents started to move away, however, he was forced to close the electrical business. Now he wanted to create a climate that would make new enterprises with their jobs and payrolls eager to locate in Camden. Speaking in industrial North Camden, fellow ticket member Frank Italiano implored his audience: "Look at the empty stores, the empty plants, the movement of our friends out of the city to the suburbs."[4]

Clearly offended by the implication that the city had suffered during his tenure, Brunner backed an alternative slate, "Home Rule for Progress," which touted its own capital improvements program. Pointing to Pierce's support from Republicans, the Brunner organization urged voters not to "let suburban carpetbaggers get a strangle hold on Camden!"[5] The powerful *Courier-Post*, which had itself relocated from Camden to the suburbs in 1955, was not impressed. Stating its general reluctance to endorse candidates, it nonetheless issued a front-page editorial backing the Save Our City slate. To further make the point, it provided an adjacent photograph of the Market Street commercial district next to City Hall, with the caption:

THIS IS PROGRESS? The election sign in the upper right hand corner of the front of the Democratic headquarters which is backing the City Hall commission ticket says the candidates are for "Progress." But the signs on the gift and jewelry shop windows below at 615 Market St. say otherwise. The merchant proclaims, "We are finished! Quitting business forever. We are thru."[6]

"We know," the paper declared, "this election will decide whether Camden continues to deteriorate and slide down the road to decay, or whether it takes a sharp turn up the highway that leads to steady municipal progress and the high rank among the nation's cities that is our proper birthright." The following day 38,611 voters—a 67 percent turnout—voted four of the five Save Our City candidates into office.[7] At last, Al Pierce had his chance to act on his vision.

According to custom, the commissioners chose among themselves the top positions for city government, and Pierce was named both mayor and director of public safety. Determined to clean up the city, he threw himself especially into the safety position, taking to riding the streets with the police, often toting his own gun on the chance that he would bring lawbreakers to justice himself.[8] Pierce went especially after the numbers operations that seemed to pervade every mom-and-pop store in every ethnic neighbor-hood. He made it clear he would not tolerate gambling, and as he had the police swoop down on the old neighborhood haunts, more than a few busi-nesses considered moving out. Such a challenge to established ways of doing business was bound to generate reaction, and in 1960 his fellow com-missioners, under pressure from the city's dominant Democratic party, voted to remove Pierce from his public safety position.[9] Pierce retaliated by seeking to change the structure of city government, from the commission form that had been in place since 1923 to a mayor-council system. Blaming the current system for contributing to the city's economic problems, he predicted that the change would attract new business and industry to Cam-den.[10] Following the new system's ratification by the voters, Pierce launched his own campaign for mayor in 1961. His challenge to the political establish-ment forced him to form a ticket for reelection that could assure him the widest possible public support. To do this, he made an effort to be inclusive, naming as running mates for city council representatives of Old Camden: Italians Michael Parulli and Andrew Corea, Jewish realtor Harry Kerr, Pol-ish Matthew Casper, and Elizabeth Hawk, from the powerful Fairview sec-tion of the city. Also on the ticket was Elijah Perry, a musician with Lionel Hampton's Band, a member of the charter reform committee and the first African American to run for citywide office. Additionally, Pierce named Mario Rodriguez the first Puerto Rican to run citywide.[11]

Perry's presence on the ticket was especially significant. The Save Our City slate would never have won in 1959 had African Americans not boy-cotted the regular party ticket after Democratic party leaders rejected their plea to place one of their number on the slate. Two years later, with their numbers approaching 25 percent of the city population, African Americans asked Pierce to adopt ward-based councilmanic elections so as to assure their representation in the new government. Pierce rejected the request, saying that he needed to back at-large elections in order to secure Republi-can support. In an effort to satisfy his critics, however, he included Perry as a running mate.[12] Even before the choice became public, word circulated in city hall that African Americans were now to be included in Democratic party politics.[13] Elected with the rest of the ticket in May 1961, Perry gained access for blacks to some share of city patronage and appointments. From that point on, as Rosemary Jackson later recounted, if you were black and wanted a job, anyone who had gone to school knew they had to see Elijah Perry.[14] Rodriguez's election served the same purpose for Puerto Ricans.

The heart of both Pierce's campaigns was the promise to launch a bold redevelopment program that he said was crucial to Camden's survival. The comprehensive plan released in 1962 laid out the vision of a revitalized city in the heart of a growing region:

A City is founded upon certain functional relationships to the people of the region. These relationships must change to meet different social, political, economic, industrial, and other human requirements. If the functions for which the city was built cease to be needed, and if they are not continuously replaced by new functions, the city will decline or disappear. If the worn out parts of the city are not replaced but are, instead, allowed to remain as a sort of urban backwash, the processes of change and new development will take place outside of the city. If the people of a city want this new growth to occur within their city, its environment must be enhanced.[15]

To achieve a "balanced environment," the plan proposed a "redistribution of functional elements," including nothing less than a whole new network of highways to connect residential areas to places of work, space for industrial expansion, rebuilt downtown residential areas, and the restoration of decaying commercial centers at such central junctions as Broadway and Kaighn in South Camden. Most central, both physically and intellectually, the plan called for rebuilding the heart of the city—160 acres in all—as City Centre. The new downtown would be anchored by a two-level shopping mall, enclosed and air-conditioned and situated over the Broadway station of a highspeed rail line connecting Philadelphia and the Camden County suburbs. This vison represented a direct response to the opening in 1961 of the Cherry Hill Mall. Another eight hundred housing units, a 15 to 20 story office building and high-rise hotel, a parking garage, and new retail shops completed the vision. Concurrently, Pierce promoted an ambitious plan to build an expansive luxury waterfront development along the northeastern shore, popularly referred to as a "City Within a City." Described as combining the best elements of urban and suburban living, the new complex was promoted for its proximity to both Camden's and Philadelphia's downtowns.[16]

The comprehensive plan revealed an unusually optimistic set of presumptions: that industry would continue to expand if only land were made available and automobile access to employment could be improved; that renovated commercial and residential areas could hold their own with suburban competitors; and that improved housing opportunities would produce "a desirable residential environment within the City which can compete with the pleasant atmosphere of the suburbs." The city's planning director even claimed that the plan would improve property values by 100 percent, and Camden could "prosper as it has seldom done before."[17] The plan was a classic progrowth renewal program, like those emerging in municipal areas across the country at the time.[18] To promote the effort, Pierce encouraged formation of an independent business organization to work in conjunction with city government. Self-consciously assuming the name of its 1920s predecessor, the Greater Camden Movement, it raised funds to publicize the effort and to recruit developers. The *Courier-Post* maintained interest in the effort by widely publicizing its presumed benefits.[19]

In order to build City Centre, Pierce first had to designate the downtown area blighted. At 1966 hearings, local businessmen facing possible displacement surprised the Pierce administration with their opposition to the plan. After the session ran well into the night, the city's planning board recessed for three weeks, enabling it to muster a carefully orchestrated array of dramatic reports from department heads on the deteriorating nature of the area. Members of the Greater Camden Movement spoke forcefully for the plan, including the president of Campbell Soup, who said its success would determine whether the business remained in the city. The *Courier-Post* chimed in to dismiss any naysaying as parochial objections that must give way to the greater good. Under the headline "Camden: A City in Pursuit of Tomorrow," it commented on the eve of the second hearing, "Five years ago, city fathers announced that Camden, a 138-year-old city, wasting on its death bed, was not going to die without a fight. Experts were called in to probe the city's complicated malady, which was draining its economic bloodstream. These experts prescribed a cure that included major surgery, a massive rehabilitation program and new transportation arteries."[20] With such backing, the Pierce administration cleared the immediate hurdle posed by the opposition of small businessmen. But it faced an even more severe challenge from civil rights activists, who, in tallying the increasing pace of demolition without the provision of adequate replacement homes, came to see a housing crisis in the city.

For years African Americans and Puerto Ricans had been confined to the oldest and least desirable housing stock in the city. Housing conditions in most distinctly black neighborhoods were inferior to those outside. As whites began to move out, homes were often rented out by absentee landlords. After the 1950 U.S. Census reported that five thousand of Camden's thirty-eight thousand homes lacked indoor toilets, the *Courier-Post* commented editorially that there were more people than it liked to admit "living under conditions like those under which millions of Asiatics live, amid filth, over-crowding and all the factors that breed disease and crime." No one, it asserted, "should be fooled by the specious arguments sometimes advanced that the victims of substandard housing conditions are the victims of their own laziness and indifference to such conditions. That argument is false. They would live decently if they knew how and had the chance. It is up to their more fortunate neighbors to see that they get the chance."[21] Conditions failed to improve, however, as Ronald B. Evans learned as a nascent activist recently returned to Camden after serving in the Korean War. Impatient with the cautious approach of the NAACP, Evans joined the Camden chapter of CORE in its early days. He was always on the street, talking to people sitting on their front stoops, who recounted the terrible conditions they encountered. In a number of properties around Cooper Hospital in particular, Evans discovered how house-hungry tenants were jammed into every available space. He heard of tenants sleeping in closets, in hallways, or on mattresses on the floor. Many cooked only with hot plates or lacked even their own source of electricity. Evans heard enough to organize a demonstration at Pulaski Square Park, adjacent to the hospital. There his crew of nearly one hundred pitched tents and said they would be staying there until they got results. City officials did not believe Evans's threat until trucks began to drive up with food, milk, and blankets for the demonstrators. The mayor never responded to their demand for a meeting, but he sent a prominent ward leader to negotiate a resolution, and Evans had his first success.[22]

Public housing also proved a bone of contention. When it was first introduced to the city in 1938, it was embraced as a highly desirable alternative to low-rent quarters in the private market. Camden politicians eagerly sought government assistance to build these projects, as they provided a ready source of patronage as well as satisfying the needs of workers, many of whose income was too low to find decent housing during the Depression. Labor backed public housing in Camden as it had nationally (particularly by supporting expanded federal investment in the landmark National Housing Act of 1937).[23] As in most other cities, however, such housing was provided only on a segregated basis, with the racial composition of the surrounding neighborhood determining who could be accommodated in each facility. The city's pioneer Westfield Acres (1938) and Ablett Village (1943) projects were placed in East Camden and were open to whites only. Two other projects—Branch Village (1941) and Roosevelt Manor—were located in South Camden to accommodate black residents. Chelton Terrace, which had been built in 1944 to accommodate white defense workers at New York Ship, was converted to African American civilian use after the war.

As the number of African Americans increased in the 1950s, pressure grew for more places in public housing. White demand for such accommodations was declining; many left for private homes as they exceeded the income limits set by the public authority. But Camden housing chief Joseph McComb, whose main paid employment came as head of the city's Central Labor Union, held fast to the color line. In 1954, the NAACP brought suit against the Camden Housing Agency for refusing to admit blacks into the newly constructed McGuire Gardens in East Camden. The plaintiffs, which included the prominent black doctor Ulysses Wiggins, admitted that in submitting applications they did not seek residence themselves. They charged, however, that because no African Americans were being admitted, the court should order a moratorium on taking any further applications until the policy changed. Superior Court Judge Vincent Haneman chose to see the issue settled voluntarily. He lifted the prohibition of further occupancy that had been approved in a lower court for McGuire Gardens, but he charged the housing authority to consider all the applications from those who originally applied for occupancy there. Four black families subsequently moved into the project.[24]

More than a decade later, the situation had not changed materially. According to a 1966 report, the city's seven public housing projects accommodated two thousand people: 765 black, 1,124 white, and 42 Puerto Rican. In South Camden, Roosevelt Manor and Chelton Terrace could be called "integrated," with one white and three Filipinos respectively, while Branch Village remained totally occupied by African Americans. In East Camden, Westfield Acres recorded three blacks, McGuire Gardens six, and Ablett Village six blacks and 44 Puerto Ricans, along with 260 white residents. The new John Kennedy Towers constructed for senior citizens listed ninety whites and only nine African Americans. The Reverend Herman Watts, who helped prompt the report by joining a demonstration organized by civil rights groups, called the projects as segregated as Georgia.[25] After two people were killed in a South Camden fire in a home riddled with code violations, the number of demonstrators increased. Addressing a crowd outside the burned-out shell, the Rev. William King, state secretary of the NAACP, proclaimed, "If we don't start here in Camden, the people of Mississippi will be ahead of us."[26]

The growing militance of the demands corresponded with an active and growing civil rights campaign in the city, which in addition to predominantly black organizations included a number of white Protestant clergy. One of the first to organize was Episcopal priest Donald Greismann, who described the St. John's parish in South Camden he joined in 1959 as located in the white hole of a donut of black and Puerto Rican residents. Seeing his own parish shrink in relevance as its parishioners left for the suburbs, he determined to engage the neighborhood. To do so, he offered local children activities and snacks. Ultimately their parents followed. A large building across the street was in bad disrepair. He located the absentee owner in Harrisburg, Pennsylvania and wrote him asking to buy it. Nothing happened immediately, but one day a man smoking a big cigar and driving a Cadillac appeared, introduced himself as the owner, and offered to let Greismann take the structure off his hands. Extracting a further commitment of $10,000 from the owner, Greismann subsequently opened the renovated building as the Episcopal Center, with the explicit intention of providing needed services to Camden's poor.[27]

Presbyterians also found themselves needing a new mission in Camden. In 1964 the Pesbytery of West Jersey established the Camden Metropolitan Ministry (CMM) with the purpose of reviving its ministry in light of new urban issues. Ministers Lawrence Black and Richard Witham and Rutgers University chaplain Samuel Appel located a building in beleaguered North Camden, from which they intended "to engage in the total renewal of the life of the city beginning with this particular neighborhood." In addition to trying to salvage the three Presbyterian parishes in the city, they used the term "urban exploration" to designate "an innovative ministry directed toward Christian involvement and citizen action to investigate and solve problems facing the urban resident—housing, the political process, public education, employment and racism."[28] CMM sought to connect suburban parishioners with Camden's growing black population. Following a particularly intense retreat held in North Camden in 1966, Judy Motely, a member of the suburban Collingswood Church of Christ and a teacher in Camden public schools, revealed the shared sense of responsibility that emerged from the meeting. "Stunned . . . overwhelmed . . . saddened . . . changed. All these inadequate words to describe emotions felt" at the retreat, she wrote in the CMM newsletter. "Be awakened then to such slumlords, rat infested houses, subdivided and subdivided again to cram human beings into despair and desolation. Watch the effects and desolation. . . . Realize this is *my* responsibility . . . *I* share the guilt. Weep for the aged, adults, children whose right to be human has been denied."[29]

Early in 1966 Donald Greismann took the lead in forming the Camden Civil Rights Coalition by including members of CMM along with his existing allies in the NAACP and CORE. Under this umbrella, Samuel Appel initiated "Project Free" to test real estate compliance with open housing legislation. Sending first white and then either black or mixed couples to inquire about listings, he began to document the ways in which the private market continued to steer clients to segregated quarters. In addition, Appel sought to address poor schools by running, unsuccessfully at first, on his own "Save Our City" slate. So intense were his pronouncements as a campaigner and at school board meetings that the board chair accused him of harassment. Appel insisted, however, that Camden received less funding per pupil than other jurisdictions, both urban and suburban, a position that was later backed by the courts. "A city cannot be rebuilt if it does not concentrate on the education of its citizenry and especially its children. Physical improvement will mean little if education is neglected," he declared.[30]

Evans, Greismann, and Appel were among those leaders who pointed out that many residents as well as businesses would be forced to relocate under the new comprehensive plan. No fewer than fourteen thousand families would have to move over the next twenty years, more than eleven thousand of them as residential structures were razed to provide industry more room to grow. Writing in the *Catholic Star Herald*, one critic reported that when he asked Camden's planning director where the poor were expected to go, the director replied, "We can't plan for social conditions."[31] Of the city's redevelopment director, Greissman later recalled, the saying went, "Save our home from Joe McComb."[32]

In September 1966, as protesters jammed a meeting of the housing authority, one activist warned that the city faced another Watts riot if it did not act soon to relieve the congested housing conditions facing African Americans. Put off by the demonstrators, a member of Pierce's reform slate, City Council member Elizabeth Hawk, retorted, "How do you expect us to build homes, with our hands? You shout and yell exactly as you are doing now. I've never heard you say you wanted to do one thing." Jersey Joe Walcott, the former boxer and now a trouble-shooter for the city, publicly complained, "The city's half-billion renaissance could be severely weakened by an uncooperative, militant, rioting Negro population."[33] The issue would not go away, however. Public housing and redevelopment were inevitably joined, not just because the housing authority maintained jurisdiction over both policy areas, but also because the true dimensions of possible displacement were finally being made public. At a June 1967 city council meeting where demonstrators disrupted proceedings by evoking the nationally known black militant chant, "burn, baby, burn," activists charged that three thousand city buildings had been demolished in the previous six years with no low-cost housing to replace them.[34]

Official documents filed in support of redevelopment plans claimed that there was plenty of available housing in the city to accommodate those displaced. But that claim was countered by, among others, Donald Greismann, who recruited a Vista volunteer to compile a damning report of escalating dislocation without adequate notice or plans for relocation. Describing a crisis "as great as that which caused the Civil War," Greismann asked the U.S. Department of Housing and Urban Development (HUD) to "obtain the immediate cessation of displacement due to urban renewal and highway construction in Camden until all individuals and families presently or about to be displaced are relocated in decent, safe housing they can afford."[35] Greismann's report provoked an angry outburst from Mayor Pierce, but the findings were confirmed by HUD, which concluded that "citizen participation in a widely representative and viable sense does not exist in Camden today."[36]

*   *   *

The night of August 30, 1967, militant black power advocate and new national president of the Student Nonviolent Coordinating Committee, H. Rap Brown, spoke before a large and vocally appreciative black audience in Camden. He was responding to an invitation from the Camden Civil Rights Coalition to speak to the issue of urban renewal and its adverse effects on African Americans. The invitation had originally gone to Brown's predecessor, Stokely Carmichael, and some in the coalition, including Father Greismann and local NAACP President John Robinson, wanted to withdraw it in light of Brown's militant pronouncements. Others, including Sam Appel, pressed forward. When Jersey Joe Walcott, acting as the city's representative, initially balked at giving Brown a platform, the coalition threatened to hold the meeting on a street corner. The city relented and authorized space at the convention center but still attempted to get a court injunction to bar Brown's appearance at the last minute. Some four thousand people showed up to hear him; perhaps 80 percent had come from outside the city. According to reports published the next day, Brown denigrated local as well as national civil rights leadership, telling the crowd that the country was in revolution and that "the only way to defend yourself is to go out and get guns."[37]

Chief Harold Melleby's deployment of four busloads of helmeted and

Figure 8. Kaighn Avenue before redevelopment, December 9, 1954, and after displacement of 39 residents and 14 businesses, May 28, 1970. Courtesy *Courier-Post*.

shotgun-carrying police quickly ended sporadic incidents of window-breaking after the meeting. Relieved that there was no greater trouble, city officials and the press revealed their antagonism to the whole process. In an editorial entitled, "What Good Was Done?" the *Courier-Post* challenged members of the Civil Rights Coalition sponsoring Brown's appearance to "examine their own actions which helped establish the climate in which hate could flourish. Possibly they are as guilty as those they accuse—the slumlord, the indifferent politician, the complacent suburbanite, who also have contributed to this climate." Pointing the way to a more acceptable approach, the paper featured the arrival of the new pastor of Camden's Berean Assembly of God Church, Augustus Davis and his comment that "we must teach love and peace, not hate and war."[38] An additional column quoted a select number of Camden activists who equated Brown's appearance with an incitement to riot.[39]

One person who never would have been identified by the press at the time, for he had no experience yet as a community leader, was Charles "Poppy" Sharp. Sharp took away an entirely different message. "Rap addressed all of us, but I felt he was talking directly at me," he recalled. "I had to make a decision in my life at that point. In making the decision, I wound up taking the suffering of the community on myself." An eighth-grade dropout in frequent trouble as a youth, Sharp had spent more than a dozen years in reformatories and state prisons. At the time the first city protests emerged, he was hustling at a South Camden bar near the church his father presided over, at Mechanic and Locust Streets. Arrested in 1967 on a charge of robbery and the threat to kill with a gun, he gained a reprieve when the complaint was withdrawn.[40] As the crowd streamed from the auditorium the night of Brown's address, a number of Camden residents pealed off to meet again at a local bar. There, Sharp took the microphone to address those assembled. Later, he admitted that he did not remember precisely what he said, but the sense of epiphany he experienced that night always stayed with him: "I felt the energy. . . . I had never experienced that type of energy. I was just going with it. I had to. There was no other choice." The effect of his comments was powerful, and an organization, Black Believers of Knowledge, formed on the spot. With additional soul searching in the following days with Walter Palmer, who had already formed his own black militant organization in Philadelphia, Sharp moved from inquiry to action and renamed his organization the Black People's Unity Movement (BPUM).[41]

Reacting to years of exclusion, BPUM initially described itself as a ve-

hicle to advance participatory democracy. Through operational unity—
"the belief that all the people in our community should contribute to positive change"—the organization set as its goals suitable housing, a decent
salary, and self-respect. Charging that "The Black community is now a col-
ony; the politics, economic and social aspects of the community are controlled for and by people outside of the community," BPUM dedicated itself to political, economic, and social self-determination.[42] Built on the
enthusiasm of mostly younger residents, including members of the NAACP
Youth Corps, BPUM quickly came to dominate Camden's public discourse
around rights issues, and Sharp was its natural, forceful, and articulate
leader.

Under Sharp's influence, protest quickly assumed a distinctly militant
character. In May 1968 he led a group of one hundred angry residents into
a Camden Housing Authority meeting, calling urban renewal "a vicious
failure" and demanding that Joseph McComb be removed as chair. In response to McComb's claim that he was not on trial, Sharp retorted that
McComb was on trial and that he was guilty. The issue most immediately
at hand was the displacement of a black family in North Camden, for whom
the city could find no alternative housing. Activists at an April 30 meeting
of representatives of CORE, NAACP, BPUM, SNCC, and several local
neighborhood organizations had voted to relocate the family to the Walt
Whitman Hotel and send the city the bill. Following a demonstration at the
hotel, City Administrator Thomas Gramigna responded that a house had
been found for the Shields family. BPUM rejected the site as inadequate,
however, forcing Gramigna to agree. The next day demonstrators marched
on the luxury Northgate apartment building in North Camden, an early
symbol of Pierce's redevelopment effort, saying that they would burn it
down if their demands were not satisfied.[43] Pierce, an early critic of Sharp
and his tactics, confronted demonstrators with a battalion of heavily armed
police, who marshaled the demonstrators out after they met briefly with the
mayor.[44] He averted an immediate crisis by locating a suitable alternative
site for the Shields family in East Camden.[45] Although the housing authority
announced within days that it was altering its relocation policy to ensure
that homes were available in advance of condemnation, Poppy Sharp continued to complain. Speaking before a U.S. Senate subcommittee on relocation days later, he charged that "Camden Negroes have been pushed into a
pocket filled with disease that is going to destroy us unless we take steps to
alleviate it." Sharp, wearing dark glasses and dressed in blue denim, "tapped
on a table for emphasis" as he told committee chairman Edmund Muskie,

Figure 9. Poppy Sharp confronts Mayor Alfred Pierce, May 7, 1968. Courtesy *Courier-Post.*

"You are forcing the black man to go into the streets to fight, to kill ourselves or to be free."[46]

Demonstrations continued in Camden, as Sharp used the Shields incident to recruit some seventy black students attending Camden High School to show their solidarity with the family by marching on City Hall. After a raucous demonstration, one group followed Sharp in another march up Broadway. There a physical confrontation with police ensued. After charging the police himself, Sharp calmed down enough to address the crowd from the top of an automobile before retiring to the Episcopal Center without further incident. Haywood Smith, cochairman of BPUM, warned, however, "From now on there will be nothing but agitation, protest or whatever means to make the city the model it can be." Days later he was arrested for inciting to riot for a speech he made in the town of Bridgeton in nearby Cumberland County.[47]

Although Smith asserted that BPUM, not the white ministry, was in charge of rights agitation now, such statements did not discourage the Camden Metropolitan Ministry from forming its own support group. Min-

utes of the April CMM meeting described BPUM as "a positive and progressive group" with aims "to promulgate Negro heritage." Noting as well
the dedication of BPUM's leaders, CMM approved a $500 donation to the
organization, the first of many financial contributions.[48] The following
month, Sam Appel took the lead in forming a Friends of the Black People's
Unity Movement, which sought to engage white suburbanites with Camden's problems:

The basic objectives of the Friends of the BPUM are to provide an instrument for
involvement of committed members of the white community in working for the
goals of social justice in areas of housing, education, employment, poverty, law enforcement, urban renewal, and in matters pertaining to good government throughout the Camden metropolitan area. We are committed to supporting and assisting
the BPUM in its struggle toward these goals, particularly in Camden, and to confront the white community with the crucial nature of the problems of urban life
and the need for radical change. We are committed to non-violent direct action to
accomplish these goals.[49]

Members of the Friends group joined BPUM in the march on the Northgate Apartments. A Cherry Hill resident, Jean Cohen, later asserted that "it
was very right and good that I, with other white suburbanites, should join
in marching through the city streets with our black friends to point out
no one would listen or act to disprove the claim 'urban renewal is black
removal.'"[50]

   As protests continued to mount, not all African Americans were
pleased with the tactics BPUM was employing. Delbert Nelson was among
a group that had been using the threat of withholding the black vote for
candidates not responsive to their needs as a means of influencing policy.
He was upset at the way BPUM activists bullied their way into the public
arena.[51] The police practice of harassing Sharp and charging him with
minor offenses such as directing profane language at officers if they had no
better cause for arrest evoked sympathy, however, even from the city's more
established black community. To reports of one incident, the Rev. Vincent
dePaul of the black St. Bartholomew's Catholic Church retorted, "Certainly
those of us in the black community of the city are not alienated from Mr.
Sharp by such evidently discrediting tactics. If anything, we are drawn
closer. You see most of us already knew of the past problems he has had
with the law and the strides he has made to his present position in our
community."[52] For his own part, Sharp remained defiant, declaring on his
release from prison for a cursing infraction, "The fifteen days in jail was

Figure 10. Demonstrators, Northgate Apartment complex, *Philadelphia Bulletin,*
April 17, 1978. Courtesy Temple University Libraries, Urban Archives, Philadelphia.

nothing. I spent 30 years in prison walking the streets of Camden."[53] In
June 1968, when detectives trailed members of BPUM to a picnic in suburban Medford Lakes, where Kenneth and Sylvia Newcomb sought to bring
members of the Friends together with the parent organization, Sharp described the incident in typically graphic form:

As I entered the road leading to the Newcombs' property there were two men in
the car preceeding me. As we drove abreast to these men, we recognized them to be
white Det. Pig Bush and Nigger Det. Pig Pugh. In their possession we noticed a tape
recorder and a camera. After seeing and recognizing the passengers in the car behind them, they immediately fled into the woods. . . . I think the presence of these
two creeps was a case of pure harassment and a violation of one's rights, freedom
of speech and freedom of movement.[54]

Two months later, Mayor Pierce and Police Chief Harold Melleby filed
a civil suit against the Friends of the Black People's Unity Movement,
charging it with inciting others to violence and conducting unlawful assem-
blies. They asked the court to restrain the organization from committing
criminal acts. The object of their charge was a May institute on nonviolent

action that had been requested by Sam Appel as a means of dealing with increasing tension between demonstrators and police. Some two hundred people gathered for this exercise, which was conducted under the direction of theology student William Repsher. The largely white and suburban group spent the weekend playing out roles, apparently depicting the police and antagonisms toward them in graphic ways.

The suit against Appel and Repsher was based on testimony provided by two infiltrators to the meeting from the Camden County Conservative Club and a George Wallace political organization. The charges were clearly trumped up, provoking an outpouring of support from fellow clergy and activists.[55] But in a deposition provided for the trial, Mayor Pierce repeated charges he and Chief Melleby had previously made, that the civil rights protest was Communist-inspired. Asserting that the meetings in question could be characterized as spreading Communist philosophy, Pierce said that he believed the Friends "are more interested in promoting civil violence and disobedience and discrediting civil authorities, than they are with the curing of the problems." The Presbyterian retreat, he claimed, "gave rise to the opportunity to spread Communist philosophy, Marxist philosophy" through the dissemination of literature that "expounded perversion or obstruction of justice and the due administration of the laws."[56]

Turmoil stemming from further demonstrations prompted the county prosecuting attorney to convene a grand jury investigation into the causes. In April 1969 the grand jury provided a surprisingly sympathetic view of the situation. While sharply criticizing specific tactics of the demonstrators and pining for leadership from "respected members of the minority community," not just from "those that yell the loudest," it concluded that the demonstrations of May and June the previous year "were at least in part, a reaction to the overall plight of the city of Camden, a city which has been abandoned by many of its businesses, much of its industry and a large percentage of its middle and upper income families, all of these having moved to the suburbs." Friends of BPUM praised the findings, adding, however, that the grand jury should have gone a step further, to encourage housing authorities in the suburbs to build and maintain low-cost housing for needy residents. Recognizing that this might appear "a pipe dream," it asserted nonetheless that "suburban communities, families and individuals, do share in the guilt of what has occurred in Camden and other areas through their apathy."[57]

Despite city officials' worst fears, no full-scale civil disorder wracked Camden. On September 2, 1969, however, the same day a grand jury indicted Appel and Repsher, violence erupted in a black section of South Camden. Accounts of the incident differed. Police attempting to arrest a man on a fugitive warrant for instigating a fight two nights earlier were confronted by a hostile crowd of some three hundred people. The father of two teenage girls involved in the crowd claimed that police instigated the violence when three officers assaulted his daughters with blackjacks. Police claimed they arrested one of the girls only after she attacked one of them with a twelve-inch butcher knife. Even as a police captain and a black minister attempted to calm the crowd, shots were fired, killing a twenty-one-year-old white police officer and a black teenage girl passing through the area.[58] The next day, Melleby directed officers to raid the BPUM headquarters. Announcing that they had recovered forty-three packets of heroin in the facility, police seized Poppy Sharp and placed him under arrest. In addition, they inflicted a good deal of damage on a clothing manufactory that had been set up recently at the BPUM headquarters. When accused of wanton destruction, Melleby countered that the damage was the result of BPUM members themselves seeking publicity.[59] Three months later, police broke into BPUM minister for development Michael Edwards's apartment in the middle of the night. As they kicked down Edwards's door, he rolled to the floor to take up his own weapon. The police had the upper hand, however, and subdued him after shooting him in the ankle and leg. Sharp fared better. He went free after ninety days, when the court threw out preliminary evidence against him. Appel and Repsher also escaped penalty when a jury failed to reach a verdict. Edwards was charged with discharging a gun in city limits and possession of marijuana. He feared he could never receive a fair trial and fled to Africa, where he subsequently changed his name to Malik Chaka.[60]

Into this charged atmosphere there soon emerged another set of provocative actions. Peter O'Connor, a young white lawyer at the Camden Regional Legal Services office, began a series of actions seeking to overturn the city's plan for urban renewal. O'Connor, who had been one of the first to offer Poppy Sharp legal assistance after his arrest, meant to "stop everything in the city until the requirement of community participation is realized." He filed a petition with the Department of Housing and Urban Development charging that it was Camden's intention "to remove the minority groups from the city through demolition of housing and ultimately to bring back the suburban white population to live in luxury housing."[61] When HUD Secretary George Romney refused requests for a full hearing, O'Connor filed suit in U.S. District Court. Plaintiffs were the Camden Civil Rights

Coalition, along with a list of active individuals starting with Poppy Sharp, CORE's Ronald Evans, the NAACP's John Robinson, and the Reverend Donald Greismann, as well as a number of Camden residents displaced by renewal policies. One of these, Mary Alice Colvin, the mother of eight and a welfare recipient, had been among those displaced by the city's first clearance project at Kaighn's Point. The area had once been the site of a ferry service to Philadelphia, but had long since become one of the densest and most concentrated black neighborhoods in the city. Colvin was relocated to North Camden where she was forced to move twice more to make way for a planned luxury high-rise project, Northgate II. O'Connor's brief asserted, "Plaintiff Colvin and her family are presently residing in substandard housing due to the scarcity of safe, decent, and sanitary housing in the City of Camden, but want to remain in Camden and live in a decent neighborhood."[62] Charging that the city had failed generally to pursue "coherent planning and programming with respect to code enforcement, physical development, housing and relocation, and constructive citizen involvement in federally assisted programs," the suit specifically charged that the city could not proceed with its program until it filed a federally required "workable program." The Camden Coalition, the suit declared, "wants to have an official plan of action for effectively dealing with Camden's problems of urban slums and blight and for the establishment and preservation of a well-planned community with well-organized living environment for adequate family life." It also sought, it said, "a feasible method for relocating individuals and families into decent, safe, and sanitary housing . . . reasonably accessible to their places of employment."[63] The court was sufficiently impressed to halt redevelopment in its tracks.

Al Pierce, faced with legal obstruction and social turmoil, retired from office in 1969. The *Courier-Post*, still speaking for the hopes vested in the renewal program, saluted him by editorializing, "Controversial or not, he takes with him the credit for giving Camden its rebirth. . . . Its rebirth is here. It is in its infancy, of course, and must be nursed carefully."[64] That challenge fell to Pierce's successor as mayor, former City Attorney Joseph Nardi. The son of a shoemaker, whose ascension in city government represented an affirmation of the American dream held by so many children of immigrants, Nardi was soon tested in that position.[65] On July 20, 1971, two Camden patrolmen arrested a Puerto Rican motorist, Horacio Jimenez, a parishioner at Our Lady of Fatima. Word quickly circulated that Jimenez had been hospitalized and was believed in a coma, the victim of a savage beating by the two patrolmen. Hispanic leaders pressed for a full investiga-

Figure 11. Protesters rally outside Camden City Hall, following the police shooting of a local Hispanic man, August 19, 1971. Civil disturbances broke out later that night. Courtesy *Courier-Post*.

tion and suspension of the police officers involved. When Police Chief Melleby refused to act and Mayor Nardi rebuffed requests for a meeting, a protest formed in front of City Hall on August 19th. Activists, including the Young Lords' Gualberto Medina, as well as the more established Hispanic leadership and Poppy Sharp, who assured Hispanics the support of Camden's black community, addressed the crowd of some three hundred, many of whom initially were women and children. As the day wore on and men leaving work joined the protest, numbers surged to as many as a thousand. Efforts to secure a meeting with the mayor during the first hours failed, and the presence of police with dogs heightened tensions. Finally, Nardi agreed to receive a delegation at 8 p.m. on the eighteenth floor of City Hall, far removed from the speeches and chanting on the street below. The mayor was going over the list of demands with his top staff later that evening when a commotion on the street became evident. A fight at a nearby bar spilled over into the demonstrating crowd, and suddenly windows were being broken, and a spree of looting began. Nardi rushed back into the conference

Figure 12. Camden police confront residents in North Camden in aftermath of civil disturbances, August 21, 1971. Courtesy *Courier-Post*.

room where the Hispanic leaders were waiting and yelled at Mario Rodriguez that he had five minutes to calm things down outside or the negotiations were over. By the time Rodriguez reached the street, the civil disturbance was out of hand. For the next three nights fires, looting, and destruction of property paralyzed the city.[66]

In this worst of situations, anticipated and feared for years and now finally a reality, Mayor Nardi was ill prepared to act effectively. The anger behind the protests—to say nothing of the violence on the streets—was simply too far removed from the values and experiences he associated with Old Camden. He had neither the personal ability nor the will to step in. For this he relied on director of public works and Democratic Party chief Angelo Errichetti. Errichetti was an early Pierce protege who had been rewarded in 1961 with an appointment as assistant city purchasing agent. In 1965 he had been named director of public works, with access to the city's richest source of patronage, and the city Democratic chairman. He was trotted out to defend the city's vision for redevelopment in 1966, and now he worked behind the scenes to defuse the situation by dealing with the

Figure 13. Unfinished redevelopment, North Camden, December 27, 1971. Courtesy *Courier-Post.*

central criticisms brought against the city's renewal and housing programs. In 1972, in a series of negotiations with O'Connor and members of the BPUM, he worked out a resolution of the lawsuit that dealt directly and forcefully with housing the city's lower income population. Most dramatically, it acceded to O'Connor's demand that a high-rise luxury building near the waterfront in North Camden, Northgate II, be reserved for low- and moderate-income residents and that it be accompanied by an additional one hundred low-rise units and recreational facilities nearby. The City Centre project was finally cleared to go ahead, but now with requirements to include subsidized housing units for residents displaced in the redevelopment process. In bringing unions into the negotiations, the Camden Coalition secured as well commitments guaranteeing 20 percent minority employment and contractors on all state and federally funded projects in the city. This provision addressed charges Donald Greismann had made before a Senate subcommittee, where he accused Joseph McComb, head of the Camden Central Labor Union as well as the redevelopment office, of directing work to unions at the expense of black construction companies

Figure 14. The suit against Camden's redevelopment is settled, June 24, 1972. Signing for the Civil Rights Coalition is BPUM's Barbara Broadwater. Looking over her left shoulder is Angelo Errichetti, over her right shoulder is Elijah Perry, Camden's first African American city councilman. Poppy Sharp stands behind her. Behind him to the right is Carl Bisgaier of Camden Legal Regional Services. Rev. Donald Greismann stands at the rear, fourth from the right. Courtesy *Courier-Post*.

and architects.[67] The *Courier-Post* thought that Camden's prospects for the future had never seemed brighter. It described the pact as one of the most liberal plans in the country for hiring and training minority workers on construction jobs.[68] When the papers to terminate the suit were finally ready to sign, Nardi asked for time to evaluate the document. Clearly in charge here, Errichetti snapped, "Just sign the damn thing."[69] Nardi soon stepped down as mayor and moved to the suburb of Pennsauken.[70]

Astute politician that he was, Errichetti recognized that the city's future stability depended on some power-sharing arrangement between old and new residents of the city. When he was elected mayor in 1973, Errichetti placed a number of black and Puerto Rican activists, including Poppy Sharp, in positions of power within his administration. In addition to recruiting twenty-three-year-old BPUM staff member Randy Primas to his successful ticket for city council, he eventually named O'Connor as a special counsel to the office of mayor. Under a headline, "New Hope for Camden," a *Courier-Post* editorial expressed confidence in a new beginning, writing, "Camden's future is by no means hopeless. The new mayor takes over a city where much of the distasteful part of urban renewal, relocating people and demolishing buildings, has been accomplished. His challenge is constructive, not destructive."[71]

* * *

Some time during his first term in office, Errichetti told one of his staff he had finally figured out how to balance the budget: sell City Hall.[72] The story may have been apocryphal, and Camden County did not, as Errichetti had hoped it would, pay the city a large fee for the right to continue sharing the half-century-old building with the city. But close followers of Errichetti agreed: he would try anything to keep the city going, and if anyone could sell the equivalent of the Brooklyn Bridge, it would be him.

Bold where Nardi had been timid, flexible where Pierce had been rigid, Errichetti brought to his position political talent not seen since the era of George Brunner, who preceded Pierce as mayor. But the situation he inherited as mayor in 1973 was dire. Federal funds for urban renewal programs had been effectively terminated. Other categorical grant programs favoring cities had been reduced in favor of revenue sharing with the states. Across the country cities faced deep budgetary shortfalls, highlighted by New York City's near bankruptcy.[73] In Camden, not only were revenues well short of meeting essential needs, the rate of serious crime had climbed to the second highest in the country.[74] Errichetti's description of his native city as he made his way down Haddon Avenue from his Whitman Park home toward City Hall for his first day of work was graphic: "It looked like the Vietcong bombed us to get even. The pride of Camden . . . was now a rat-infested skeleton of yesterday, a visible obscenity of urban decay. . . . The years of neglect, slumlord exploitation, tenant abuse, government bungling, indecision and short-sighted policy had transformed the city's housing, business and industrial stock into a ravaged, rat-infested cancer on a sick, old industrial city."[75]

Errichetti's dire picture of Camden could have come from any number of his fellow white ethnics, who had already left the city or were counting on him to stem the tide before they might decide to leave too. What he offered in response was a commitment to a brand of politics that was sufficiently inclusive to diffuse social conflict and a knowledge of government

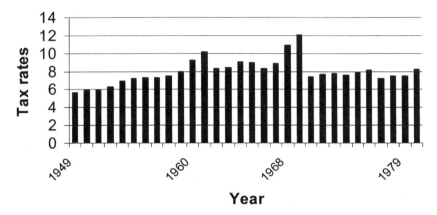

Figure 15. Camden tax rate (per $100 assessed value), 1949–1980.

capable of identifying the resources necessary to hold the coalition together. With a federally funded redevelopment strategy no longer possible in Camden, Errichetti had to rely on old-fashioned politics. Following the Brunner mode, he did all the personal networking necessary to sustain support. He extended his role as dispenser of favors as both city Democratic chairman and mayor well beyond normal office hours, receiving constituents for hours into the evening at a local bar. But what he had to dispense, he knew, was limited by the city budget, and in this he had a very different hand to play than Brunner.

Until his last year in office, continued increases in city property values had enabled Brunner to keep taxes from rising too rapidly. In 1959 those values dropped significantly for the first time, by $300,000. To balance the budget, the tax rate rose by 68 cents, to $8.64 per $100 in assessed value. As property values continued to decline in 1960 and 1961, tax rates went up again, to a postwar high of $10.12 in 1961, the first year Pierce presided as mayor under the revised form of city government. Pierce managed to reduce the rate over the next two years on the basis of a revaluation of existing properties completed shortly before he took office. He admitted that some property owners suffered the consequences of increased payments, but he claimed that the next two years would bring between ten and twenty million dollars in additional taxable properties as a result of his redevelopment efforts. As those projects lagged and the tax rate climbed again to over $9.00 in 1964 and 1965, he continued to claim that the city would be financially restored even as it was physically renewed. Remaining staunch in its support, the *Courier-Post* commented sympathetically in 1966, "Looking at the broad picture, the mayor notes that City Council and the people must accept hard, cold facts—that industries of this city cannot afford financially to remain here without a great rebuilding program sufficient to add new ratables and provide the favorable tax base industries must have."[76]

Even as Pierce held out future prospects, he still had to balance the budget, and in 1966 he introduced the dangerous strategy of selling off city assets, starting with WCAM, the city-owned radio station. As the sale of that property lagged, in 1967 Pierce drew on $1.2 million in surplus funds from separately budgeted water and sewer rents. The *Courier-Post* worried publicly that Pierce was relying too much on one-time "tricks," but it remained supportive, writing, "Many communities are enticing business and industries still located within cities to move to new areas to take advantage of what now are better tax rates. A challenge is presented to any city administration to try to maintain a tax climate attractive to business and industry while at the same time fighting to produce new sources of income and revenue so vitally necessary to a city's welfare."[77] Even so, the tax rate rose another 60 cents to $8.92 in 1967, and to $10.92 a year later. It reached $12.06 in Pierce's last year in office, underscoring how damaging the delays to proposed redevelopment efforts were to the city's economy.

Joseph Nardi found the fiscal problems he inherited devastating. Lacking either Pierce's cleverness or aptitude with finances, he was forced to accept a tax rate of $14.36 in announcing his first city budget in 1970. "I must tell you I am not proud of this budget," he told city council. "I still have that pride in Camden, and with the budget—though it is burdensome and inadequate—I will continue to do the best I can." True to its past stand, the *Courier-Post* declared, "There seems to be no escaping the conclusion that Camden taxpayers must shoulder the financial burden until, through the promise of urban redevelopment, the city hopefully makes its comeback." Nardi's announcement that Lit Brothers Department Store would not be leaving the city, as previously reported, allowed the paper to express hope that "this could be the depth from which Camden comes back."[78] Nardi, however, never mastered the situation. Although the tax rate fell to nearly half for the next three years, it did so only because the city increased its actual levy from 50 to 100 percent of property valuation. A new $2.4 million Campbell Soup research facility that came on tax rolls in 1971 softened the impact, but it could not overcome the continuing loss of businesses, which by the end of Nardi's term included both Lit Brothers and Sears department stores.

It was this situation that Errichetti knew well clouded his prospects as mayor. To keep the remaining white population in the city, he had to prevent taxes from rising. To satisfy the black and Puerto Rican constituents with whom he had allied himself, he had to deliver services. As property values plunged, despite his best efforts to attract new business to the city, it remained for Errichetti to draw on his most masterful political resources to make the city run. Because the Camden Democratic vote remained important in the state as well as the county, Errichetti could in early years tap considerable resources to meet the city's budgetary needs. His early support of Democrat Brendan Byrne in 1977 opened the door for Byrne to the governor's office. The grateful Byrne during his first year in office supplied more than $1 million in state aid to cover Camden's deficit. When county Democrats failed to deliver necessary resources, Errichetti made sure Republicans had enough votes to win county office, receiving valuable patronage in return.[79] He made sure that revenue-sharing funds made their way through the state's new Department of Community Affairs to meet neighborhood needs, while at the same time using federal funding to employ workers who otherwise would have to be paid for by the city. Most dramatically, he built on the precedent set by Al Pierce in selling off city assets. First, he transferred responsibility for parks and recreation to the school system, with its separate budget. Then, he engineered a sweetheart deal in which he sold an antiquated municipal waste plant to the county, which planned to build a new facility in the city to serve the whole county. The city received $2.5 million a year for four years, and that money was a major factor in bridging the gap between revenues raised through local taxation and total costs.[80]

Errichetti's tenure had its difficulties. Early in his first term he was indicted for alleged improprieties in his position as director of public works. Although the charges were ultimately dismissed, his court battle demanded much of his attention for nearly two years. In 1976 he added considerably to his political influence by being elected state senator, a position he held in addition to those of mayor and city Democratic chairman. As a member of the appropriations committee, he could help assure further increases in state funding for the city.[81] He managed to convince Cooper Hospital not to leave the city at a crucial time, making a convincing case for the utility of building up a central medical complex around the original site with the addition of the New Jersey School of Medicine and Dentistry nearby. The withdrawal of a desperately sought after federally funded Veterans Administration hospital, promised by President Gerald Ford, withdrawn and then promised again by

Figure 16. Abandoned buildings along Broadway, once Camden's commercial spine. *Philadelphia Bulletin*, August 19, 1978. Courtesy Temple University Libraries, Urban Archives, Philadelphia.

Jimmy Carter before being finally killed by Ronald Reagan, proved costly to the city. The *New York Times*, in a laudatory 1979 article, may have proclaimed of Errichetti's ability to address Camden's situation, "Hell may have a floor," but city finances remained precarious. Noting that the city's property values had fallen to $277 million (compared to Cherry Hill's $1.1 billion for a much smaller population), Errichetti pushed openly for a tax revaluation.[82] While taxes did not have to rise significantly in 1980, when Errichetti left office he handed his successor a huge deficit to make up.

The myth still surrounds Errichetti—one that he has encouraged—that he alone could have saved Camden, if he had only been given the chance to do so.[83] But two perceptive articles by the *Courier-Post*'s Dennis Culnan at the time of Errichetti's departure revealed the difficulty he would have had. As long as Errichetti was important to both Democrats and Republicans, the former who counted on his getting out the vote, the latter who wanted him to keep it home, he retained significant political leverage for the city. But a precipitous decline in the city vote undercut that position. While Camden in 1960 cast one-third of the county vote, in 1980 it cast only 16 percent. In contrast, Cherry Hill's portion of the county vote rose from 10 to 18 percent in the same period. As long as the Great Society persisted, social programs could be tapped to supplement the city's declining revenues. "Everyone," Culnan wrote, "wanted to throw money at the lame, poor, blacks, Hispanics, and downtrodden that Camden represented to the white middle-class psyche, guilty for abandoning cities like Camden all over the country. Errichetti was willing to play the poverty hustle and to subtly blackmail the conscience of white suburbia, meanwhile assuring it that he was keeping the poor—particularly the blacks—home on the city reservation." But as Cherry Hill and the rest of South Jersey gained in political strength, wealth, and population, Camden became both poorer and weaker politically. By 1980 the day of Great Society bailouts was over. The country was ready to let cities like Camden shift for themselves, and without the political strength it once had, Camden was in no position to dictate the terms of political rewards. "I tried to use mirrors to give the image of strength of the city," Culnan quoted Errichetti as saying, "but the smart people could see the real numbers. . . . Camden's no longer the hub of south Jersey or the county; it's just a spoke."[84]

Chapter 4
From City to County: The Rise of the Suburban Power Structure

They have a problem out there in the suburbs, and that is that they have no landfill space. So, they're going to build an incinerator, and 127 trucks a day will drive through this neighborhood bringing the trash of the county in to be burned amongst us. The people went away and sent us back their rubbish; they sent us back their trash and their sewerage and . . . anything they didn't want. And then they say to us, "Well, how come you're not coming back?" Well, I want to say, "You got your foot on my neck; that's why I can't stand up."

—*Father Michael Doyle,* 60 Minutes: Michael Doyle's Camden, *March 20, 1983*

Angelo Errichetti's departure from office coincided with Ronald Reagan's election as president and with a national assault on domestic welfare programs. The succession of African American mayors who subsequently assumed leadership were largely limited, as Poppy Sharp put it, to "managing decline."[1] This was partly because national policy trends sharply curtailed the resources these mayors had to draw on. Even more important in determining Camden's fate in the aftermath of the city's industrial decline, however, were state and especially local political structures and the power they assumed. In the post-industrial era, suburbs assumed new responsibilities for managing resources that determined the quality of life of residents in the region. Great as were the hopes African Americans harbored for Camden's self-determination, then, the shift of resources out of the city made that goal especially difficult to achieve.

Traditionally, one way cities had dominated their regional neighbors was by providing services whose operating costs were beyond the budgets of smaller jurisdictions. Many an early suburb consolidated with a central city in order to receive water, sewer, or other central services. Although that pattern practically ceased in the older cities of the Northeast and Middle West by the early twentieth century, it continued in growing areas of the West and throughout much of the rest of the country.[2] As noted in Chapter 1, Camden's aspirations in the 1920s to bring its suburban neighbors under its jurisdictional control failed. The rising awareness of environmental concerns in the 1970s and 1980s, however, provided new imperatives for regional cooperation, which Camden's leadership was determined to exploit. Water and air pollution did not respect jurisdictional boundaries, and as federal rules became tougher, both for adequate disposal of waste and for the control of air- and water-borne pollutants, new facilities were called for. Camden proved successful in achieving the right to provide both wastewater and trash treatment facilities. But over time, what had once been seen as a benefit to the city turned to its detriment. These facilities, sought after as the sources of both power and patronage for the city, in the end added to Camden's environmental degradation even as they fell under suburban control. While suburban politicians reaped financial and political rewards from these maneuvers, Camden's decline only accelerated. Its leaders acceded to external demands or they were driven from office. Not incidentally, Camden's residents bore the burden of this reversal of fortunes.

*   *   *

No doubt, the environment demanded attention throughout the built-up areas of South Jersey in the 1980s. Stream and river pollution in Camden County was as bad as any in New Jersey. Camden's existing sewage facility was under orders from the state department of health to upgrade its secondary treatment. According to an assessment in the *Courier-Post*, costs would increase fivefold without a consolidated regional system. Detailed reports of the effects of sewage dumping practices throughout the county, including vivid descriptions of "dirty, foul-smelling and generally repulsive conditions" in area streams, appeared in the suburban press.[3]

As both director of public works and City Democratic chairman in Camden in the 1960s, Angelo Errichetti was acutely aware of the importance of public utilities as sources of political power and patronage. As discussions about the need for a regional sewer authority arose, he made clear his intent to assume control. His ambition, however, clashed with that of the equally determined chair of the Camden County Democratic Party, James Joyce. A bare knuckles politician of the old school, Joyce brought his own political muscle to the issue through his position as head of the Stratford Sewer Authority in the suburban central section of Camden County. Each man institutionalized his ambition by forming his own regional sewer authority in the late 1960s, Joyce under the authority of the Camden County Board of Chosen Freeholders, Errichetti simply through his own powerful position as head of the city Democratic organization.[4] Suburban jurisdictions strongly resisted giving up their independence to join either authority, and as a consequence Errichetti and Joyce competed fiercely to gain their cooperation. The first contest came in Cherry Hill, whose growth, wealth, and increasing political influence made the township strategically important. There, in 1969, Joyce offered to assume more than $2 million in the township's outstanding bonds in return for its joining his system. Cherry Hill's mayor resisted, asserting antagonism to any outside authority that would usurp local authority and reduce the township's taxing ability. Bowing to practicality, however, the township, citing lower costs, subsequently announced it would be joining Errichetti's Camden authority.[5] Formally announcing the new Camden City Municipal Utilities Authority shortly afterward, Errichetti called for a new plant costing $14 million, 57 percent of which would be state or federally funded. At the same time, he called for the regional collection of trash.[6] Buoyed by his alliance with Cherry Hill, Errichetti got the county freeholders to issue a report in July 1971 urging Joyce's County Sewerage Authority to abandon its plans. Joyce attempted to retaliate by organizing ten municipalities under his political control to say they would go to court rather than join the city authority. But the county agency lacked a single customer and had little choice but to dissolve. A relieved *Courier-Post* expressed its hope for the end of partisan infighting, political quagmire, and stagnation.[7]

Nine months after the county agency dissolved, a new consolidated authority formed. The new organization, the Camden County Municipal Utilities Authority (CCMUA), echoed the name of Errichetti's authority. The five board members, appointed by the county freeholders, however, represented a blend of the two existing authorities. Errichetti still held the upper hand as the authority's executive director.[8] Although he left that position to run for mayor of Camden in 1973, he managed to sustain control of the authority by securing his own selection over Joyce for an open seat on the authority board. Although Joyce outwitted him by striking an alliance with Republicans and one dissident Democrat on the board of freeholders to reorganize the commission,[9] Errichetti managed nonetheless to achieve his ultimate goal of getting the Camden sewer facility funded. In December 1975, CCMUA agreed to pay Camden $2.5 million immediately towards the $11.3 million purchase of its two existing sewage treatment plants, with the final payment to be completed by the end of 1978.[10]

The contest between Errichitti and Joyce was not yet done, however. With payment in hand not just to secure a plant in Camden but to relieve the city's budgetary problems, Errichetti challenged CCMUA's leadership. Exercising influence both at the state and county levels, he secured indictments against both Joyce and his closest ally as CCMUA chairman, John Nero. Although Joyce was ultimately cleared of the charges that he had bribed an engineering firm seeking business with the commission, he nonetheless felt obliged to resign his position as CCMUA vice-chairman.[11] Nero suffered a similar fate. He managed initially to stave off charges that he had improperly favored another engineering firm by holding back final payment for the Camden sewage plant. In December 1976, however, following Errichetti's successful effort to replace Joyce as county Democratic chairman, the all-Democratic county freeholder board removed Nero and two other commissioners from office.[12]

Errichetti's triumph was short-lived, for Camden County politics was poised to take a new direction. For some years, Errichetti had nurtured a new breed of leadership outside the city. Most visible in the new cadre was James Florio, a native New Yorker, who supported himself while studying law in Camden at Rutgers by taking a series of political jobs. He was elected to the state assembly in 1960 and to Congress in 1974, each time with Errichetti's strong support. Florio, ambitious and hard-working, believed he had Errichetti's backing to replace New Jersey's retiring Democratic governor in 1977. That this was not so was revealed in the worst possible situation. Each year Errichetti hosted a lavish banquet on the eve of the convention of New Jersey Municipalities in Atlantic City. Florio was already seated when Errichetti arrived late, walking arm in arm with powerful state senator John Lynch and his candidate for governor, Richard Coffey. When Errichetti announced that Coffey was his candidate, too, Florio turned white as a sheet.[13] Without Errichetti's support, Florio showed up a weak fourth in the primary. Determined to bury that humiliation, Florio joined with the rising suburban Democratic leader Louis Katz, another Errichetti protege who had secured his base as both a county freeholder and chairman of the Cherry Hill Democratic party, to challenge Errichetti for county control in 1979. Together they organized their own slates for assembly and freeholder positions. Such was the nature of change that James Joyce now joined Errichetti in defending the established order. In the battle between generations, the Florio forces won by effectively organizing the suburbs, succeeding par-

Figure 17. Pols before the storm. Angelo Errichetti with Rep. James Florio,
November 16, 1977. Courtesy *Courier-Post.*

ticularly in new apartment buildings where allies, often already known to residents for providing free legal advice, got out the vote.[14] Florio's success in that contest and Errichetti's indictment in the ABSCAM scandal effectively signaled a new era in county politics. Although he narrowly lost the 1981 governor's contest to Republican Tom Kean, Florio emerged the titular Democratic party leader in Camden County and in South Jersey.

During the 1979 contest for Democratic party control, one rival commented that he thought Florio's poor showing in the gubernatorial primary two years earlier had convinced him of the need to exercise greater control over party patronage.[15] CCMUA, which remained a primary source of valuable contracts as well as appointments for the county, attracted Florio's intense interest. Following the 1981 gubernatorial campaign, CCMUA hired Florio's campaign manager, Ray Hoban, as its fiscal officer. Only months later, with a former Florio aide, Joseph Roberts, as freeholder-director, the county freeholders voted to expand the number of commissioners from five to nine. Although Roberts claimed the effort was intended to give better representation to the southern end of the county, the effect was to put the commission fully in the control of Florio forces. Were any further confirmation necessary, the authority subsequently contracted with state Democratic party chairman and former Florio law partner James Maloney and M. Allen Vogelson, former Camden County freeholder-director and a Katz ally from Cherry Hill, to handle legal issues associated respectively with acquisition of easements and renovation of the main sewage plant in Camden. Other campaign aides took important county positions, notably Steven Weinstein as full-time county counsel and Nicholas Rudi, Florio's 1981 campaign treasurer, as county administrator and treasurer.[16]

To this point, the pattern of securing political patronage was familiar enough, but a new dimension appeared as well. In 1984 Weinstein and Rudi left government service. Weinstein opened a New Jersey office as a partner in the Philadelphia law firm of Blank, Rome, Comisky, and McCauley. Rudi formed a new company, Consolidated Financial Management (CFM), designed to advise municipal organizations on finances. Within a year, Joseph Salema joined Rudi as a new partner at CFM. Salema's rise from chauffeur to manager of Florio's home office made him the person closest to the congressman. With high interest rates finally receding, it was now possible both to issue new bonds and to refinance old issues in order to bring projects like the county sewer system—still not connected with the Camden plant—to fruition. As CCMUA prepared to finance construction through $600 million in bonds, it replaced its New York bonding firm with Rome, Comisky—a contract worth close to $1 million in legal fees—and named CFM its financial consultant, a deal that provided CFM with over $360,000 by 1987. Both Rome, Comisky and CFM became generous contributors to Florio's congressional reelection campaigns.[17] Thus was born—for South Jersey, at least—a pattern of politically connected payouts and reciprocal campaign contributions between politicians in public agencies and private firms that came to be known as "pay to play."

CCMUA was not Rudi and Salema's only important client. While still in county government, the two men, along with Camden County freeholder-director Joseph Roberts, determined to build on Florio's reputation as an environmental reformer to devise new means for disposing of garbage. Under a 1978 state mandate to develop a county master plan for trash disposal, these men sought alternatives to existing landfill operations where new pollution controls were raising costs. In 1981 Roberts led a county delegation to inspect a pioneer trash and sludge burning facility in Harrisburg, Pennsylvania. In 1983, New Jersey adopted measures to encourage new incinerators by authorizing dumping fee surcharges to subsidize construction and payments to host communities. Camden County determined to be the first in New Jersey to use the new technology.[18] In order to finance the effort, without adding to the county's existing indebtedness, the freeholders created a semi-autonomous organization, the Pollution Control Financing Agency, with its own powers to issue bonds and to contract with a private company to build the plant. As with the CCMUA, the freeholders named the directors. Allan Vogelson subsequently became the authority's counsel, ultimately receiving an $80,000 contract to negotiate with the owner-operators of the plant. CFM was named financial consultant, receiving $66,589 for its advice on the project and another $110,000 for consulting on the authority's sale of $108 million in bonds.[19] It was in this environment, giving suburban-based politicians new economic as well as political tools over county actions, that Camden's first black mayor, Melvin "Randy" Primas, took office.

* * *

Primas, elected to succeed Errichetti in 1981, could be considered part of a handful of urban executives who assumed office identified as civil rights activists, including Richard Hatcher in Gary in 1966, Kenneth Gibson in Newark in 1979, and Marion Barry in Washington, D.C., in 1980. Primas was a 1971 business graduate of Howard University, and he liked to tell the story of how he had passed up an offer from the RCA Corporation in favor of a position with the Black People's Unity Movement's new business development arm. His parents wondered about the wisdom of the decision, but Primas had witnessed the devastating 1968 riots in Washington that followed Martin Luther King's assassination, and he felt a strong pull to address social needs rather than to make money. "That was a defining moment for me," he asserted.[20] As mayor, he framed his administration accordingly, by invoking Martin Luther King's name at his first and final official acts in office.[21] He might have been expected, then, to have followed BPUM's declaration at its inception of political independence and embraced the leading manifesto on black power in the era, Stokely Carmichael's charge to pursue collective action to enhance the material well-being of the entire black community.[22] But neither his background nor his options within the austere environment of the 1980s would lead Primas in that direction. As BPUM activist Malik Chaka later noted sharply, Primas was not part of the movement, joining demonstrations and fighting for civil rights.[23] Rather, the business arm of BPUM was pragmatic, more in line with Primas's own temperament. His rise to power owed more to his mentor Angelo Errichetti than to any particular cause. Moreover, his election in 1981 coincided with recognition in Camden as well as nationally that deindustrialization was a harsh fact of life and that Camden had lost its position of regional primacy. Even as Primas honored local NAACP activist Ulysses Wiggins at a ceremony dedicating a waterfront park to his memory, he used the occasion to warn his audience that the price of financial neglect would have to be paid. At his first state of the city address four months later, he described the situation he inherited as "the most troubling financial times we have faced since the Depression."[24]

Primas attempted to project a progressive agenda addressing the as yet unmet needs of the city's black majority, but he was haunted by the overpowering legacy of financial disinvestment. With the city facing a major deficit, New Jersey stepped in immediately to take charge of Camden's finances. The state closed the $4.6 million shortfall but required a staggering 88 percent increase in taxes in return. In order to regain budgetary control, Primas had to provide the state with monthly financial statements; to obtain approval for any city contract or purchase exceeding $4,500; to submit approval for all municipal appropriations; to obtain approval for any new financial obligations, such as bonds and notes, assumed by the city; and to limit such borrowing to an amount equal to the total amount of state aid received by the city.[25] Even then, he had to identify new funds to meet the continuing gap between local revenues and costs. He would have preferred to have introduced a payroll tax, but the state did not allow such taxes for cities as small as Camden. As a consequence, he embraced an offer of $3.4 million in state funds in return for giving up valuable land on the North Camden waterfront for a new state prison.

The state had indicated its determination to build a high security prison somewhere, most probably in Camden, but it had held back any announcement until after the city's elections because of local opposition to the idea, including that of Primas as chair of Camden City Council.[26] Once the proposal was official, citizen reaction was predictably negative. Speaking before a city council that was largely favorable to the development, Gualberto Medina, who had entered Camden's activist community as a leader of the militant Young Lords Puerto Rican organization while still a student at the Rutgers Camden campus, charged, "Camden is a dumping ground and every time somebody wants to get rid of something, they throw it to Camden City."[27] Neighborhood residents, declaring that a prison would aggravate North Camden's already precarious economic situation, picketed the mayor and actively sought to block the new building. Primas held fast, however. As he told the *New York Times*, "The prison was a purely economic decision on my part. I saw the $40 million in construction, the 400 jobs, $450,000 spent annually among local businesses outside the state bidding process and $1 million a year in taxes, and I sold it to the city through a public education program."[28]

Primas's conflict with North Camden residents was particularly telling and not confined to the prison issue alone. Despite the victory in securing Northgate II apartments for low- and moderate-income residents as part of the 1972 redevelopment settlement, North Camden continued to decline physically in the 1970s, not least because homes were old and banks refused to lend in the area. Many owners simply left their homes rather than continue to pay high property taxes against declining values. By the time Primas was elected, seven hundred of the area's two thousand homes had been abandoned. North Camden residents, aided by resurgent religious organizations, took matters into their own hands. In 1978, they formed Concerned Citizens of North Camden (CCNC) to lobby the city for assistance. When Mayor Errichetti told them he could not help unless they formed their own agenda, they organized an effort to board up abandoned properties, securing some Community Development Block Grant money to sustain the effort. Faced with a low-income population of blacks and Hispanics who needed housing themselves, CCNC began to urge residents to squat in some of the homes they had secured. Shortly after Primas became mayor, they sought to embarrass him into granting title to the properties. Primas initially resisted, repeating a belief he had articulated at the time of his election, that the city could not be sustained as a community solely of poor people.[29] He finally acceded to community pressure, however, and directed additional block grant money to the effort. Over the next five years, 142 families received title to the best vacant houses in North Camden.[30]

The director of CCNC (and a constant thorn in Primas's side) was Tom Knoche, a disillusioned Baltimore city planner who had been recruited to work in North Camden in 1981 by Hans Goebel, rector of Grace Lutheran Church, who had known Knoche in Baltimore. Knoche kept the pressure on the mayor to respond to squatters' demands by organizing sustained protests at City Hall as well as in North Camden. Six years later, when Primas began to promote the redevelopment of the Bergen-Lanning Square area of South Camden near Cooper Hospital and the waterfront as the best hope for attracting middle-income residents back to the city, Knoche again reacted angrily. Primas intended to direct nearly half a million dollars in Community Block Development Grant funds to subsidize the site. Knoche claimed that this was "reactionary" and could "only mean massive displacement of Camden's poor and working people."[31] He was only echoing community sentiment. Among those also speaking out were former BPUM activist Malik Chaka, back from Africa, and neighborhood activist Brian Medley, who compared the council vote in favor of the project to the infamous Philadelphia bombing of the radical MOVE organization, saying the council had carelessly, callously, and cunningly voted to adopt a plan "designed to force us out of our homes and businesses and into homes that cannot compare with our present homes." Hispanic activist Freddy Alvarado, fearing that displacement would roll through his neighborhood just to the south, joined the criticism.[32]

These later events are worth noting as a means of understanding Primas's responses to county actions that brought additional nuisance industries into the city. Like the prison, the proposed new sewage facilities generated controversy and opposition in Camden. CCMUA's plans for its expanded facilities called for plants to provide both primary and secondary treatment in Camden before treated wastewaters were conveyed to the Delaware River. As progress in funding and building the second plant lagged, residual byproducts of the processing—sludge—began to accumulate at the Camden plant. Initially, these products were treated with wood chips and chemicals in a separate, open-air facility completed in 1978. The goal was to

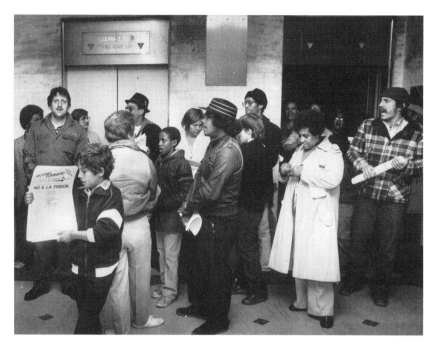

Figure 18. North Camden Concerned Citizens protest, City Hall, November 13, 1981. Tom Knoche is at the left facing the camera. Behind him, with the hat, is Carlos Callazo, organizer of the protest. To the right of him in the rear in white is Milagros Castillo, once of the leaders of the squatter movement. *Philadelphia Bulletin*, November 13, 1981. Courtesy Temple University Libraries, Urban Archives, Philadelphia.

resell the end product as compost. Fears that dangerous chemicals, including mercury, had not been filtered out dampened demand, however, with the result that waste accumulated, bringing with it noxious odors.[33] With 2,000 tons of compost accumulated at the treatment plant at Second and Jackson Streets, only several blocks from the Sacred Heart parish school, CCMUA asked the Environmental Protection Agency for permission to dump five million gallons of sludge in the Atlantic Ocean. Denied that request and facing protests from several suburban mayors who objected to the odor associated with the practice of dumping sludge on county parklands, the authority sought alternatives.[34]

The commissioners relied on trucking the material out of the county in the short term and began to discuss construction of a cogeneration facil-

Figure 19. Demonstrators in North Camden protest plan to evict a squatter, November 11, 1981. Courtesy *Courier-Post*.

ity, which would incinerate both sludge and trash.[35] The idea was abandoned in 1983 when estimates for building a cogeneration plant reached $126 million. CCMUA resolved instead to construct an enclosed composting plant at half the cost.[36] While this suggestion was being pursued, the authority was embarrassed by stories reiterating the bad effects of continued open-air composting. Linda Delengowski, a native resident who had not left the city, told the commissioners that her pupils at Sacred Heart knew it was bad to breathe the air. "Don't you know too?" To the reply of the CCMUA chairman that he was concerned about costs, the *Courier-Post* commented editorially, "Had the authority not spent so lavishly on itself and its chosen professionals over the years, that lament might receive a more sympathetic hearing. As it is, our sympathies lie wholly with the children."[37]

Given such poor environmental conditions near his church already, it was not surprising that Sacred Heart pastor Michael Doyle became an early critic of county plans to locate an incinerator nearby. When he attended Freeholder-Director Joseph Roberts's 1981 tour of a model facility in Harrisburg, Doyle complained that Camden had already become "a dumping ground, for prisoners, sewage, the poor, the elderly and now the prospect of millions of tons of trash from all over Camden County." Unmoved by Doyle's complaint, in December 1982 the freeholders unveiled plans for an incinerator that would turn both sewage sludge and solid waste to steam that could be sold to industrial users for electricity. The proposal provoked considerable dismay from Camden residents, including Doyle, who called the idea "a monstrous operation." Despite reassurance from CCMUA executive director Herman Englebert that the facility could be at any one of eighteen possible sites and that location "doesn't have to be based only on the best engineering," Doyle remained skeptical. "I don't trust that you have the poor people of Camden in mind," he charged. "You will build it no matter what we say, but which one of you would want it in your neighborhood?"[38] His pointed message reached a national audience in 1983, when CBS's *60 Minutes* featured Camden's distress under the title "Michael Doyle's Camden." Referring to the new sewage treatment plant, Doyle snapped, "Camden has the biggest concentration of people in all the county, and yet there is where they're going to send in this sewerage. Eighty million gallons a day. I see in my mind, out there in the suburbs and all over Camden County, there are millions of toilet bowls, and the pipe is just set up for us. And everytime you flush, you send to Camden, to Camden, to Camden." The program presented such an unflattering picture of Camden that Mayor Randy Primas enlisted Poppy Sharp, among others, to protest its unfairness.[39] Within a year, however, Primas was himself forced to grapple with the effects of the new waste authority.

In January 1984, faced with the prospect that fees could rise as high as $600 a household per year, a sixfold increase over previous rates, Randy Primas went to court to try to block a proposed $255 million bond issue that would allow construction of CCMUA's system. Tellingly, he appeared motivated as much by the adverse effects high rates would have on attracting new business to the city as by the effects they would have on individuals. Primas made his case with the backing of the city's largest consumer of water, Campbell Soup, which joined in seeking a subregional alternative to CCMUA. Thanks to new regulations, CCMUA was obliged to appear before the state's Local Finance Board, which rejected its request after Camden aired its concerns.[40] More than a year of contention followed, in the courts and through a court-appointed mediator. The result was an agreement that all users would pay a uniform fee, a position that Camden had argued was

Figure 20. Father Michael Doyle, of Waterfront South's Sacred Heart Roman Catholic Church, at the time he was featured in *60 Minutes*. Courtesy *Courier-Post*.

necessary to prevent its users from paying twice what suburban customers were charged.[41]

Having achieved a victory, at least in part for Camden residents, Primas nonetheless became a forceful advocate, even over sustained local opposition, for the proposed trash-to-steam incinerator. Again, he was motivated by fiscal more than social concerns. The facility, Camden County freeholders announced in the fall of 1984, would be located at the bottom of the new I-676 interconnecting highway between the Walt Whitman and Benjamin Franklin bridges, a short distance from the CCMUA processing plant. Under the proposed terms for attracting a for-profit company to build and run the facility, profits had to be guaranteed for twenty years, a goal that could be reached satisfactorily only by directing sufficient trash to the site to keep fees at an acceptable level. Despite the economic risks, Mayor Primas argued that as a poor city Camden needed the facility both to create new jobs and to control trash disposal costs. He reported further that the city would receive back $3 for every ton of trash burned, a host benefit estimated to be worth $900,000 a year. Speaking to a skeptical South Camden audience in 1985, he asked, "What if we put up a plant that employed city residents, had no odors and allowed the city to have its trash fee zero?" To the further question, "Would you mind?" Camden resident and internationally acclaimed haiku poet Nick Virgilio retorted, "It might happen in Utopia."[42]

Such promises failed to sit well either in Doyle's Waterfront South neighborhood, where a local organizing group continued to fight the effects of accumulating sludge, or in the nearby Fairview neighborhood, which for the first time had now to encounter an environmentally destructive intrusion. There, the issue caught hold. Two young mothers, Linda McHugh and Suzanne Marks, formed an organization, Citizens Against Trash to Steam (CATS), which circulated petitions, picketed meetings, and attempted, unsuccessfully as it turned out, to secure a citywide referendum on the proposal. They pressed their case over a period of six years, often encountering organized political opposition in the form of Democratic Party loyalists who went out of their way to disrupt their public statements.[43] Although dumping costs continued to rise, the New Jersey Department of Environmental Protection approved the permit to build the facility in December 1987. Five months later, Superior Court Judge Paul Lowengrub dismissed the CATS lawsuit to overturn the decision, ruling that the state approval preempted the rights of the municipality and its citizens to challenge the decision.[44]

Figure 21. Protesting the trash incinerator, Nancy Welch of Collingswood and Milton Rogers of the Fairview section of Camden, October 1989. Courtesy *Courier-Post*.

Protests continued, as estimated dumping costs rose to $88 a ton and additional concerns arose. Residents worried about the arrival of as many as three hundred additional trucks a day to the area and about proper disposal of the residual toxic ash and stack emissions containing heavy metals. Unmoved, the county proceeded to present the city of Camden with a check for $1 million in March 1989, in exchange for the eighteen acres of city-owned land where the new facility was to be built. Describing the initiative as one of the major accomplishments of his administration, Primas reported that the funds would become part of the city's general revenue for fiscal 1989, thereby helping to offset a gap of $10 million in his spending plan.[45] Republican successes at both the state and county levels threatened to derail plans for a Camden incinerator, but a bipartisan compromise that included funds for recycling as well assured completion of the project. The $112 million plant finally fired up for the first time in March 1991.[46]

County freeholders had made plans to build another incinerator in nearby Pennsauken which they subsequently dropped. Working under the compromise plan they had crafted to direct unburnable wastes to the township's landfill, they purchased the site for $49 million and authorized payments to Pennsauken of $3.1 million a year for the next twelve years, to compensate the town for the waste that other municipalities would dump there. The payout effectively relieved the township of costs that had been incurred to plan its own incinerator and enabled it to reduce taxes to levels before the debt was incurred.[47] The decision to build an incinerator only in Camden clearly pleased suburbanites elsewhere as well. In Cherry Hill, tipping fees were expected to rise from $54 to $73 a ton as a result of the decision, but Mayor Susan Bass Levin claimed the extra cost was worth the environmental advantages to the township.[48] Indeed, it was not long before the press was reporting rising incidences of asthma among Camden's children, a problem critics immediately linked with the presence of the incinerator. Citing concern for the health of her daughter, CATS cofounder Suzanne Marks put her Fairview home on the market and moved to the suburbs herself. Linda McHugh also left the city.[49]

Randy Primas failed to respond to citizen protests against the incinerator, and in the summer of 1989 his decision to accept yet another nuisance industry provoked still further outrage. The New Jersey Department of Corrections wanted to build a second medium security prison in North Camden to house between five hundred and eight hundred inmates. The proposal for the $55 million facility slated for a site once occupied by the Knox Gelatin Company was embraced both by the Black People's Unity

Movement, whose efforts to develop the site had faltered, and by Mayor Primas. "I don't think I would fight it," he commented. "I view the prison as an economic development project. In addition, I think the surveillance from the two prison towers might stop some of the overt drug dealing in North Camden." He received editorial support from the *Philadelphia Inquirer*, which argued that the city could not afford to reject a promised $2.8 million in annual subsidies and an estimated three hundred jobs for Camden residents: "Understandably, residents of the area would prefer to have a less gloomy tenant on the 20-acre site overlooking the Cooper River. The problem is that officials responsible for balancing the city's budget can't wait."[50]

Primas indicated that he wanted to meet with residents before fully agreeing to the proposal, and what he encountered was sheer hostility. Community organizers formed a second protest organization, Save Our Waterfront, to oppose the prison. Asserting that another prison would bring the number of incarcerated up to a quarter of North Camden's residents, SOW argued forcefully for alternative uses of the land to serve the community and within a month put up $35,000 in earnest money to buy the site itself. Primas still defended the state proposal. At a meeting that drew three hundred angry residents, he explained "I have to deal in the real world. We operate a $70 million budget and collect $11 million in property taxes. A million dollars (from both state prisons) is 38 percent of every tax dollar we collect. I have to look at that. I need revenue to run a city. I don't think a prison is as negative as people make out to be. It would create jobs, create revenue and would have a positive effect on the drug problem here. It's not the solution to Camden's problems, but it's realistic." To this, Rev. John Randall retorted that any depressed city that ever revived "built on its waterfront. It didn't give it away."[51]

This time the protests had their effect. The otherwise development-friendly *Courier-Post* opposed the project, which it compared to "dumping cyanide into the recovering pond." Why, the paper asked, should Camden "put another human warehouse in North Camden when the neighborhood and, in fact, the city, needs so many other things—housing, industry, a boost in morale—far more"? The paper urged the city and the Black People's Unity Movement to get serious about developing a viable economic plan for the site.[52] Additional support came both from area clergy, including Catholic Bishop James McHugh, and area Democratic politicians, including James Florio during his successful run for governor that fall.[53] When Primas agreed to join the new Florio administration as Commissioner of Community Affairs, the state relented. Describing Primas as the only local backer of the prison, the state corrections department said it would abandon plans to locate the facility in Camden.[54]

Throughout his seventeen years in office in Camden, especially in his nine years as mayor, Primas found himself increasingly at odds with his natural black constituency. Forced to improve the city's finances, he accepted compromises and pursued goals that inevitably put him in opposition to a range of city activists. Challenged in primaries in both of his successful reelection campaigns as mayor, he turned to the new county power brokers for help, most notably George Norcross, III. The son of a powerful labor leader, Norcross had worked his way up the system, first by assisting several state legislators, including Angelo Errichetti. Errichetti had appointed Norcross director of a reconstituted Camden Parking Authority in 1978, when Norcross was only twenty-two. Building on his labor and political connections, Norcross developed an insurance business that gave him the financial leverage to help direct Democratic politics in Camden County. He provided Primas with a crucial $15,000 loan in 1984 to fend off a primary opponent.[55] Benefiting from his insurance contracts with the city, he became Primas's biggest backer in 1989. Of the $93,000 raised on Primas's behalf, $78,000 came from Norcross's organizations. Only two contributions came from individuals living in Camden, two thirds of that in the form of a $1,000 check from Primas's former boss at BPUM, Harvey Johnson.[56]

Primas's relationship with Norcross waned but did not end in 1990. Even as Primas assumed his position in Governor Florio's cabinet, Norcross became the new chairman of the County Democratic Party. His selection in 1989 came in response to the victories giving Republicans control of the county freeholders for the first time in a generation. Given the challenge, Norcross became the master builder of the bridge between politics and contractors, so often referred to as "pay to play." Still new to the countywide business of raising funds in 1991, Norcross took out a personally backed $200,000 loan that helped finance a last-minute television blitz assuring election of his handpicked candidate to oppose state senator and Camden County Republican leader Lee Laskin. Norcross singled out Laskin for blocking the appointment of his father, an avid horse racing fan, to the New Jersey Racing Commission.[57] Norcross's success in this effort inspired him to raise both total giving and the amount coming from individual contributors dramatically over the next two years. According to a 1993 analysis of state election enforcement commission records by the *Courier-Post*, Nor-

Figure 22. George Norcross, January 9, 1989, as he took the helm of the Camden County Democratic party and made South Jersey a major force in the state. Courtesy *Courier-Post*.

cross raised $1.7 million through two political action committees. Nicholas Rudi and Joseph Salema's Consolidated Financial Management came in close to the top givers at a generous level of $22,500. Rudi gave an additional $14,000 himself. Close behind with a donation of $22,100 was the engineering firm of O'Brien-Kreitzberg, which had made an estimated $1.3 million in the previous two years from contracts with CCMUA, and James C. Anderson Associates, which was paid at least $568,000 in 1992 and $1 million the previous year for engineering consulting work with the Pollution Control Finance Agency. Topping the list, however, was the law firm of Parker, McCay, and Criscuolo, which made at least $272,000 in fees for handling a county lawsuit over faulty construction at the county jail and contributed $38,000. Norcross's brother Philip was the firm's managing partner.[58] Rudi and Salema's business dealings subsequently drew an investigation from the Securities and Exchange Commission, forcing Salema's resignation as Governor James Florio's chief-of-staff in 1993. Both men paid substantial fines, and Salema served six months in a half-way house.[59] That did not hamper

Norcross's continued success, however, and a good part of the reason is revealed in several contributions not included in the *Courier-Post* report. Especially noteworthy was a gift of $1,500 from Vernon Hill, president of Commerce Bank in Cherry Hill. Another $5,000 was listed from Site Development, a company headed by Hill's wife. In Vernon Hill, Norcross found a new and especially powerful ally.

Vernon Hill got his start as a young man studying at the Wharton School at the University of Pennsylvania. He worked part-time during his school years at the People's National Bank in Haddon Township, New Jersey, a hometown institution founded and run by William Rohrer, who operated the bank just as he had run a successful automobile sales business for years, through personal customer attention. Hill left the bank in 1968 to form Site Development, a Cherry Hill firm that could locate development sites for other businesses, including franchises seeking to expand. In 1973, aged only twenty-seven, he formed an investment group to start Commerce Bank in nearby Evesham. The bank grew quickly, from only $1.5 million to $720 million in assets and over five hundred employees during the 1980s. In 1992 the bank set a record for earnings, with $10 million.[60] But Commerce took an even bigger step in the early 1990s. Hill, a registered Republican, was put off enough by state bias against the southern portion of New Jersey to back James Florio in his successful bid for governor. His aggressive fundraising tactics in that race offended at least one builder, who felt he was being pressured by the president of a bank on which he relied for funds to complete a major project. Some bank officers complained in addition that they were pressured into buying tickets to Florio's inaugural after being told the size of their bonuses depended on it.[61] Hill's support nonetheless paid immediate dividends, as Commerce received a $24,000 commission on a controversial Camden County Freeholder decision to refinance $72 million in debt.[62]

During this period, Hill drew close to George Norcross. Following a U.S. Supreme Court decision allowing banks to sell insurance, Hill made Norcross's Keystone National Insurance part of Commerce Bankcorp. Norcross became an executive of the larger company in 1997 and a member of the thirteen-member central board of directors in March 2002. Hill drew Randy Primas into the Commerce empire as well. Following James Florio's reelection defeat in 1993, he helped put Primas in charge of Cypress Securities Corporation, operating out of Commerce's headquarters in Cherry Hill. The company subsequently joined Commerce Bankcorp as Commerce Capital Markets. Together these two new subsidiaries brought the bank an unequaled range of services, not just to hold deposits but to broker insurance policies, float bonds, and give investment advice.[63] Randy Primas's success in rising to lucrative as well as powerful positions outside the city affirmed the opportunities within the new county structure of politics. Equally revealing were the less happy fates of his two immediate successors as mayor.

*   *   *

The new suburban organizational muscle was never so vividly demonstrated as in the selection of Aaron Thompson to fill Primas's unexpired term as mayor in 1990. A retired telephone company technician and college dropout, Thompson had gained a seat on the city council by running on the Primas ticket in 1988. Less than two years later the party organization plucked him from obscurity and made him mayor. Honest and well-intentioned, Thompson had very little idea how to run the city. As his executive aide, Charles Ashley, later reported, Thompson was so unfamiliar with office work he did not even know what an "in-box" was.[64] The real power in the city resided in the hands of Theodore Hinson, who, like Errichetti before him, had risen from a position as public works director to that of Democratic Party chairman. Coincidentally, he succeeded party ally George Norcross as executive director of the Camden Parking Authority.

The county organization's support for Thompson immediately became an issue when he prepared to run for a full term as mayor in 1990. Although a number of candidates initially indicated they would challenge him, by November the leading opponent to Thompson was Jose Delgado, an independently elected member of the Camden Board of Education, who bore his independence from the organization and his Puerto Rican heritage as signs of his promise to give Camden a new beginning. Blaming the mayor for failing to defend the welfare of Camden residents, he promised to stop construction of the county's incinerator and spoke out against the injustice of the efforts to incarcerate more prisoners in the city. The *Courier-Post* pointed to the difficulties of unseating the new political machine, however, noting as the election neared that Thompson was outspending his two opponents five to one. As in 1988, political action committees associated with George Norcross provided the bulk of the incumbent's campaign fund, some $145,000 of the $170,000 at Thompson's disposal.[65]

Delgado managed to energize a number of the city's growing Hispanic residents, now about a third of the population. Registrations rose sharply in parts of North and South Camden as well as in the Cramer Hill neighborhood where Hispanics were concentrated. But the Democratic organization fought his candidacy aggressively, circulating, among other things, last-minute flyers charging him with egregious moral violations. On election day, many of the new voters reportedly had trouble gaining access to the polls or tabulating their votes correctly. Although turnout was significantly up from 1985 and 1989, Delgado still fell short, securing just 5,161 votes to Thompson's 6,328. A third candidate received 2,009 votes, leaving the organization victorious but without a majority.[66]

Delgado's strong showing, and the loss to Republicans of three contested county freeholder positions in the 1990 election, convinced Norcross of the importance of securing the Hispanic vote in Camden. Following the Errichetti model of incorporating dissidents into the system, he arranged a meeting with Delgado shortly after the election to ask him to become part of the organization. When Delgado refused, Norcross went around him to enlist another Hispanic activist, Israel Nieves. In exchange for support at the polls, Norcross promised that the organizational ticket for city council would include a Hispanic and that Hispanic representation on the Democratic city committee would be increased from thirteen to thirty-five.[67] The arrangement worked for Norcross. Not only did Hispanics fall in behind the organizational slate, Nieves's opposition helped defeat Delgado's bid for reelection to the school board. With his defeat, the school board replaced the lucrative insurance contract assigned to Delgado supporters Benjamin Calif and Gene Alston with another minority firm. Noting that Norcross's Keystone National Insurance Company retained the remaining school coverage, Delgado supporters were quick to describe the decision as political retaliation.[68]

Further opposition to county influence in the city formed under the banner of an organization named Democrats for the People, which contested both city Democratic Party elections and a shift in the rules for city elections supported by the county. Neither effort gained much ground. As a sign of the further power of the county, even Aaron Thompson fell out of favor after he attempted to assert control over key city agencies, most notably public works.[69] When he announced his intention to run for reelection, the county organization gave its support instead to Superintendent of Schools Arnold Webster. Explained one Democratic committeeman, "The mayor was not able to be a team player. For whatever reason, he wasn't willing to communicate with the people who put him in power: the City Committee and the City Council."[70] With strong organizational backing and no major blemishes on his record, Webster trounced Thompson in the spring Democratic primary, by a four-to-one margin. The headline of a *Courier-Post* editorial described the situation well: "Like a River, Camden's Machine Keeps Rolling Along."[71]

The new mayor lacked both the personal skills and the energy to navigate the issues of a persistently declining city. An educator by training, he was not used to the give-and-take of daily policy-making situations. While Webster did much to shape that reputation for himself while in office, he opened his term with surprising independence and vision for one selected by the county organization. He quickly sought to channel community activism into a new $21-million program funded by a federal Empowerment Zone granted jointly to Camden and Philadelphia. He also created a Waterfront Development Council and bargained his way into participating in decisions about waterfront redevelopment. Previously, the waterfront had been controlled by the independent Cooper's Ferry Development Association, about which Aaron Thompson complained, "They had no respect for me. They have never had any respect for any Afro-American mayor of the city."[72] Webster crafted his own redevelopment effort and declared his independence in his first state of the city speech stating, "Needless to say everyone is beginning to recognize the so-called shadow government is out of business."[73] These early efforts to assert control, however, managed mainly to ruffle potential allies. Within months, both the board chair of the Camden Redevelopment Agency and the city's business manager, a former managing director of the Cooper's Ferry Development Association, had resigned. Both actions signaled the withdrawal of county political support.

Webster also suffered from poor relations from an increasingly assertive Hispanic constituency, which blamed him for excluding Hispanics from important roles as city managers or as directors of the Empowerment Zone. Carlos Peraza, director of the Latin American Economic Development Association (LAEDA), expressed a commonly held sentiment in the Hispanic community: "There are [black] individuals who fought very hard to get where they are, so naturally there is resistance to sharing those gains. But it's going to happen, whether they like it or not. . . . If they don't share, it will be taken anyway." The *Courier-Post*'s Kevin Riordan, whose coverage of Camden in the 1990s was especially well informed, subsequently reported a widespread belief among African Americans that the county organization was using Hispanics as surrogates in the effort to undermine Webster.[74]

A primary agent of that effort was a young businessman, Milton Milan. Elected to city council in 1995 when the black vote split among two candidates in East Camden, Milan was immediately elected chair of the council with the support of two fellow Hispanics and the lone white member, a longtime county employee, Michael Devlin. For the next two years, Milan and the council majority made it difficult for Webster to execute any of his initiatives. As Webster prepared to run for reelection, Hispanic leaders organized an unofficial "Hispanic primary," with the candidates each pledged to give way to the winner in the formal election. Jose Delgado made the effort to rally Hispanics to his side once again, but Milan won a three-way contest when a last minute box of returns put him over the top.[75] Although there was also discussion of holding a similar "African American primary," Webster resisted. When two other black candidates entered the race, his natural constituency further split and Milan eased to victory. Like Thompson before him, Webster blamed what he called the behind-the-scenes powers in the county Democratic Party. "He said he lost the race," the *Philadelphia Inquirer* reported, "because he stood up to powerful forces who had run the city for decades. He blamed the same forces for backing Milan and putting 'spoilers' in to split the black vote."[76]

Webster may well have exaggerated the effect on his reelection of county politicians, which by some accounts were otherwise preoccupied that year. Still, the short-lived political careers of both Thompson and Webster represented the perils of independence in the modern era. The contrast with the upward trajectory of Primas's career could not have been clearer. Just as clear was the confirmation of the shift of power away from the city and its consequences. With the new regional equation spelling imbalance in favor of the suburbs at every juncture, even the best city-based efforts to revitalize the city faced considerable obstacles to success. The next three chapters will assess those valiant yet limited efforts.

PART III

Shifting Strategy

Chapter 5

The Downtown Waterfront: Changing Camden's Image

This is the site of the $42 million aquarium, a symbol of the city's hope. If the dreams of state and city officials and residents come true, the aquarium will lure millions of visitors back to Camden and stem the flight of its population. . . . Then, as the project develops over 10 years, the city hopes to see housing and economic development spread to its neighborhoods, making Camden a place people would want to come back to—to live.

—Philadelphia Inquirer, *1989*

I'm telling you, Camden is happening. It's not going to be the poorest city 10 years from now. Our property, which was once the symbol of blight, will be the symbol of a remarkable revival. How could it fail, with all the energy and creativity—and cash—flowing into it?

—RCA Victor building developer Carl Dranoff, February *2003*

Before his successful campaign for governor of New Jersey in 1981, Tom Kean had never visited Camden. His first impression, during a campaign visit, was one of shock. The entire city appeared visibly blighted, and, as he noted later, it seemed that nothing was happening to reverse the trend. Once elected, he placed Camden high on his list of troubled urban areas demanding attention. Acting in the best spirit of what has since become a central element of redevelopment theory, he felt it necessary to build on existing assets.[1] In the northern part of the state, with which he was much more familiar, Newark needed a new downtown anchor. Jersey City, he believed, could take advantage of rising real estate prices in Manhattan to develop housing within easy commuting distance. Without question, Camden's greatest asset appeared to be its waterfront, then a mix of still vibrant industrial use at Campbell Soup and RCA, a viable port, and

Figure 23. Sign, "Camden, Changes Its Image," November 10, 1973. Courtesy *Courier-Post.*

plenty of open space for redevelopment at the heart of the greater Philadelphia metropolitan area.[2] Its conversion, with Kean's strong support, from industrial to leisure-time use for tourists and visitors followed a popular contemporary approach, one that used public incentives to attract private investment. Between 1976 and 1986, cities constructed as many as 250 new convention centers, sports arenas, community centers, and performing arts facilities downtown at a cost exceeding $10 billion.[3] Such efforts lacked the public accountability of previous redevelopment efforts, but according to a respected evaluation of the process, the rewards could be considerable. Public-private dealmaking may not have fully saved cities given up for dead, but they marked "a turning point that brought the middle class back to town, added a glow to specialized office districts, and turned downtown into a resource that can make life better for city people."[4]

By the turn of the new century, by almost any account, the twenty-year process of reinvestment in Camden's waterfront had been successful, if still incomplete. A new state aquarium, named for the governor who made it happen, opened in 1992. A regional entertainment center, a new

minor league ballpark, and the city's first market-rate housing in a generation followed. The influx of visitors, Camden's boosters could claim, was
helping alter the city's negative image, an essential prerequisite to attracting
additional investment.[5] Still, there were disturbing aspects to the story. The
industries that first generated plans for the area did not remain as central
partners. The financial returns to the city were not nearly enough to reverse
the city's structural deficit. While waterfront facilities brought jobs, they did
not lift the financial prospects of significant numbers of Camden families.
Conceived as the heart of the downtown, the waterfront still remained into
the early twenty-first century an area apart from the rest of the city. Despite
promises that increased downtown investment would ultimately aid the
neighborhoods, that prospect had yet to be demonstrated. Not surprisingly,
in a process that revolved around dealmaking, neighborhood interests lost
out. As in other cities that sought to tap the market potential of their waterfront, most notably models in Baltimore, New York, and Boston, particular
contingencies determined the fate of the projects. But instances of redevelopment, when not linked to broader revitalization strategies, repeatedly ran
the risk of reducing cities merely to tourist destinations. Camden's waterfront history serves as a cautionary tale about the limits to what investments
in a single sector of a city can do for the whole.

*   *   *

Historically, industrial uses had crowded the downtown waterfront, taking
advantage not just of immediate access to the Delaware River, but also of
rail facilities dating back to the nineteenth century that promised to move
passengers as well as goods along the north-south industrial corridor. At
the height of production, RCA Victor owned eleven buildings clustered at
the river. Campbell Soup operated facilities on thirty nearby acres. With so
many workers congregated together, a host of restaurants, bars, and other
service facilities operated nearby, at the lower end of Market and Federal
Streets. Housing demand in inner city neighborhoods remained high. As
those employment opportunities shrank, however, all elements of a once
viable waterfront area weakened considerably. As early as 1961 the waterfront had "become an eyesore and a community trash can," and Mayor
Alfred Pierce made redevelopment there a high priority.[6] He sought to
make land available for industrial expansion, even as he envisioned mixed
residential and commercial use nearby.[7] Although those plans faltered entirely after the courts suspended the redevelopment process in the late

1960s, Angelo Errichetti revived interest in the waterfront during his term as mayor. He commissioned a 1978 study that called the area a unique opportunity "to reverse the flow of population to suburban areas; to appeal to the New Jersey counterpart of the social and economic mix of people that have made Philadelphia's Society Hill a success; to develop as socially and economically balanced a residential community as possible within the feasible limits of market-rate housing; to add to Camden's tax base, and to stimulate and provide support for other development."[8] In 1980 the county broke ground for a new waterfront park, which Errichetti hoped would serve, along with the clearance of the old rail yards, as a backdrop for attracting reinvestment.

Randy Primas's election as mayor in 1981 marked a new era. Although he was immediately saddled with state supervision of the city's finances, he attracted the interest and support of a group of energetic newcomers to the Camden scene. These included the new president of Cooper Hospital, Kevin Halpern; Campbell Soup president Gordon McGovern; and RCA's John Rittenhouse. Together with Primas's young city business administrator, Thomas Corcoran, whom Errichetti had recruited directly out of the Wharton School, and with the active interest of Governor Kean, this group breathed new life into a relic of the Pierce redevelopment era, the Greater Camden Movement (GCM). Boosted by investments from both Campbell Soup and RCA, the GCM commissioned a comprehensive plan for the entire waterfront site. Impressed with progress being made in Baltimore's conversion of its Inner Harbor, it hired the American Cities Corporation, a subsidiary of the Rouse Corporation, to prepare a comprehensive development plan.[9] In a March 1983 report, American Cities noted that Camden still possessed significant assets despite its reversal of fortune. Principal among these was its location directly across the Delaware River from Center City Philadelphia, convenient access by public transportation, and the presence of strong higher education and medical facilities, as well as the two remaining major corporations. With its market analysis demonstrating that the city was unlikely to reverse the flow of either manufacturing or retail activity to suburban locations, American Cities stressed the creation of "an attractive, secure, and lively urban environment" as a key factor in retaining existing industries and attracting newcomers. By creating what planners described as an induced market in the form of mixed-use development, it would be possible to "capture the full potential of the Camden riverfront as well as instigate a dramatic reversal in Camden's position as a viable urban center."[10]

While planners spoke of modest improvements Camden might expect in capturing white-collar employment, it reserved its greatest enthusiasm for what it called a public attraction facility: "This could be potentially critical in stimulating the induced market effects stipulated in the projections of market support, and in generally establishing a quality environment for the project area." Most important, "a major public attraction will act as the focal point for the overall project and will significantly improve Camden's image,—critical to stimulating market support." Creating such a facility, the report claimed, could dramatically contradict pervasive negative perceptions of Camden and require it to be "regarded in a new light as offering certain opportunities that can not be obtained elsewhere."[11] In a follow-up report in October, American Cities became more specific in calling for the creation of a mixed-use development called the Pavilion at Cooper's Ferry. The new development prototype, building on Rouse's own efforts at Baltimore's Inner Harbor, would include a specialty retail center, a hotel, and an Omni-theater complex. The primary objective of the Pavilion would be "to engage the imagination of the visitors in a totally entrancing and exciting environment where a single visit would be insufficient to experience everything, and everything should be experienced two or more times." This approach, it claimed, "will afford Camden, and its redevelopment efforts, a high visibility way beyond the Philadelphia metropolitan area. Within the Philadelphia area, the Pavilion will be known as an exciting place for shopping and family entertainment, at a very attractive riverfront setting with dramatic views of the Philadelphia skyline. It is this image which will provide a unique environment, and, therefore, a competitive edge, for occupants of the new office and research projects. The overall impression will be one of an exciting and secure environment, and will greatly enhance Camden's image as a location for development and investment."[12]

Cooper's Ferry Pavilion never materialized, but the underlying thrust of the report remained exceedingly powerful. Henceforth, the driving force for redevelopment would no longer be industrial, or even primarily office development, but that of a powerful entertainment district with wide regional appeal. One further element in the report, a recommendation that a private development corporation with exclusive responsibility for the waterfront be created, was acted on right away. Even as American Cities Corporation joined with the Greater Camden Movement to announce its preliminary $100 million plan for the waterfront, Thomas Corcoran was drawing up papers for the Cooper's Ferry Development Association, so named for the initial ferry link across the Delaware that marked the modern origin of Camden City.[13] Corcoran launched the organization in July 1984, operating with a single secretary and "the single-focused mission," as he later described it, "of planning and coordinating all of the public and private investment decisions necessary to achieve over a twenty year period a high quality, high density redevelopment of Camden's downtown waterfront."[14] As much heft as the new effort had behind it, it was a stroke of luck that initially boosted Corcoran and his supporters when that originally unspecified "special attraction" identified by American Cities as central to Camden's future literally fell in their laps.

For some time, Philadelphia Zoo director William Donaldson had been seeking a site for an aquarium and had not been satisfied with prospects in West Philadelphia or at the undeveloped Penn's Landing site on the Philadelphia waterfront. At the invitation of Campbell's Gordon McGovern, he looked at Camden. With the help of a $600,000 grant from Philadelphia's William Penn Foundation, he undertook preliminary planning to locate on the waterfront. The project clearly needed public funding to succeed, but in order to be convincing, Cooper's Ferry's Corcoran and Kevin Halpern (chairman of the Cooper's Ferry board in addition to his hospital work) felt there should be a private partner. Campbell Soup had outgrown its main office facility and needed approximately 150,000 additional square feet. What better plan than to locate its new world headquarters on the waterfront beside the new aquarium?

Even before supporters could approach Governor Kean with the idea, another lucky break came their way. Legislators were debating a contentious issue as to whether the New Jersey Sports and Exposition Authority would assume responsibility for the rehabilitation of the failing Monmouth Park racing facility. The vote was completely deadlocked when Guy Musiani told supporters he would switch his vote in favor in return for adding a commitment to locate an aquarium in South Jersey, presumably at Wildwood in his district. The bill passed by voice vote on December 31, 1984, without notice in the press, but news of the action got to Corcoran and his party. When they met with Kean in March 1985, he seemed surprised that legislation already authorized an aquarium in South Jersey. Apparently unaware of any commitment to Musiani, he quickly saw the possibilities for Camden as they were presented.[15] By the end of the month, Gordon McGovern had made public Campbell's determination to build its new headquarters on the waterfront and to modernize its nearby flagship processing plant at Front and Market Streets. Stressing the facility's role as an educational institution, Governor Kean said he would ask every school in the state to visit the aquarium, urging an enthusiastic audience to take the message with them that "Camden is coming back. That something good is going on here. That if you want someplace exciting to go—to develop, to grow, come to Camden, because that's where the future is." For his part, Randy Primas called the new plan the most significant accomplishment of his four years as mayor. Following the logic of the American Cities report and the success he perceived to have followed from Baltimore's Inner Harbor redevelopment, he noted, "The reality is, I don't believe you're going to find private sector investment in the neighborhoods, given Camden as it is today. The only way to change that is by creating a viable downtown and having it grow from there. There's no financial incentive for the private sector to come in any areas of Camden and rehabilitate housing when you've got a population that has so many unemployed. It all works together." He closed his remarks by projecting as many as 2,500 new jobs from waterfront development.[16]

Writing under the title, "The Faint Beating of the City's New Heart," the *Courier-Post* reacted cautiously to the new effort, citing the failure of Camden's chief educational and medical institutions, Rutgers and Cooper Hospital, to contribute significantly to the city's rebirth through their own expansions. The best the paper could muster in reacting to the new effort was appreciation that Campbell Soup was not leaving the city.[17] The paper would become notably more enthusiastic over the years as waterfront plans began to materialize, but nothing was easy after the first apparent victory. Although the New Jersey Sports and Exposition Authority, an autonomous agency with its own funding, allocated $1 million to plan the aquarium, the estimated $25–30 million in state funds needed to build the facility were not immediately forthcoming. It was more than two years before a plan even materialized to authorize the Sports and Exposition Authority to secure $32 million in revenue bonds to complement the $10 million Governor Kean had managed to set aside in state funds.[18] With the funding finally secured, Corcoran claimed that the investment would more than double Camden's current tax base and Governor Kean said that it could trigger nearly $500 million in new investment and generate as many as eight thousand new jobs during the next decade. As city and state officials converged on the waterfront to mark the groundbreaking on December 22, 1988, Governor Kean declared, "Everything is here, everything, to make it work."[19]

By the time Kean made his announcement, the initial plans for the seventy-five-acre waterfront redevelopment had broadened to include an amphitheater, a marina and dry dock, a 250-room hotel, and a Festival

Market in the mode of the Rouse Company's successful projects in Boston and Baltimore. The heart of the project remained the aquarium, however, and public officials invested the new facility with high expectations. A review of waterfront plans appearing in the *Philadelphia Inquirer* the following spring cited hopes that "the aquarium will lure millions of visitors back to Camden and stem the flight of its population." Primas repeated expectations for $500 million in new investment, adding his hope that, with proper use of training funds, there would be new jobs for many unemployed Camden residents. With one million paying customers drawn to the aquarium annually, the number originally hoped for in the American Cities report, he expected the addition of new retail opportunities not just on the waterfront but for all downtown Camden as well.[20] National columnist Neal Peirce described Camden's effort as "the ultimate test," noting that "in a town where good news is as hard to come by as a movie ticket, the aquarium is supposed to draw one million visitors a year and be the linchpin of redevelopment including a marina, hotel, and international trade center."[21] Even as the picture of a revitalized waterfront began to fill in, however, hopes for the anticipated revitalization received a significant setback.

On November 1, 1989, Campbell Soup announced the early retirement of Gordon McGovern, the single most important business supporter of waterfront redevelopment. McGovern had been known as an innovative manager who diversified the Campbell product line, but the company's stockholders, dominated by the Dorrance family as descendants of the founder, reportedly wanted greater return on investment. Thus, even as Governor Kean announced a long-awaited land swap between Campbell and RCA that would enable Campbell to build its world headquarters on the waterfront, the press reported doubts about the soup company's commitment. On his first day as Campbell's new president, in January 1990, David Johnson fulfilled the worst prophecies when he announced that the company was abandoning plans for the waterfront headquarters. Thomas Corcoran, considering this a disaster, quickly drafted a letter for newly elected governor James Florio and had it delivered to Johnson by state police. Florio wrote that he intended to uphold the obligations of his predecessor and that he expected Johnson to do the same. After a courtesy visit with Johnson, the new governor remained outwardly optimistic. A year later he claimed that the occasion marked the beginning of New Jersey's economic revitalization, saying, "I had the people from Campbell Soup in my office. We looked each other in the eye and worked out an agreement that was good for the people of New Jersey."[22] Those remarks were made at the time of the resolution of what had appeared to be yet another potential blow to Camden, with the threatened departure of RCA's successor company, General Electric Aerospace.

Even as Campbell's commitment to the waterfront appeared to be weakening, General Electric indicated that it was planning to move its 3,300 employees to either Cherry Hill or Valley Forge in Pennsylvania unless it could obtain a low-rise office building at an attractive rate. Damaged by problems that arose after the company abandoned buildings at its Schenectady, New York, plant, General Electric insisted as a condition of staying in the city that Camden buy and demolish as many of its old buildings as possible. Thomas Corcoran immediately appealed to Governor Florio's treasurer, Richard Wright, who together with the Camden County Freeholders secured enough public funding to pay half the initial estimated cost of $65 million for a new facility.[23] With the freeholders pledging $13 million in bonds and a consortium of state agencies providing the rest of the financing, General Electric agreed to stay. Officials marked the arrangement with a ceremony in March 1991, using the desk that had once belonged to Victor Talking Machine founder Eldridge Johnson to sign the agreement. Touting the creation of five hundred construction jobs and the retention of an $86 million annual payroll, a press release from the governor's office proclaimed, "This development project will shine forth as an example throughout New Jersey of what we can do when we work together and fight for what the people want: jobs and economic opportunity." Camden's redevelopment agency agreed to demolish the buildings and repay the loan it received from the county as the site was sold or redeveloped under the Cooper's Ferry Development Association's guidance. Built on the twenty-acre site where the Campbell Soup company plant had been located, the new building ultimately opened in 1995 with seventeen hundred employees dedicated to the assembly and testing of government communications systems. With yet another ownership shift, to the Martin-Marietta Company, construction costs rose to $80 million, and the annual payment in lieu of taxes was set at $600,000, somewhat below the $1 million Governor Florio had predicted. Although Cooper's Ferry's John Shannon stressed the new facility's role in bridging the waterfront area to the central business district, the building's self-containment, with its own cafeteria, health club, and parking, created more of a separate campus environment.[24]

While Governor Florio could initially take credit for keeping major corporations on the waterfront, Campbell Soup did not keep its commitment. Faced with a recession, the company laid off four hundred of its sixteen hundred office workers, eliminating the need for a new headquarters building. In March 1991, the company declared it would be closing its last Camden processing plant, laying off an additional nine hundred workers. Florio managed to convince Campbell to enter into an agreement with a private developer to build the now unnecessary office tower, by promising to have the state lease space in the building in order to make it financially viable. His defeat for reelection in 1993, however, effectively scuttled that commitment. The death of John Dorrance, patriarch of the Campbell family, removed the last supporter for the new headquarters.[25]

There was still one bright spot in the redevelopment of the waterfront, however. The opening of the aquarium in February 1992 was hailed as a major event for Camden. The *Philadelphia Inquirer* crowed, "The city without hope finally has reason to be hopeful." Governor Florio promised that investment in the waterfront would eventually reach Camden's neighborhoods, while Assemblyman Wayne Bryant, a prime backer of the effort, asserted, "For our young folks, this is the new Camden. It says, 'Yes, there are opportunities here.'" Camden High School principal Ruthie Green-Brown added that "the aquarium signals a rebirth of the city that will give it new life, revitalize the complacency of its people and be the stimulus to move the city forward." The *Inquirer*'s architectural critic, Thomas Hine, however, worried, "there probably has never been such a building that has been asked to do so much as this one."[26]

No building, in fact, could sustain such expectations. The aquarium did well in the first year, as 1.2 million visitors flooded the facility. "People find it's easy to get here, attractive and safe," Thomas Corcoran asserted, "and then they tell others, creating a ripple effect that's changing Camden's image." The aquarium, he added later, enabled the city to "win its most important battle: to prove that people would come to Camden for certain types of activities despite what the skeptics believed. The area is viewed as safe, clean, and attractive."[27] The excitement wore off quickly, however, and attendance dropped significantly over the next two years, to under 550,000. Having made a conscious decision to make New Jersey's own local marine species the centerpiece of the facility, aquarium planners necessarily excluded a number of attractions that might have caused more interest. To broaden the scope of the exhibits cost the aquarium another $3.7 million, and even then its staff discovered what other theme attractions were learning, the need for continued reinvention to sustain the interest of repeat visitors.[28] Additionally, the facility suffered as the partnership between the New Jersey Academy for Aquatic Sciences, which managed the facility and provided its educational programs, and the Philadelphia Zoo soured and dissolved. The zoo, reeling from the death of its president William Donaldson (who would also have presided over the Academy's board), failed in responsibilities for membership and marketing and proved a drag on the aquarium's institutional development.[29] Most important, the lack of nearby restaurants, retail facilities, and hotel spaces left the aquarium isolated and without the synergies the American Cities report had identified as critical. The problem was well illustrated through the prolonged and ultimately unsuccessful effort to lure a professional sports facility nearby.

In 1989, Governor Kean initiated plans for construction of a new arena on land owned by the South Jersey Port just north of the Walt Whitman Bridge. Offering to provide $65 million in state financing for a new $100 million facility and further incentives to develop an additional sixty adjacent acres, Kean gave Philadelphia's basketball and hockey teams incentives their hometown found difficult to match.[30] Surprisingly, the *Philadelphia Inquirer* favored the move, noting that the teams would remain at the heart of the region and would be more accessible than at the existing site in South Philadelphia. Besides, the paper asserted, "This is not a case of the rich suburbs stealing yet another asset from a financially troubled city. Camden is a far more hurting place than Philadelphia. Its waterfront development is its only hope for a brighter future, and it's a pretty dim hope at that."[31]

Despite what appeared a promising match, efforts to finalize the arrangement faltered during the early months of the Florio administration, as other issues, most notably a looming state deficit of $550 million, occupied the new governor's attention. Trying to keep the effort alive, government aides introduced the idea of a special zone around the site, known as a tax increment financing district. Local sales and possibly property taxes generated by the new arena would be directed toward repaying bonds issued to cover costs. Reacting additionally to concerns that the proposed port location would jeopardize the twenty-three firms and their six hundred employees there, Florio proposed shifting the location to the downtown waterfront. Unnamed aides argued that a downtown site would provide better access and, as one put it, the aquarium area looked nicer and would do more for the city of Camden: "At Broadway you go in and out without really seeing too much of Camden. It's kind of like going in the back door of a hotel."[32]

Such efforts kept New Jersey's hopes alive, but Pennsylvanians were not willing to give up immediately. As a result, negotiations dragged out on both sides of the river into the last months of Florio's term. Then, in October 1993, New Jersey appeared to have triumphed, as newly elected Philadelphia Mayor Edward Rendell announced that his city was too broke to further sweeten the offer to assist the construction of a new arena adjacent to the existing facility. In December, even as he prepared to give up the office in defeat, Governor Florio announced that arrangements with 76ers owner Harold Katz, who had broken with the Flyers ownership to act independently, were virtually settled. Republican governor-elect Christine Todd Whitman, while she acknowledged her desire to review the arrangements, seemed disposed to support the deal.[33] In the next few weeks, however, she began to question openly the financial feasibility of the project. Alarmed, the Democratic-controlled Camden County Freeholders stepped in, offering to raise up to $25 million of the $110 million in costs and to take the greater risk by subordinating their interests to those of the state.[34] On January 12, 1994, Whitman announced she would not support the project. Under a banner headline, "Whitman Dumps Sixers Deal," the *Courier-Post* reported that she was not convinced that the facility could pay for itself. Determined not to let the opportunity slip away, the county freeholders sought alternative financing, including $50 million in bonds, $11 million from Campbell Soup, and a piece of waterfront land worth an estimated $3 million.[35] Despite this last effort, the 76ers' Katz announced the following month that his team would be staying in Philadelphia. The final inducement was a $175 million stadium, Spectrum II, adjacent to the existing location. To be financed largely through private funds for luxury seating, the arrangement nonetheless brought with it $20 million in Pennsylvania state funding as well as a $6.5 million low-interest city loan to build a parking garage. A photograph accompanying news of the announcement showed a beaming Mayor Rendell clapping as Katz made his presentation at the podium.[36]

In all the commentary about the location of the sports team, the financial benefit to Camden was not always clear. The prospect of having competing arenas on either side of the Delaware River, each needing to recruit additional acts to generate revenue when the teams were not playing, raised reasonable doubts about the financial viability of the basketball-only facility in Camden. Noting their exclusion from negotiations, Camden officials worried about their ability to generate revenue for the city from the facility. The active interest of Camden County Democrats, including County Chairman George Norcross, provided yet another indication that city interests might not be preeminent. Although early reports of negotiations revealed that the Philadelphia teams were offered corporate tax credit for hiring Camden residents for certain jobs, that commitment was not sustained over time, prompting additional fears that employment opportunities for local residents would be relegated to part-time work.[37] Still, the setback represented a major blow to waterfront aspirations. Cooper's Ferry's Corcoran initially downplayed the impact, saying such an activity had never been planned in advance. Nonetheless it was hardly coincidental, in the effort to keep expectations high for the area, that on the same day Harold Katz confirmed his decision to stay in Philadelphia Corcoran revealed initial discussions with the Sony Corporation to develop a high-tech theme park on both sides of the Delaware River. The Philadelphia side was expected to include movie theaters, virtual reality games, and restaurants, at the long-delayed Penn's Landing site. That effort was intended to complement Sony's recent commitment, in association with the Blockbuster Entertainment Corporation and Pace Entertainment Group based in Houston, to build a $40 million amphitheater adjacent to the aquarium in Camden.[38]

Designed to accommodate up to eighteen thousand summer spectators (beyond the seven thousand that would be accommodated under a year-round weatherproof shed), the facility was conceived as the premier state-of-the-art option for major concerts in the greater Philadelphia area. The state quickly insisted that the facility be combined with a performing arts center for the South Jersey area. As a result, estimated costs rose to $54 million. To cover the additional expenditure, the Sony-Pace-Blockbuster partnership increased its commitment of $20 million by another $10 million, for which it was granted a ten-year tax abatement to cover the additional debt service. After that, the partnership was required to pay a per-ticket fee that was expected to generate approximately $600,000 a year starting in 2005 and rise to as much as $2 million in the last ten years of the thirty-year lease. The center opened in 1995 and quickly achieved the status of the second highest such entertainment venue in the country in both gross revenue and attendance.[39] It generated twenty permanent and four hundred part-time jobs. Although the economic impact was thus limited, public officials looked beyond employment alone for the building's importance. Even though visitors stayed at the theater only a few hours, Camden Redevelopment Authority Director Thomas Roberts noted, its presence "is positive in terms of changing the image of the city. It makes the city a more attractive place for investment. The city has a tough image. If people can come in, have a good time and leave safely, it shows Camden is not a terrible place to be."[40]

In the early 1990s, several other important facilities opened on the waterfront. With the assistance of a $7 million Urban Mass Transportation Administration grant, a new 740-car garage went up across from the aquarium. Thirty-five percent of the construction jobs were filled by minority workers and 20 percent by Camden residents. In addition, Cooper's Ferry hired fourteen unarmed security guards to patrol the waterfront from a pool of two thousand unemployed residents.[41] John Shannon admitted this was a "drop in the bucket for a city where unemployment is so high but," he noted, it was "a step in the right direction."[42] Wiggins Park was extended at a cost of $3.1 million, while another $3 million county investment secured completion of a fifty-slip circular marina between the aquarium and the entertainment center. Most significant, a $30 million eleven-story office building—conceived as the first of four office towers surrounding the new garage—opened in 1996. It was designed by New Jersey's internationally renowned architect Michael Graves primarily for the use of the joint Pennsylvania-New Jersey Delaware River Port Authority. By bringing an anticipated five to six hundred office workers to the waterfront, Cooper's Ferry board chairman Kevin Halpern predicted, the new building would provide a market not just for a restaurant planned for the building but for additional shopping and eating facilities.[43] Although significant gaps in downtown waterfront redevelopment still remained, the shape of a revitalized urban core had begun to take form. Enthusiastically as this vision was being received in the mainstream press, however, the effort did not please everyone, most notably Camden's activists.

Even as officials broke ground for the new aquarium in 1989, a volume of case studies of downtown public-private partnerships appeared to warn against creation of an "hourglass economy," one that creates a few technically demanding, highly paid professional positions and many unskilled, low-paying jobs disproportionately held by racial minorities. "The fundamental long-standing inequality that has always prevailed in joint public-private ventures," editor Gregory Squires concluded, "has also informed the activities of contemporary partnerships. A key question [is] 'For whom are we saving the cities?'"[44] Rutgers University professor Michael Lang struck a similar note several years later in commenting on the aquarium: "You need to do something that has a high visibility to attract people who have left the city back into the city," he told an Associated Press reporter. But by segregating the downtown tourist areas from decaying neighborhoods, as was the case in Camden, he said, "It tends to set up an uneven development. It doesn't trickle down and filter into the lower-income neighborhoods."[45] Camden activists hardly needed to be aware of such pronouncements to reach similar conclusions. Among those protesting the opening of the aquarium was Jean Brooks, who commented brusquely, "We're paying for water that's polluted and the fish are swimming in clean water." "The aquarium's a beautiful thing," North Camden housing organizer Luis Galindez told the *Inquirer* a short time later, "but nobody's going to benefit from it. We got two and three families living in one house and beautiful fishes living in tanks by themselves. We could really have used that money." Pointing to the $52 million spent on the aquarium when more than 1,700 city homes lay abandoned, Lillian Ubarry, organizer of Concerned Citizens of North Camden, charged, "This city has to get its priorities straight."[46]

The central issue was the number and type of jobs created. The fact that Camden residents filled thirty-five of the aquarium's eighty-two full time jobs was itself significant. The Academy for Aquatic Sciences made efforts to increase that number, too. Because many younger residents lacked good backgrounds in science, the Academy secured funds in the next year to train youngsters. A number who started at the aquarium in high school ultimately made their way into full-time supervisory positions.[47] Nonetheless, local residents initially were disproportionately found in nonprofessional positions, not surprisingly, given the low educational levels among the majority of city residents. While Camden residents held eleven of forty-seven professional and managerial positions, they held all the positions listed as clerks, custodians, and security guards. Cooper's Ferry executive vice president John Shannon admitted the aquarium did not provide many jobs itself, but he claimed the aquarium would act as a diamond on the Delaware, luring private businesses that would offer more opportunities and more jobs. Pointing to the failure to train Camden residents for more technical jobs, as originally envisioned at Camden County College, activist Roy Jones retorted that if the waterfront could not produce jobs for city residents or produce business opportunities for them, "then it's a waste of time. It will serve a political value for some people, but for the majority of people in the city, it is a sign of disrespect."[48] In his opinion, Camden was well on its way to becoming another Atlantic City, with poor neighborhoods entirely set apart from a secure entertainment area.[49] Similarly, the loss of nine hundred Campbell production jobs was not entirely made up by the retention of some seventeen hundred jobs at the GE Aerospace facility. Tom Knoche was among those questioning how the state could use $65 million in public funds to benefit two healthy multinational corporations without getting commitments to increase use of city-based vendors and suppliers or to provide special programs to prepare Camden minorities for the high-tech jobs available at GE's Camden plant.[50]

Even as ground was broken for the aquarium, activists identified another point of contention with waterfront development as they sought to save an affordable housing complex located only a few blocks away. The 93-unit Royal Court, constructed in 1974 as part of a federal rent-to-buy experiment, was a shambles within a few years.[51] In 1984, resident Charlotte Robinson won a class action suit in federal court requiring the U.S. Department of Housing and Urban Development to make available $1.3 million for repairs. Despite sporadic attempts at improvement, the homes were scarcely any better six years later, even with an additional commitment of $350,000 in Community Development Block Grant funding. Armed with a report that the costs of rehabilitation would exceed HUD's maximum allowance, Martin McKernan, attorney for both the city's housing and redevelopment authorities, attempted to apply the remaining funds available for Royal Court to demolish the complex and build twenty new units for remaining residents. The rest of the land would be sold for private redevelopment. Armed with their own report that the buildings were structurally sound enough to meet HUD's guidelines, residents organized, picketing McKernan's office and pressuring city officials to seek new funds.[52] They revealed the heart of their distrust with city authorities in a press release issued as Charlotte Robinson returned to court in November 1990: "The location of the complex near to the waterfront site makes it highly desirable for developers. Royal Court families are convinced that the City and the Housing Authority have abandoned them in the hope that the entire complex would become vacant, and available for profit-making."[53] Bolstered by a new HUD program and additional state funds, rehabilitation finally went forward, although the new units did not open until 1999.[54] Despite the victory, the prolonged battle helped fuel antagonism between community-based activists and waterfront planners.

Also contentious was a Camden City Council proposal to form a special improvement district at the waterfront, a plan critics charged only affirmed the determination of waterfront planners to set an entertainment district entirely apart from the city. Aquarium and waterfront development plans were sold to the public largely on the strength of benefits expected to spill over into the rest of Camden. Adina Abramowitz, executive director of the Cooperative Business Assistance Corporation, charged that "The Special Improvement District makes that harder to believe." Collecting more than 3,000 signatures on a petition seeking a referendum on the improvement district ordinance, activists managed to kill the idea in one of the few victories they managed in contention with waterfront supporters.[55]

Thomas Corcoran admitted that Cooper's Ferry had been heavy-handed in attempting to rush the special improvement district through the city council.[56] He contended, however, that the issue was not merely one of priorities. "Tom Kean did not call Randy Primas and say, 'I have $52 million. Would you like to build housing or an aquarium?' The state made a decision years ago that there would be an aquarium in New Jersey. We at Cooper's Ferry put together a team that won the competition. It could have gone to Atlantic City, Liberty State Park, or the Shore. We brought in money that would not have come to Camden for any other purpose and we're proud of what we have accomplished."[57]

In fact, Corcoran, who remained a Camden resident himself, shared the belief that neighborhood issues ought to be addressed directly and not as mere spillover. In a proposal he sent to *Courier-Post* executive editor Everett Landers in April 1992, he stressed the importance of waterfront development beyond the downtown, in creating more revenue and generating jobs for Camden residents, but also in helping "create a better image of the City to investors and developers interested in projects outside the downtown area." After addressing citywide issues of public safety, the creation of industrial parks, and the expansion of small business development, he proposed a new, citywide nonprofit housing development corporation. Composed, as he put it, of "credible community groups engaged in grass roots housing efforts," in addition to representatives of area banks and public officials, he believed such an organization could leverage start-up grants from area foundations.[58] Several years later, Camden-area state legislators from both parties joined to back a bill that would dedicate half of all sales taxes collected within a proposed waterfront Municipal Development Financing District to a fund for Camden's neighborhood redevelopment. The concept, originated by the late state senator Walter Rand, was expected to generate $1.2 million in its first year. The other half of the money collected would be dedicated to shoring up Camden's public safety. Although the fund never materialized, both Corcoran and Mayor Arnold Webster, who themselves had been fighting over control of waterfront redevelopment, supported the measure.[59]

Even as periodic attempts to link waterfront and neighborhood redevelopment faltered, by the early 1990s the course for waterfront development had been set to establish a premier family entertainment center. That was no more clear than in plans for the redevelopment of the Campbell

Soup site immediately south of the Benjamin Franklin Bridge. In 1992 Cooper's Ferry convened a high-level team, including Philadelphia planner David Wallace and architect Michael Graves, to envision future possibilities for the waterfront. Their vision was quite comprehensive, encompassing specialty retail, restaurants, a hotel, and an ambitious infill housing program for the adjacent Cooper-Grant neighborhood in addition to an entertainment center. Few of the details of the plan were realized. Its spirit lived on, however, in its most emphatic statement, "We believe that highest and best use of the waterfront acreage is to make it a quality leisure-time and entertainment center for Philadelphia and Camden, one of the five largest markets in the U.S." Urging themed development to capture "the intrinsic aspects of life on the waterfront," it urged laser and light shows, fireworks, barge entertainment, wateredge private parties, and water celebrations. The payoff, it suggested, could be attendance levels of as many as 8 million visitors, three to four thousand new jobs, and "a strong regenerative influence on the life of the city."[60] This report was extended and deepened through a 1995 consulting agreement with MRA International, a leading firm specializing in urban entertainment destinations. MRA called for additional visitor attractions in Camden and direct linkage between the area and Philadelphia's Penn's Landing as a historic district capable of supporting unified programmatic development.[61]

Such a strategy turned waterfront development and marketing even farther away from the city of Camden and toward Philadelphia. This effort was facilitated especially through a change in the charter in the Delaware River Port Authority (DRPA). Following the model of the powerful New York-New Jersey Port Authority on the Hudson River, the DRPA was granted the right to reinvest funds generated from tolls in redevelopment projects. Although promoters of the measure initially stressed DRPA's potential role to promote more traditional economic development through creation of industrial parks,[62] the logic of current development swiftly shifted investment toward cultural and entertainment venues. The rationale was that such investments would be returned not just in increased revenues as visitors sought improved destinations but in more general increases in area prosperity. This concept ultimately materialized in the marketing theme "Two Cities—One Waterfront," and naming the entire area Independence Harbor. As early as 1996 Thomas Corcoran was predicting an increase from 8 to 10 million visitors annually.[63]

By the time of the 1992 plan, ferry service already had been reintroduced by a nonprofit corporation, to connect tourist sites on each side of the river. Although ridership dropped to about half the first year's level of 583,535, it picked up again to an average of 325,000 as more waterfront attractions became available.[64] In 1999 the Delaware River Port Authority authorized a $7.9 million plan to develop a barge-based light-and-sound show intended for display on one hundred nights from May through October. Expensive as that was, the cost paled next to a $23 million tram designed to move 3,000 people an hour from Penn's Landing to Camden. The tram, viewed not just as a transportation link, was intended to become the "icon" identifying the combined destination, much as the Liberty Bell or Independence Hall had done for Philadelphia's historic district. Together with the proposed light show, the ride 160 feet above the Delaware, promoters asserted, would offer riders an experience unmatched anywhere else in the United States. Most of these ambitious plans, including the light show and the tram, failed to materialize.[65] What was realized, however, fully supported the direction of family entertainment.

In a rare example of incorporating a community-based organization into waterfront development, a $7 million Camden Children's Garden opened at the entrance to the aquarium in 1999. The garden was the vision of Michael Devlin, a long-time Camden County political appointee and a member of Camden City Council, and his wife, Valerie Frick, and was built with funds from the DRPA. In addition to employing a significant number of Camden residents, the garden directed fees to support community gardens and grow labs—hands-on classroom gardening programs that emphasized science and math. Although it existed in somewhat uneasy relationship with its larger neighbors, especially the aquarium, the garden became an important addition to family entertainment on the waterfront.[66] Camden waterfront backers also managed to secure quite another kind of attraction, the *U.S.S. New Jersey*, retired from the Navy after distinguished service. To secure this prize, the South Jersey Port Alliance, a coalition of influential area politicians (including George Norcross's brother Donald) had to wrest it away from competing interests north in Bayonne. To do so, proponents of the Camden site had to contend with efforts to exploit Camden's image as the nation's murder capital, among other charges.[67] With the aid of $30 million in grants, including funds from Camden County and the Camden Empowerment Zone as well as DRPA, the ship opened as a museum at a newly constructed pier just south of the waterfront entertainment center in October 2001.[68]

Even as the *New Jersey* was being towed to dock, yet another entertainment venue came to realization with the opening of a minor league baseball stadium in May 2001. Originally conceived as a potential partnership with the Phillies in 1996 and 1997, the opportunity fell to a former banker turned developer, Steven Schilling, who proposed an independent league team. County freeholders wanted a team from another league, which would play only half the number of games and locate in Camden's suburban neighbor of Pennsauken. Thomas Corcoran was already committed to Schilling when the alternative idea arose, but he opened the opportunity of developing a site immediately south of the Benjamin Franklin Bridge to bidding anyway.[69] Only Schilling submitted a proposal, and he built the stadium with a $9 million loan from Sovereign Bank, a $6.5 million loan from the Delaware River Port Authority, and $2 and $3 million grants from the New Jersey Economic Development Authority and Rutgers University respectively. Under terms the state required, the field was to be owned by Rutgers, which could use it for its Camden games. The university coincidentally opened adjacent playing fields, for which the city retained first right of use during the summer months. Schilling's company, Quaker Construction, built and managed the stadium, gaining an additional $3.5 million from Campbell Soup for the naming rights. In exchange for a tax exemption, the owners agreed to pay the city fifty cents per ticket, an estimated $180,000 in the first year of play.[70] Faced with considerable competition, with the Phillies across the river, the Wilmington Blue Rocks to the south, and eight additional minor league teams in New Jersey, the Camden Riversharks, as they were christened, presented some considerable risk, not the least in their Camden location. Despite the challenge, the sparkling new stadium, with its magnificent views of Philadelphia and of the Benjamin Franklin Bridge, prompted a wave of favorable publicity. As *Courier-Post* columnist Phil Anastasia put it, "This team and its gem of a ballpark, they really are about life in South Jersey, about the ongoing development of the precious resource that is Camden's riverfront, and about the complicated and continuing dynamic of this dying-to-be-reborn city's relationship with the suburbs."[71]

Perhaps even more important psychologically to the waterfront's future was the announcement in 2000 that Philadelphia developer Carl Dranoff intended to convert the abandoned RCA Nipper Building to market-rate apartments. Offering a luxury residential option not envisioned for the city since the construction of the Northgate Apartment complex in the early 1960s, Dranoff's project, Thomas Corcoran asserted, "will give the Waterfront a whole different feel." Expected to compete well in price with similar structures on the Philadelphia side of the Delaware, the Nipper promised the first real influx of middle-class residents in a generation. They would be provided with parking inside the building, a fitness facility, and a 24-hour concierge. In addition, commercial outlets at ground level were expected to enliven the largely empty streetscape around the structure.[72] The owners of Triangle Liquor at the dying intersection of Broadway and Kaighn were among the first to put their names before the developer as possible tenants. Dranoff managed to secure full financing for the project, but not without a struggle. What he offered was a quality structure that would be largely self-contained and a residential island in an otherwise deserted downtown.

Camden's waterfront became one of the few success stories to emerge out of the city during the 1990s. One measure of that success was the degree to which changed conditions altered at least part of the city's image. The director for economic development for Flint, Michigan's Chamber of Commerce could easily have been talking about Camden when he said, "The only thing working against us is our name. . . . If people didn't know this was Flint they would probably like it."[73] In Camden, it was not unusual for performers opening their acts at the waterfront entertainment center to greet their audiences, "Hello, Philadelphia!" If a portion of those present could forget, even temporarily, that they were in Camden the same could not be said of the city's residents. For Camden, like Baltimore, continued to witness overall population loss and further decline among its older neighborhoods despite the success of its waterfront revival.[74] The waterfront remained something entirely apart from their daily lives, along lines suggested by Christine Boyer of New York's South Street Seaport market:

Devoted to entertainment and wish fulfillment, city tableaux on the margins of reality are designed explicitly for escape and gratification. They emphasize their own lack of seriousness by claiming, as spectacles do, that their business is show business. These tableaux separate pleasure from necessity, escape from reality. They widen the gap between the city on display and the city beyond our view. And in so doing they sever any connection they might have had to the art of building real cities, for, after all, these city tableaux only claim to be special places for fun and entertainment, areas of the city to explore during periods of play, which promise not to burden the spectator with the seriousness of reality.[75]

Camden's waterfront did not have the capacity to spur development elsewhere. The view that the benefits of rising tourism would ultimately spill over into the city's residential areas by the time the new century arrived had not been confirmed. Indeed, the very distance between the two sectors prompted police to line streets at gametime or during concerts to assure that visitors to the city did not stray into unknown territory. Such a situation was not unusual in the post-industrial era. As Dennis Judd comments, "Where crime, poverty, and urban decay make parts of a city inhospitable to visitors, specialized areas are established as virtual tourist reservations," what he further labels "the tourist bubble."[76] Because that separation remained so distinct, Camden residents kept their own distance from the waterfront, except on special occasions. The city had proved it could attract visitors, but it failed to convince either current or potential residents that this set of investments was capable of uplifting the city as a whole.

Chapter 6
The Neighborhoods: Not by Faith Alone

Neighborhood initiatives have often been viewed as a kind of antidote to the casualties of capitalism, including its tendency to undermine local communities. The history of neighborhood initiative also reflects American society's persistent tendency to ask those who have the least role in making and the largest role in bearing the brunt of society's economic and social choices to deal with the effects of those choices.

—*Robert Halpern,* Rebuilding the Inner City, *1995*

Nearly a quarter of a century after America's post-industrial cities hit bottom as both private capital and public programs appeared to have abandoned the effort to reverse the situation there finally appeared to be good news. "The American inner city is rebounding—not just here and there, not just cosmetically, but fundamentally," Paul Grogan and Tony Proscio declared in their 2000 book, *Comeback Cities.*[1] The inner city, Harvard research fellow Alexander Von Hoffman added in a 2003 study, "is no longer the lurid nightmare portrayed for so long on the local eleven o'clock news. . . . In the 1980s a scholar examining inner-city neighborhoods found only 'islands of renewal in seas of decay.' Today researchers write of 'islands of decay in seas of renewal.' As startling as it may seem, across the United States inner-city neighborhoods are being reborn."[2] Government was not the party responsible for neighborhood renewal, these studies asserted, but rather a broad array of largely nonprofit organizations, which managed in a variety of ways to tether new human and monetary resources to the benefit of places previously left behind.[3] In terms of talent, creativity, and dedication, Camden's community organizers stood among the nation's very best for their ability to address huge problems and to make a difference in people's lives. Like their peers elsewhere, they formed community development corporations, reinvented old organizations—notably those associated with parish churches that had once served white ethnic groups in the city before its transformation—and tapped state and national sources of expertise and capital. But an observer of Camden's neighborhoods would have been hard pressed to declare victory. By the turn of the new century Camden's neighborhood improvements remained largely pockets in a sea of decay. Indeed, by 2000 no neighborhood in the entire city had escaped the dire effects of disinvestment. Camden remained, in urban commentator David Rusk's terms, a "city past the point of no return."[4]

Why was Camden unable to rebound? Certainly, the ability to attract new investment and visitors to the waterfront signaled some progress in reversing Camden's fortunes. An entertainment district does not a self-sustaining city make, however. For Camden to join the company of success stories, it had to become a good place to live as well as to visit. This proved a particularly daunting challenge, and not only because of ineptness in city government or a bad economy. Cumulative changes that had left Camden with the worst of all worlds—inadequate services, high taxes, and undesirable environmental conditions—undercut even the best efforts to make the city a preferred place of residence once again. Moreover, a shift in national policy away from public investments aimed at the elimination of poverty and toward attracting private capital again put social activists at a disadvantage. The strength they once possessed in bridging divides, between races and between city and suburb, declined in an era of greater personal as well as policy privatization. Many made their adjustments to these shifts as well. Still, however impressive group efforts were in improving neighborhood conditions and however generous outside help became, Camden residents found themselves in a situation best described again by David Rusk: attempting to ascend a down escalator.[5] Lacking neither social capital nor new sources of monetary investment, they nonetheless faced too many external forces against them to assure their well-being as long as they remained in place. Many objected strenuously when *Time* featured Camden in 1992 under the title, "Who Could Live Here?" but the story continued to have a ring of truth to it into the first years of the new century.[6] Nor was their situation unique. Grogan and Proscio dismiss Rusk's metropolitan prescriptions for dispersing poverty as impractical, but they do not contest his arguments that even the best community development efforts have failed to reduce poverty significantly in inner city areas. As reviewers noted, these contemporary urban boosters were all too quick to commend physical changes which only masked continued poverty.[7] To Rusk, praise for community work stuck him as serving mainly to relieve guilt, not poverty:

My exasperation stems from the way in which the CDC paradigm allows powerful institutions to shirk once again their responsibility to confront racial and economic segregation. It is easier to pair corporate money and volunteers with inner-city schools than to allow inner-city students to attend the schools that the corporate executives' own children attend. It is easier to give foundation grants for affordable housing projects in inner-city neighborhoods than to demand a "fair share" of low- and moderate-income housing in neighborhoods where many foundation executives dwell. . . . Easier? Not easier at all, if the goal is to achieve substantial progress. It is "easier" only in that this path is more socially and politically comfortable.[8]

*   *   *

Single mother Donza Harmon moved to the Westfield Acres public housing complex in East Camden in the early 1980s, seeking a place where she could bring up her son in relative security at an affordable price. Public housing was not new to her. In childhood she had lived with her mother at Chelton Terrace, a defense housing complex built during World War II in the Centerville section of South Camden. Westfield had been built in 1938 and was both the first and largest public housing project built in Camden. By the 1980s, it had seen better days. But the neighborhood around it was relatively stable, and in her first few years at Westfield the complex met Harmon's expectations. Then the scourge of drugs set in. Westfield's grouping of buildings around open spaces, yet cut off from service streets, provided plenty of room for dealers to operate. So many outsiders jammed the entrance to Harmon's apartment that she found herself constantly urging them to move away simply so she could get about her business. One night, when the commotion was especially evident in the stairwell, she got out of bed, poured some vegetable oil into a glass, took up her Bible, and went outside where the dealers congregated. It was 2 A.M. She did not say a word to her tormentors. She simply began reading the Bible as she touched the surrounding ground with the vegetable oil, as though she were anointing the area. The dealers moved off right away and did not come back.[9]

Whether one attributes Harmon's success to God's purpose, as she did, or to more practical considerations, her act of faith was but one of countless such efforts sustaining Camden residents through the most difficult of circumstances. At the time this happened, a *Courier-Post* reporter described Westfield in the direst terms: "For the 1,450 people who reside there—800 of them children—life is a constant battle to stay alive. Drug gangs, vandalism and aging, and deteriorated buildings combine to produce a grim existence."[10] Yet Harmon persevered. Her poverty had paralyzed her for years, but she found she could become motivated when she got angry. Facing conditions no one would have chosen and observing cruelty and indifference to those circumstances, she was moved to act. As she recalled years later, she finally was able to put her depression on the back burner. She got involved, first in the tenants association, which she soon headed, then in providing programs for Westfield's children. Not just for herself but as a model for her son, she completed work for a college degree in 1999.[11] Faith, determination, and working associations with other people facing many of the same hardships intertwined to make a world not of her own making, if not pleasant, at least tolerable and open to promise.

Harmon's journey to greater self-sufficiency coincided with the emergence in Camden, as in many other inner city areas, of a remarkable complex of neighborhood-based efforts designed not just to cope with the harsh social and physical conditions associated with concentrated poverty but to improve them. Many of the most impressive of these efforts were church-supported, providing evidence for claims at the turn of the new century that faith-based institutions held the key to ending the debilitating culture of poverty that had persisted now over several generations. Such institutions, some argue, provide the key to overcoming the "quiet riots" of drug, alcohol, and personal abuse, by providing moral solidarity as a substitute for narrow self-interest.[12] As Harmon's own story indicated, however, faith had to confront a material world. To do so required a range of secular tools and the enlistment of many whose faith in improvement came from other sources. For after a generation of losses in social and monetary capital, Camden's residential leadership needed all the help it could get.

Camden's first neighborhood-based initiative derived not from any moral imperative but from the practical realization among supporters of the renewal process in the 1960s that the turmoil created from displacing residents threatened the whole process. The second wave of redevelopment activity thus sought to complement physical renewal with associated social programs.[13] In 1967 business leaders, including a former vice president of Campbell Soup, the president of the Greater Camden Movement, and the chairman of the First Camden National Bank, announced formation of an organization to rehabilitate abandoned homes for new occupancy. Funded initially by $20,000 contributions each from Campbell, RCA, First Camden National, and the Dorrance Foundation, Camden Housing Improvement Projects (CHIP) received its first state funding three months later and quickly formed a close relationship with the city's Interfaith-Interracial Council of Clergy. A CHIP study showed that 10,500 of the city's 35,000 residential units needed rehabilitation. The *Courier-Post* praised CHIP's effort as essential to the success of renewal plans and painted the first CHIP property to open (in North Camden in March 1968) in glowing terms. This "gleaming white and blue row home" was eligible for sale, thanks to a revolving loan fund, for only $200 down and $65 a month to any buyer with an annual family income under $5,280.[14] Further positive reports of new homes opening later in the year followed. Only three years later, however, the paper reported a host of complaints about faulty construction and utilities.[15] Real estate records for the time demonstrate a marked pattern. Families, many of them headed by single women, occupied the homes for a short two- to four-year period before they abandoned the homes. News accounts suggest they lacked the funds either to sustain payments or to maintain the properties. Taken over by the Department of Housing and Urban Development, soon the homes were back on the city's abandoned property lists.[16] While some individuals managed to make the most of their new investments, as a whole the program failed. Scattered housing rehabilitation had done nothing either to stem the pace of abandonment in tough neighborhoods like North Camden or to anchor a new group of investors in their communities. Several smaller rehabilitation efforts undertaken at the same time also failed. Neighborhood-based housing, without organization behind it, clearly was not sufficient to stem the corrosive effects of poverty.

Despite its origins as a militant protest organization, the Black People's Unity Movement adopted a similarly practical approach. As the thrust of the original organization's militance waned with the absorption of key leaders into city government, their focus shifted to promoting black businesses. The incorporation papers for the BPUM Corporation described as its primary purpose "to provide relief of the poor, the distressed and the underprivileged . . . by developing and expanding the opportunities available to underprivileged persons or groups comprised substantially of such persons to own, manage, operate and gain employment in business enterprises."[17] According to Harvey Johnson, who became the organization's first and only director after receiving his law degree from the University of Pennsylvania in 1969, the Bedford Stuyvesant Development and Services Corporation offered a powerful model in the 1960s. Few other organizations could command similar levels of funding, however. More relevant, he suggested, was Cleveland's more modest program promoting black businesses, including a law firm and a credit union. Using the organization's political muscle, BPUM managed to advance some promising business deals, including plans for an industrial park in North Camden and a share of a regional corporation, U.S. Vision. Daycare centers operated at four locations, including suburban Lindenwold. Over time, however, BPUM entrepreneurial activity withered away, as even a Burger King located adjacent to the Rutgers campus closed. With the final sale out of bankruptcy of the industrial site in 2001, only Johnson's own law firm survived as a for-profit activity. In Camden, as Robert Halpern has suggested more generally of inner city areas, the loss of resources was so swift and dramatic in the 1970s and 1980s that even those capable of getting financing encountered high levels of community suspicion and resentment in an atmosphere shaped largely by patterns of coping merely to survive.[18]

BPUM's decline did not signal a total collapse in grassroots organizing, however, as demonstrated in North Camden. There, in direct contrast to CHIP's corporate sponsorship, a series of organizations formed out of a protest movement. Although Grace Lutheran Parish's pastor, Hans Goebel, had the idea of forming Concerned Citizens of North Camden and Lutherans remained central partners in efforts to rebuild North Camden, early organizational activity stemmed from immediate and pressing material needs. The first protests, including the efforts to block the waterfront prison and to secure from the city abandoned homes that could be rehabilitated, were largely improvised affairs. They grew more out of a sense of anger than out of any singular vision for the future. Just as Donza Harmon had been energized by a reaction to injustice, much of a whole neighborhood began to act collectively in ways largely unknown since the dissolution of white ethnic domination. Out of this protest was born an organizational structure to carry the movement forward and to build a long-term agenda.

In 1984 members of Concerned Citizens of North Camden formed the North Camden Land Trust (NCLT). Even before this, Concerned Citizens had managed in a half dozen years to convert some one hundred vacant properties to homeownership. Continued disinvestment and a rash of fires, however—many of them believed to be set by owners hoping to receive insurance premiums when no buyers were available—continued to ravage the community. A new organization was needed to manage the considerable problems associated with acquisition, rehabilitation, and sale of these properties in an area where the median income, at $11,000, was less than a third that of the county.[19] The organization embraced a land trust formula, a way of combating speculation by requiring owners wishing to sell to offer the property first to the trust, so that it could be resold eventually to another low-income buyer. "The message that is being sent to speculators," Tom Knoche asserted, "is: the best you can hope to accomplish here is not to create a new community but rather a mixed one."[20] In 1989 the trust received a grant from New Jersey's Balanced Housing Program and a loan from the Philadelphia-based Delaware Valley Community Reinvestment Fund. The immediate goals were to extend neighborhood rehabilitation and to rebuild the 400 block of State Street, a row of stately properties, once a premier block occupied by substantial business and professional offices and homes. Leaders of Grace Lutheran Church, located at the corner of Fourth and State, had long harbored hopes for reconstructing the block, and they encouraged the Camden Lutheran Housing Corporation's decision to join NCLT in assembling the finances to transform sixteen shells into thirty-two three-bedroom homes.[21] Because the concept of single-family ownership did not fit with the multiple-family use of the structures, NCLT introduced a cooperative model through which tenants could build up equity in their homes, receiving credit if their homes were well maintained at the end of their tenure. The model was subsequently extended to the majority of properties NCLT converted to rental occupancy.[22] Neighborhood residents were hired to do the work, even when delays ensued as crews struggled to meet federal preservation regulations that required the State Street houses to maintain their historical character.

Over most of a decade NCLT maintained its own construction crew of fifteen community residents, who were assisted by a licensed plumber and a licensed electrician. Among those included was Charles Rutherford, a former truck driver with no construction experience who had been homeless for a while before gaining shelter and a chance to work through the North Camden organization. In 1993, grants from the Catholic Campaign for Human Development, the Diocese of Camden, and the Chemical Bank of New Jersey allowed the organization to provide more thorough training for workers. These funds also made possible a maintenance service for Land Trust homes and a rehabilitation and home repair service for other homeowners and organizations in North Camden.[23] Two years later those seed funds enabled NCLT to incorporate North Camden Community Builders as a for-profit subsidiary.

Improved housing has been a staple of many community development corporations nationwide. The strength of these organizations, however, has been to engage the community in larger social issues, and to do this the North Camden leadership determined to establish its own long-term plan. Like the previous North Camden efforts, this one involved an active grass roots effort—a committee of some two dozen neighborhood residents as well as representatives from neighborhood churches and organizations, charged with making sure the plan "is consistent with the hopes and desires of the people who live in North Camden."[24] As the active force in launching Concerned Citizens of North Camden, community organizer Tom Knoche became the lead organizer for the effort born out of the 1989 battle to defeat a second state prison. The planning process began simply with alternative suggestions for use of the North Camden waterfront. Among the primary principles stated were that the planning process must involve the whole community, residents must benefit from development decisions, public access to the river must be maintained, and further affordable housing must be supported.[25] From these initial concepts, relatively narrow in focus, grew a more comprehensive effort, starting in March of 1992. With the movement's growing maturity, the planning effort gained financial support from a range of sources, including in addition to the Delaware Valley Community Reinvestment Fund, the Pew Charitable Trusts, the Fund for New Jersey, and the Camden County freeholders.

The seventeen-month planning process involved active engagement with city officials as well as a number of outside consultants. In addition to the grassroots oversight committee, the process involved both a technical review group, including representatives of the city's division of planning and the redevelopment agency, and the North Camden Task Force, composed of North Camden leaders and city officials. Thus, even as they set an agenda determined to free North Camden from outside interventions not to their liking, the plan's proponents were determined to gain it sufficient status to assure its acceptance into law. Announced in September 1993, the North Camden Plan stated its goal to provide "a guide for North Camden's transformation from its present situation to a bright and exciting future." That it had to ask its readers to imagine goals and services, such as parks, basic health and day care, shopping, and the presence of fire and policemen, indicated how far from the depths of disinvestment North Camden had to come. The plan called for $85 million in new investment over a 15 to 20 year period. This included funds for a 35,000 square foot supermarket-anchored shopping center, an outdoor plaza, new and rehabilitated housing, a police substation, and a linear greenbelt connecting the neighborhood to other recreational sites in the city and county.[26] The redevelopment authority and city council quickly approved the plan, and in July 1993 Save Our Waterfront took over its implementation.

The plan's very presence made possible the infusion of significant new funding to meet its goals. With the added inducement of credits through the federal Community Reinvestment Act—one of the few federal programs created in the aftermath of the 1960s directed at redressing the injustice of past discriminatory practice—five area banks signed a compact to loan $34 million toward a redevelopment effort now estimated at $92 million. The infusion of private capital was expected to bring an additional $44 million from public agencies and another $14 million from other private sources. In addition to funding commercial revitalization, funds were directed at a 65-unit lease-to-own complex, Cooper Waterfront Housing, and at an additional affordable housing complex, Grace Homes, at North Fourth and State Streets. Both complexes were to be built by Camden Lutheran Housing. The event marking the arrangement was significant enough to draw the presence of New Jersey Governor Christine Todd Whitman.[27]

Like any plan, the North Camden proposal met its share of obstacles. Cooper Waterfront Housing was completed on schedule in 1997 and proved a vital addition to the neighborhood's stock of solid but affordable housing. The first eight units of a projected twenty-four at Grace Homes opened two years later.[28] Rehabilitation continued under the direction of the North Camden Land Trust. By the late 1990s, however, continued problems with drugs, fire, and abandonment meant that the organization was doing well if new units just kept pace with those being lost to occupancy. Although hopes for a new shopping center appeared close to fruition when the North Camden plan was announced in 1993, work had still not started on the site a decade later. The director of the North Camden Land Trust, Luis Galindez, was murdered in his home in 1994, his assailant never identified.[29] Save Our Waterfront's director Gloria Lyons, a constant presence at neighborhood meetings of all kinds, died of cancer in 2002. The transition from creating the plan to implementing it tempered the enthusiasm and energy that comes from the early stages of dealing with a crisis. With both human and physical obstacles of tremendous magnitude, the community nonetheless stayed generally on course for effecting changes it had demanded. Joined by strong social programs offered by Holy Name Catholic Church and Respond day care center, North Camden's secular and religious institutions continued to press a broad agenda to accommodate and to sustain Camden's poor residents and to make them increasingly self-reliant. In doing so, they set an especially high and clearly defined standard that maintained a commitment from the 1960s to fight poverty and to do so through inclusive grassroots organizing.[30]

For the Catholic Church, the lines of continuity were not so unified. Bound by canonical law as well as tradition to maintain parish boundaries, parishes were not so free as other denominations to follow their constituents as they moved from one place to another.[31] As a result, parishes were forced to adapt if they wanted to survive. Clergy responded differently to the dramatic social and economic changes in their neighborhood parishes. St. Joseph's Polish parish in Whitman Park did what it could to hold on to its largely dispersed and aging members. Once a year, at Christmas, former members returned from the suburbs for Midnight Mass. Brightly lit streets and a strong police presence encouraged those who might otherwise have been wary about returning to their old neighborhood. So too, at the old Italian parish, Our Lady of Mount Carmel (now merged with the Puerto Rican Our Lady of Fatima), an Italian American priest, Salvatore Scuderi, promoted a dual strategy of administering to his Hispanic parishioners' needs even as he encouraged former Italian parishioners from the suburbs to maintain ties with the church. His efforts to restore the church, which included converting the old Mecca funeral home across the street into a parish center, impressed many of the church's former parishioners who came back for the Mecca property dedication.[32] Once a year, former residents gathered for mass and a church dinner at Christmas time. For a few years, too, Father Sal blessed the wine for a pre-Easter party of former Camden residents hosted by Joseph Biasi, a second-generation Camden roofer, who continued to work from his father's worksite a few blocks from the church. Former residents helped finance these projects, but support for the immediate needs of neighborhood residents came from elsewhere.

In 1997, the Christian Brothers order of Catholic priests, with Father Sal's encouragement, opened the San Miguel School where the Mount Carmel parochial school, closed since 1978, had previously been located. Open to boys whose parents could not afford the cost of other parochial schools, San Miguel sought to give structure and direction to children whose exposure to Camden's unsavory social conditions put them especially at risk.[33] Father Sal helped neighborhood youth in other ways, too. He hired young men to do restoration work in the church and on other buildings tied to the old parish, including the Young Men's Catholic Club. Getting a community development organization launched was more difficult, however. His current parish, already beginning to disperse to the suburbs itself, lacked the catalytic event that had launched North Camden's effort. With Yolanda Aguilar DeNeely, a longtime lay leader in the parish, out of work and committed to the effort, however, it gained momentum in 2002.[34] More successful was the annual San Juan Bautista (St. John the Baptist) parade, which had been started in 1957. By the 1990s, it had grown to encompass a month-long series of events and the award of college scholarships. This particular

Figure 24. The San Juan Bautista parade, conducted annually starting in 1957, revived the tradition of church processions through the city. Courtesy of Yolanda Aguilar DeNeely.

reinvention of Catholic tradition served the Puerto Rican community especially well; it gave many of its members an important role in sustaining social capital, even as new monetary investments in the city remained hard to come by.

Many of the efforts at St. Joseph's and Mount Carmel-Our Lady of Fatima were pragmatic responses to changing social conditions. At Sacred Heart, Father Michael Doyle took a more starkly moral tone, tying his campaign to improve the surrounding South Camden neighborhood to tenets of social justice well honed in the 1960s. A member of the "Camden 28" who had broken into draft headquarters in Camden to destroy records there in protest of the Vietnam war in 1971, Doyle alternated slides of Vietnam and Camden to argue at his trial two years later that the destruction of neither area could be morally justified.[35] Never afterward avoiding the chance to brandish Camden's negative image to prod whoever would listen into taking up the cause of ending poverty in the city, he explained,

"There's a sadness in me about how the lives of the people of Camden are so abused. There's no real national ache or pain over the urban body bag count. We have to ask ourselves how this could happen in a country such as this."[36] In this, he was eminently successful at attracting white suburban parishioners who still felt some responsibility for addressing the unfinished social agenda of the 1960s. Each year Doyle recruited seventeen hundred financial sponsors to support the parochial school. At Christmas, the church raised funds for and prepared baskets of food and gifts for needy Camden children.[37] Once a year, individual parishioners bearing the names of Camden's murder victims over the previous year devoted a service to helping heal their survivors.

Doyle's proselytizing possibly reached its height in 2000, when he tapped special county funding to mark the millennium to commission a symphony for Camden's recovery. Tracing the sounds of Camden's rise and fall, the symphony celebrated, in Doyle's words, "the raw and the rough, the clang of broken bits in the scrap yard morgues of the City, the cry of the victim, the shouts of success, the crushing blows of demolition, the vibrant hammers of restoration."[38] Played to a full house at the Camden waterfront entertainment center, even as hail from a sudden storm added an ominous thunderclap on the tin roof, the event confirmed Doyle's unmatched capacity to extend his message of the immorality of concentrated poverty in the city to a wide audience.

Beyond charity and proselytizing, however, Doyle's church entered an active housing rehabilitation program through its subsidiary community development corporation, Heart of Camden. Run for some fifteen years by Sister Margaret Hynes—Sister Peg, as she was universally known—Heart of Camden used the promise of better housing for community members to secure their involvement in the larger good of the neighborhood. Each tenant, before moving into a rehabilitated structure, agreed to give back five hours of community service each month. Although performance was uneven, Sister Peg admitted, Heart of Camden had only five evictions among its first one hundred relocated tenants.[39] In yet another revival of an old tradition, in 1991 Sacred Heart's Bromall String Band led a two-block procession to a site where parishioners marked the opening of eleven restored homes.[40] Although unsavory conditions continued, the effort helped combat an especially corrosive environment, both socially and physically. In addition, the church fully supported the formation of South Camden Citizens in Action, a small but active community organization intent on planning a better future for the neighborhood.

Across town at East Camden's St. Joseph's Procathedral, Camden native Monsignor Robert McDermott adopted yet another approach to accommodating neighborhood changes. Unlike Sacred Heart, most of St. Joseph's weekly parishioners were Camden natives, though by 1985 these were mostly Vietnamese and Hispanic immigrants and their descendants. Like Sacred Heart, St. Joseph's had to rely on outside contributions to sustain its parochial school, a vital institution for the strongly Catholic community in the immediate neighborhood. St. Joseph's provided a number of select social services, but the heart of its effort to deal with social problems associated with the area's poverty lay in its subsidiary community development corporation, the St. Joseph's Carpenter Society. Formed by McDermott shortly after he arrived at St. Joseph's, the Carpenter Society grew out of his frustration when he struggled to find housing for a Vietnamese family with eight children. Choosing a property from among the many abandoned buildings in the neighborhood, McDermott borrowed $8,000 from a friend, had the property fixed up, and sold it to the family for the same $8,000. He put that money back into rehabilitating another shell, and as that modest pattern of reinvestment was repeated, an organization was born.[41] When the Carpenter Society built seventeen two-family homes in East Camden in 1990, they represented the first new housing construction in Camden in twenty years and so long that city officials could not even remember the appropriate tax assessment procedures.[42]

Once it was formally organized as a community development corporation, the Carpenter Society made its mission to help low-income families improve their quality of life and to create safe neighborhoods through homeownership. Initially, it directed reinvestment at properties located near the church, a practical decision to protect the chief institutional sponsor of renewal from the harmful effects of continuing decline. Over time, investment outward attempted to stabilize the strongest remaining portions of East Camden, nearest the Pennsauken border to the east. The goal was both to ensure enough neighborhood stability to keep owners from leaving the area and thus taking their social skills with them, and to revive market forces, which had become so depressed in Camden as to offer virtually none of the homes in East Camden the usual advantage of ownership and the prospect of achieving greater equity. As Sean Closkey, a young Wall Street broker who left his position to become the second director of the Carpenter Society in 1995, later pointed out, homes worth $20,000 at sale simply were not appreciating as long as abandonment continued on the same block. As areas stabilized, however, the average appraisal of Society properties rose from $27,000 to $45,000 between 1994 and 1998. Moreover, by more than keeping pace in converting vacant to occupied properties, Closkey could look forward to seeing the first of the targeted portions of East Camden completely rehabilitated.[43] Recognizing the unfamiliarity many former renters had both with home maintenance and with strategic means of saving, the Carpenter Society, with sponsorship from Campbell Soup, launched a homeowners' academy. In twelve classes instructors taught prospective buyers, who had to complete the course to qualify for a home, lessons that former residents of CHIP homes could well have used.[44] Commending the dozen families who utilized the training in 1995, the St. Joseph's Carpenter newsletter proclaimed, "They have taken up residence in this East Camden community, enrolled their children in area schools, and begun to play a part in the life of their neighborhood. In each case they represent a thirty-year commitment to the life of their community. What a wonderful sign of HOPE!"[45]

As the pool of new owners grew, the need to confront rising crime became increasingly evident. In response, the Carpenter Society organized a series of neighborhood demonstrations at known drug sites and bought up the abandoned properties that had served as points of contact or concealment. Parishioners at St. Joseph's Procathedral used the Stations of the Cross processions enacted every Good Friday to point out trouble spots in the neighborhood. Such efforts to secure the area, Closkey argued, were essential to a longer range goal of attracting to the neighborhood higher income buyers, who in turn could do more to support local retail establishments.

No doubt Closkey was moved by moral considerations. As he told a Philadelphia reporter, the presence of so many degraded homes was unacceptable: "Why in God's name does a child have to live there? Because it's too expensive to rehab? Because it's too difficult to work through the legal process? Those are shallow reasons to allow a child to grow up without dignity. . . . When a young child walks on broken glass, and that child's dignity is degraded, I'm degraded."[46] Yet, unlike the North Camden or even the Sacred Heart leadership, money more than morals underlined his calculations as he sought to make the market work in poor people's favor again. As long as the housing market remained so stagnant in Camden, the city's poor would be denied a crucial means of upward mobility. By getting the market to work again, he believed, the Carpenter Society could assure that homeownership, properly managed, would benefit not just new buyers but their neighbors as well as values rose. While job strategies to increase income were essential, he believed, they would be nicely complemented by homeownership because, as he said, "only income that is stored rather than consumed becomes wealth." People who buy more consumer goods, especially at high rates of credit, can easily dissipate their gains and leave nothing for the next generation. A property that gains in value, however, can help break the generational cycle of poverty, by allowing an investment in a child's education, an inheritance, or new cash resources through sale to another family. Depressed values and reduced interest fees made possible through the Community Reinvestment Act, he argued, made it possible to purchase homes at lower income levels than would otherwise be possible.

Camden's high taxes, which narrowed the difference in monthly payments between houses in the city and comparable properties elsewhere, and requirements attached to subsidies that resales go to other low-income families, complicated the goal of generating new wealth inside the city.[47] Nonetheless, the Carpenter Society advanced with considerable success, drawing funds from federal, state, and foundation sources. When the organization marked the completion of its one hundredth property in 1994, the new owner, Doreen Jones, a nurse's aide, spoke of her pride after believing for years that she would never own her own home. The two hundredth house restored, in 1999, went to the extended Otero family. Carlos, employed at a Philadelphia warehouse, and Marisol, a Camden hospital worker, saved up for two years to purchase the property for $62,500. Both credited the homeowners' academy for preparing them for their purchase. Closkey and the Carpenter Society were recognized at the White House in 2000 with the President's Service Award, one of the nation's outstanding honors for volunteer service. In 2002, the organization completed reconstruction of its three hundredth property, even as newly elected Governor James McGreevey tapped Closkey to become director of the New Jersey Mortgage and Home Finance Agency.[48]

Before he left, Closkey made the crime-ridden Westfield Acres public housing project a central object of attention. When an application for Hope VI funding to completely demolish and rebuild the complex was rejected in Washington, St. Joseph's Carpenter Society stepped in to help rewrite the grant. In June 2000 the Department of Housing and Community Development approved the request for $35 million to construct 523 new townhouses on the tract. The state added another $33 million in matching funds, and demolition on the troubled complex began the following summer. Organizers envisioned a mixed-income community to be known as Baldwin's Run. The buildings would be low rise and integrated into the surrounding neighborhood by cross streets and shared facilities, making them fully in line with both Closkey's long-term goals and new federal guidelines. The state granted an additional $8.8 million to build 25 duplex homes in Carpenter Hill, an associated development immediately adjacent to Westfield. Three hundred of the new homes were to be rental. The remaining three-bedroom homes were projected to sell at prices between $60,000 and $80,000. Closkey's successor, William Whelan, who had gotten to know the organization through his role as a bank's lending officer, managed to get local residents employed in the projects at a rate of 30 percent. With fully $100 million at its disposal, new school construction, and a proposed stop on a new light-rail line, the organization seemed strong.[49]

With further support from a local investor, St. Joseph's Carpenter contracted with Urban Design Associates of Pittsburgh to prepare a strategic investment plan for the area. The report called for further housing adjacent to Baldwin's Run as the means of creating the critical mass necessary to attract "high quality private investment." Calling for between 250 and 400 new rental and homeownership units, the report pointed the way to public investment by identifying infrastructure improvements, land acquisition, and some demolition. "After a decade of meticulous incremental improvement conducted unit-by-unit by the Saint Joseph's Carpenter Society," it said, "East Camden is ready for a bold, market-rate residential initiative." Such investment, the report concluded, "will enhance the city's revitalization immeasurably," and to achieve the goal of critical mass it urged development of a large contiguous site of at least ten acres.[50]

The efforts described in these three Camden neighborhoods were not alone among neighborhood redevelopment efforts, but by the mid-1990s they represented the city's most mature and most clearly defined, by philosophy as well as action. Quite different in their own ways, their decision to formally associate in 1993 helped sustain a sense of common purpose. The same year the Delaware Valley Community Reinvestment Fund facilitated further cooperation in forming the Cooperative Lending Initiative of Camden, in partnership with seven commercial banks that agreed to pool $3.2 million to help nonprofit organizations build or renovate up to 250 houses. Seeking to reestablish a private lending system in Camden's badly undercapitalized neighborhoods, Fund director Jeremy Nowak explained, "We're trying to restore the marketplace, to make it a more normal situation."[51]

Outside observers have often emphasized the importance of intermediary institutions—organizations with proven national track records, that can leverage funds for local employment. Among the most prominent is the

Local Initiatives Support Corporation (LISC). It might have served such a role in Camden, but Nowak did not want an outside organization to move in after he and others had done so much to form a base there.[52] Instead, in 1995, Camden formed its own organization dedicated to securing national funding, the Camden Collaborative. Former mayor Randy Primas was the president and A. Ahada Stanford, an urban planner associated with Nowak, was the director. The Ford Foundation chose the organization as one of five nationwide to participate in its expanded Community Development Partnership Program. The William Penn and Pew foundations and the Fund for New Jersey, the Robert Wood Johnson and Campbell Soup Foundations, and Nowak's organization, renamed the Reinvestment Fund, all made significant contributions. In its first three years, the Collaborative helped fourteen nonprofit groups in the city finance $3.5 million worth of real estate projects, including 299 homes valued at $38 million.[53] By providing both predictable revenue resources and technical assistance to both established and emerging community organizations, the Camden Collaborative intended to increase the capacity of community development as a whole. In the words of an early circular, it supported "groups that take a comprehensive community-based development approach: Community-based as reflected by active participation and the accountability to citizens that reside in the target community; comprehensive in approach, as demonstrated by being engaged in efforts that address the economic, physical, and social needs of the community, as a soul [sic] undertaking or acting in partnership."[54]

To advance the cause of coordinated neighborhood-based recovery, local activists did call on another national organization, the Pacific Institute for Community Organization, for help in coordinating faith-based neighborhood redevelopment efforts. The resulting organization, Camden Churches Organized for People (CCOP), which met initially in 1983, described its mission as a covenant. The group pledged to address the city's many social problems and to take the Bible "as a serious guide for involving ourselves in the community in order to promote love and justice and to enhance the dignity of every member of our congregations and community." Lay committees fanned out through different neighborhoods to survey needs, prioritize and research issues, and promote actions to get problems resolved.

The initial test of the organization came in 1987 as it entered a four-year campaign to roll back water and sewer rates for Camden residents. The first public meeting on the subject, at St. Joseph's Procathedral in March

1988, drew 1,500 residents, an unheard of number in a city widely presumed to be apathetic to its dire circumstances. Working to confront the Camden County Municipal Utilities Authority over continued complaints of foul odors and to secure the support of a Republican governor, Thomas H. Kean, and Democratic county politicians, CCOP forged an agreement for $2 million in relief each from the county and the state.[55] Responding to reports that the decision would raise rates in their jurisdictions, a group of suburban mayors rebelled. As the mayor of Haddon Heights put it, "Here is another situation where the suburbs get hit on the head to take care of a problem in Camden City. The well is dry. There's just not the money in the suburbs to take care of Camden all the time."[56] The courts accepted their argument that the county commitment was invalid without state enabling legislation. Thus spurred to take their case to the legislature, CCOP argued it was precisely the absence of such nuisances in the suburbs that facilitated higher property values there at the expense of the city. "We have put up with the injustice of an awful stench that has created an environment where children become ill and cannot play or study. . . . We have put up with the injustice of a corrupt utilities authority that has squandered public funds, pays no taxes and sits on 17 acres of prime waterfront property," a CCOP circular to state legislators declared. Their request was for relief that "creates an opportunity for an historic model of justice that rewards communities for shouldering the burden of an entire county," a plea that ultimately proved successful in spurring legislation that saved $300 million in payments for 19,000 Camden households.[57]

Even as CCOP sought the financial compensation of a host benefit, it joined the opposition to a second North Camden prison. Subsequently, it worked to stabilize city neighborhoods, through increased police protection and the clearance of abandoned homes and lots, which bred drug traffic as well as other illegal activities.[58] Using a tried organizing technique, CCOP enticed a reluctant Mayor Aaron Thompson to a public meeting on the subject of abandoned homes in 1992. CCOP co-chair Rosa Ramirez told a crowd of one thousand residents, "We want the public officials in Camden to give as much attention to the drug problem as they do the Aquarium. We want to make sure that the downtown development doesn't come at the expense of our neighborhoods."[59] Responding to the city's lack both of adequate numbers of inspectors and funds for demolition, CCOP organized a Camden Community Housing Campaign composed of both public officials and residents and committed to community-based planning. Volunteers surveyed every neighborhood, then commissioned a Rutgers team in

Figure 25. Rosa Ramirez, with the bullhorn, leads a CCOP march on the CCMUA, April 9, 1989, seeking a resolution to provide the City of Camden host benefits as the site for the sewage plant. Courtesy *Courier-Post.*

New Brunswick to assess the results. Not surprisingly, they showed a high correlation between incidences of crime and the number of deteriorated structures.[60] Evidence in hand, CCOP raised the visibility of the issue and got both state and city officials finally to act on their request for more timely intervention. In addition to new funds committed to demolition and rebuilding by Governor Christie Whitman, the mayor and city business administrator agreed to monthly meetings with CCOP and appropriate department heads to monitor the situation further.[61] Pressure for reinstituting community policing practices, long in disuse in the city, followed.[62] By the mid-1990s, CCOP had become a leading voice in connecting city residents with public officials.

A 1996 evaluation of five intermediary-assisted community organizations, including CCOP, concluded that the religious basis of these efforts was a distinct strength. Noting that such institutions "brought a complexity and stability that goes beyond a ready-made base of people, money and in-kind resources," the report commended an "organizational culture [that] harnesses and leverages congregations' social capital for social change." In some neighborhoods of color, it concluded, "congregations are the only social glue preventing a total unraveling of the communities' social fabric."[63] Not all residents felt comfortable, however, in channeling their energies through religious institutions. Partly as a consequence, another organization, Camden Neighborhood Renaissance, formed in 1996, also with the goal of empowering Camden residents.[64] In line with national neighborhood-based organizing trends at the time, the most immediate impetus to action was the city's soaring murder rate—the highest per capita in the county in 1995. Authorized by a resolution offered by Camden City Councilman Angel Fuentes that November, law enforcement officials, city department heads, clergy, business, and educational leaders formed a task force to reduce crime, drugs, and violence in the city. A group of volunteers surveyed residents about what issues mattered most in their daily lives. Lack of jobs, difficult juveniles, and drug activity, all of which pointed to the need for greater law enforcement, topped the list. A detailed, four-part strategy followed. First, police were to sweep a targeted neighborhood, identifying locations of high drug activity, including vacant buildings where drugs were stashed. Tough code enforcement inspections and prosecution of violations would follow. Then, neighborhood residents would be enlisted in clean-up campaigns as the first step toward more sustained civic involvement. This plan became the cornerstone for the organization's mission statement: "The Camden Neighborhood Renaissance will develop a holistic approach building upon the relationships in the community to eliminate the drug activity in one specific area at a time, to impact on the economic/social issues of that area, and to improve, ultimately, the quality of life for that neighborhood."[65]

Using the talents of a committed white suburban activist, Carol Dann, as an organizer, the organization launched two initial projects in 1996. Starting in Parkside, after a police sweep and code enforcement effort had been deployed, residents cleaned up the area, starting with a particularly troublesome alley running between Eleventh and Twelfth streets. Once the area had been secured from drug activity, more than one hundred residents joined together to remove twenty truckloads of debris, including nine hundred vials of crack cocaine. The effort concluded with a community barbeque and an interfaith service the following day. Subsequently, two buildings in the area were torn down and another seventy boarded up.[66] Several months later, residents followed a similar plan in the Cramer Hill neighborhood, focusing on a notorious drug corner at Twenty-eighth and Hayes.

Twenty additional truckloads of debris were removed, and an apartment building burned beyond use eight years earlier was torn down. Small initial grants of $10,000 each from the Camden County Freeholders and the Delaware River Port Authority kept the largely volunteer effort going until a $100,000 grant from the William Penn Foundation for a peacemakers program boosted revenues. After city errors delayed funding, Renaissance was finally successful in 2000 in getting federal "weed and seed" money designed to "weed" out drug dealers and "seed" social services in their place.[67] Although block-based maintenance efforts existed previously in the city, Camden Neighborhood Renaissance systematized the effort.[68]

Over the next two years, eleven neighborhoods qualified, by reason of active citizen interest, to participate. A single member of the County Prosecutor's staff, Timothy Gallagher, became the full-time liaison between residents and police. Other law enforcement officials joined the Renaissance board. In meetings with neighborhood residents, Gallagher recorded information about unlawful activity, ranging from drug sales to abandoned cars, made sure the information got to the right authorities, and returned the next month to see what progress had been made. Although the purpose of the organization was relatively narrow, its effect, like improved rates of homeownership, was potentially wide in making neighborhoods more attractive and safe to live in. Among the most heavily targeted neighborhoods were those that had traditionally been stable but were now showing all the signs of social and economic decline. Fairview and Parkside both initiated "walk and talk" exercises, in which residents joined together to confront drug dealers on their corners. In both neighborhoods, residents spoke forcefully, saying that they would rather die than continue to tolerate horrible conditions so close to their homes.[69] In each area, the ability to mobilize citizens around issues of security lead to broader organizational efforts.

Throughout the period of initial disinvestment, Fairview was the neighborhood that changed least. Constructed as the planned community of Yorkship Village to accommodate shipworkers during World War I, the area became part of Camden in 1918, changing its name to Fairview in 1922.[70] It retained its social as well as physical distinctiveness well into the late twentieth century. It was not until the real estate revaluation of 1992, when older residents suddenly faced much higher property taxes and were induced to move, that the area began to diversify, both racially and economically. As in earlier years, the shift was unsettling, and one black family who moved to the area faced ugly discrimination in the form of a burning cross on their lawn.[71] Those determined to stay in Fairview, however, were pragmatic enough to realize that they needed to work with their new neighbors, and they attempted to do so initially through the community's chief civic organization, the Fairview Historic Society. Through such vehicles as a welcome wagon and other outreach activities, organizers attempted to assimilate new residents though dissemination of information both about design guidelines for the historic district and prevailing social mores of cooperation and neighborliness. Inevitably, not all newcomers responded as hoped, and as levels of homeownership declined and social mores diverged, the historical society sought out additional tools.

To deal with a rising crime rate, a product not just of the area's changing population but of its growing attraction for the sale of drugs to suburban buyers, members of the historical society applied through Camden Neighborhood Renaissance to become part of a weed-and-seed program. The neighborhood was committed as well to developing partnerships to attract new investment as another means of reversing economic decline as well as social volatility. In 2002 the Fairview Historic Society secured a $40 million grant from the New Jersey Department of Community Affairs to work with a for-profit development company, RPM of Montclair, New Jersey, to upgrade the physical face of the community and to institute a number of related social and recreational programs. News of that investment spurred immediate activity among speculators, who began buying up some of the neighborhood's 250 abandoned properties, putting new pressures on the historical society's staff to manage development. Although not without its moments of mistrust and misunderstanding, the society attempted to strengthen its position by entering a partnership with Rutgers University. The partnership used an initial $450,000 grant from the First Union Regional Foundation in Philadelphia to form a community development corporation to help manage the project.[72]

Although its population shifted significantly in the 1960s from white to African American, Camden's Parkside neighborhood also maintained its reputation for stability well into the 1990s. After the 1992 revaluation, however, Parkside also began to witness abandonment and housing decline.[73] The Parkside Business and Community in Partnership (PBCIP) began work on the first ten of a projected one hundred-property renovation campaign in 1999. Civic participation was at first minimal, and it took a concerted organizing effort to begin to engage the community fully. By 2002, however, a community-based planning process was underway, which culminated in a plan approved by the city's planning board within a year.

Taken collectively, Camden's neighborhoods had, in the course of several decades, established the elements experts agree are necessary for community revitalization, including affordable housing opportunities for ownership as well as rental; improved prospects for local retail services; improved safety; and strong community institutions.[74] Prospects for providing jobs for neighborhood residents were generally implicit in plans rather than addressed directly, but they were still there. That being said, "progress" had its costs as well. The demolition of Westfield Acres brought with it considerable displacement. Among those forced to move was Donza Harmon. Because there were not sufficient alternative public units available in the city, she was granted a voucher to subsidize her rent outside the city. After many trials and tribulations, she secured a new apartment in suburban Pine Hill twenty miles from her native city physically and light years in terms of environment. Some might count her displacement a plus: an African American woman had made it out of urban decay to the suburbs. But Harmon had no real reason to go there. Her grown son could not benefit from suburban schools. In two years of living outside the city, she made virtually no new friends. She was too far from the medical facilities she needed for her severe health problems. Diabetes took most of her sight, then a foot, then a leg, and finally her life. She died in 2003 at age forty-six.[75] Many other Camden residents would have jumped at the chance to leave. When the city issued a limited number of vouchers in the summer of 2002, residents lined up around the block to apply.

Of those who stayed in Camden, by choice or necessity, not all invested as much time and energy in their communities as Donza Harmon had. For those who did, the frustrations were immense. Rehabilitation rarely kept pace with abandonment. One safe corner gave way to drug dealing at another spot nearby. Elements of urban infrastructure others might take largely for granted—streets, sewers, and water—remained problematic at best. Like community development generally, as Anthony Downs summarized such efforts, Camden found it difficult to reach a sufficient scale to affect conditions in more than one or a few distressed neighborhoods.[76] The Camden Collaborative ran out of funding in 2001. No effort was made to extend its life. The North Camden Community Builders organization folded in 2002, a victim not just of a bad economy but of insufficient management capacity to remain solvent. Tom Knoche, put off by some of the pragmatic compromises made by North Camden organizations, left his formal positions with them to concentrate on his work at the Leavenhouse homeless shelter and to join a community organizing effort seeking to link predominantly black Morgan Village with the racially changing area of Fairview. Sister Peg Hynes died in a tragic 2002 automobile accident in Cherry Hill, the victim of a suburban driver high on drugs.[77] These setbacks did not destroy either the material or spiritual dimensions of community organizing in Camden. Much of the social capital that had been weakened or destroyed in earlier years was refurbished through hard organizational work. Talented, dedicated, and persistent as the best community organizers were, however, they could not pull Camden up by its own bootstraps. The broader economic and political forces mustered against them were simply too great. In this situation, Camden fell into the condition, described by David Rusk, of generating admirable commitments inside and outside the city, but without the effect of altering basic rules which continued to hold city residents in check.

Chapter 7

The Courts: Seeking Justice and Fairness

The Congress hereby declares that the general welfare and security of the Nation and the health and living standards of its people require . . . the realization as soon as feasible of the goal of a decent home and a suitable living environment for every American family.
—*National Housing Act of 1949*

Gladys Blair spent the 1960s in the Parkside area of Camden, moved to the suburbs for a while, and, after separating from her husband, returned to Camden, where she bought a house on Fairview Street in the four-block square area of South Camden known as the Terraces. Located directly across from the site where New York Ship had been located, the area had once been a preferred home for shipworkers, many of them skilled, who saw the advantages of a comfortable row house within easy walking distance of work. Blair's home had previously been occupied by two Polish shipworkers, who moved to predominantly white Gloucester City just beyond the Camden city line after the yard closed. At the time, she considered her purchase a good one. Despite the substitution of African American for white homeowners, the area was well kept and showed few signs of the larger malaise that had overcome much of the city. But the advantages of this residential area did not last long. The completion of I-676 linking Camden and the Benjamin Franklin Bridge crossing to Philadelphia with routes to southern New Jersey brought heavy traffic and increased air pollution to the area. The municipal waste plant built in 1977 and the trash-to-steam incinerator that followed worsened air quality further. As environmental quality declined, so did the neighborhood. Residents abandoned homes. The city began to tear down parts of the Terraces, but ran out of money to complete the job. A few homes remained dotted among grown-over lots littered with trash. A few remaining shells attracted drug dealing, and periodically police swat teams would sweep the area, passing through high grasses with guns poised in a scene reminiscent of Vietnam.[1] Like many of her neighbors, Blair suffered respiratory problems, coughing frequently as she spoke. A 2002 state report told her what she already knew: water quality literally stank too.

Blair faced a dilemma. She had returned to Camden, not the least to take advantage of its range of affordable housing opportunities, by one estimate nearly half the total stock available in the whole county.[2] Now, as environmental conditions declined, she wanted to move, but her choices were severely limited. Demand for low-cost housing remained high in Camden, where so many people of limited income resided. The suburbs, despite the landmark *Mount Laurel* court decisions requiring every community to provide its fair share of regional affordable housing opportunities, offered even fewer options than Camden. Ironically, it appeared that the appearance of another polluter in Blair's neighborhood would finally provide a solution. In order to counter objections to its 1999 proposal to build a new plant in the area, the St. Lawrence Cement Company hired a local attorney, Morris Smith, to work with residents. A former Camden City Attorney and an African American who was well versed in community organizing, Smith did all the right things. He invited community participation in an advisory board, hired Villanova University to do an independent test of emissions effects from the new plant, and, most important, secured a promise from the company not only to hire and train Camden residents, but also to offer relocation assistance to those remaining in the Terraces.[3] Blair said she trusted Smith and another St. Lawrence supporter, the Rev. Al Stewart, who ran the Camden Rescue Mission nearby in South Camden. She joined Stewart and other neighbors in supporting St. Lawrence in demonstrations called to counter protests organized by established environmental groups in South and North Camden.[4]

St. Lawrence got the permits it needed to build its plant. With that success, it offered the forty households remaining in the Terraces a total of $300,000 to support their relocation. Appalled by the paltry sum that could scarcely give them a new start in life, Gladys Blair and her neighbors joined other Camden organizations in suing St. Lawrence. In doing so, she joined a time honored tradition recognized as early as the 1830s by the astute French observer, Alexis de Tocqueville, when he described the courts as necessary checks on what he called the tyranny of the majority.[5] In the twentieth century, the courts, especially at the highest level, proved crucial in overturning segregation sanctioned by local authorities. As the twentieth century advanced, however, the issues were not so sharply drawn. In a society that extended rights to many different constituencies, it was not always easy to arrive at just solutions when one set of expectations clashed with another. Civil rights themselves became more difficult to define, especially as overt segregation was replaced with more subtle forms of discrimination.

No issues were more highly contested than those revolving around the home, its location, and its amenities. As Thomas Sugrue demonstrates so forcefully in his examination of Detroit, one of the central legacies of the New Deal was the competition, manifest most centrally in housing policy, between the ideals of providing assistance to the disadvantaged, on the one hand, and supporting the expansion of opportunities for those who already had significant resources on the other.[6] As this conflict shifted from city to suburb, from public to assisted and mandated housing in metropolitan areas across the country, the issues were never better illustrated or more fiercely contested, in the end, than in New Jersey. Problems redressing the effects of suburbanization in leaving the poor behind in declining cities had their origin in Camden and simply would not go away. By the first part of the new century, as Gladys Blair struggled to sustain her life in the most difficult of circumstances, the Camden area had become a leading national battleground for the rights of homeownership in a decent environment.

*   *   *

The latest challenge in Camden's struggle for environmental justice had its origin in the South Jersey Port Corporation's decision to lease space to the St. Lawrence Cement Company, a Montreal-based worldwide leader in the industrial production of its product. A state authority that now operated the old New York Ship terminal, the port corporation was under pressure to increase tonnage to justify its state subsidy, and St. Lawrence was attracted by the inducement of relief from local taxes by means of operating on state land. The first suit intended to block the decision was filed by Camden Regional Legal Services on behalf of South Camden Citizens in Action, the community organization that had formed initially to fight CCMUA and the trash-to-steam facilities. Legal Services lawyer Olga Pomar charged that the New Jersey Department of Environmental Protection had violated the 1964 Civil Rights Act when, in issuing air permits for the new plant, it had failed to take into account either the 90 percent minority concentration in the Waterfront South area or the environmentally hazardous activities already in place there. Pomar asked the court to consider the context of the proposed site and the history of previous decisions affecting it and provided

data demonstrating a stark pattern of racially disparate impact in the distribution of pollution facilities in New Jersey. Camden's Waterfront South
area was in the ninety-seventh percentile—meaning that only 3 percent of
the state's zip codes had more of such facilities. Although Pomar accepted
St. Lawrence's claim that it would meet existing air pollution standards, she
pointed to the presence of neighboring facilities as complicating factors.
"Waterfront South is visibly environmentally devastated," she asserted,
"with abandoned contaminated sites, smokestacks spewing pollutants into
the air, noxious odors, and high volume of diesel truck traffic."[7]

St. Lawrence was clearly aware of community opposition to potential
polluters, as evident from its decision to hire Morris Smith as a lobbyist.
The company stressed the economic benefits it promised local residents
through taxes and wages. But its plans promised considerable environmental damage. The plant was to process granulated blast furnace slag, which
was to be shipped to the city's Beckett Street terminal from Italy, then
trucked three miles south on diesel trucks to the Broadway terminal across
from the Terraces. The grinding facility would operate all day, every day,
processing 848,771 tons of slag and emitting nearly 60 tons of fine dust annually. In addition, it would emit other pollutants, including silica, lead,
mercury, manganese, radioactive materials, carbon monoxide, volatile or-
ganic compounds, and sulfur oxides.[8] It would increase traffic through the
area from some 20,000 to 77,000 truck movements a year. Those trucks, an
angry Rev. Michael Doyle charged, are "taking our space, our clean air, our
lungs, and our children's safety. And they're not even paying a penny of
taxes, while people in their houses here struggle every day to pay theirs. We
are nothing but a tax shelter for this multinational company. To say otherwise is a bunch of lies."[9]

Because the land was owned by the South Jersey Port Corporation, St.
Lawrence was allowed to bypass local agencies and apply directly to the
state for permits. In November 1999, the state Department of Environmental Protection allowed construction to begin. Not until August 2000 did the
first, poorly publicized public hearing on the proposal take place, one the
citizens suit charged did not include advance notice in Spanish, despite the
fact that nearly 17 percent of the area's residents were Spanish speaking.[10]
Protests built into 2001, when court papers were filed. When Camden City
Council took the unusual step of backing the plaintiffs, Morris Smith responded, "Council's action is sad. It sends a message to businesses . . . that
they are not welcome even when they follow the rules."[11]

On April 19, U.S. District Judge Stephen Orlofsky stunned St. Lawrence and its supporters by ruling for the plaintiffs that air emissions permits constituted a civil rights violation and were thus invalid. Criticizing the department for not considering the effect on area ozone levels of diesel fumes from the expected influx of trucks or the impact of PM-2.5 emissions—smaller particles that lodge even more deeply in the lungs than the PM-10 particles the DEP had accounted for—he allowed the department thirty days to conduct an analysis of whether issuing the permit had a discriminatory effect on African Americans and Hispanics. Meanwhile, he prohibited the $50 million plant, which was nearly complete, from operating until further court order. "The Civil Rights Act of 1964 is alive and well, and can actually be put to use," Camden Legal Services's Pomar declared.[12] Her euphoria did not last long, however.

Four days later the U.S. Supreme Court, in an unrelated Alabama case, appeared to invalidate Orlofsky's position by ruling that private individuals could not use federal regulations promulgated under the civil rights act to sue government entities. The decision changed the course of civil rights litigation dramatically. Although courts had for thirty years accepted discriminatory impacts as proof of violations of Title VI of the Civil Rights Act, the court majority now insisted that private plaintiffs would have to prove not only impact but direct intent to discriminate.[13] Not to be deterred, Judge Orlofsky on May 10 upheld his own injunction, citing U.S. Code 1983, adopted after the Civil War and used for decades in constitutional law cases to protect citizens from "deprivation of any rights, privileges or immunities secured by the Constitution."[14] Some legal scholars viewed the case as "the most important environmental justice case currently pending in the United States." Morris Smith, on the other hand, declared that the decision could discourage "responsible corporate investment" not just in Camden but throughout New Jersey.[15] St. Lawrence immediately appealed to the Third Circuit Court in Philadelphia, which quickly lifted the injunction, thereby saving the company $500,000 a week while the court continued to review the case. The plant opened three days later.[16]

Nearly a dozen business and industry groups, including the National Association of Manufacturers, the American Chemistry Council, the U.S. Chamber of Commerce, and the National Black Chamber of Commerce, filed supporting briefs for St. Lawrence, charging that shutting down the plant after it had been built could have a chilling effect on urban redevelopment nationally. Describing the suit as "environmental do-gooding run amok," *Business Week* warned that environmental groups, emboldened by Judge Orlofsky's decision, were "plotting bigger things," namely lawsuits in

California, New York, Michigan, and elsewhere in New Jersey. "After years of being minor annoyances to business, environmental justice activists are setting off alarms in boardrooms. With George W. Bush in the White House, industry thought it was relatively safe from 'green' assaults. Now, companies are rushing to fight back."[17] On the plaintiffs' side the NAACP, the American Civil Liberties Union, and the Natural Resources Defense Council joined ten local citizens organizations, including Concerned Citizens of North Camden and the New Jersey Environmental Federation to file amicus briefs. Charging that "Camden traditionally has suffered undesirable uses and activities that . . . prosperous, suburban communities would not tolerate in their own backyards," the Camden organizations rejected the proposition that the provision of a handful of jobs for local residents justified the threat to the health of an entire community.[18] Additionally, in a separate but complementary suit, thirty-five of the Terraces residents (representing 28 of 41 remaining households and including Gladys Blair) filed suit in Superior Court, asking that the St. Lawrence facility be declared a nuisance and its operations stopped. "They didn't come through," fifteen-year Terraces resident Pearly Good declared about the company's false promises of relocation assistance. "We really feel like they are taking advantage of us. Our houses are falling apart, and a lot of people are sick from the smoke. We can't live in this kind of contamination."[19]

On December 17, the appeals court, in a 2-1 decision, ruled in favor of St. Lawrence. Senior U.S. Circuit judges Morton Greenberg and Thomas Ambro, citing the Alabama case and other Supreme Court decisions, ruled that Section 1983 could not be used as a remedy for redressing violations of federally guaranteed rights assured through regulation, "unless the interest already is implicit in the statute authorizing the regulation."[20] Company attorney Brian Montag hailed the decision, saying, "This ruling really does send the message to industries across the country that if you invest in inner cities and urban areas, and if you go through all the right permitting processes, you can rely on those processes." Added Morris Smith, "A legal defeat would have sent a wrong message to the investment community and the investment community will play a crucial role in Camden's comeback." "Rest assured," *Business Week* asserted, "if the largely minority political leadership of Camden, N.J. hadn't wanted the $50 million St. Lawrence Cement Group plan in the first place, it wouldn't have been built."[21] The following month, by a 10–3 vote, the court rejected a request for review by its full membership. Not surprisingly, the U.S. Supreme Court six months later refused to hear an appeal.[22] Gladys Blair and her few remaining neighbors had no immediate recourse. They might have looked to the suburbs for alternatives; but even as the St. Lawrence case came to a head, the applications of state "fair share" housing rules were being fiercely contested in the courts.

*   *   *

New Jersey's landmark "fair share" housing law was crafted in two state Supreme Court decisions in 1975 and 1983. Known as *Mount Laurel I* and *Mount Laurel II* for the town, some fifteen miles east of Camden, where the original suit was filed, these decisions led to state laws that prohibited local zoning practices that had the effect of excluding low- and moderate-income housing and required suburbs as they built out to provide their "fair share" of their region's affordable housing opportunities. Political pressures resulted in two key modifications to the rulings. First, responsibility for overseeing the process shifted from court-appointed judicial monitors to a state administrative agency, the Council on Affordable Housing (COAH), made more sensitive to political pressures through its selection by the sitting governor. Second, the legislature approved a device, known as a Regional Contribution Agreement, through which any one community could be relieved of up to half its affordable housing obligation by paying a fee to another community. What followed was a protracted process of negotiation and litigation as communities across New Jersey challenged both the state-mandated low- and moderate-housing obligations set for their areas and the means available to achieve them.

To their credit, New Jersey's Mount Laurel rules fostered construction of 26,000 new units and the rehabilitation of another 10,000 units of affordable housing.[23] Such numbers fell well short, however, of state need, originally estimated at 145,707 in 1987, revised to 83,313 in 1993.[24] Furthermore, a thorough analysis of the process published in the *Seton Hall Law Review* in 1997 showed that the effort had done virtually nothing to assure the deconcentration of the state's urban poor minorities. Those who took advantage of the new suburban units were overwhelmingly white and already living in suburban areas. Of the mere 182 families in a 1996 sample totaling 2,675 households identified as having moved from city to suburb with the program's assistance, 66 percent were white. Only 23 percent were black. Only three Latino families, 2 percent of the total, moved out. Of the 30 families who moved from suburb to city, none were white, 90 percent were black. The net effect was that, while 81 percent of all suburban units identified were occupied by whites, 85 percent of all urban units were occupied by black or Latino households.[25] As implemented, it seemed clear, the law had been most helpful in providing starter homes for young white suburbanites or the elderly seeking lower costs to meet limits set by retirement incomes. "It's not that there isn't a need to provide housing for these groups," Arnold Cohen, a coordinator for the state's Affordable Housing Network commented. "But when it began, one of the main ideas of the program was to provide lower income people with an opportunity to live where there were more jobs." With 300,000 households in New Jersey using more than half their income to pay for housing at century's end, he believed the need remained unmet, especially after the state reduced its target to 83,000 new units.[26] As another commentator put it, while administration of New Jersey fair share housing laws "has accomplished some good, it has failed to integrate neighborhoods and, indeed, has perpetuated segregation."[27] The law's failure to open up the suburbs to the urban poor was nowhere better illustrated than in the Camden area.

The initial suit challenging exclusionary zoning derived, like the St. Lawrence Cement case, out of the Camden Regional Legal Services office. There, in the 1960s, a group of young white lawyers gathered, "beads, ponytails, ideals in all," as Allen Zeller later recalled of the group of which he was a part. They were anxious to take on the most difficult poverty and civil rights cases. While Peter O'Connor initially focused on efforts to bring Camden's redevelopment process to a halt in order to stop the displacement of the urban poor, his colleague Carl Bisgaier became equally consumed with an effort to prevent displacement of African-Americans at the other end of the development continuum, in Mount Laurel, a traditionally rural area in nearby Burlington County. The opening of a New Jersey turnpike exit in 1952, and completion of Interstate 295 nearby a few years later, cut up farm land and displaced many tenants. Given the rising home prices that came with suburbanization, these tenants, the great majority of whom were black, had little choice but to concentrate in a part of town known as Springville, a motley group of residences that had been converted from chicken coops to accommodate the influx of military personnel at Fort Dix after World War II. Surveying the area in preparation for possible litigation, Allen Zeller said he was immediately reminded of conditions he encountered a few years earlier while working in a registration drive in Mississippi.[28]

The pace of progress prompted Mount Laurel to condemn and demolish the bulk of the Springville homes. One of those who feared the effects

Figure 26. Springville shanties, Mount Laurel, where New Jersey's affordable housing battle started. *Philadelphia Bulletin,* October 6, 1969. Courtesy Temple University Libraries, Urban Archives, Philadelphia.

of displacement on the next generation was Ethel Lawrence, one of eight children whose family could trace its roots in Mount Laurel back six generations. Fearing that she and her family would have no alternative other than to relocate to what she considered slum areas in Camden, Lawrence became involved in the formation of the Springville Action Committee. Seeking federal funds to build subsidized low-income housing in Mount Laurel, the committee retained Camden Regional Legal Services to secure a revision in the township's zoning laws to overturn a prohibition against multi-unit apartments. Mayor Bill Haines's report of the town's response to the request, delivered to Lawrence and fellow parishioners in historic Jacob's Chapel, could not have been more insulting: "If you people can't afford to live in our town, then you'll just have to leave."[29] In a similar vein, Lawrence recalled, a town councilman, recently moved to the area, commented, "If you can't afford to live in Mount Laurel, pack up and move to Camden!"[30] With that Bisgaier and O'Connor filed *Southern Burlington County NAACP v. Mt. Laurel.*

After four years of litigation, the New Jersey Supreme Court ruled in favor of Lawrence and her fellow plaintiffs, establishing the doctrine requiring "each . . . municipality [to] affirmatively . . . plan and provide, by its land use regulations, the reasonable opportunity for an appropriate variety and choice of housing, including . . . low and moderate cost housing, to meet the needs, desires and resources of all categories of people who may desire to live within its boundaries."[31] As committed as the court was to opening the suburbs to poor minorities, it did not initially believe it should impose specific remedies. It was therefore left to Mount Laurel and the state's other municipalities to act in good faith to revise their zoning codes. Given the firestorm that greeted the state's decision, the failure of the doctrine to take hold was not surprising. Although the case has been compared to *Brown v. Board of Education* in significance, some supporters of the decision feared right away that the same pattern of noncompliance that characterized the South's resistance to *Brown* could be expected in New Jersey.[32] Indeed, fifty mayors swiftly gathered in Mount Laurel to declare they would seek to overturn the decision, even if it meant amending the state constitution. Mount Laurel itself proposed only minimal changes, potentially opening one percent of the town's land to build 103 low-income units. Across the state, as legal scholar John Payne reports, *Mount Laurel I* "prompted furious political opposition, municipal intransigence, and a flood of lawsuits, but very little actual progress toward breaking the back of exclusionary zoning."[33]

With such a dreary record, the plaintiffs returned to court, and in 1983 the New Jersey Supreme Court determined in the *Mount Laurel II* decision not just what the law should be but how it should be achieved. In what one critic has called "one of the most extraordinary judicial opinions ever written,"[34] the court established strict criteria to assure compliance. Affirming the state's control over land use, all land use, Chief Justice Robert Wilentz declared:

In exercising that control it cannot favor rich over poor. It cannot legislatively set aside dilapidated housing in urban ghettos for the poor and decent housing elsewhere for everyone else. The government that controls this land represents everyone. While the state may not have the ability to eliminate poverty, it cannot use that condition as the basis for imposing further disadvantages.[35]

Municipalities that did not adopt acceptable zoning revisions would be placed under the supervision of one of three specially assigned trial judges.

These judges had the power to determine numerical goals to meet each growing community's fair share obligation in its region. To provide incentives to get such housing built, the ruling authorized a "builder's remedy," granting developers the right to greater building densities in projects where they agreed to set aside one out of every five units for low- or moderate-income occupants. This marriage of private profit to public interest, to paraphrase Charles Haar's phrase, broadened the field for reform.[36]

Among the many communities resisting the process to assure equal access was Mount Laurel itself. From a farming community of some 11,000 residents when the original case was filed, Mount Laurel grew over the next quarter century to a suburb of 40,000. In that time, none of the apartments sought in the first suit were built. Only 140 of the 950 units required by the state were completed. In 1997, Peter O'Connor offered to build a $15 million low-income complex on sixty-three acres that his Fair Share Housing Development had purchased in 1985. Residents flooded planning meetings to object to a proposed project, named in honor of Ethel Lawrence, claiming it would be a threat to their taxes, their schools, and the quality of life that had attracted them to the township in the first place. Speaking for the residents of nearby Holiday Village East, a retirement community where a number of older white former Camden residents now lived, attorney Ted Costa asserted, "My clients are not selfish people. They are concerned that the developer of this project is more interested in making money than he is in the welfare of the people who will live there. They could be condemning these people to a plantation of poverty."[37] Seeing no escape from the court mandate, however, the township settled with O'Connor. Having gained some 10,000 jobs in the 1990s alone, the town agreed to provide only 345 new affordable units.[38] It met its remaining obligations through renovation of 180 units for senior citizens, for double credit under state rules, and relief of 85 units through payment of $1.7 million to nearby Beverly City under a Regional Contribution Agreement. A year later, the township sought to relieve its obligation by another 52 units through another Regional Contribution Agreement with Beverly.[39] The day after he received the township planning board's approval, O'Connor promised to involve nearby community residents, including his antagonists at Holiday Village East, saying, "That way I think the fear and apprehension of the unknown will gradually dissipate."[40]

The challenge did not end there, however. For the next four years, O'Connor continued to fight the township, in court as well as in countless zoning and planning meetings, to get clearances for both the Ethel Lawrence Homes and the 180-unit senior center, which was to be located on part of a ten-acre site owned by one family for the previous twenty years. Although the proposed Lawrence site incorporated many of the best amenities found in any modern complex, including open space and community facilities in addition to counseling services, antagonism to the project did not die with its approval. Facing repeated obstacles to the project's permit applications as well as vandalism to the property, the effort nearly failed to make a deadline to assure sufficient investment credits to make the financing possible.[41] Finally, in November 2000, the first twenty-four units opened to, among others, a handful of former Camden residents. By the time NAACP national chairman Julian Bond spoke eloquently about the unfinished civil rights revolution at the Ethel Lawrence Homes dedication in August 2002, the project was receiving considerable praise in the local press.[42] The hard-won victory, however, was unique among neighboring suburbs. Nearby Cherry Hill told another story.

In 1986 the state's Council on Affordable Housing (COAH), established under the Fair Share Housing Act of the previous year, assigned Cherry Hill 2,295 new units of affordable housing, the sixth highest amount in New Jersey. The township immediately objected. In challenging COAH's figure, the township's solicitor argued that Cherry Hill's existing requirement, dating from 1974, requiring new multi-unit developments to set aside 20 percent for low-cost housing, had been successful enough that already low and moderate-income residents occupied 2,619 units. Because Cherry Hill was between 92 and 94 percent fully developed, it would be nearly impossible to satisfy the state unless the township created, as Mayor Maria Barnaby Greenwald described it, a vertical ghetto within the township.[43] Asked to submit a revised proposal, Cherry Hill did so in December, only to rebuffed again by COAH for, among other things, attempting to claim barracks in temporary use by stable workers during the summer months at the Garden State Race Track. The township then prepared to enter an agreement to pay Trenton $4.5 million dollars to relieve 165 units of its state-mandated allotment.[44]

Even as Cherry Hill contested its obligation, Peter O'Connor made his presence felt, in planning meetings, at COAH sessions, and before the courts. As early as March 1987, he sought imposition of an order, authorized under COAH regulations, restraining the township from further development of its scarce remaining open areas until its affordable housing obligation had been met. When Susan Bass Levin succeeded Greenwald as mayor in 1988 and said both that she intended to comply with the township's obligation and that she would drop plans to enter a Regional Contribution Agreement, O'Connor responded tersely that Levin's decision was the first positive step the township had made in the past sixteen years toward fulfilling its fair housing share.[45] Accommodation was not lasting, however.

When Cherry Hill continued to balk at COAH numbers, O'Connor sued the township, getting it placed under the supervision of Superior Court Justice Anthony Gibson, one of the three trial court judges named under the *Mount Laurel II* decision. In 1988 Judge Gibson ruled that developed communities like Cherry Hill could not escape fair share housing just because they were running out of land. Two years later the New Jersey Supreme Court ruled 7-0 against developer's fees imposed in Cherry Hill and four other New Jersey towns as substitutes for including affordable housing in multi-unit projects, although the Court indicated such fees would be acceptable should COAH establish regulations providing for their imposition. Frustrated by the Courts, Cherry Hill lobbied for legislative action, completed in 1993, imposing a cap of one thousand units on any township, a move that affected only five communities in the state. With the help of a court-appointed mediator, Cherry Hill gained approval for a revised figure of 787 new units. Resentment, a local reporter noted, remained on both sides. O'Connor continued to believe that the township intentionally used open space laws and zoning restrictions to keep the nonwhite poor out of town. Cherry Hill officials charged O'Connor with using his lawsuits to drum up business for the Fair Share Housing Center.[46]

O'Connor continued to press the township over the decade, arguing that two properties (Short Hills Farm, which the township intended to be a park, and Sergi Farm) should be held open for affordable housing. Holding firm on preserving the first property, the township acceded to a plan for 129 affordable units on an isolated portion of Sergi Farm. The units would be surrounded by homes valued up to half a million dollars, and the compromise satisfied nobody. When the Garden State Race Track closed, making its site available for redevelopment, the argument came to a head.

The Garden State Track had opened in 1942, when what was then Delaware Township was largely undeveloped. It served for a generation as a premier regional destination, spurring the development of hotels, restaurants, and other entertainment venues and helping to create a new and specifically suburban alternative for leisure time activity for Philadelphians as well as for residents of South Jersey. A fire that destroyed the grandstand in 1977 and voter approval for gambling in Atlantic City the previous year took a severe toll on the track. Although Garden State reopened in 1985, it was never profitable again. Secondary businesses associated with the track closed. Once the track closed, the 223-acre property, which had long represented a financial drain, had become the most desirable property for development in the township (or, as the developer claimed, in the entire Delaware Valley). Excited about the prospect of generating new tax revenue, Mayor Levin announced immediately that the township would not mandate construction of low- or moderate-income housing on the property. "We are looking for something upscale," she said. Specifically, what developers proposed were 1,191 housing units, none of them selling below $200,000, along with a corporate complex, a hotel, and a renovated commuter train station. In place of affordable housing, the township earmarked $4.3 million in developers' fees, which the township intended to apply to projects elsewhere, including in Camden.[47] When the Fair Share Housing Center indicated that it would insist that the project include affordable housing, the developer sought a declaratory judgment authorizing its stated plans.

The case came before Judge Theodore Davis, an African American and Camden resident who succeeded Judge Gibson on his retirement in 2000 as the supervising judge for Cherry Hill's fair share housing plan. O'Connor challenged the legality of closing off yet another scarce resource in the form of developable land before Cherry Hill's future obligations towards low-income housing had been finally determined. When Judge Davis, confining his ruling to the appropriateness of the developer's fee, sided with the developer, O'Connor appealed. In an unusual action, the New Jersey Supreme Court took the case without awaiting judgement at the appellate level, presumably so that the Cherry Hill situation could be considered in conjunction with several other affordable housing cases, including *Toll Brothers v. Township of West Windsor*, for which O'Connor provided a powerful amicus brief in support of the builder's remedy sought by the developer. As the press noted, Mount Laurel appeared to be heading to another historic judgment.[48]

While both sides in the Garden State case focused on central points of law, each took the occasion as well to address larger philosophical issues. Taking a strict view of the long process of the litigation, Cherry Hill claimed that the Garden State Park could not be held responsible for providing affordable housing, because the court had not previously designated the site for future affordable housing units. More broadly, the township pointed to actions it had taken for affordable housing that could not be counted toward the state-mandated obligation because they had occurred before 1980.[49] Then, in the most overt of the defense's philosophical points, Cherry Hill planning board attorney Allen Zeller (O'Connor's former associate at Camden Regional Legal Services) argued that money should be spent to improve broken cities rather than forcing the dispersal of the poor. "Moving families out of the cities that they have forever called home and planting them in large suburban rental housing that Plaintiffs envision building in the suburbs, is not a sensible way to battle urban decay," he charged in his brief. "Whether Plaintiffs want to believe it or not, many such people do not want to move and live in the suburbs and do not want their children to attend school in the suburbs."[50] Pointing to his law partner and co-signatory on the brief State Senator Wayne Bryant's own recovery legislation pending in the legislature designed to pump new money into Camden, the argument affirmed an unambiguous preference for gilding the ghetto over dispersing it.

Plaintiffs argued that Judge Davis had erred both in his reading of prior court decisions on developers' fees and in ignoring the larger issue of the exclusion of yet more developable property for future affordable housing development. More significant, the plaintiffs used the case to try to evaluate the overall effect of the *Mount Laurel* decisions. Fair Share Housing's brief blamed legislative actions, including Regional Contribution Agreements, the 1,000-unit cap on any individual municipality, and permissive COAH regulations for the suburbs' failure to integrate:

In *Mount Laurel II*, the Court, as reflected by Chief Justice Wilentz's vision, responded courageously to government abuses that could not be addressed, nevermind resolved, by the political branches. By requiring all municipalities to plan, zone, and take affirmative measure to promote the development of their fair share of affordable housing, the Court's *Mount Laurel* decisions sought to curb the use of governmental powers that promoted the migration of the middle-class to suburbia and the resulting urban segregation of the poor. The court elevated to constitutional significance our State's obligation to avoid and redress the social devastation that results when governmental policies contravene the 'general welfare' and promote racial and economic stratification. The Court's 1975 recognition of a constitutional right to freedom from exclusionary zoning was profound, its commitment to redressing discrimination and social problems through responsible governance unparalleled. When the Court in 1983 affirmed the necessity of the builder's remedy and subsequently deferred to COAH, the intended result was a more efficient provision of more units in more places.

But the poor still have not benefitted. Camden and its sibling New Jersey cities over the past twenty-five years have grown more racially and economically segregated. Whereas the *Mount Laurel* doctrine was bold on paper, in application it has been neutralized. COAH, sometimes with the judiciary's acquiescence, and at other times because regulations have gone unchallenged, has succeeded in making *Mount Laurel* more palatable to suburbanites by removing the parts of the doctrine that were most likely to lead to social change and, unfortunately, thus exacerbating the racial and economic segregation in our urban areas.[51]

In contrast to Allen Zeller, O'Connor took a consistent view that integration, not gilding the ghetto, was crucial to urban revitalization. In a separate brief challenging a Regional Contribution Agreement that authorized the transfer of 152 units from the rapidly growing suburb of Washington Township in nearby Gloucester County to Camden, O'Connor challenged the wisdom of subsidizing housing in what the brief called "one of the most crime-ridden, murderous, environmentally-unsound, impoverished, dysfunctional, and at times downright scary census tracts in New Jersey, if not the nation.[52] The brief even challenged the high court's action requiring additional funding for urban school districts with concentrated poverty, the school equalization measure known as the *Abbott* decision.[53] "Like ships passing in the night, *Mount Laurel* calls for the use of resources to promote regionalization while *Abbott*'s massive allocation of resources are focused on funding racially-segregated schools in a manner that does not produce equality and fails to promote regionalization and racial and economic integration," it charged. "Unless the Court recognizes a comprehensive and unified constitutional standard in those cases, our urban centers will continue to deteriorate, and the poor, especially poor children, will too often be destined to a life of despair in impoverished, segregated neighborhoods." Calling the plaintiff's *Mount Laurel* vision " a diatribe," Cherry Hill claimed it misrepresented the facts and "should be addressed by the Legislature and not by this Court."[54]

In decisions only days apart, the New Jersey Supreme Court ruled in favor of the plaintiffs in both the Toll Brothers and Fair Share Housing cases, upholding the builders' remedy in the first case and striking down the use of a developers' fee in Cherry Hill while the township still faced an unmet obligation. Speaking for the court in the Cherry Hill case, Justice Gary Stein declared, "The Legislature's delegation to COAH of the duty to determine a petitioning municipality's fair share obligation would be undermined irreparably if a municipality could, in effect, exempt choice parcels of land from its affordable housing obligation by the simple expedient of imposing a development fee."[55] Yet while O'Connor claimed that the ruling assured low- and moderate-income housing at the Garden State site,

Cherry Hill's attorney immediately asserted that the township would fulfill its obligation at other locations. In a theme increasingly used to counteract high-density construction favored by the builder's remedy, township planning board lawyer Zeller made the dubious claim that the ruling would contribute to further suburban sprawl. Even as it supported the court's decision, a *Courier-Post* editorial sought assurances that "the project doesn't end up overwhelming already overburdened taxpayers."[56] And while there were no polls of suburban reaction to the decision, one letter to the *Courier-Post* captured residents' ongoing resistance to "socialistic" equal housing: "When did I suddenly wake up in China? The builder at the track should pack up and leave rather than build homes that no one would want." Striking an especially familiar refrain, the writer contended, "The only housing that anyone is entitled to is that which is earned."[57]

Such resistance comes as no surprise to scholars, who have long acknowledged the many ways Americans who fled aging cities after World War II sought to defend their new suburban investments from any changes that might harm their property values or their access to basic amenities. Summarizing a generation of such change, Lizabeth Cohen reports, "As residents retreated into suburbs defined by the homogeneity of their populations and the market values of their homes, the barriers they erected against outsiders grew higher, and their conception of 'the public good' correspondingly narrowed." "Fair Share" housing decisions like *Mount Laurel,* she concludes, "cannot be considered important because they have racially altered suburban landscapes but rather because they attest to how deeply entrenched socioeconomic stratification, and the local authority that supports it, remains in the early twenty-first century."[58] Extending his own analysis beyond New Jersey to other contentious court decisions requiring housing integration in Yonkers and in Chicago, Yale law professor Peter Schuck concludes, "A court demanding the implementation of a diversity idea that a neighborhood's residents do not share, and will strenuously resist, cannot conscript the housing market to do its bidding as it might be able to do with a public bureaucracy. . . . A court that mandates this diversity over such resistance is bound to impair its legitimacy and effectiveness."[59]

In Camden County, local authority became predominately Democratic, but the meaning of "Democratic" changed over the years. The party had been a champion of the less privileged at least since the Great Depression, but in the postwar years it became more diversified. Well-trained professionals concentrated in New Jersey suburbs. Their representatives, in-

Figure 27. Peter O'Connor, surrounded by neighborhood children, at the opening of the park developed as part of the urban renewal settlement of 1972, adjacent to the Northgate II apartment complex. Courtesy Northgate II, Inc.

cluding Cherry Hill's Susan Bass Levin and Woodbridge mayor James McGreevey, whose town was also granted a 1,000 COAH limit on affordable units, went along with constituents when they resisted aggressive affordable housing campaigns. When Levin and McGreevey were elevated to State Director of Community Affairs and Governor, respectively, in 2001, neither was inclined to press the case for accelerating an already lagging record on the issue. McGreevey spoke of legislative alternatives to the builder's remedy, and Levin, whose responsibilities included overseeing COAH, delayed announcing new obligation goals based on the 2000 census, lest her office, she said, make a mistake in methodology. O'Connor charged that the new administration was delaying its report so as not to upset suburban constituents before the 2003 legislative elections, where the narrowest possible degree of Democratic control in both houses would be at stake. Saying McGreevey and Levin needed to "shed their mayoral attitudes and realize that they're now representing all the people in the state," O'Connor petitioned the courts to compel COAH to act.[60]

While court battles continued, Camden's fate and that of many residents like Gladys Blair remained very much subject to the will of local political power. As Carl Bisgaier wrote on the tenth anniversary of *Mount Laurel II*, the courts had succeeded in forcing politicians to grapple with the problem of affordable housing. Yet, he noted, the poor could not expect all that much from the courts, as they lacked the machinery to implement social programs.[61] Another decade later, as activists marked the decision's twentieth anniversary, Peter O'Connor was just as critical of the situation, but he was still going to court.[62] The real ability to change things, however, lay with the politicians, and unfortunately for Camden that political power was concentrated almost entirely outside the city.

PART IV

Shifting Prospects

Chapter 8
The Politics of Recovery

It is cumbersome to ask for help, especially [of] those who live in the suburbs. Together with Camden residents, we need to make the city the economic powerhouse it deserves to be. Remember your parents and/or grandparents and/or family members who worked for RCA and Campbell Soup or Camden's shipyard. They made it and owed it to Camden City. It is not too late. We can save Camden. Yes, we want the middle-income people [to come] back to Camden.

—Angel Fuentes, President, Camden City Council, 2002

On a hot day in July 1992, Bill Clinton and Al Gore's eight-bus caravan arrived in Camden to mark the first stop in the candidates' whirlwind tour marking their nominations for national office. As the local paper noted, the candidates could have used the occasion that day to speak about a number of issues: drugs, poverty, crime, and rebuilding American cities. Instead, Bill Clinton chose to highlight a state grant aimed at helping retain some of the four thousand workers laid off from the General Electric aerospace plant during the Bush presidency. Such "government in partnership with private industry" would prepare skilled workers for other occupations, Clinton said. It was an example of the "third way" approach between traditional liberal and conservative policies that ultimately marked his time in office.[1] Clinton's emphasis was in fact not entirely new. The previous Democratic president, Jimmy Carter, had also promoted public-private partnerships, especially an urban development action grant program aimed at leveraging private funds through public investments. Clinton's major urban policy initiative, the creation of a limited number of empowerment zones around the country, was both a modification of a Republican idea and his own attempt to use tax incentives to attract private investment. Toward the end of his tenure, he extended his vision by traveling with a group of businessmen to a number of distressed post-industrial cities, including East St.

Louis, Hartford, and Newark, to stress the new market opportunities such underserved communities offered for investors. The private sector, he said, was poised to do the work at which the public sector had failed. As Clinton asserted in East St. Louis, "Government's not going to do it."[2]

When Al Gore returned to Camden as a presidential candidate eight years later, he neither addressed the city's obvious problems as the third poorest in the nation, nor did he set foot beyond the new entertainment center, where the Democratic National Committee had brought Cher and a number of other luminaries to help boost party coffers on Gore's behalf. Despite an early commitment to issues of sustainable development in his campaign, he touched on none of those issues in his few hours in Camden.[3] He was no more engaged that night with the issues roiling the city than the Republicans had been only months before when they had gathered on the waterfront in huge numbers to kick off their national nominating convention in Philadelphia.

Such was the level of indifference at the national level to the ongoing decline in the nation's post-industrial areas at the millennium. That situation, however, did not eliminate policy formation for such areas, especially at the state level, where rising deficits requiring ever larger state subsidies were raising serious concerns. Both Republicans and Democrats in New Jersey's statehouse struggled with urban deficits for most of a generation. Superficially, the two parties differed, with Republicans stressing fiscal discipline primarily through management reform and Democrats calling for new public expenditures as the means of stimulating new private investment. By the mid-1990s, as Camden's situation in particular reached desperation, state officials acted. After a long and contentious process, the legislature finally approved a bipartisan $175 million recovery package for Camden that appeared finally to address the city's problems in a comprehensive manner. Approved in July 2002, the effort was hailed in the press as a triumph and the best possible hope for the city and the region. Such were the times, however, that recovery was cast within the same constraints that characterized national discourse. The new legislation, although it addressed the effects of concentrated poverty, was crafted primarily to reduce the city's deficit. Although the means to this end were contested by opposing political parties, each seeking its own advantage, the chief goals were generally agreed on. To assure Camden's renewal, recovery proponents, like Bill Clinton and others before him, sought private investment, and they did so by making deals. Those most in need of support and attention were neither partners in the negotiations nor the primary beneficiaries. As much as neighborhood-based activists attempted to influence the process, from the start the balance for renewal was skewed in favor of the private over the public and nonprofit sectors. That this imbalance was not widely recognized at the time was largely the result of disproportionate attention paid to the dramas played out between personalities and between political parties that often hid underlying points of agreement. Following the process of the debate closely allows us to identify the true principles behind the recovery legislation as well as the structures of power that determined its final form.

*   *   *

No drama was more widely followed or commented on than that which pitted Camden's first Hispanic mayor, Milton Milan, a Democrat raised on the tough streets of Camden, and Republican governor Christine Todd Whitman, born to wealth and, true to her party philosophy, an ardent proponent of cutting taxes and expenditures. Elected over incumbent James Florio in 1993 on a strident anti-tax platform, Whitman became concerned early in her administration about Camden's continued deficit, which forced the state to provide more money each year to balance the city's budget. Annual city audits repeatedly emphasized administrative problems that Camden officials simply ignored. Building on legislation introduced by Camden County Republican Assemblyman Lee Solomon in 1992 to provide greater state oversight over communities guilty of mismanagement while receiving high levels of state aid,[4] Whitman began to speak about taking over certain municipal functions in Camden. In a tough-minded series of extended essays and editorials, "Camden at the Crossroads," the *Courier-Post* endorsed the idea. "Gov Whitman, perhaps, is reluctant to take over the entire city," a March 1995 editorial declared, "because some may call her racist; however, she shouldn't care. Pulling the race card without cause is what desperate people do when they can't defend themselves with facts."[5] In an effort to stop the hemorrhaging, as Whitman budgetary advisor Mark Lohbauer put it, the governor directed the New Jersey Department of Community Affairs to conduct its own audit of the city.[6] Released during the administration of Camden mayor Arnold Webster, the report savaged the management of city finances and contributed to Webster's defeat. Concurrently, Whitman began to initiate her own reinvestment programs in Camden, most notably in housing, and to seek cooperation with community organizations, notably Camden Churches Organized for People and Camden Neighborhood Renaissance, which she described as more reliable partners than the city government.[7]

By the time Milton Milan succeeded Webster in 1997, the Whitman administration, working with sympathetic Republican majorities in both houses of the New Jersey legislature, had secured approval for a financial review board to supervise Camden's spending and to review its financial procedures. The board operated under the authority of the New Jersey Department of Community Affairs and was directed operationally by Steven Sasala, who had been Camden County's administrator during a brief period of Republican control of the freeholders in the early 1990s. Sasala and the other Republicans named to the board had a history of criticism going back over a decade of Democratic control of both the city and the county. An unstated assumption, revealed privately, was the desire to thwart powerful Democratic politicians representing the area in Trenton, most notably State Senator Wayne Bryant, from continuing to exploit the Camden situation for their own advantage. The *Courier-Post* suggested the reasons for that criticism when it declared, "The fact is: A great deal of taxpayers' money went to Camden. A few well-connected people got rich and most of them don't live in Camden. Meanwhile, the Camden poor stay poor and are ignored—until their votes are needed."[8]

Governor Whitman felt she could work with Milan.[9] She thus made him a voting member of the financial review board and encouraged Sasala as chair of that panel to give the city enough leeway to effect a partnership in the recovery effort. For his part, Milan indicated a willingness to accept increased state oversight of city affairs in return for more money to balance the current and next several budgets.[10] Although the board's initial guidelines recognized the presence of a structural deficit that Democrats insisted was at the heart of Camden's problems, they also made it clear that the state would rely more on internal reforms than on the creation of new revenue streams. "It is hoped," the section on social impact concluded, that "more prudent fiscal management will help return Camden to its status as a strong, vibrant urban center." Similarly, the document counted on fiscal discipline to "help improve the status of Camden as a commercial center," a theme frequently repeated during the Whitman administration.[11] Not surprisingly, then, the state's emphasis from the start was on reducing the city's budget. Even with state funding constituting 70 percent of anticipated revenue, the city was $12 million short of meeting its $112 million budget.

For most of a year, the oversight board and city officials sparred over expenditures and their documentation. As the prospect for new funding faded, Milan became increasingly uncooperative, either challenging his fellow board members or not showing up at all. While the board did approve a city request for more police, it quibbled about the smallest of items, spending two entire meetings, for example, arguing about funds for street cleaning machines.[12] The arguments especially galled Milan, who following the "broken windows theory" that the prosecution of small violations could reduce the prospect of greater crimes, had made strict code enforcement, clearance of abandoned property, and especially cleaner city streets the keystones of his administration.[13] While the *Philadelphia Inquirer*'s review of his early tenure in office raised some questions about his ability "to make a permanent break from Camden's tradition of patronage and incompetency," the paper urged Governor Whitman "to give the City of Camden something besides a tight fist and hard funding decisions."[14] Instead, the state insisted on imposing additional restrictions on spending the following spring, as a condition for granting the funds needed to close the deficit at the end of the fiscal year. In response, Milan, against the advice of the city comptroller, declared bankruptcy in July 1999.[15] Although Milan was not the first Camden politician to threaten such action, his actual declaration proved a terrible mistake. "Milton Milan," the *Courier-Post* predicted, accurately as it turned out, "will be known as the mayor who rebelled against state fiscal oversight by paving the way for a complete state takeover of the city."[16] He may not have made himself irrelevant by his act, as the paper claimed, but he managed both to gain the governor's enmity and to damage the city's credit without forcing the state to give the city new resources. Moreover, Milan took his stand at a point when he was personally most vulnerable.

Within days of his declaration, the press reported that a grand jury was investigating work done by city contractors on Milan's house at no cost. Several weeks later, federal investigators raided both Milan's home and his office. More press reports appeared, about the misuse of campaign funds for a vacation trip to Puerto Rico and about favors from mob associates who hoped to get city contracts.[17] When independent councilman Ali Sloan El brought a resolution for Milan's resignation before the city council, however, Milan received the support not just of a large and vociferous Hispanic crowd, but of every member of council but Sloan El.[18] Democrats allied with the county, it appeared, were not about to have a Republican governor drum out their sitting mayor. When a grand jury delivered a 54-page indictment on March 30, 2000, Milan remained defiant. To U.S. Attorney Robert Cleary's charge that "The mayor designed this pay-to-play system for his own selfish benefit, and the people of Camden be damned," Milan retorted that the charges were politically motivated.[19] The indictment nonetheless provided the Whitman administration with the final argument it needed for fully taking over the city. As a deadline passed for providing financial information the state had demanded, the New Jersey Local Finance Board voted unanimously to place the city under direct state supervision. Milan called the decision that of a "kangaroo court," but in June the Superior Court affirmed the Local Finance Board's powers. "The decision," the *Courier-Post* observed, "means the nation's second-wealthiest state now must determine how to repair and revive the country's second poorest city."[20]

The state now sought full control of daily operations in the city, a goal that required special legislation. To bolster the state's case, Commissioner of Community Affairs Jane Kenny contracted with the National Academy of Public Administration to examine municipal operations and to prepare a plan for the city's recovery. In line with the Whitman approach to Camden, NAPA president Robert O'Neill stressed at a press conference that getting the city's financial house in order was the key to attracting new investment.[21] While that work was going forward, the state introduced legislation authorizing, as the *New York Times* noted, "the biggest city takeover in the country since the Great Depression." The proposed legislation transferred powers normally accorded the mayor and the city council to an appointed Chief Operating Officer, who would retain exclusive authority over city business for a minimum of five years. The language of the bill was explicit in declaring, "The chief management officer may override any action of the governing body if the chief management officer determines that the action is contrary to the rehabilitation and supervision of the municipality." The city was given the right of appeal to the New Jersey Local Finance Board, but the judgment of that board (also appointed by the governor) was to be final.[22] This was a bald assertion of state control. Not surprisingly, Democrats denounced the approach. Legislators representing the city accused the governor of imposing a "dictatorship."[23] Camden City Councilman Israel Nieves put overtly what the state legislators were diplomatic enough not to express, that Republicans were attacking the county Democratic Party's traditional source of money and power in Camden City.[24] Outside Camden, the New Jersey League of Municipalities, fearing a bad precedent for state interference, joined the opposition.

The Whitman administration quickly realized it would have to show some level of support within Camden. Even before the recovery legislation effort, the administration had been courting the city's most prominent city-wide religious organizations. At a June meeting in an East Camden church attended by more than one thousand city residents, Camden Churches Organized for People and Concerned Black Clergy of Camden City presented a list of objectives aimed at recovery to Commissioner of Community Affairs Jane Kenny and Republican Assembly leader Jack Collins, then a presumed candidate to succeed Whitman as governor.[25] These ranged from public safety, public education, and social service needs to community and economic development and the need to incorporate Camden residents into the revitalization process. The public reading of the group's vision statement somehow left out the key point that "additional resources must be made available to the city administration that do not presently exist," perhaps not so inadvert a mistake as organizers claimed, for neither Collins nor Kenny offered any concrete commitment to tapping new funding sources. Despite that omission, both organizations stood by the concluding statement that they were "willing to support an immediate and full takeover of the city by the State of New Jersey provided that the above conditions and outcomes are agreed to."[26]

Bolstered by this visible support, the Whitman administration continued to press for full takeover authority, even as it extended its immediate control. In October, it forced on the city its own choice for the important position of business administrator, despite Milan's effort to name his own appointment. Once again, Superior Court confirmed the state's authority.[27] The following month the state released its own commissioned plan for the city's recovery. The document claimed that the city's structural deficit could climb as high as $30 million by the year 2004. To meet the crisis, the plan called for considerable financial resources—$102 million in new capital investment—but only if tied to extensive management reforms and savings. There were to be achieved largely by a freeze in city employee wages and a rollback in benefits. According to the plan's complex carrot and stick approach, the city could achieve fiscal stability within four years. Funds designated for emergency aid would gradually shift to pay for the projected capital improvements.[28] The approach owed much to Democratic Mayor Ed Rendell's success in rolling back union costs in Philadelphia. Not surprisingly, Camden politicians quickly joined New Jersey unions in opposing the approach.

Commissioner Kenny did not immediately embrace the plan's particulars, saying only that it could provide guidance once new leadership was in place.[29] Her caution stemmed from the shifting fortunes of the principal antagonists. Milan was on the verge of conviction and jail. His crimes, which totaled $30,000 in payoffs from the mob, some thousands in improvements to his home, and a $7,500 vacation trip, prompted one attorney to describe them as "the K-mart of criminal activity." Yet even as the state managed to remove a chief obstacle to its intent, Governor Whitman prepared to leave office herself. News headlines the day of Milan's conviction revealed that she was about to be named George W. Bush's administrator of the Environmental Protection Agency.[30] The removal of the two chief protagonists in the takeover drama changed the political dynamic. It did not, however, entirely change the direction of discussions.

Now it was Democratic State Senator Wayne Bryant—an early target of the takeover legislation himself—who stepped in. A severe critic of Whitman's legislative approach,[31] Bryant prevailed upon senate president and now also acting governor, Republican Donald DiFrancesco, to support revised legislation. Introduced almost exactly a year after the first takeover bill had surfaced, the new proposal expanded the amount of money New Jersey was willing to invest in the city, to $150 million in state-backed bonds. To this was added another $50 million in funding from Camden County, to assume responsibility for city parks, the city's 911 emergency system, and to make necessary investments in crumbling sewers and streets. Gone was any discussion of reducing city workers' wages and benefits. The bill's language avoided discussing state takeover and instead emphasized recovery through a city-state partnership. Calling the effort "a plan for South Jersey," the acting governor declared, "A revitalized Camden will give the entire region a reborn economic, social, educational and cultural center."[32] True to a letter Bryant had written Governor Whitman early in her term, the effort included new funds for Camden's chief medical institutions, as a way of expanding Camden's job base; additional investment in infrastructure; and new initiatives directed at bringing the middle class back to the city.[33]

In outline as well as emphasis, the plan reflected the Camden Initiative introduced by James Florio shortly before his defeat for reelection in 1993. As befit a situation where Bryant had to work with a Republican governor and legislature, however, the new approach represented some power sharing across party lines. In fact, it was a precarious political balancing act. The Democratic county organization, to whom Camden's new mayor, Gwendolyn Faison (the seventy-five-year-old former chair of city council) owed her election, gained potential patronage through new investments in streets and sewers. The Republican-controlled Delaware River Port Authority gained the lion's share of responsibility for overseeing redevelopment. Other important downtown constituents—colleges and universities, hospitals, and the Cooper's Ferry Development Association—all received allocations for favored projects, and proposed redevelopment favored plans supported by the city's religious organizations. Had everything been worked out in advance with the interested parties, the package might have gained full consensus. One sticking point remained, however: the state's continued insistence on the appointment of a Chief Operating Officer. Under the terms of the new bill, the mayor retained many traditional responsibilities, including the right to make appointments to municipal authorities and to veto minutes of any independent local board. The power to make both financial and personnel decisions for the city, however, shifted to the Chief Operating Officer. Camden City Council would be allowed to choose from two state nominees, but would only be able to override COO decisions by a two-thirds vote. In such instances, the disputed issue would be referred to a special judicial mediator, whose decision would be final. Superior Court Judge Francis Orlando, who had already ruled twice in the state's favor in arbitrating the exercise of contested powers to govern, was to fill that role.[34]

Even the staunchest supporters of the new approach recognized the folly of pressing legislation without enlisting wide support in advance. Devised by Senator Bryant chiefly in association with DRPA vice-director Glenn Paulson and Acting Governor DiFrancesco,[35] details of the proposal came to the attention of Mayor Faison only days before the official announcement, and that by way of an anonymous fax. Although she joined the governor's news conference, she nonetheless expressed misgivings about giving up powers in the position to which she had just been elected. Within days, she was actively opposing the bill. Declaring that she was "no Milton Milan" needing state supervision and that she was not about to relinquish rights her father had risked his life for in the southern civil rights movement, she secured a unanimous vote of city council opposing the bill.[36] Other city officials also complained about their exclusion from crafting the legislation. Saying that Senator Bryant had betrayed city residents, Councilman Israel Nieves further charged that the proposal did more to shore up Republican patronage through contracts that would be let by the Delaware River Port Authority than to address city problems. "Right now you have a line of consultants, Republican consultants, waiting in line to get a piece of the millions of dollars that will come to Camden. It is the big special interests that are going to benefit from this."[37] Camden County Freeholder-Director Jeffrey Nash followed by claiming that the county had never agreed to assume responsibility for city parks and pointedly suggested that an acceptable compromise would have to wait until after the election of a new governor in the fall.[38]

Nash was not just being partisan. By the time DiFranscesco introduced the new legislation, he had already dropped out of the race for governor himself after being embarrassed by a series of revelations about his previous real estate dealings. A maverick, Bret Schundler, had upset the party's endorsed candidate in the Republican primary, and Democrat James McGreevey was widely perceived to be the frontrunner. Faison assumed that a Democratic administration would be more sympathetic to her position. Five members of council joined her in a public rally against the bill.[39] The bill languished, and the legislature adjourned on June 30 before holding either a hearing or a vote.

During the summer, Republicans agreed to reduce DRPA's control over state spending from $150 million to $63.5 million, for demolitions and neighborhood beautification projects. As a result, Democrats in the city and county reversed their opposition and began to press hard for the bill's passage. The shift in the Democratic position was attributed to Freeholder-Director Jeffrey Nash, whose close ties to George Norcross were well known. In addition, Nash secured approval to direct the remaining state funds to a recovery board, which, under a change of administration would be controlled by Democrats. Because all but one member of city council owed their jobs directly or indirectly to the county Democratic organization, the council followed Nash's lead. At a carefully orchestrated hearing before the State Senate, a stream of potential beneficiaries appeared to support the bill. A small protest group meeting outside the capital complex, lead by the only member of Camden City Council still opposing the bill, Ali Sloan El, charged in a circular that the city was being punished because it had become "a threat to the financial looters who wish to capitalize on Camden's current conditions by changing our form of government and returning to a time of the past where voting is reserved for a particular race or class of people."[40] This time the targets of criticism were Democrats, not Republicans, but neither the rally nor Sloan El's remarks before committee were reported. Other opposition, including that of Mayor Faison, was relegated to the end of a long afternoon of testimony. To her remark that the legislation was "arrogant, undemocratic, and racist," Senator Bryant retorted that some power concessions were needed. "You can't keep the status quo and expect this kind of investment," he stated. The bill subsequently passed the

State Senate with only three dissenting votes, all Republicans from rural areas.[41]

The new recovery legislation retained one powerful and somewhat surprising opponent, Governor-elect McGreevey. First drawn out in public on the issue when campaigning in Camden in September, McGreevey heightened his initial opposition after his victory, when it became clear that the state faced a historic deficit. Part of his stated objection lay in the perception that both the Camden bill and a closely identified measure to provide funding for new professional sports facilities in Newark were loaded down with costly concessions to South Jersey. Included in the recovery legislation were $20 million each to support a civic arena designated for Pennsauken, where George Norcross and Assemblyman Joseph Roberts were partners in an effort to launch a minor league hockey team, and for a sports facility at Rowan University, in Republican Speaker Jack Collins's district. McGreevey needed look no further for affirmation of his position than an unusually blunt September editorial in the *Philadelphia Inquirer*, subtitled, "Camden Recovery Plan Falls Victim to Politics and Grabs for Pork." By the time the revised bill reached committee, however, the *Inquirer* had joined the establishment as a supporter, writing, "Mr. DiFrancesco is doing his successor a big favor by performing the arduous groundwork needed to win local and state support for such a controversial takeover. He will then leave the more politically agreeable part of investing money in neighborhoods to Gov. McGreevey." Senator Bryant argued that in a state budget of nearly $23 billion, the cost of Camden's recovery could be as little as $11 million a year to pay back bonds. McGreevey remained unmoved, however. Rejecting the plea of Camden clergy as well as the press to support the legislation, he promised only to take up the issue again in the first six months of his administration. Given the state budget crisis, the product of generous Republican-backed spending at the end of DiFrancesco's term as well as a souring economy, he suggested relying on new tax incentives for Camden rather than state investment. At his insistence, Democrats in the assembly held back a vote on the legislation.[42]

The mounting state budget preoccupied the new governor in his early months in office, and he did not appear in Camden until early March. When he did, it was before a town meeting of some 1,300 people organized once again by Camden Churches Organized for People and Concerned Black Clergy. Joining the swaying choir in song in front of a packed Antioch Baptist Church, McGreevey did his best to exude sympathy and concern for the plight of the city. In their self-appointed role as representatives of the people, the Camden religious organizations played heavily on the continued drama of concentrated poverty and disinvestment. One speaker after another pleaded for the infusion of state funds A handout circulated at the meeting claimed that "every family in New Jersey is paying $108 *just to keep Camden on life support.*" The flyer declared that every child in Camden should "live in a vibrant neighborhood free of abandoned buildings, drug trafficking and gangs; feel safe in their homes and on the streets of their neighborhood; and receive a well-rounded education that will lead to a job or career that pays a decent wage."[43] St. Joseph's Carpenter Society executive director Sean Closkey provided the hard statistical evidence that underlay the emotional appeals from city residents. The meeting reached a peak when a group of school children carried in on a stretcher a figure meant to represent Camden, bloodied and dying. "Let it be said in your name and power, O God, that this seventh day of March 2002 is like no other day in the sad story of our city," intoned Msgr. Michael Doyle. "Let us declare that the long, painful waiting is over, that the State will take responsibility, that the decline will end, and that ways and means will surely be found to restore this city. . . . As you did of old, raise up a new David, with the courage to use even inadequate resources and yet overcome the massive problems of the city."[44]

McGreevey's presentation was notable for the absence of specifics. He announced immediately that one hundred new state police would be detailed to Camden at a cost of $600,000 to help assure resident safety. Shortly thereafter he appointed Closkey executive director of the New Jersey Housing and Mortgage Finance Agency, with its critical role in distributing tax credits to organizations working in housing redevelopment projects. He refused, however, to detail what a recovery bill for Camden might look like. Instead, he promised only to return with proposed legislation within sixty days and to push any bill through the legislature before adjournment.[45] With the exact nature of the recovery bill left open to interpretation, different parties began to press for their own views of appropriate legislation. Camden's six medical and higher-education institutions, at Senator Bryant's request, circulated a glossy brochure prepared by the equally politically connected former Camden County administrator Louis Bezich. It claimed that "we are the stimulus that attracts the private sector" and charged that "Years of state-funded assistance to Camden have only led to greater need. Investment in our plan will lead to economic independence." The institutions followed up with a presentation to senior McGreevey officials that stressed the number of jobs and additional income that the state's investment would produce.[46]

A small group of activists spearheaded by Councilman Sloan El and calling itself the Camden Community Recovery Coalition prepared its own proposal. Calling the Bryant bill part of the "same failed approaches" that had been tried for years, the group urged entirely new legislation combining massive public investment with extensive community input. State legislation, the activists declared, must address foremost the city's environmental degradation, the needs of its youth, and the means to prepare Camden residents for employment opportunities. With an $810 million pricetag and an activist role for government, the proposal was unlikely to gain favor in Trenton and did not even receive any notice in the press.[47]

Used to the special access they had experienced with Republicans, the Camden clergy began to fret as time passed without a clear indication of intent from the new Democratic governor and with no further efforts to consult them. Mayor Faison claimed that she was similarly excluded from decision-making.[48] The local press reported in early June that the emerging legislation, despite Governor McGreevey's earlier antagonism to the approach, would look very much like the failed Bryant bill. On June 13, the governor returned to Antioch Church to announce his proposal. Significantly, while the location remained the same as the March meeting, the time shifted from the evening to mid-day, and many fewer residents appeared at the announcement. Quite clearly, this was the governor's moment, not the Camden clergy's, and it was orchestrated as such.

Introducing Senator Bryant as the moral force whose vision was responsible for bringing recovery to the city at last, McGreevey embraced every central element of the bill he had appeared to reject only months earlier. Proposing a $175 million package of improvements, the governor stressed his own vision of making Camden a university city similar to New Brunswick, a goal he hoped to achieve by directing $41.1 million from the state's Economic Development Authority to new buildings for educational institutions and medical centers around the city's central business district. This money would be matched with an additional $45.3 million in investments by local hospitals, colleges, and universities, including Rutgers, Camden County College, Rowan University, and the University of Medicine and Dentistry of New Jersey. Although the emphasis was new, the projects were not, and the governor proceeded to list each of the other elements contained in the original Bryant bill: $45.8 million for downtown improvements; $35 million for a neighborhood improvement fund; and $43 million for demolition and redevelopment. Another $25 million was subsequently added back into the legislation to support the expansion of the New Jersey Aquarium.[49] A provision for a Chief Operating Officer remained in the bill after Mayor Faison said that the governor had satisfied her that her powers over day-to-day operations remained intact. City Council endorsed the legislation that night, even before all the details had been laid out. Only Councilman Sloan El voted against it. McGreevey said he would draw funds for the recovery package largely from existing state revenue sources. Within days, however, Senator Bryant was revising the bill in committee to be funded, as he had insisted all along, through government-backed bonds.[50] One element McGreevey appeared to have inserted on his own was the governor's right to veto the minutes of the elected Board of Education, thereby exercising in effect direct control over school construction and spending decisions. Moreover, he insisted, over Bryant's initial objection, that he and the mayor have the right to phase in their own appointments to the board, leaving only three of nine members to be popularly elected. This would allow for the board's reorganization over a two-year period.[51]

With the Camden Board of Education and a small group of activists who could mount only a modest protest rally outside Senator Bryant's Camden office the only dissenters, the legislation moved quickly through committee. The measure gained enough bipartisan support for passage despite Republican Assemblyman Joseph Malone's denunciation of it as "one of the biggest political pork barrels in the history of the state of New Jersey."[52] The recovery legislation gained final approval just as the legislative session and the requirement for a balanced budget came to a head at the end of June. Referring to the failed urban renewal plans of the 1960s, Assemblyman Joseph Roberts, who spearheaded the legislation in the lower body, asserted, "Unlike prior plans, this bipartisan measure has the vision and true potential to help Camden and the entire South Jersey region. . . . The Camden plan is more than a legislative measure; it is a vision for a revitalized community."[53]

Beyond its more publicized components, the recovery legislation contained some extraordinary elements. To some degree, the bill was directed at existing Camden residents, through modest funding for job training ($1.5 million) and a requirement that unions working on Camden projects increase the number of apprentices on the job, thus opening the door some to residents previously denied union access. It also offered some tax relief and neighborhood renewal, although it remained unclear how much of that effort would be directed at existing as opposed to new constituents. Powers

Figure 28. Old friends, May 10, 1989. Celebrating Randy Primas's reelection for mayor in 1989 are assemblyman Wayne Bryant, directly behind Primas, and Gwendolyn Faison, behind Bryant's left shoulder. Together they played central parts in a new chapter in Camden's history with the state takeover. Courtesy *Courier-Post.*

granted to encourage land assembly for redevelopment projects suggested the possibility of displacement and gentrification. Indeed, a strategic revitalization plan called for in the bill was specifically charged with ensuring "a full range of housing choices." Another provision prohibited Camden from entering any further Regional Contribution Agreements, as Roberts explained, "to stop Camden from being a magnet for poverty" while "new housing incentives are established to attract moderate- and upper-income residents to Camden." An associated measure aimed at building a middle class offered newly hired fire and police officers, who under state law dating from 1972 were exempt from a residency requirement, a 10 percent bonus on their salary for as long as five years for purchasing a home in Camden and making it their primary residence. Funds for environmental remediation and assurances through state control of accountability in the public school system could be seen as additional efforts to appeal to prospective home buyers from outside the city.[54] Together these measures offered the means to achieve the city's own stated goal to attract 20,000 new residents.[55] Another provision, for a regional impact council, promised assistance in stemming the spread out of Camden of problems such as crime and increased blight, while offering hope that more difficult issues of affordable housing would be taken up on a regional basis. The overall vision offered by the new bill, then, was one of restoring Camden to normalcy. In Roberts's words, Camden would once again become a city "where residents can breathe clean air, drink clean water and send their kids to superior schools . . . a city where residents can earn an honest living and take pride in their community."[56]

Questions quickly arose about the political implications of the new measure, particularly about the influence of Camden County Democratic leader George Norcross. Although Norcross's involvement with the recovery legislation was initially perceived to have related only to the companion measure to fund a hockey arena, there appear to have been other areas of influence. Holding on to the Camden Board of Education insurance contract mattered to him. After independents on the board terminated that arrangement in 1996, he turned to backing his own candidates for the board. Somewhat surprisingly, these efforts failed at the polls, even though some of those elected as independents later became his allies. His candidates in 2001 were no more successful than they had been in previous years. It could not have been surprising, then, that Rosemary Jackson, who had been responsible for terminating Norcross's contract with the school board, immediately charged that McGreevey's insistence on appointing school board members was aimed at reestablishing Norcross's control. Much more than a single insurance contract was at stake, she pointed out, as the schools would soon have $437 million to spend in new construction money available as a result of the New Jersey Supreme Court's latest *Abbott v. Burke* school equalization decision.[57] Although some found Jackson's argument strained, new provisions in the recovery legislation giving the Economic Recovery Board considerable control over school finances seemed to support her contention. Under the revised bill, the recovery board was granted powers to negotiate bond financing and to "maintain reserve and insurance funds" for school and other facilities, as well as "to purchase, acquire, attach, seize, accept or take title to any project or school facilities project by conveyance or by foreclosure, and sell, lease, manage or operate any project or school facilities project for a use specified in this act."[58]

That Norcross could have exercised such power with McGreevey seemed surprising. The previous summer he had been closely identified with a failed effort to block McGreevey's nomination when U.S. Senator Robert Torricelli jumped into the gubernatorial race. Norcross had already suffered defeat in the 1997 Democratic gubernatorial primary when his candidate, Congressman Robert Andrews, lost to McGreevey. Norcross lost his second battle when McGreevey picked up endorsements from several southern New Jersey county organizations and convinced North Jersey powerhouse and Newark mayor, Sharpe James, to drop his support for Torricelli.[59] Norcross's unmatched ability to fundraise, however, put McGreevey back in his debt after the election. Although Norcross failed to secure from McGreevey every Democratic leadership position he wanted in the new legislature, he did manage to push out North Jersey's Joseph Doria as Assembly Majority Leader and replace him with Camden's Joseph Roberts.[60] Moreover, Camden County Democrats gained the key financial positions in the legislature. Wayne Bryant became co-chairman (in a body evenly divided by party) of the Senate Appropriations Committee. Louis Greenwald, son of the late Cherry Hill mayor and county freeholder Maria Barnaby Greenwald, assumed the chairmanship of the Assembly Budget Committee. Given the state's fiscal crisis, the new governor could scarcely expect to execute his budget without the support of Camden County Democrats. Such were his allies in key committee assignments, the *New York Times* later reported, that the arrangement enabled the promotion of a "broad political agenda—some bills that would benefit their constituents in South Jersey, and others that seem specially tailored to boost Mr. Norcross's business ventures."[61]

Just as important, perhaps, was the quiet elevation of McGreevey's political mentor from Middlesex County, former state senator John Lynch, as a regional director at Commerce Bank, where Norcross was an officer and a director. Also joining Norcross on Commerce's board as he retired from office was Donald DiFrancesco.[62] In a final assurance of a connection, McGreevey appointed James P. Fox his new chief of staff early in 2003. A former chief of staff for Senator Torricelli, Fox had actively collaborated with Norcross in Torricelli's effort to secure the gubernatorial nomination. In the following months, Norcross had paid Fox $40,000 as a consultant to state legislative races.[63] After McGreevey's election Fox had become Secretary of Transportation, which allowed him to intervene on behalf of a billboard company in which Norcross had an interest.[64] Fox's elevation to chief of staff only further enhanced Norcross's access to the governor's office.

As early as December 2001, when the DiFrancesco version of the recovery bill was pending, the press began to speculate that Randy Primas would be named Camden's Chief Operating Officer. An early version of the bill called for a national search, but that provision was later dropped, and no other name ever surfaced. Primas was appointed in July 2002.[65] As the city's first African American mayor, as James Florio's Commissioner of Community Affairs, and in the 1990s as president of the Camden Development Collaborative, Primas clearly had the credentials to fill the COO position. Just as significant, however, he had an incontestable alliance with Norcross, who had been his chief financial backer when he ran for mayor and his career patron. Primas's Commerce Capital Markets, as a result of a merger with Commerce Bank, was the most active underwriter of short-term municipal bonds in New Jersey for six straight years through 2002, issuing $1.3 billion in bonds in 214 issues in 2002 alone. In that year, the company was named co-manager to secure the bonds to close McGreevey's last $1.1 billion budgetary gap, a controversial issue against tobacco settlement fees.[66] That McGreevey needed the support of Camden County legislators to close the state's budget deficit, that he acceded in a Camden County version of recovery, and that he appointed the most likely representative of the county's chief power broker as COO all added up to a mutually beneficial arrangement.

Certainly Norcross's support for the legislation was no secret. A *Courier-Post* editorial went out of its way to thank Norcross, despite his lack of a single public statement on the matter, declaring, "he put his considerable political influence behind a bill that is for the good of all South Jersey. . . . when his clout was needed, he delivered for South Jersey." The *Inquirer* added later what was becoming common wisdom when it noted, "The $175 million Camden recovery plan was a direct result of hard bargaining by Norcross and the newly ascendant team of South Jersey legislators who snap to his command."[67] Evidence that this was the case came from a totally independent source.

During the early controversy over the state's determination to assume control of Camden, Msgr. Robert McDermott, rector of St. Joseph's Procathedral and founder of St. Joseph's Carpenter Society, became an active and visible proponent of takeover legislation. After years of dealing with city government ineptitude and inaction, he came to support state intervention. Writing that "there may be other avenues that take us to the necessary goal of building local government's capacity to meet the needs of residents and business," McDermott nonetheless asserted, "The system now in place is broken. Brave and radical steps need to be taken."[68] While Whitman was still governor, he asked Senator Bryant to become the city's champion by supporting the Republican-led effort. Bryant rejected the challenge out-right, publicly calling Whitman's effort "plantation politics," a phrase pop-ular in the black community and later used by Rosemary Jackson to oppose Bryant's own support of the revised legislation. McGreevey wanted to break the package apart, pulling out the hospitals, universities, and the aquarium, and letting them fend for themselves. Bryant refused. A graduate of Rutgers Law School in Camden, he had close ties to the institution, which put con-struction of a new complex at the top of its agenda for recovery money. George Norcross served as vice president of the Cooper Health System. Too much had been invested to knock these downtown institutions out of the bill.[69]

McDermott admitted that he did not like the politics of the situation, but he felt he had to protect the interests of neighborhood activists by as-suring that money would be available for the reconstruction of their areas. As he explained, he learned earlier in the fight to reduce sewer fees for Cam-den residents that one has to exploit self-interest in order to achieve desir-able goals. On that occasion, CCOP had wide public support on a moral plane. But in order to secure necessary state enabling legislation, the organi-zation had to seek Norcross's help. CCOP made the case, he said, that the loss of revenue might be tolerable but not the bad publicity that emerged after the plaster ceiling at Sacred Hearth church school collapsed in 1985 as a result of trucks rumbling by on Ferry Avenue to build CCMUA's plant. Only chance prevented a human disaster as the children had left the room minutes before to play outside.[70] Responding to the CCOP plea, Wayne Bryant, at Norcross's insistence, took the lead to secure the necessary legis-lation, and CCOP had its victory. Although in both instances church orga-nizations had to rely on county power brokers, keeping public pressure on them to serve the community had its effect. We learned, McDermott con-cluded, that power is never given, it has to be taken away.[71]

With all the evidence available to link Norcross to the Camden recov-ery legislation, it was no surprise that Rosemary Jackson and other long-term critics of the Camden county Democratic organization contested the legislation in court. Much to the shock of the recovery legislation's support-ers, state Superior Court Judge Andrew J. Smithson struck down the section of the bill relating to schools, saying that it failed constitutionally because it represented special legislation for which only Camden was eligible. Saying that "a legal maneuver can't be allowed to impede progress," Senator Bry-ant led an effort to broaden the bill's applicability through amendment, gaining the legislature's approval with relative ease.[72] Just as significant,

Randy Primas settled a festering tax dispute with Mark Willis, owner of the old Sears building on Admiral Wilson Boulevard. Willis had long believed county politicians were set on seizing his building for tax arrears. As a result, he had been a donor to independent candidates for school board, including Rosemary Jackson. He also helped fund the successful legal challenge to the recovery legislation. But when Primas offered to settle on better terms than Willis had proposed himself, Willis called off his opposition. "I just want you to know . . . that there has been a complete cessation of hostility," he declared in October 2002. "The city's claim of $2 million in back taxes has been reduced to $689,000. The war is over. I know they're already saying I've sold out. But in Camden there are only two sides. You're either on the inside or the outside. I've laid down my tomahawk."[73]

Such accommodation did not end the war, however. Although the effort was delayed, activists headed by councilman Sloan El and Camden County NAACP chairman Colandus "Kelly" Francis secured the services of a new lawyer to file what they described as a citizens' suit against the recovery legislation.[74] Now the court had under consideration three suits concerning the recovery legislation, including the city's appeal of the school ruling as well as a separate complaint filed by activist and frequent independent candidate for city office, Frank Fulbrook.[75] The situation was made all the more precarious for defenders of the legislation because yet another suit pending in the state Supreme Court threatened to block any further bond issues without prior submission to public referendum. Primas warned that the state could not issue bonds to back the recovery plan unless Sloan El dropped or amended his lawsuit. Sloan El responded with terms linking institutional funding to the needs of Camden residents. Instead of considering the proposal, the government reacted by questioning Sloan El's disability status, acquired through a terrible elevator accident while working for Camden County in 1986, and putting a lien on his home, forcing him to scramble to refinance his mortgage.[76] Around the same time, Rosemary Jackson was reprimanded by the state for ethics violations and suspended for two months from participating in deliberations of the Board of Education.[77] Additionally, news reports suddenly appeared that Frank Fulbrook had failed to use funds he received in a legal settlement for charitable purposes as he had claimed he would. The charges were largely taken out of context, but, linked as they were to a company owned by the politically connected family of Lewis Katz, they served to more fully flesh out the picture of a political effort to beat back opposition, however it might be done.[78] If such efforts did not soften the opposition, Judge Smithson's ruling in March that Bryant's revised legislation, "by significantly expanding the number of cities that could qualify for aid," was valid. Although other features of the bill clearly constituted special legislation, the judge, who had to consider the effect of his decision on his own reappointment, clearly had taken the issue as far as he was willing to. In only a matter of days, the state issued the bonds necessary to put the recovery program into effect.[79]

It would be some time before the funds not already committed would be made available and the full nature of the bill's impact would be revealed. But right away, some of the more worrisome political elements of the legislation became evident. Most notable were the actions of the bill's primary sponsor, Senator Bryant. Within months of the bill's clearance in the courts, the press revealed a hidden clause in the complex legislation that required up to $1 million designated for Cooper Hospital to pass through to a "federally qualified health center operating in Camden." The only such qualifying program was CAMcare Health Corporation, run by Wayne Bryant's brother Mark. Ali Sloan El charged that the organization was not doing an adequate job of providing services to under and uninsured patients and that Cooper Hospital was better suited to provide that service. Yet the recovery legislation specifically excluded Cooper from using the money to establish or expand family-practice facilities, making CAMCare the only possible beneficiary. Despite the controversy, Governor Mc-Greevey used the groundbreaking of CAMCare's $10 million facility to praise both Bryants for their efforts in the process. Shortly afterward, further reports surfaced that Senator Bryant had been retained by several of the bill's prime beneficiaries: the University of Medicine and Dentistry of New Jersey, which had agreed to pay him $35,000 to "improve communications and relations with local governments," and Rutgers University Law School, which made him a special guest lecturer for an additional $30,000. Together with his salary as senator and the $53,000 he earned as attorney for the Gloucester County Board of Social Services, Bryant was receiving close to $170,000 in public funds, not counting work that came to him through his law firm.[80] Such activities were in keeping with Bryant's reputation, at least as it was characterized by his Republican critics.

Details of the aquarium expansion were more complex. During the long controversy over the legislation, the $25 million designated for the aquarium attracted little notice. This was surprising, not least because the Delaware River Port Authority had already set aside the same amount as an enticement to a private developer to double the facility's size and to assume its management. The Democrats who came onto the DRPA with the change

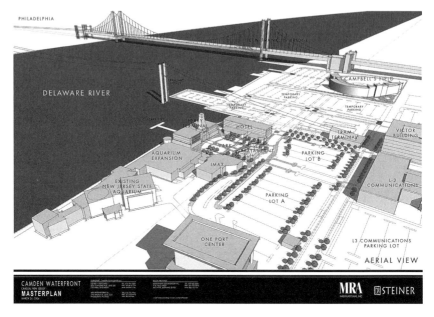

Figure 29. The Downtown waterfront, as it was to be built out with funds from the recovery legislation. Courtesy Development Design Group, Baltimore.

in state administration in New Jersey counted on that money being available through the recovery legislation, which meant that DRPA's original allocation could be distributed to other projects. Indeed, Democrats made their intentions clear even before the recovery legislation had been cleared in the courts, by trying to force out DRPA's executive director and replace him with Democratic loyalist and former Camden County administrator Louis Bezich. That effort failed when the new governor of Pennsylvania, Ed Rendell, stepped in by naming himself chairman of the commission, thereby dashing any illusions that New Jersey Democrats would be running the operation.[81] With the developer threatening to drop the project if delays in signing a final agreement continued, the DRPA committed $18.3 million for the project and the state another $10.6 million out of the funds reserved under the recovery legislation, leaving some but not all the anticipated funds of each entity to use for other purposes. Only three months later, with the developer complaining once again about delayed payments, the Economic Recovery Board voted to authorize the full $25 million payment, bringing the total subsidy to $43 million. When Rosa Ramirez, the representative of Camden Churches Organized for People on the recovery board, pressed developers for assurances that Camden residents would benefit, developers promised job training and 50 cents a ticket for the city. This payment was the same amount being made by the Riversharks baseball team, despite the fact that prices at the aquarium were expected to be considerably higher than baseball tickets.[82]

The chief beneficiary of the arrangement was Steiner and Associates of Columbus, Ohio, described by the DRPA as "leisure time destination" developers.[83] Although the state would continue to own the aquarium, it arranged to lease the facility under a twenty-five year renewable contract. Steiner was supposed to put up $5 million toward the facility's expansion. In fact, it put up only $1 million of its own funds and received an additional $1.5 million from the state to supervise construction, a role that the state treasurer's office normally would have done itself. Although the press repeatedly described Steiner's commitment as $9 million, $4 million of that came from a firm committed to putting a restaurant in the expanded facility. Another $4 million was already committed independently for an IMAX theater. Moreover, the company qualified under recovery legislation for a refund of up to 75 percent of its state corporate business taxes for up to ten years.[84] The Academy of Aquatic Sciences, which had run the aquarium from its inception under a lease from the state, was eased out in the process over its objections. As State Treasurer John McCormac put it, "I don't want to beat them up. We just can't afford to pay the debt"—$8 million built up in the early years when there were no other facilities on the waterfront.[85] Unless the state paid that debt, the Academy would lose the $3 million endowment, on which it was expected to continue to operate. Once the deal was completed, the state saved about $1 million a year in operating revenues and Cooper's Ferry got Steiner's commitment to bring another $113 million in investment over the next decade for commercial and residential facilities to fill in the waterfront. Although he served as secretary on the Academy board, Randy Primas made no effort to intervene on the Academy's behalf, saying that was really a matter for the state to determine. The Academy's educational programs that had served Camden children so well for years were the probable victims.[86]

Yet another element of the recovery effort highlighted the ways in which political influence triumphed over economic need. On December 11, 2001, the day before Governor-elect McGreevey succeeded in postponing the pending recovery bill, the legislature approved a bill introduced by Assemblyman Joseph Roberts authorizing private vendors to collect taxes for those municipalities failing to sustain good collection rates. The effort represented a shift from the original Bryant-DiFrancesco approach, which had given the DRPA the power to dispose of delinquent properties or to assign them to a state agency such as the New Jersey Economic Development Authority. In providing enabling legislation for the private collection of taxes as well as the sale of liens in bulk, the bill met a requirement in the recovery legislation for a tax collection audit in preparation for a demolition funding plan.[87] Instead of the weeding out of bad properties among good called for by CCOP, however, this approach pointed more to the kind of discredited wholesale redevelopment characteristic of the 1960s. The only company to come forward was one formed in 2000 by Roberts's early political mentor, former governor James Florio. Camden City Council promptly awarded the company, Xspand, a no-bid contract, with incentives running up to 25 percent to collect $100 million in back taxes.[88] With the city's own tax collecting process clearly inadequate to the task and precedents in other states for outsourcing the function, there was clearly a case for such intervention. Furthermore, following the terms of the legislation, Florio announced a program to help residents refinance their homes.[89] Many Camden residents, however, were not eligible for such assistance, because of their advanced age or credit history. Asked about the prospect of residents losing their homes, Randy Primas replied, "If some people don't qualify, I can't say I have an answer for that problem."[90]

With that response, activists seized on the spectre of residents being pushed from their homes. Following the lead of Councilman Sloan El and the president of the Camden City Taxpayers Association, William Jenkins, they formed an opposition effort, Camden's Forgotten Homeowners Coalition. Pointing to the hardship and injustice of cracking down on homeowners who had remained in Camden during hard times while corporations were being given big tax breaks for relocating to the area, they urged an amnesty program for residents.[91] Pressed to support a resolution on the subject on the eve of an election when his seat was being challenged by Frank Fulbrook, City Council president Angel Fuentes sidestepped the issue by referring it to an ad hoc committee for study. Fuentes proceeded to crush Fulbrook in the election only days later, drawing on more than $77,000 in funds from the Democratic City Committee for his ticket. Campaign election reports indicate that more than 500 people were paid to get out the vote in an election that involved only several thousand. A Washington-based consultant produced highly inflammatory fliers directed at Fulbrook, whose greatest threat appeared to be his willingness to second motions raised by the body's only independent member, Sloan El.[92]

The Camden recovery legislation represented a creative alternative to the budget slashing that was the fate of so many cities burdened with the fiscal burdens associated with post-industrial decline.[93] If successful, the *New York Times* proclaimed, the effort could serve as a model and propel Governor McGreevey into the national spotlight. Undoubtedly, the effort as it developed was not all that it should have been. At the same time, the active involvement of faith-based community organizations in the advocacy process prevented the winners in the partisan battle from limiting the focus simply to physical improvements. The people of Camden had both mobilized for the recovery effort and asserted their interests in securing better homes, a safer environment, and greater economic opportunities. The legislation as passed offered possibilities for realizing those goals, yet as early actions on the measure suggested, those priorities were not necessarily favored in the incessant search for personal or political gains. Certainly, the influx in new money did not itself address Camden's biggest problem: the concentration of poverty and all the social problems that flowed from that fact. The question remained, what alternatives would emerge within the existing framework to make the recovery work, and who would be able as well as willing to assume this challenge?

Chapter 9

Future Camden: Reinventing the City, Engaging the Region

Camden is the best visual aid in America of what went wrong. If you could turn it around, it would be the best visual aid of what went right.
—Msgr. Michael Doyle, 1992

Once Camden's recovery legislation had been secured, there was suddenly no lack of willing partners to direct the city's future. Investors and bankers who had for a generation avoided the city became once again very much a presence. Foundations perked up and considered how they might make a difference. Activists sharpened their strategies and girded for new battles. Planners, critics, and the press weighed in. A solid plan, directed at central needs and built out of a growing consensus across geographic as well as ideological interests, could well have provided a blueprint for Camden's future. Policy seldom emerges in such a fashion, however, and this was no exception. Politically charged as it was, the recovery legislation failed to secure consensus. Its very success as a stimulus bill directed at attracting new investment set off the first wave of controversy as local residents fought the specter of gentrification. Its initial failure to embrace the requirement that Camden's problems be addressed in a regional context prompted still more criticism. Because the bill contained so many elements that could be seized by different constituencies, the effort to set its direction became highly contested. In the process serious questions emerged not just about Camden's future, but about the state of contemporary urban policy.

As the first major urban revitalization initiative of the twenty-first century, Camden's recovery effort took place in a different social and policy context from the one that framed the urban renewal programs of the 1950s and 1960s. Battles to stem the outward flow of population and capital had already been lost. Older industrial cities remained greatly diminished actors in their larger metropolitan areas. Their suburbs held economic, environmental, and political advantages well beyond those acquired a generation earlier. Under the circumstances, cities could scarcely expect to compete with their suburbs on their terms. They had to build on their own existing assets, of location, of exercising naturally centralized functions for entertainment and services, and of providing specialized functions such as higher education and skilled medical care. At its core, the recovery legislation did just that, helping enhance the city's position as an important regional destination. Building on waterfront successes in breaking down suburban reluctance to enter the city, these new expenditures could be expected to increase the daily inward flow to Camden and thus provide a spur to business investment.

Encouraged by the direction cast by recovery legislation, the Greater Camden Partnership, revived and reconstituted from earlier iterations in the 1920s and 1960s, presented a vision statement in April 2003 that spelled out $800 million in new investment in the downtown area adjacent to the waterfront and suggested many projects to come.[1] Describing downtown as "the economic engine of Camden's revitalization," it identified a series of overlapping districts—for education, health sciences, high-tech, recreational activity—that could together enliven the downtown if properly planned with shopping, restaurants, and other amenities. Such a mixed-use strategy, the report claimed, "can be the catalyst for making Downtown a place to linger after visits to the government, employment, education, healthcare or recreation districts. After hours and weekends it can and should be the gathering place for casual visitations providing pedestrian connections to and from the nearby campuses, tourist attractions and residential neighborhoods."[2]

Other new investment possibilities reinforced the sense that Camden, finally taking full advantage of its location directly across the Delaware from Philadelphia, would revitalize at its core. Passage of the bill alone had been enough to secure financing for Carl Dranoff's conversion of the old RCA Nipper Building—renamed the Victor—to market-rate apartments.[3] The state's commitment to the aquarium's expansion prompted him to say he would also build one thousand new houses and condominiums on the waterfront over the ensuing decade. A month later, as he began to show the Victor apartments, he was encouraged enough by the flood of applications to announce that he would soon begin the conversion of a companion building and that he would consider converting the high-rise board of education facility, also a former RCA building, should it become available. "I've changed streets, I've changed neighborhoods," he commented with the first arrivals, "but I've never had the opportunity to be the catalyst for changing a city."[4] Only days later, news reports appeared that the Cigna Corporation, one of the last major companies based in Philadelphia, was considering relocating its fifteen hundred employees to a Camden waterfront site. Equity Bank, a regional company with headquarters in suburban Marlton, indicated it was interested in moving into Dranoff's second converted building when it was ready.[5] So charged was the climate for waterfront reinvestment, that serious discussions arose about removing Waterfront State Prison—a suggestion whose irony was not lost on city activists who had fought the prison when it was imposed on impoverished North Camden.[6]

If rasing Riverfront Prison seemed farfetched, a proposal from the Builders League of South Jersey appeared more immediately practical. The League announced its intent to build up to three thousand new homes, along with new business and school facilities. Focusing first on the Lanning Square area adjacent to the downtown and waterfront areas, the League called for "an imaginative approach to new urbanism" that would both attract new middle and upper income residents to the city through market-rate homes and accommodate existing residents through subsidies backed by the kind of homeownership training required by the St. Joseph's Carpenter Society in East Camden. Prompted by a request by Cooper's Ferry's Thomas Corcoran, the Builders League's proposal encompassed all of South Camden, including Waterfront South, and offered itself as a model for other sections of the city. Once completed, the effort promised to bring another $500 million in new capital investment to the city.[7]

Even as these initiatives built on success at the waterfront, every proponent for recovery knew that downtown revitalization would not be sufficient alone to secure renewal. Severe blight and worse reached into every Camden neighborhood. It would be here, as Randy Primas asserted repeatedly, that the recovery effort would be tested, and it was here that different visions for Camden's residents would be contested. Three competing approaches emerged, each rooted in the city—and the nation's—recent history. The first, seeking foremost to improve the city's fiscal position, sought, like those urban renewal programs of the 1950s and 1960s, to make the city more attractive to middle and upper income people, to live and work in as well as to visit. With fewer public funds at hand, however, this goal could be achieved only by leveraging private investment. The cost of rebuilding cities to standards desirable to targeted buyers was simply too great for the public sector to bear. A second approach emerged out of Camden's own struggle with the effects of disinvestment in the 1990s, epitomized especially in the work of the city's nonprofit sector. These organizations, instead of trying to attract newcomers, were in the process of growing the assets of existing city residents, upgrading their housing, mediating environmental intrusions, and encouraging the pursuit of better educational and training opportunities. As painfully slow as the approach was, there were demonstrable results—enough to give hope to the city's faith-based organizations that recovery would build on those efforts. Finally, a third alternative stressed improved opportunities for Camden residents but in a regional context in which individuals would be given options to move closer to existing opportunities in the suburbs as well as waiting for them to appear in the city. Built on the efforts of the fair share housing campaign of the previous quarter century, this element based its hopes for achieving greater regional equity on provisions in the recovery legislation for a regional impact council and a prohibition against accepting Regional Contribution Agreements in Camden. Because each approach had its strong advocates, the issues were raised in clear and forceful fashion for Camden and its region.

*   *   *

The recovery legislation required Randy Primas as the Chief Operating Officer to be guided by the Camden Recovery Board, a body top heavy with government representatives but including representatives of business and labor as well as three Camden residents: CCOP activist Rosa Ramirez, Concerned Black Clergy chair James C. Jones, and Rodney Sadler, chair of the Camden planning board and an unsuccessful Norcross-backed candidate for school board in 2002. As a signal of how important the effort was to the state, Governor McGreevey named State Treasurer John McCormac the chair. The board in turn was to be guided by a strategic revitalization plan commissioned by the New Jersey Economic Development Authority.[8]

Although the revitalization plan released in April 2003 addressed the depths of Camden's social problems, much of it was directed at attracting the middle class back to the city. While it stated its first priority as the creation of jobs for Camden residents and detailed some of the challenges in employment readiness, it used the politically popular "smart growth" rationale for combating suburban sprawl by directing resources back to older urban areas as an argument for attracting new residents through ties to their employment. In the report's words, good job generating strategies would have the benefits of reducing "high levels of commuter traffic while increasing expenditure potential in the city's neighborhoods. It is the link required to join economic development with community development."[9] While the report identified improved neighborhood housing conditions as its second priority, it again favored the recruitment of newcomers over solutions for current residents. If institutional employers would provide buyer programs for their employees, the report argued, the city could reap more taxes from these higher income families and could also benefit from the new leadership and institutional connections such residents would bring.[10] Although the report emphasized the need to provide a regional solution to Camden's problems, it failed even to discuss matching Camden residents to other employment centers outside the city, let alone the regional impact council that had been called for in the recovery legislation.[11]

Clifton Henry, the chief architect of the plan, made his public presentation at two sessions. The first, held during the day at the city's Office of Economic Opportunity facility as part of a regular meeting of the recovery board, drew a number of the legislation's critics. Among those using the question and answer period to challenge the very premise of the revitalization plan was Roy Jones, an economic consultant who had worked with Councilman Sloan El on an alternative to the Bryant recovery plan. Jones argued, in line with his earlier criticisms, that the $35 million set aside for neighborhood reinvestment should be put on a par with the $800 million targeted for the downtown. Tellingly, when the recovery board reconvened that evening at the waterfront entertainment center, where residents were invited to hear the presentation, its members removed themselves from the floor level to a distant stage. When it came time for questions, no one was allowed to speak from the floor, as Jones had in the morning. Instead, questions were submitted in writing. The result was a less contested and less substantive exchange. The public was invited to submit further questions and concerns in writing over the ensuing two months.[12]

Among the issues most troubling to representatives of many of the city's nonprofit organizations was Henry's division of city neighborhoods into two tiers. "Priority areas" would be given precedence over the first five years of recovery, whereas "transitional areas" were targeted for planning and further preparation for later recovery efforts. The criteria for immediate preference, Henry said, was a neighborhood's ability to attract investment. Aside from Lanning Square, close to downtown, the four priority neighborhoods were all residential areas at the city's suburban borders: Cramer Hill, East Camden, Parkside, and Fairview. In these neighborhoods, relatively new nonprofit organizations were pursuing promising plans for rehabilitation. They were no further ahead in organizational terms, however, than North Camden, whose community-based plan had set a standard for Camden for more than a decade, or Waterfront South, where Sacred Heart's Heart of Camden organization had commissioned, with Cooper's Ferry's assistance, a redevelopment plan from the same leading national firm that had assisted East Camden's St. Joseph's Carpenter Society. Despite strong records of planning for recovery in both neighborhoods, the revitalization plan relegated them to secondary status.[13] The revitalization plan also relegated Waterfront South to the second tier of redevelopment.

Camden's nonprofit community was used to banding together. By the time Henry returned to Camden in June to present a final plan for approval to the Economic Recovery Board, it had convinced him to amend the revitalization plan to reserve 10 percent of the entire $175 million in funding for Tier II neighborhoods and to accept the additional goal of targeting up to 5 percent of new housing as affordable.[14] Previously, the emphasis of the report had been entirely on market-rate investments. The recovery board accepted those changes, promising as well to name a community advisory board, as called for in the recovery legislation.

In spite of this responsive attitude, the planning consultants completely failed to address Camden's most pressing social concerns in a regional context. Peter O'Connor, representing the Fair Share Housing Center, had used the advisory period to submit a strong argument for addressing the metropolitan structural systems that had kept cities like Camden marginalized for so long. His letter quoted Myron Orfield's regionalist manifesto, *American Metropolitics*: "Until the problems of the cities are placed in their true, metropolitan geographical context, in-place initiatives will remain palliatives—a series of small, broken arrows in an increasingly empty quiver."[15] Not surprisingly, O'Connor urged the board to pursue regional affordable housing opportunities as the means both to advance integration and to deconcentrate poverty. The Economic Development Authority ignored O'Connor, however, and the recovery board approved a revised document without addressing the issue. The legislatively required regional impact council had not even been appointed, let alone consulted, and EDA Executive Director Caren Franzini said she had no idea where the creation of the council stood.[16]

The board's failing on regionalism was especially ironic given the chief influences on the plan. Most readers of Henry's report found it muddled enough that they could not discover any underlying philosophical rationale. It is possible in retrospect, however, to discern the influence on the document of Jeremy Nowak. Nowak's Philadelphia-based Reinvestment Fund had been a major contributor to neighborhood revitalization in Camden, first in North Camden and subsequently in East Camden where he worked closely with St. Joseph's Carpenter director Sean Closkey. At Closkey's request, now acting as director of the New Jersey Housing and Mortgage Finance Agency and a technical advisor to the revitalization plan, Nowak was commissioned to assess the state of Camden's resident population. Most striking in that analysis was the magnitude of Camden's isolation. After nearly a decade of rising prosperity in the nation, the region, and in Camden County, Camden residents were even further behind their contemporaries than they had been a decade earlier. Moreover, their separation from opportunities outside the city was virtually complete. Very few residents commuted to Philadelphia, despite its easy access just across the river. Residents relied heavily on public transportation. As a consequence, few took advantage of growing employment centers in nearby suburbs, many of which were inaccessible or inconvenient to reach by public transportation.[17] As a self-professed believer in "expanding the geography of opportunity for poor people," Nowak recognized the need to reintegrate not just the city but its residents into the regional opportunity structure. Such efforts could include affordable housing opportunities close to job clusters, in line with O'Connor's own strategy to deconcentrate the poor.[18] Just as pertinent, however, to use Nowak's words, were public and private investment strategies that "will reposition distressed places as locations of choice." Older cities, like Camden, could become assets to their regional economies once again if they managed to improve their market competitiveness in three realms: as sites for residential investment and development, as sites for business location, and as sites for labor market skills.[19] The goal of Nowak's analysis, submitted in early 2003 to Closkey and to Clifton Henry for consideration in the revitalization plan, was to remake Camden as a location of choice once again.

Nowak recognized that residents clearly needed much more than the small measure of training offered them through the recovery legislation.[20] He perceived a strategy by which the city could be revitalized, however, building from such strengths as had already had been demonstrated in Closkey's own efforts through the St. Joseph's Carpenter Society in East Camden. Using a sophisticated geo coded data base for real estate and social indicators in Camden and its nearby communities, he classified areas into three categories of relative market strength: those in need of large-scale reclamation; those that were distressed but still responsive to intervention; and those transitional markets in need mostly of further protection of their existing assets.[21] The neighborhoods Nowak had identified as transitional had to be tackled first, for they held the best hope of attracting private investment. Although he used different terms, Clifton Henry clearly absorbed this concept and incorporated it into the revitalization plan.

The revitalization plan thus confirmed first and foremost the central premise of the recovery legislation that state money was needed to do more than simply meet the gap created by a structural deficit; it must also reduce it by generating new revenue.[22] Randy Primas had made this point himself in the first public meeting reviewing the strategic revitalization plan. Nowak was explicit (as Primas, Henry, and the recovery board were not), however, about the need to make these decisions within a regional framework. "For the City of Camden to become reintegrated into its surrounding metropolitan area, its extreme poverty must be reduced and its concentration of poverty dispersed," he wrote in a February application to the Ford Foundation for funds to participate in the recovery process. "This can happen in several ways: poor, unskilled residents can be trained for and linked with living wage, career path jobs that are mostly being created in the suburbs and in Philadelphia; higher-income residents can be enticed to move into Camden; and surrounding jurisdictions could build affordable housing so that Camden residents could move to places that provide more opportunity. A combination of these tactics would likely provide the best results for Camden and its residents, and regional collaboration at the individual, institutional, and government level would be necessary for any of these scenarios to unfold."[23]

Although it may not have been designed as such, Nowak's strategy appeared primarily to compensate for the conceptual weakness as well as the political biases of the original legislation. In fact, Ford Foundation officers hoped their investments might help make Camden a model for conversion to a sustainable post-industrial condition.[24] To further pursue that goal, Ford underwrote several efforts designed to advance greater regional equity in Camden and throughout the rest of New Jersey. In addition to providing funds to CCOP and Concerned Black Clergy to widen their own regional compasses, Ford underwrote an organizing effort by the newly formed New Jersey Regional Coalition. Working with the advice of Myron Orfield and john a. powell, the director of a center on race and ethnicity at Ohio State University, Ford program officers became convinced that New Jersey, despite its fractured system of local governance and its reputation as a premier example of suburban sprawl, was primed for a policy breakthrough. Ford supported the publication of *New Jersey Metropatterns*, a report prepared by researchers working under Orfield and the New Jersey Regional Coalition. The coalition described its mission as "promoting an anti-sprawl, pro-redevelopment, socially equitable and environmentally friendly agenda of research, organizing and policymaking." Listed first among the common values of its members, which included O'Connor's Fair Share Housing Center, was deconcentrating poverty and its impact on New Jersey communities. Promoting social and racial equity was another common value.[25]

Like Orfield's previously published work, the New Jersey study identified a number of at-risk suburban as well as declining urban communities and blamed low-density growth for "a devastating pattern of social stratification that divides communities by income and race." While it praised the intentions of the 1992 New Jersey State Plan to foster greater social and economic balance through reinvestment in older areas,[26] the report reinforced what other observers had noted, that it lacked teeth. Describing regional and statewide initiatives as crucial to reform, the report called for "greater tax equity to equalize resources among local governments; smarter land-use planning to support more sustainable development practices; stronger affordable housing rules to expand opportunities for low- and moderate-income residents and promote integrated schools and neighborhoods; and institutional reforms to encourage local governments to cooperate on regional and statewide goals."[27] Urging community organizations to join together in promoting "a regional equity agenda," the report claimed such efforts would offer relief to all communities: "For cities, they mean enhanced opportunities for redevelopment and for the poor. For fiscally stressed suburbs, they mean stability, community renewal, lower taxes and better services. For developing bedroom communities, they offer sufficient spending on schools and clean air and water. Affluent suburban communities also stand to gain from regional efforts to preserve open space and reduce traffic congestion."[28]

The report spoke directly to the situation in the greater Camden area. During the 1990s, the suburbs immediately adjacent to Camden, most notably Pennsauken, but also Collingswood and the western portion of Cherry Hill, began to be affected by the same patterns of blight and unsettling demographic change that affected Camden's outer residential areas. In both Pennsauken and Collingswood, the area between the Camden border and U.S. Route 130 (running north to Trenton) began to look more like Camden, both physically (with more rental units) and demographically. As a sure sign of change, the presence of black and Hispanic children in Pennsauken schools increased to 46 percent in 1995 and 68 percent in 1999.[29] White flight was beginning in Pennsauken. When one family, the Bonifacios, decided to leave for Cherry Hill, the sale of their home was delayed because only minority buyers who found financing difficult to obtain considered the house.[30] As early as 1987, some white homeowners had begun to express alarm. "I'm afraid the value of my property will depreciate because East Camden is moving in slowly," one commented. "You can see it coming. I'm talking about drugs, theft, noise."[31] Quipped one Pennsauken resident only a few years later, "Let's face it, everyone is moving out of Pennsauken: just ask a realtor. There are more than 600 houses for sale in Pennsauken."[32] Suburban support for the state's recovery legislation built precisely around the perception, as Senator Bryant reported, that Camden's problems were spilling over into adjacent communities. In rallying support for the state proposal while she was still mayor of Cherry Hill, Susan Bass Levin told a large gathering in her township, "The success of Camden is linked to all our communities in Camden County . . . and anybody who doesn't believe that is a fool." Noting that the problems of abandoned housing and businesses and eroded neighborhoods "know no boundaries," Collingswood Mayor James Maley described the Camden legislation as "the single most important step in the continued progress of Collingswood and the entire region in the last 50 years."[33]

Pennsauken, and to a lesser degree Collingswood and the older sections of Cherry Hill, were good examples of what Orfield called inner ring and subsequently at-risk suburbs. Characterized by growing numbers of children eligible for free school lunches as well as by stagnant or falling property values and an aging housing stock, these areas typically failed to qualify for federal or state programs directed at similar problems located in urban areas. As a state legislator in Minnesota, Orfield had advanced coalition building between cities and their older suburbs, crafting legislation that would make them eligible for revenues shared from regional districts.[34] That cooperation, born from perceived shared interests as well as strong leadership, did not exist in the Camden area in the 1990s. Responding to the perception that crime was spilling over from Camden into their township, Pennsauken officials in 1994 instituted spot police checks of cars crossing the border. Only when Camden Mayor Arnold Webster, backed by a constitutional expert who saw racism in Pennsauken's actions, objected strenuously did the practice stop.[35] Even then, other dubious strategies continued. In Collingswood, the borough aggressively converted troubled apartment buildings, where minority presence was rising, from open occupancy to specialized use, usually for seniors, or had them torn down.[36] Pennsauken instituted its own special policing program in the troubled neighborhoods near the Camden border, though officers claimed they had no intent of profiling Camden residents. Additionally, they instituted in 1999 a $500,000 housing fund to deal with dilapidated properties, which, as one town official put it, if not checked would expand like cancer: "At first, it's only a few cells, but then it spreads."[37] Both Pennsauken and Cherry Hill pursued aggressive reinvestment strategies to improve properties on their western edges, and, in the case of Pennsauken, to distinguish suburban sections of continuing streets from the Camden portions of the same streets. Collingswood hired an outside organizer to upgrade its commercial shopping districts, gaining a good deal of praise for the results.[38]

Not all reactions were so stringently negative. In 1996, Pennsauken resident Lynn Cummings responded to the appearance of a number of "for sale" signs after the first black family moved to her block by forming Neighbors Empowering Pennsauken, with the idea of protecting the township's diversity. With the assistance of Donald DeMarco, whose Fund for an Open Society had helped promote integrated neighborhoods in Shaker Heights in Ohio and South Orange in New Jersey, her organization obtained a grant to assist the township in forming a Stable Integration Governing Board.[39] Establishing the goals of sustaining a robust housing market and high quality schools, the organization set out both to keep white homeowners in the township and to attract more potential buyers among whites. While he recognized the awkwardness of promoting the effort to fellow African Americans, board president Harold Adams believed that it was in his own self-interest to prevent the resegregation of Pennsauken. Moved by the prevailing wisdom that without white buyers prices in the area would fall, his organization, with the township's financial support, advertised the community with some success in the predominantly white Northeast section of Philadelphia.[40] Much like Camden's Fairview neighborhood, Pennsauken thus wrestled with the uneasy equation between accepting new minority residents and the effort to attract, or at least to retain, significant numbers of whites.

Other suburbs suffered as well, especially those built up along transportation corridors a generation earlier. As garden apartments aged and use of Section 8 housing vouchers expanded in these areas, social problems accumulated. Lindenwold, at the end of the PATCO Speedline to Camden and Philadelphia completed in 1969 emerged as a particularly visible troubled suburb. Referred to frequently as "Little Camden," it became the target of police investigations for drug use and associated crimes.[41] Figures released with *New Jersey Metropatterns* identified other at-risk suburbs, including a number of towns located along the Black Horse Pike (NJ 168) and U.S. Route 130, highways which had been bypassed by alternative routes and, as a consequence, had declined both commercially and residentially. Towns located along both corridors actively pursued funds for reinvestment, especially in declining commercial properties.

Organizational efforts to form a regional alliance began at the end of 2002, when the New Jersey Regional Coalition hired Paul Scully. Scully had roots in labor and community organizing and had recently handled, with the support of the Gamaliel Foundation, a particularly difficult organizing effort among Northwest Indiana's suburbs of East Chicago, Gary, and Hammond.[42] Scully's initial steps in New Jersey were to meet with Catholic priests in Camden and its suburbs. At a meeting in Pennsauken in May 2003 he introduced the findings of *New Jersey Metropolitics* to some fifty attendees, pointing out that more than 60 percent of the area's parishes were located in inner cities or at-risk suburbs. The Catholic Church, he argued to a generally responsive audience, had a direct interest in addressing proactively the spread of poverty and its consequences. Reverend Robert Vitillo, national executive director of the Catholic Campaign for Human Development, endorsed the goals of the regional coalition. Citing Pope John Paul II's concern about the "exacerbation of inequalities between powerful economies and dependent" ones, he reported that he had signed a pastoral letter supporting a similar Orfield report in Connecticut. That report asserted, in part,

Our Tradition of Catholic Social Teaching calls us to look outside ourselves and to act beyond ourselves and to act beyond our comfortable, human constructed boundaries. These may be historical town lines on a map or ways we define ourselves and others by income level, racial or ethnic background, religion or parish, or any of the other ways we too often label and separate those whom God loves. We are interconnected geographically by the water, air and land we share in common, as well as by our economy. We are all children of one God and must express solidarity in practical ways.[43]

Although not everyone in the room embraced the particular elements of the day's message, the occasion did provide Scully with both a moral and practical means for moving ahead with his organizing. The next step was the regional coalition's statewide conference a month later. While Orfield called for regional tax sharing among other innovations and urban consultant David Rusk pointed to the ill effects of concentrated poverty on educational attainment and upward mobility, john a. powell addressed the hardest issue of all: why African Americans should embrace such changes despite the potential dilution of their political strength in inner city areas. Noting that the process of black suburbanization was already well under way, powell argued that what was missing was a conscious strategy to link that movement to the realization of greater educational as well as economic opportunities. This argument built on one he had spelled out in a previous essay:

What distinguishes a mobility strategy from a dispersal strategy is its intent; while mobility strategies do disperse population, they do so with the aim of moving people toward opportunities that lie elsewhere in metropolitan areas. In a sense, mobility strategies can be seen as a positive subset of dispersal strategies, because they attempt to break down geographic barriers to housing, education, employment, and wealth creation for communities of color. Advocates of mobility strategies believe that if people who are segregated and isolated by race and poverty can move into neighborhoods with adequate community resources, they will gain access to the means and mechanisms of progress.[44]

Favoring a federated approach to regional equity that both preserved existing communities of color and linked them with regional opportunities, powell nonetheless had been explicit about the altered nature of the challenge to racial justice:

The racial justice advocacy community has seen racial subordination mutate from explicitly racist laws and covenants to, more recently, the superficially race-neutral policies that reproduce the isolation of people of color from opportunities. The most devastating manifestations of racism today take structural forms—in tax policy, in student assignment policies, in exclusionary zoning, in the gentrification that displaces people of color—requiring that advocacy strategies be structurally focused, multiple and adaptive.[45]

In that spirit, attendees, including a substantial presence of African Americans and Hispanics, made the pledge at the end of the day to form organizing efforts in each of three sections of the state: North, Central, and South. Regional organizing meetings began the following month.

Coincidentally, Peter O'Connor took his opposition to concentrated urban poverty to a new level. In 2002, O'Connor challenged the allocation of tax credits—funds that reduce builders fees so they can afford to charge lower rents—by the New Jersey Housing and Mortgage Finance Agency

(HMFA).[46] Arguing on behalf of the Southern Burlington and Camden County branches of the NAACP as well as his own Fair Share Housing Center, he charged that disproportionate funding for segregated inner city areas—$12 million of the $16 million awarded—had the effect of maintaining poverty in place. "By totally ignoring the segregative effects of its funding decisions, and by focusing on funding poverty in place," he charged, "HMFA's administration of the federal LIHTC [Low Income Housing Tax Credit] program perpetuates and exacerbates racial segregation in a state that already is one of the most racially segregated in the nation."[47] O'Connor wanted more tax credits directed to the suburbs. HMFA's response strongly contested O'Connor's characterization. It argued both that such funds were necessary to meet housing needs in older cities and that suburban requests for funding were many fewer.[48] Not satisfied with the response, O'Connor filed suit. Frightened at what the loss of funds for inner city redevelopment might do, city officials in Newark as well as the national office of the national low-income housing intermediary Local Initiatives Support Corporation filed in HMFA's defense.

In making his original case against HMFA's allocation plan, O'Connor cited national and state responses to the civil disorders of the late 1960s, including the Kerner Commission report:

Enrichment must be an important adjunct to integration, for no matter how ambitious or energetic the program, few Negroes now living in central cities can be quickly integrated. In the meantime, large scale improvement in the quality of ghetto life is essential. But this can be no more than an interim strategy. Programs must be developed which will permit substantial Negro movement out of the ghettos. The primary goal must be a single society, in which every citizen will be free to live and work according to his capabilities and desires, not his color. The major goal is the creation of a true union—a single society and a single American identity. Toward that goal, we propose the following objective for national action: Opening up opportunities to those who are restricted by racial segregation and discrimination, and eliminating all barriers to their choice of jobs, education and housing.[49]

While the HMFA could counter that contemporary policy demanded investments both to boost those remaining in undesirable inner city conditions and helping at the same time to secure them better opportunities elsewhere, O'Connor argued that the effort to direct resources at the inner city as an "interim strategy" had gone on long enough. From his perspective, the Camden recovery effort should have combined coordinated and substantial assistance—well beyond that provided in the state legislation—to those desiring to stay in the city, including counseling as well as health and other assistance, with a concerted effort to allow those wanting to relocate to do so.[50] In this, there was a basic level of agreement between himself, Nowak, and others who were thinking regionally about the plan. What such thinking came up against, however, was a political bias to address Camden's poverty in place. As such, as the NAACP's Kelly Francis explained in defending his role as a plaintiff in the tax credit case, "All of the poor and the minorities are being warehoused in the cities instead of allowing the wealthier suburban cities to share the burden."[51]

In taking this controversial step, O'Connor acted on criticism leveled most consistently by Myron Orfield, that the failure to make more progress in deconcentrating urban poverty was because so few civil rights organizations were raising the issue as central to a regional agenda. Describing direct confrontation of race as the "hard path" to redevelopment, as compared to "soft path" measures attempting to address poverty in place, Orfield admitted such efforts could be highly controversial. Indeed, an independent assessment of the sustained effort to deconcentrate poverty in Minnesota's Twin Cities suggested how controversial such efforts could be in suburban areas. The very use of the term "deconcentrating poverty," Edward Goetz argues, "gives rise to a politics that is not conducive to regional cooperation, not supportive of low-income populations, and unlikely, in any event, to achieve its stated goals."[52] Orfield disagrees. If cast as providing people of color the same rights as whites and if linked to the self-interest of older suburbs threatened to be overwhelmed with poor leaving the cities, he believes that regional deconcentration of poverty could gain broad support.[53]

In addition to reasserting his unwavering commitment to racial integration, O'Connor's controversial tax credit case represented a further response to the judgment that the court's *Mount Laurel* decisions had failed to achieve their intended result. That position received additional confirmation through a damning July 2003 report issued by the smart growth and environmental advocacy organization, New Jersey Future. Reiterating the New Jersey Supreme Court's determination to assure housing opportunities close to jobs, research director Tim Evans reported that state trends were heading in just the opposite direction. While a dozen state communities—mostly cities with declining economic opportunities—hosted more than half the housing affordable to low income people, the forty-six towns that gained at least two thousand private-sector jobs in the 1990s had only one in twelve affordable homes. Moreover, communities hosting both jobs and affordable housing recorded declining employment. "If the conditions that perpetuate and intensify the need for affordable housing—chronic, concentrated poverty and disappearing jobs—are ever to be ameliorated," the report concluded, "it is critical that lower-income households have access to new job opportunities." Calling for an overhaul in state housing policy, the report proposed quite a different approach from the one O'Connor was embracing. The "growth share" formula it advocated would require affordable housing in conjunction with new commercial and residential development. Under such arrangements, it asserted, "affordable housing goes where growth is going, so that households on the lower end of the income scale are not excluded from newly developing areas and are not kept isolated from new job opportunities." Additionally, the report called for the elimination of Regional Contribution Agreements, describing them as serving "only to perpetuate the concentration of poverty and to widen the spatial divide between new jobs and the low- and moderate-income households who need them."[54]

The timing of the New Jersey Future report was not accidental. Two years earlier, a statewide coalition on affordable housing and the environment had submitted just such a growth share proposal to the Council on Affordable Housing (COAH) for its consideration. The approach owed much to Rutgers-Newark law professor John Payne, a frequent commentator on the *Mount Laurel* decisions, who argued that existing rules determining each community's affordable housing obligation represented both bad politics and bad planning. By shifting the determination of the obligation from projected future development to actual growth, a new formula, he suggested, could be devised that would allow communities greater flexibility in meeting their obligations while at the same time linking housing opportunities with employment growth. Promising to bring assistance both to inner-ring suburbs, through redevelopment, and to growing outer areas, such an approach, he argued, had a reasonable chance of overcoming the political opposition that inevitably arose in every community forced to build more homes than they wanted. "By combining the solid, constitutional 'general welfare' underpinnings of the *Mount Laurel* doctrine with a simpler, more realistic way of calculating fair shares, the growth share approach focuses a moral clarity on the responsibility of local governments for the consequences of their own planning decisions," he wrote. While such an approach did not eliminate entirely the controversial builder's remedy, it shifted the leadership role back to local communities. Moreover, he thought, a variety of programs, including tax credits, would continue to be available to for-profit developers to make such housing possible.[55]

Within weeks of the New Jersey Future report, COAH announced that the new rules it was proposing to govern the next round of fair share housing requirements was based on the growth share concept. Using language similar to Payne's, COAH chair Susan Bass Levin claimed that the obligation to build one affordable unit for every ten new homes or thirty new jobs was a more effective and less contentious way of providing affordable housing while at the same time eliminating inducements for additional sprawl that critics of *Mount Laurel* had charged were brought on by the builder's remedy. The effect of the decision was quite different, however. The 10 percent formula represented a dramatic cutback of the standard one-in-five homes under previous rules that already had fallen well short of need. The new rules also prohibited communities from using tax credits to meet their fair share obligations. Moreover, not only did the new rules retain RCA agreements, they doubled the number of units that could qualify for seniors without children, a preferred practice since such building did not increase school costs through additional enrollments. Under such rules, a community could avoid accommodating any poor or working class families at all by devoting half its obligation to retirement living and relieving the other half through a Regional Contribution Agreement. Fair Share Housing's Kevin Walsh was quick to denounce the proposed regulations for nullifying the *Mount Laurel* decisions, claiming, "It will result in the continued 'ghettoization' of Camden, Trenton and Newark."[56] John Payne was equally appalled by the proposed rules, writing, "Yesterday was a Chinese-curse day. I got what I wished for, and now I pay the consequences."[57]

The proposed rules were subject to comment and change. The fact that COAH was not obligated to act until after the tightly contested legislative elections took place, however, meant that the McGreevey administration had immediately removed a contentious issue from potential suburban opposition. Moreover, the new rules combined with other factors to paint a bleak picture for Camden's lower-income residents. The same day that Levin announced her proposal for revised COAH regulations, a survey of home sales in Camden revealed an accelerated pace of speculation as both individuals and investors bought up vacant properties.[58] Combined with successful efforts to delay any public intercession on behalf of those facing the loss of their homes due to unpaid taxes, the news amounted to a notice to Camden's lower income residents that should they be forced to leave their homes, they were going to have difficulty finding alternatives inside as well as outside the city. The situation Gladys Blair faced as an individual, still seeking alternative housing to her home in the Terraces in Camden, was now writ large for Camden's residents. That reality became ever more evident as the redevelopment process heated up in its second year.

*   *   *

In any ambitious redevelopment effort, even the best of plans fall short of realization or take entirely unanticipated directions. Camden was no exception. The plan to lure Cigna employees from across the Delaware collapsed in the spring of 2004, as had the plan for the 76ers twenty years earlier, when Pennsylvania made a strong counter offer.[59] The South Jersey Builder's League proposal to remake much of South Camden proved more a vision statement than a fully developed plan. Still, within that structure individual companies, encouraged by the city's willingness to designate much of the area for takings through eminent domain, moved on ambitious plans to bring new businesses as well as market-rate housing close to the downtown. The new buildings for both Rutgers and Rowan lagged, though they appeared to be back on track by the time Cigna made its announcement. A $117.2 million expansion of Cooper University Hospital was assured with further funding from the Camden County Improvement Authority.[60] Complete plans issued in December 2003 by the Greater Camden Partnership indicated that even more development could be expected in the downtown, thus confirming the hopes that a critical mass of activity would reestablish the importance of the urban core.[61] Now attention shifted to the neighborhoods, and in contests that followed the true philosophy of recovery as well as its potential effects became clear. The tale can be told in the fate of two areas, Cramer Hill and Waterfront South. Each fronted potentially valuable waterfront property. Each developed ambitious plans, which envisioned both new homes and retail activity as well as environmental remediation. Cramer Hill, however, was designated as a Tier I neighborhood and received priority treatment. Waterfront South, as a Tier II area, was neglected. In neither case were residents pleased with the city's plans. Politics had some influence on what decisions were made, but the most important element proved to be public acquiescence in what private investors were willing to do.

Nestled within a bend of the Cooper River directly above East Camden, Cramer Hill had long been a working-class neighborhood of homes on relatively large lots, which gave the area a suburban feel. As white occupancy gave way to African American and eventually Hispanic domination, the area suffered the effects of disinvestment without being completely devastated. A vacancy rate of about 6 percent was well below that of the rest of the city. Empty lots and a number of abandoned businesses, especially along the waterfront, cried out for organization, however, and this came in the primary instance through the Camden Office of Economic Opportunity, with roots deep in 1960s activism, and especially through the leadership of Thomas Holmes, a development officer for the OEO and longtime former resident of the area. With his assistance, several local institutions banded together in 1997 to form the Cramer Hill Neighborhood Advisory Committee (later a community development corporation). Although the effort acknowledged the North Camden organizing effort as an influence, in spirit it followed a less ideological course, close to that set by Camden Neighborhood Renaissance. A strategic plan, *Cramer Hill Tomorrow*, completed in January 2000, stressed the physical stabilization of homes and increased security; a gateway shopping center close to a light rail stop; and extensive waterfront improvements to convert abandoned industrial, government, and commercial properties to parks and housing. In all, the plan called for investments over a ten year period of $140 million, $54 million of that in private funds.[62] The effort received an early boost from a highly competitive $750,000 grant from Fleet Bank for waterfront redevelopment.[63] With the help of the Cooper's Ferry Development Association, it secured additional funds to establish design guidelines for the area's commercial corridor.[64] It was these efforts, along with its prime waterfront location, that earned the area a Tier I designation and an early call for redevelopment proposals.

The winning bid emerged in December 2003 as a $1.2 billion plan to reconstitute virtually the entire neighborhood around a golf course that would replace a long-abandoned municipal landfill.[65] The plan was personally announced by Governor McGreevey and embraced effusively in the press.[66] In addition to a marina and office complex, it envisioned five thousand new homes, some near the waterfront in the $200,000 range, as well as replacement housing for the twelve hundred families expected to be displaced by the project. A good portion of those designated for relocation occupied public and low-cost rental apartments on the periphery of the neighborhood, where a retail complex of some 500,000 square feet was expected to draw boutique shops, restaurants, and family entertainment. Describing the effort as consistent with the state's smart growth vision, the developer, Cherokee Investment, claimed it would "become a model for urban revival and brownfield development throughout the United States." Promising to assume, with its partners, 90 percent of the estimated project

Figure 30. Demolition Man. Randy Primas as mayor, inspecting a site being cleared. October 20, 1982. Courtesy *Courier-Post*.

costs, the company projected that more than a billion dollars in new assessed property value would follow.[67] Working with the Cramer Hill Community Development Corporation, the city and the COO marshaled a respectful if somewhat concerned audience at an initial public meeting in March 2004. Randy Primas assured the audience right at the start that new homes for anyone who wanted them would be available elsewhere in the neighborhood, along with public access to the waterfront, no gated communities, and use of the golf course. "The relocation issue has everyone concerned," he told the five hundred residents at the meeting, assuring his audience nonetheless, "This is going to be a process of working together."[68]

Just as the Cherokee effort seemed charmed, blessed by its Tier I designation, Waterfront South seemed cursed. This area also solicited a redevelopment plan, again with the encouragement and financial support of Cooper's Ferry. The Waterfront South Strategic Plan, released in July 2003, called both for additional affordable housing and for remediation of the serious environmental problems plaguing the area. The proposal reflected what residents wanted, but many officials worried that it was ambitious and potentially costly. In reality, it was no more ambitious than the Cramer Hill plan, but it came from visionary consultants rather than a developer prepared to make the vision happen. In fact, Randy Primas described the vision as irresponsible because of the environmental costs involved, and in October he informed Sacred Heart's Msgr. Michael Doyle that the city would not sign off on further funds to support rehabilitation efforts in the neighborhood. "I believe it wrong and disingenuous to populate an area where people can't breathe the air, where folks can't sit out back," Primas later explained publicly.[69] Residents were appalled. "Now those great powers that be who, for decades dumped heavy industry on valuable waterfront property and said it wouldn't hurt us, suddenly are saying Waterfront South is unlivable and that there will be no money for remediation—no money for rehabilitation of our neighborhood," the president of South Camden Citizens in Action retorted.[70] Invoking the memory of Heart of Camden's Sister Peg Hynes, Doyle used his February 2004 newsletter to call the alarm to his fifteen hundred readers. "They will kill Sacred Heart. . . . They intend to crush Sister Peg's dream of a neighborhood revived and an environment restored for all the people of South Camden."[71]

As might be expected out of a church so well connected in the area, Doyle and his allies put up a good fight. Seeing its influence over the redevelopment process receding before the power of private investment, CCOP rallied to Waterfront South's defense, bringing some eleven hundred people to gather at the same church where Governor McGreevey had revealed his own recovery plan in 2002 to confront Primas and his position on the area's future prospects. Meeting there only one day before Primas first addressed the Cramer Hill plan in public, CCOP leader and Recovery Board member Rosa Ramirez described the meeting as a "defining moment," explaining that CCOP fought hard to bring these resources to Camden. "We're not going to let our neighborhoods be sold to the highest bidder."[72] Doyle, as expected, tore into Primas, describing his actions as a "rule of tyranny" and charging him with bringing CCMUA and trash-to-steam to the neighborhood and only now becoming concerned about the environmental impact. Clearly uncomfortable with the pressure, sweating as he spoke, Primas nonetheless held his ground. He promised not to bring any new heavy industry into the area, but he did not budge on his decision to deny funding to Heart of Camden's rehabilitation effort. Only when the city council, miffed by its own exclusion from some central decisions affecting redevelopment, held up Primas's request to clear all of Waterfront South as a redevelopment area, did he relent on the smaller issue of releasing funds to

Heart of Camden. Determined to secure that designation in order to have the authority to clear the Terraces area across from New York Ship, he threatened to appeal the council decision to the court master established under the recovery legislation if the neighborhood continued to block his plan.[73] Waterfront South remained a low priority for help.

In the new climate of publicly assisted redevelopment, community-based nonprofits had a hard time competing with proposed development that promised to return significant revenue to the city. No one was more aware of that than Todd Poole, a talented and experienced African American who was named director of economic development for Camden following his role as Governor McGreevey's chief liaison with the recovery legislation before it passed. Both versed in economic development and aware of the history of unwanted social consequences of wholesale redevelopment, Poole wished there had been more time devoted at the start of the process to think through all the elements of the revitalization effort. Once into it, he described lagging social efforts, including employment retraining, as visible problems he might glimpse as in a rear mirror. With all the political pressures to achieve tangible results before the governor stood for reelection, however, he felt he could not turn back lest he be run over from the onrush of development. He was confident much more private investment was coming, but he described the situation as a lot like that faced by the chief American administrator, Paul Bremer, in Iraq: "We're an occupying power from the outside. We have only a short time to get things done. We're bound to be unpopular with local interests. Let's just hope the shooting doesn't begin."[74] Metaphorically, that was already starting to happen.

Despite what appeared to be initial acceptance of the Cherokee proposal in Cramer Hill, the number of people displaced and the radical transformation of the area involved was bound to create dissension, some of it predictably from community activists who had not been consulted in the early process. As opposition signs began to crop up in the neighborhood, those disposed toward the effort blamed disgruntled businessmen who were likely to lose their properties, none more than William Hargrove, whose recycling plant connected to his extensive demolition business in the city was a primary target for taking.[75] But fear and dissatisfaction were deeper than was generally recognized. As neighborhood opposition to the plan mounted, Jeremy Nowak's Reinvestment Fund detailed staff member Graciela Cavicchia to help move the effort along. Working with the Camden Redevelopment Agency, she came to realize that the city had failed to anticipate and deal effectively with community opposition to the redevelopment process. In the month following Primas's appearance, she considered it too late to get the community to buy into the plan. At best, she hoped to make the developer sensitive to community concerns. At the last moment, she managed to get some details about relocation into the preliminary redevelopment plan, a move she hoped would ease community concerns.

With Primas continuing to insist that the project be approved as a test, "whether we intend to go forward or keep the status quo," community dissent finally spilled out in May when the redevelopment agency presented its proposal to the city's planning board to designate all of Cramer Hill a renewal area.[76] What might normally have attracted a dozen or so citizens for comment drew three hundred and fifty, half of whom had to wait outside City Hall for a chance to speak. The meeting lasted so long it could not be reported in the next morning's papers, and another hearing had to be scheduled for the following week. Held this time in Cramer Hill, the second meeting attracted six hundred residents, many of them listening in Spanish translation. In presenting the case for redevelopment, director of neighborhood planning Charles Lyons admitted the survey taken to determine neighborhood conditions was not done at a professional standard and that the designation of only 4 percent of the homes in the area as "good" was too low. Mistakenly pointing to the area's designation as a state enterprise zone as an adequate justification for renewal,[77] he fended off repeated criticisms from the audience that the area was not blighted. After hearing a host of speakers denounce the plan, including long-time white as well as black and Hispanic residents and several businesses that had been in Camden for more than one hundred years, the board voted to approve the renewal designation. The vote was delayed slightly when one member of the board asked what the issue was. Despite having sat in the dark through two hours of testimony, he joined other board members in approving the renewal designation. Only one board member dissented by abstaining.

In the second part of the meeting, to take up the redevelopment plan, Charles Lyons claimed that it built on the city's master plan as well as the community-based *Cramer Hill Tomorrow* plan by bringing to the area new homes, businesses, employment and recreation activities. He did not answer criticism from the audience that the earlier Cramer Hill plan had consciously sought to avoid displacement. Nor did he acknowledge that the Cramer Hill Neighborhood Advisory Committee had removed from its original recommendations the demolition of the Ablett Village public housing complex now just so designated under the redevelopment proposal.[78] To deal with displacement, Lyons repeated earlier promises made by Randy

Primas and the mayor that every resident would be guaranteed replacement housing at equal or better value and outlined how relocation would proceed, following Cavicchia's outline. Rehabilitation and replacement housing would be built first in the lower section of the neighborhood. Residents living near the north waterfront area could then move south before their area was cleared and rebuilt. This scheme, however, would involve massive subsidies, including $280 million for residential housing, at least $100 million of which was expected to come in the form of tax credits from the New Jersey Housing and Home Finance Agency. Although news accounts had previously emphasized tax benefits from anticipated private investment, they failed to report the public funds necessary to make the Cherokee investment possible. Now, the planners' own report revealed that total to be in excess of $1.2 billion. The same document failed to specify any level of private investment, a figure that still needed to be negotiated with developers.[79] Although a few speakers, including a representative of the community development corporation, spoke up for the plan, the overall reaction was hostile. Summing up the five-hour meeting, Cramer Hill resident Carmen Ubarry Rivera charged that the board was "shredding people's lives." Added long-time activist Roy Jones, "It was obvious they (the board) didn't take the people into consideration. These are people in office to serve us, but they're serving some other interests."[80] Incongruously, the president of Cherokee, who did not attend the meeting, responded with a letter appearing afterward in the *Courier-Post* seeking resident input to the plan. Approached by the *Inquirer*, he declared that "If there were enough opposition, we would abandon it. We're not in the business of stuffing things down people's throats."[81] Now the planning board had done just that.

One hurdle yet remained before the Cramer Hill plan could be put into effect: approval by Camden City Council. In the weeks intervening between the planning board and council votes, the plan's supporters mounted an aggressive advocacy campaign, including advertisements in Spanish print and radio outlets and meetings with individual opponents of the effort. When a much smaller crowd showed up for the final council hearing and vote at a downtown location, Randy Primas remarked that residents must have come to accept the plan. Nothing in the public comments before the vote supported that view. Not only did Cramer Hill residents, with a single exception, adamantly oppose the proposal, speakers from other neighborhoods, fearing similar renewal efforts where they lived, joined the criticism. Following more than an hour's testimony, only councilman Sloan El raised any questions about the proposal. Without further consideration of the public comments or copies of criticisms submitted for the record, the council voted, with only Sloan El dissenting, to approve the plan.[82]

There would still be many details to work out before the Cramer Hill plan could be realized. What its proponents had for the moment was an important precedent in clearing the way for wholesale renewal. In that triumph, planners harked back to the unsuccessful "City Within a City" plan of the 1960s. Also evident was the belief, apparently unchanged over a generation, that wholesale redevelopment was necessary to attract the middle class. Removal of existing housing and the incorporation of a golf course as a buffer to the wealthiest homes were intended to do just that, at current residents' expense. If anything had changed over the generation, planners were more sensitive to their obligation to accommodate those forced to relocate. In this, they faced major obstacles, however. A brief submitted to the planning board at its first meeting in May by South Jersey Legal Services pointed out that plans to demolish Ablett Village, when combined with other conversions of public units to mixed-use, would reduce the number of units available to low-income residents by half. The Bush administration's determination to freeze funding for housing vouchers made it unlikely that the large number of people requiring subsidized housing in the open market would find the help they needed. The critique identified both the inadequacy of planning for relocation and the failure to conform with the *Mount Laurel* requirement that municipalities use their zoning powers "consistent with general welfare."[83] Matters were only made worse by a parallel trend in the older suburbs toward reducing the number of affordable housing units. Lindenwold provided a case in point.

Concerned about the declining state of older rental apartments, Lindenwold officials embraced their own draconian redevelopment plan to permit the acquisition and demolition of some two thousand apartments. Despite the strong opposition to displacement expressed by many residents and by Robert Barhum, the town's lone African American councilman, the planning board decided to replace the complex with a mix of homes, stores, and offices. Drawing on a "smart growth" rationale and claiming that the decision was not "against people" but against the bad planning that had located so many apartments close to the PATCO Speedline terminus in the late 1960s, Mayor Frank DeLucca, Jr., sought to create an attractive destination like the successful main street areas of Collingswood and Haddonfield.[84] Affected were 2,200 apartments and condominiums. African American and Hispanic residents faced displacement out of proportion to their presence in the town. Although Mayor DeLucca adamantly denied any prejudice on his part, the effect of moving out minorities prompted more than one charge of "racial cleansing." Certainly the process paralleled the situation in the 1960s that led critics to describe urban renewal as black removal. The reasons were much the same, even if the location had shifted. Older, less desirable housing also tended to be more affordable, thus drawing those with limited incomes. As ghettos formed, they became targets for renewal. The twenty-first-century version of this process pitted older suburbs against newer, expanding suburban areas in a contest for ratables which Myron Orfield, at least, would describe as unwinnable. Lindenwold was certainly not alone in its dilemma as similar efforts proceeded in nearby Mount Holly and in the Ventnor area just outside of Atlantic City.[85]

Despite the obvious problems in Lindenwold and elsewhere, the Mc-Greevey administration continued to cling to its inadequate affordable housing strategy. Opposition from housing advocates continued, however. Peter O'Connor finally secured through the courts 214 units of affordable housing out of 1,659 units planned in the Garden State Park's redevelopment in Cherry Hill, but he lost his case to redirect tax credits toward the suburbs.[86] The court ruled that even if the disproportionate allocation of tax credits to distressed urban areas had a discriminatory effect in further concentrating minorities there, the legislative intent in forming the Home Mortgage and Finance Agency to serve the lowest income tenants in qualified census tracts overrode other considerations. Most pertinent to Camden's situation, the court applauded HMFA incentives to encourage mixed income housing in cities through the HOPE VI program to reconstruct public housing, commenting:

Urban revitalization programs, including programs that replace dilapidated low-income housing with mixed-income housing, should promote integration in the long run and make our cities vibrant communities for people of all races and economic means. . . . Upgrade of housing stock in cities, combined with commercial endeavors, should spark eventual gentrification and return to the cities of higher-economic people of all races.[87]

Integration was to be served, then, by bringing middle class people into the city, not facilitating the relocation of African Americans or Hispanics to suburban locations. What was to happen to those displaced by urban renewal, the court did not say.

Clearly the latest recovery effort was not simply a revival of earlier initiatives. It was both more comprehensive and better funded as well as more centralized through the introduction of the Chief Operating Officer. With powers centralized over both land reclamation and redevelopment Randy Primas gained tools he might have wished for but did not have when he served as mayor. The latest effort offered the promise of finally getting the job done. To say this happened without the county Democratic Party taking a lead role would have been naive. It took a while, but in the spring of 2004 the last elements fell into place when city council finally granted Primas's request to chair the redevelopment agency, and the school board, with new appointments offered by the mayor, reorganized under county control.[88] Now clearly, the genius of Randy Primas's appointment as COO was apparent. His association with George Norcross was anything but a detriment. With the governor's ratings in the polls remaining very low throughout most of his term, it was Norcross, many believed, who would be around for the long run and whose power to make things happen could be counted on. With his close ties to South Jersey's premier power broker, Primas wielded authority not just as COO but as the primary influence on the city's revamped redevelopment agency.[89] With proposals to create numerous redevelopment areas before him, each one complete with powers of eminent domain and each the target of a tax recovery program,[90] Primas could determine as much as one billion dollars in contracts. In the process, he was in a position to remake much of the physical city. What did this mean in the larger arena of urban redevelopment?

Clearly, the convergence of political control rooted in the suburbs with a successful effort to generate interest in reinvestment tipped the balance for recovery towards the first of the three approaches to renewal. The greatest economic as well as political returns were not in the incremental approach offered by nonprofit organizations. Although interest existed for extending the concept of regional equity, organizers still faced a major hurdle to get suburban leaders to commit to efforts that would make their towns additional sites for relocating some of the area's poorer residents. Notably, an effort to marshal help for Camden from the Jewish suburban population, much of it with direct roots in the city, focused on what could be done in the city, not close to home. The resulting direction of recovery, shaped nationally by a reduction in money and support for a vigorous public sector, was a "partnership" that gave much to the private sector and minimized appreciation for what "the courageous civic organizations," as a 1993 *Courier-Post* editorial had called them, had done to prepare the way for recovery.[91]

Among those who could still speak hopefully about the process was Camden County Freeholder-Director Jeffrey Nash. He spelled out his expectations for the city by remembering how his first exposure to Camden's distress had come when he viewed the 1983 *Sixty Minutes* program, "Father Doyle's Camden." "It is my prediction," he wrote in the *Courier-Post*'s special section looking to the future, "that in 2015, *60 Minutes* will return to Camden to report on a city revitalization that will serve as the national model for urban renewal. Camden will be emerging as South Jersey's economic engine once more. A middle-class foundation will take root and will stand alongside residents working hard to participate in and benefit from the recovery. And Monsignor Doyle's prayers for success will have become prayers of thanks."[92]

In practice, this was hard to achieve. Many Camden residents rightly feared that Camden might be "saved" at their expense. Yet, the fact that physical construction and market revitalization advanced at the expense of securing greater means of social equity should not have been surprising. For this latter challenge remained the single most difficult issue before metropolitan America in the new century. Powerful patterns of public as well as private action had entrenched suburban privilege for over a generation. As Peter Schuck writes, "Although racism's extent and intensity have declined markedly in recent decades, the residential patterns it produced have great staying power. Because people make large investments in their housing and plan to occupy it for many years, the effects of individual, group, and neighborhood choices may persist much longer than the racial attitudes that originally influenced them."[93] Without the kind of tax sharing Myron Orfield and other supporters of regional equity have advocated, it remained rational, apart from any racial reasons, for wealthier communities to resist dilution of their local tax base by discouraging residents who would consume more in services than they would repay in taxes.[94] As long as inequality of place remained protected in law and sustained by popular and political opinion, then, the poor would continue to suffer disproportionately.

Conclusion

Taking issue with a Cramer Hill residents organization that was suing the city to prevent the reconstruction of its community, the *Courier-Post* acknowledged the validity of its concerns about displacement, about designating good homes "blighted," and about "the callousness of the process involved." The paper pointed, however, to the project's potential in tax ratables and for "effecting economic revival." Camden's chief executive, the paper asserted, "cares about the homeowners." But his concern was greater. "The committee is trying to save homes and he is trying to save a city."[1] The project in question was not Cherokee Investment's, but a proposal from a Philadelphia developer to create a new "City Within a City." The executive was Al Pierce, not Randy Primas. The year was 1966, and yet almost forty years later history seemed to be repeating itself. Could so little have changed?

In fact, over a generation much had changed, both in Camden and nationally. After reaching new heights of commitment to addressing urban problems in the 1960s, the federal government had virtually abandoned any effort to reverse the fortunes of cities besieged by social and economic restructuring. Because even the most liberal challenges to concentrated poverty had been fleeting and inadequate, activists had few foundations to build on. As influence over policy affecting their lives shifted to the states and, increasingly, to the private sector, they were forced to adapt. As a consequence, black militance no longer presented the chief challenge to privately induced development and redevelopment. African Americans took a more pragmatic turn, and in this Randy Primas could be described as only a little ahead of his time. By the late twentieth century even black critics were embracing revenue-building strategies over the more ideologically driven social welfare practices embraced by the first generation of black big-city mayors.[2] Neighborhood-based organizations, deprived of federal subsidies available only briefly during the Great Society, adjusted as well. They became less ideological and willing to form partnerships with the private sector themselves. Their most important legacy, community development corporations, Robert Halpern reports, proved "to be a relatively flexible and enduring strategy," capable of attracting capital back to inner city neighborhoods and demonstrating "how investment can address social as well as individual needs."[3]

Pragmatism had its rewards. Despite the lack of federal funding available for urban renewal, community as well as downtown organizations found new ways to attract new investment. These successes prompted the optimistic view at the start of the new century that the nation's post-industrial cities were experiencing renewal at last. In one city after another—Cleveland with its waterfront development including the Rock and Roll Hall of Fame, Newark with its performing arts center, Trenton with construction of a new hotel complex—such investments were considered sure signs that prosperity would ripple through the city as a whole. Supporters of New Jersey's recovery legislation for Camden spoke confidently of adding the city to the list of "comeback cities." Both by creating funds to leverage private investment and by concentrating power in the position of the Chief Operating Officer over management as well as redevelopment, they hoped to overcome decades of inaction and ineptitude.

For Camden, as for other cities David Rusk has labeled "beyond the point of no return," such hopes, to date, have proved illusory. Even as modern physical improvements have helped banish entrenched images of decline and decay, they have failed to alter the position that left these older cities—downtown as well as in their neighborhoods—weakened elements in their larger metropolitan regions. The changes at hand have not been sufficient either to restore central cities to the primacy they once had or to materially lift the fortunes of their residents. As David Perry points out, citing Buffalo's experience, once corporate ownership locates outside a city and that city's resources fail to attract capital investment on its own, such areas require increasingly generous public subsidies. The worse the situation, the more expansive the incentive offered to private investors. "Indeed," Perry writes, "most forms of economic development policy and planning deliberately eschew any direct distributional or equity issues. The conditions of deindustrialization and economic distress are viewed as evidence in the United States of a lack of attention to the needs of capital. Profit, and not equity, is the issue of the day in contemporary urban America."[4]

Not surprisingly, Camden followed the same trajectory in its recovery efforts. To keep General Electric in the state, New Jersey underwrote its new facility on the Camden waterfront. To build an entertainment center, the state relieved the Sony partnership of paying any taxes for a decade. To eliminate the annual subsidies required to maintain the New Jersey Aquarium as an educational facility, the state virtually gave it away to for-profit investors intent on converting it to family entertainment. Such efforts could not provide anything but trickle-down benefits, as repeated claims for the waterfront demonstrated. In the dozen years since the aquarium's opening launched a new era of waterfront redevelopment, Camden residents had attained only 150 full time positions throughout the entire complex of new institutions.[5] Associated claims under the recovery legislation for Camden's educational and hospital institutions were similarly expansive but lacking in plans to make new employment—especially for poorer residents—probable. Instead of lifting the fortunes of the poor, "recovery" represented quite the contrary. As plans for Cramer Hill showed so starkly, advantage always went to the investor, whose insistence in this case that the environment be so fully upgraded for middle income residents required that more than one thousand existing residents would have to move. Similar prospects lay in store for residents in the Bergen and Lanning Square neighborhoods located near the waterfront.[6] Refusal to direct public resources to Waterfront South, where no private investment for housing was available, represented the other side of the same coin. Long the victims of a regional imbalance in resources, residents of beleaguered cities like Camden were unlikely to succeed without a basic change in rules, or as Rusk puts it, a rewiring of the down escalator that makes it so difficult for the poor and their communities to move up.

Major changes, such as forming regional governance structures and effecting property tax reform, come slowly, as a number of accounts have indicated.[7] Politicians necessarily demand quick results, in line with election cycles, not with long-term objectives. To have expected the recovery legislation to have embraced radical changes that would have challenged New Jersey's fierce commitment to home rule in particular was unrealistic. Few politicians of either party wished to challenge the existing imbalance in resources, for fear of the kind of firestorm that had resulted in California and elsewhere when suburban residents were asked to pay for the consequences of uneven development, either in the form of higher taxes or subsidies to promote open housing.[8] Indeed, the legislation as effected did everything it could to assure suburbanites that they would not have to encounter displaced Camden residents suddenly showing up in their communities. That is why the Cramer Hill plan was so telling. Despite the strain on public resources, the city's Chief Operating Officer was promising to accommodate all those displaced nearby. That his audience was not just Cramer Hill but the larger metropolitan area was revealed months earlier when the chief of neighborhood planning laid out the plan for residential revitalization. For those displaced in prime development areas, alternative housing would be created in rehabilitated structures in Parkside, Centerville, and Fairview as well as a designated area of Cramer Hill.[9] This would be renewal without the massive displacement of the 1960s. But could it be? And what chances were lost in advancing such a strategy?

As the Cramer Hill plan also indicated, successful redevelopment required high levels of public subsidy as well as private investment. Even should public resources be found for such a massive project of relocating those displaced, how might it be said that the lives of residents would be better? Neither levels of funding for training nor for the infusion of jobs accessible to those of limited education were sufficient to meet the city's high unemployment rate. Simply rehoused, especially in highly segregated areas, the prospects for improving their life's chances did not appear materially better.

Rusk has placed his hope beyond established politics. He is an enthusiast for church-based coalitions because they can add a moral dimension to planning debates that too often can be mired in dry, technical language. More broadly, he perceives the emergence of a new citizens movement. "By the mid-1960s, the civil rights movement had succeeded in changing the rules in order to advance the cause of racial opportunity," he writes. "By the mid-1970s the environmental movement had succeeded in changing the rules in order to advance the cause of clean air and water and to protect endangered animals and plant life from extinction." Now the civil rights and environmental movements were merging as a regional movement: "The issues of social stewardship and environmental stewardship are inextricably interwoven. The connecting link is America's environmentally and socially destructive land development patterns. To win today's civil rights battles as well as today's environmental battles one needs to change the same set of rules."[10]

Rusk made just such a case in Camden, speaking at the annual meeting of the Fund for an Open Society in October 2004. Joined by Myron Orfield at the same auditorium in which he had addressed the South Jersey Summit in 1999, Rusk reiterated the need for a new regional balance sheet, where affordable housing could be found throughout the area, not just concentrated in Camden and a few older suburbs nearby. That evening more than five hundred people allied with faith-based organizations throughout South

Jersey gathered in Cherry Hill to present the case to city and state representatives, not just for improving the rules governing the *Mount Laurel* affordable housing decisions, but also for reforming a system that assured unequal returns to communities of varying wealth through heavy reliance on
property taxes. That meeting, organized with Ford Foundation support,
represented the first prominent effort locally of the New Jersey Regional
Coalition to demonstrate its political influence on behalf of regional equity.
As its third issue, organizers demanded that the regional impact council
required in the Camden recovery bill be formed within thirty days. Here
was the chance, finally, to force Camden's recovery effort to address the
larger context of the city's decline.[11]

Within weeks, Assemblyman Joseph Roberts redeemed the pledge his
representative made that night by calling the first meeting of the regional
impact council. As had been previously rumored, the new organization assumed as its core the group of suburban mayors who had been meeting for
several years under a smart growth grant to the Camden County Freeholders. Known as the Hub group for their proximity to Camden, council members chose one of their own number, Collingswood Mayor James Maley, as
chair, thereby also making him their representative on Camden's Economic
Recovery Board.[12] Known for his skill in prompting the revival of his town's
commercial sector, Maley was hardly likely to advance an equity strategy. A
member, with George Norcross's brother, in a politically connected law
firm and an advisor to aggressive redevelopment efforts in Lindenwold and
other older suburbs, he could be counted on to define smart growth in
terms of economic redevelopment. Once again, the limits of electoral politics showed, but the alternative of court action remained.

Because of its formation more than two years after passage of the
Camden recovery initiative, the regional impact council had not been available to review the recovery plan submitted to the Economic Recovery
Board, as required by the legislation, nor had it been represented on that
board in subsequent decisions on grants. Pointing to that violation of legislative intent, the same legal services office that brought Alfred Pierce's
urban renewal program to a halt in the 1960s sued the state to stop the
Cramer Hill plan. The Camden Legal Services complaint, filed on behalf
of a new citywide organization of neighborhood representatives, Camden
United, cited the same failures in planning that had plagued earlier redevelopment efforts: inadequate resources for replacement housing, failure to
take into account citizen concerns, and violation of existing laws as well as
statutory authority. Like the lawsuits against St. Lawrence Cement and

Mount Laurel before them, this complaint sought a commitment to social justice not incorporated into campaigns for private investment. Although the suit naturally focused on Camden, by citing among its chief complaints the state's failure to create the regional impact council it forced the issue of regional planning.[13] Similar suits filed concurrently in suburban Mount Holly and Lindenwold, where predominantly minority residents also faced displacement to make way for new development, further highlighted the regional nature of the issue.

As the results of the *Mount Laurel* decisions have revealed, even the most progressive courts find it virtually impossible to engineer social changes that majorities do not embrace. Even if this latest lawsuit succeeded, it remained to be seen what remedies would be offered to incorporate the primary needs of residents into the planning process. Such legal action did, however, provide yet one more confirmation of a reality that has too often been ignored in contemporary discourse: people of modest means are neither passive about their fate nor incapable of asserting their hopes for achieving a decent life. They may not know the particulars, but they are aware of the promise, enshrined as far back as the National Housing Act of 1949, that every citizen have a decent home in a suitable living environment. It is the same American dream that motivated generations of immigrants before them. Their organizational efforts in Camden to grow resident assets, to reverse the environmental degradation that has been brought on by policy decisions not of their own making, and to counter crime and exploitation runs counter to every conservative stereotype propagated over the last quarter century. Once such efforts are recognized for the positive contributions they are, policymakers can proceed with building on them rather than pursuing programs that pretend these human resources either do not matter or do not exist.

Camden's situation is not much different from that of many other cities similarly burdened by years of disinvestment. The desperateness of their social as well as their physical conditions may be exaggerated in the press and in popular imagination, but there is little doubt that they are inferior to the condition of neighboring suburban jurisdictions. Those who live in declining cities may well choose to do so for rational as well as emotional reasons offering them shelter at acceptable prices and tying them to family and friends. But the conditions they encounter every day would be unacceptable to most Americans. Many who have had the means have moved away, not just decades ago but on a continuing basis. In New Jersey, two court decisions affirmed that it was in the best interest of the public welfare to facilitate access to alternative locations offering rich opportunities for affordable housing, education, security, and environmental amenities. Taken to a logical extreme such efforts, if successful, without complementary urban reinvestment, would empty out declining cities. Such efforts, however, have been sharply limited. Camden's recent experience provides more evidence why.

Clearly, it is no longer productive to speak simply about gilding the ghetto or dispersing it, as has been argued from the time of the Kerner Commission report of 1968. Disinvestment and its effects on individuals is not an isolated problem. It is embedded in metropolitan frameworks that have changed dramatically over the past half century. Comprehensive renewal efforts must seek to improve both the fiscal imbalance of cities and the access of all citizens to the larger framework of regional economic opportunities. In Camden, full recovery would thus direct resources toward improving options for current residents even as it sought to attract middle class residents back to the city. That has not happened to date. Seeking new investment without assuring that it lifts the fortunes of residents as well as the place where they live represents only half the equation. Alternatives have been posed for a more equitable outcome. It will be up to those outside the current system of power and prevailing decision making to make that happen. If it does, Camden will represent not just one more failed policy initiative but a national model for future renewal efforts.

Note on Sources

During the course of this work, I have gathered material from a number of sources, including files which *Courier-Post* journalist Kevin Riordan and Professor Robert Beauregard collected for their own reporting on Camden. I have consolidated these materials and put them on deposit at the Camden County Historical Society. They are arranged topically as part of the Gillette Camden Collection and referred to in the text by file name and location with the abbreviation CCHS.

References to the *Philadelphia Inquirer* refer to the New Jersey edition after 1996. Some articles cited in this work may not appear in the Pennsylvania editions. When articles have appeared in the Sunday New Jersey section of the *New York Times*, I have so indicated in the note. Otherwise, articles cited appear in the national edition of the paper.

Notes

Preface

1. William Dean Howells, *Hazard of New Fortunes* (1890; reprint, Blooming-ton: Indiana University Press, 1976), 66, cited in Amy Kaplan, *The Social Construction of American Realism* (Chicago: University of Chicago Press, 1988), 50.

2. *Philadelphia Inquirer*, April 21, 2004; *Courier-Post*, April 25, 2004.

Introduction

1. For background as well as cogent criticism of the limitations of the War on Poverty, see Michael B. Katz, *The Undeserving Poor: From the War on Poverty to the War on Welfare* (New York: Pantheon Books, 1989), Chapter 3. See especially Katz's conclusion on page 91, that among the most debilitating contradictions in the effort "was the translation of a structural analysis of poverty into a service-based strategy."

2. Kerner Commission, *Report of the National Advisory Commission on Civil Disorders* (New York: Bantam, 1968), 1.

3. See, for example, Paul S. Grogran and Tony Proscio, *Comeback Cities: A Blueprint for Urban Neighborhood Revival* (Boulder, Colo.: Westview Press, 2000).

4. Douglas S. Massey and Nancy A. Denton, *American Apartheid: Segregation and the Making of the Underclass* (Cambridge, Mass.: Harvard University Press, 1993), 2.

5. Sheryll Cashin, *The Failures of Integration: How Race and Class Are Undermining the American Dream* (New York: Public Affairs Council, 2004), xvi. See also the extensive report in the *Philadelphia Inquirer*, "The Great Divide," May 16–19, 2004.

6. David Rusk, *Cities Without Suburbs* (Washington, D.C.: Woodrow Wilson Center Press, 1995), 76–77; comments and tables submitted in the summer of 2003 as part of a brief challenging the State of New Jersey's allocation of tax credits, courtesy Kevin Walsh, Fair Share Housing Center. Although eleven of the twenty-four cities on Rusk's list closed the income gap with their suburbs in the prosperous 1990s, another dozen cities declined significantly enough to qualify for an expanded list. Only Chicago, among those originally listed, could truly qualify as a "comeback city." Camden, Newark, and Trenton all continued to decline in all three categories.

"These three (along with Hartford, East St. Louis, and Benton Harbor [Michigan]) share the cellar of American cities," he concluded.

7. See Katz, *Undeserving Poor*, 137–65, covering such important tracts as George Gilder, *Wealth and Poverty* (New York: Basic Books, 1982) and Charles Murray, *Losing Ground: American Social Policy, 1950–1980* (New York: Basic Books, 1984).

8. Norman Fainstein, "Black Ghettoization and Social Mobility," in Michael Peter Smith and Joe R. Feagin, eds., *The Bubbling Cauldron: Race, Ethnicity, and the Urban Crisis* (Minneapolis: University of Minnesota Press, 1995), 137. For the origins of the term "underclass," see Herbert J. Gans, *The War Against the Poor: The Underclass and Antipoverty Policy* (New York: Basic Books, 1995), Chapter 2, "The Formation of the Underclass Label," 27–57. For a summary of the "underclass" debate, see Michael B. Katz, "The Urban 'Underclass' as a Metaphor of Social Transformation," in Katz, ed., *The "Underclass" Debate: Views from History* (Princeton, N.J.: Princeton University Press, 1993), 3–23, and Alice O'Connor, *Poverty Knowledge: Social Science, Social Policy, and the Poor in Twentieth-Century U.S. History* (Princeton, N.J.: Princeton University Press, 2001), especially Chapter 10. See also Lawrence Mead's attack on a "culture of dependency," *The New Politics of Poverty: The Nonworking Poor in America* (New York: Basic Books, 1993). According to a forthcoming study from Carl Nightingale at the University of Buffalo, this book had a major impact on the debate that culminated in the 1996 welfare legislation, which forced long-term welfare recipients into the workforce.

9. See Jonathan Rieder, *Canarsie: The Jews and Italians of Brooklyn Against Liberalism* (Cambridge, Mass.: Harvard University Press, 1985), especially Chapter 4, "The Lost People," 95–131.

10. Fred Siegel, *The Future Once Happened Here: New York, D.C., L.A., and the Fate of America's Big Cities* (New York: Free Press, 1997). Siegel wrote as a prominent member of the Manhattan Institute, which had helped subsidize and promote Charles Murray's *Losing Ground* and provided advice and support to Republican Rudy Giuliani in his successful campaigns and in his terms as mayor of New York. See also Heather Thompson's discussion of the work of Jim Sleeper and Jonathan Rieder, as well as Siegel, "Rethinking the Politics of White Flight in the Postwar City: Detroit, 1945–1980," *Journal of Urban History* 25 (January 1999): 165–66.

11. See the essays included in Gregory D. Squires, ed., *Organizing Access to Capital: Advocacy and the Democratization of Financial Institutions* (Philadelphia: Temple University Press, 2003), and the *New York Times*, March 17, October 22, 24, 1999.

12. Sugrue points especially to tensions within rights-based liberalism in the area of housing. "In cities like Detroit," he writes, "social reformers and federal officials fought to erect public housing sufficient to meet the needs of those whom the market failed to serve. But public housing advocates were repeatedly stymied by homeowners who asserted their own interpretation of New Deal social policy. They demanded that the government privilege the stability of their homeownership, over and above its support for public housing." Thomas J. Sugrue, *The Origins of the Urban Crisis: Race and Inequality in Postwar Detroit* (Princeton, N.J.: Princeton University Press, 1996), 59.

13. Lizabeth Cohen, *A Consumer's Republic: The Politics of Mass Consumption in Postwar America* (New York: Knopf, 2003).

14. Peter H. Schuck, *Diversity in America: Keeping Government at a Safe Distance* (Cambridge, Mass.: Belknap Press, 2004), 205.

15. David Dante Troutt, "Ghettoes Made Easy: The Metamarket/Antimarket Dichotomy and the Legal Challenges of Inner City Economic Development," *Harvard Civil Rights-Civil Liberties Law Review* 35 (Summer 2000): 429, 432–33.

16. Paul A. Jargowsky, *Poverty and Place: Ghettos, Barrios, and the American City* (New York: Russell Sage Foundation, 1997), 144, 48. Also relevant to Jargowsky's conclusion is the work of William Julius Wilson, including *When Work Disappears: the World of the New Urban Poor* (New York: Knopf, 1996), especially Chapter 3, "Ghetto-Related Behavior and the Structure of Opportunity," 51–86.

17. Massy and Denton, *American Apartheid*, 8.

18. Myron Orfield, "Comment on Scott A. Bollens's 'In Through the Back Door: Social Equity and Regional Governance,'" *Housing Policy Debate* 13, 4 (2003): 663.

19. Andrew Wiese, *Places of Their Own: African American Suburbanization in the Twentieth Century* (Chicago: University of Chicago Press), 255. The most optimistic reading of this trend appears in Stephan and Abigail Thernstrom, *America in Black and White: One Nation, Indivisible* (New York: Simon and Schuster, 1997), especially Chapter 8, "Cities and Suburbs," which challenges specifically the dire predictions of the Kerner Commission. Wiese's study, along with Myron Orfield's *American Metropolitics: The New Suburban Reality* (Washington, D.C.: Brookings Institution Press, 2002), provide a much starker picture of metropolitan separation by race and income. Even open housing legislation, because it is based on the ability to pay regardless of race, has contributed further to the isolation of the poor, as those who could afford alternative locations left the inner city. See Wendell E. Pritchett, "Where Shall We Live? Class and the Limitations of Fair Housing Law," *Urban Lawyer* 35 (Summer 2003): 399–470.

20. New regionalism is defined by Sherryl D. Cashin in "Localism, Self-Interest, and the Tyranny of the Favored Quarter: Addressing the Barriers to New Regionalism," *Georgetown Law Journal* 33 (July 2000): 2028, as "any attempt to develop regional governance structures or intralocal cooperative agreements that better distribute regional benefits and burdens."

21. See Neal R. Peirce, *Citistates: How Urban America Can Prosper in a Competitive World* (Washington, D.C.: Seven Locks Press, 1993); William H. Barnes and Larry Ledebur, *The New Regional Economics: The U.S. Common Market and the Global Economy* (Newbury Park, Calif.: Sage, 1997); and Peter Calthorpe and William Fulton, *The Regional City: Planning for the End of Sprawl* (Washington, D.C.: Island Press, 2001).

22. Manuel Pastor, Jr., Peter Dreier, J. Eugene Grigsby III, and Marta López-Garza, *Regions that Work: How Cities and Suburbs Can Grow Together* (Minneapolis: University of Minnesota Press, 2000), 15, 95, citing Joan Walsh, *Stories of Renewal: Community Building and the Future of Urban America* (New York: Rockefeller Foundation, 1997), iv. In making the connection between bonding and bridging, Pastor and his associates parallel the discussion of social capital addressed by Robert

Putnam, *Bowling Alone: The Collapse and Revival of American Community* (New York: Simon and Schuster, 2000), 22–23, which I take up in Chapter 1.

23. Pastor et al., *Regions That Work*, 8, 182.

24. John Goering and Judith D. Feins, *Choosing a Better Life? Evaluating the Moving to Opportunity Social Experiment* (Washington, D.C.: Urban Institute Press, 2003), 27–29, 383.

25. Pastor et al., *Regions That Work*, 16; Al Gore, Foreword to Bruce Katz, ed., *Reflections on Regionalism* (Washington, D.C.: Brookings Institution Press, 2000), ix–x.

26. Myron Orfield, *Metropolitics: A Regional Agenda for Community and Stability* (Washington, D.C.: Brookings Institution Press, 1997), chapter 7, 104–55.

27. Orfield, *American Metropolitics*, 153.

28. Edward Goetz, *Clearing the Way: Deconcentrating the Poor in Urban America* (Washington, D.C.: Urban Institute Press, 2003), 107–11.

29. U.S. Department of Housing and Urban Development, *The State of the Cities 2000: Megaforces Shaping the Future of the Nation's Cities* (Washington, D.C.: Department of Housing and Urban Development, 2000), Table 4, "Doubly Burdened Central Cities"; Rusk, *Cities Without Suburbs*, 76–77.

30. Reported in *Courier-Post*, November 11, 1999. See also the editorial, November 9, 1999.

31. See Primas's essay, "Regional Cooperation Is the Key to Reviving Camden—and the Region," *Courier-Post*, April 30, 2000.

32. Telephone interview, February 16, 2004.

33. Sugrue, *Origins of the Urban Crisis*.

34. Wendell Pritchett, *Brownsville, Brooklyn: Blacks, Jews, and the Changing Face of the Ghetto* (Chicago: University of Chicago Press, 2002); Jefferson Cowie and Joseph Heathcott, eds., *Beyond the Ruins: The Meanings of Deindustrialization* (Ithaca, N.Y.: Cornell University Press, 2003) provides further testimony to common themes of urban decline in a number of disparate places, from Oakland, to Youngstown, to Atlantic City

35. Robert O. Self, *American Babylon: Race and the Struggle for Postwar Oakland* (Princeton, N.J.: Princeton University Press, 2003).

36. I made this the basis of a conference held at Rutgers-Camden April 22, 2001, and associated web site (camdencommunity.rutgers.edu) that highlighted community building strategies on either side of the disinvestment divide.

Chapter 1. A City That Worked

Epigraph: Camden Chamber of Commerce, *Camden, New Jersey: the City's Rise and Growth* (Philadelphia: Shelton Company, 1904).

1. Alan Ehrenhalt, *The Lost City: The Forgotten Virtues of Community in America* (New York: Basic Books, 1995).

2. Robert B. Putnam, *Bowling Alone: The Collapse and Revival of American Community* (New York: Simon and Schuster, 2000), especially 18–25. For a discus-

sion of the origins of the term and its contemporary use, see Robert E. Lang and Steven P. Hornburg, "What Is Social Capital and Why Is It Important to Public Policy?" *Housing Policy Debate* 9, 1 (1998): 1–16.

3. This is the argument Douglas Rae makes in *City: Urbanism and Its End* (New Haven, Conn.: Yale University Press, 2003). Using the term "civic fauna" much as others have used "social capital," Rae suggests that the loss of this historically grounded urban resource makes the contemporary city virtually ungovernable.

4. *Camden Courier*, Greater Camden special issues, 1909, 1917.

5. Campbell Gibson, "Population of the 100 Largest Cities and Other Urban Places in the United States, 1790–1990," U.S. Census Bureau, Population Division Working Paper No. 27, available at www.census.gov/population/www/documentation/0027.html.

6. *Camden First*, May 1924, 13; *Camden Courier*, July 1, 7, 1926. For Hurley's background as a progressive influence in Camden's business community, see Jeffrey M. Dorwart, *Camden County, New Jersey: The Making of a Metropolitan Community, 1626–2000* (New Brunswick, N.J.: Rutgers University Press, 2001), 118.

7. The negative view of the bridge was articulated as early as 1939 in *The Works Progress Administration Guide to 1930s New Jersey* (reprint. New Brunswick, N.J.: Rutgers University Press, 1986), 227–28, which reported that the bridge's construction "cut into the heart of what was then the fine residential section and pushed many of the more prosperous citizens to new homesites in the suburbs." In much the same spirit, it repeated a quip attributed to Will Rodgers at the bridge's dedication that "Now we have a bridge we can get out of Camden when we want to." Much later, Sacred Heart Parish's Msgr. Michael Doyle frequently cited the bridge's bad effect on the city, as did former state senator Alan J. Karcher, who wrote, "Prior to 1926, at the height of enthusiasm for the Greater Camden Movement, the power axis of the county ran North to South along the waterfront. The opening of the bridge radically shifted the axis to one that ran east to west." *New Jersey's Multiple Municipal Madness* (New Brunswick, N.J.: Rutgers University Press, 1998), 160.

8. Charles Leavitt, "Camden in Planning for Growth in Systematic Manner Goes Long Way in Assuring Health and Happiness of Citizens," *Camden First*, October 1924.

9. *Philadelphia Evening Bulletin*, July 29, 1935.

10. Edna Martin letter, February 10, 1998.

11. *Courier-Post*, August 18, 1943.

12. Interview, Camden, April 25, 2002.

13. Telephone interview with Lee Large, February 23, 1998.

14. Letter from Deborah Large-Fox, February 8, 1998.

15. *Courier-Post*, December 2, 1952; telephone interview with Fiore Troncone, Tony Mecca's nephew, December 18, 1997.

16. *Courier-Post*, March 12, 1946.

17. Inez Balestra Pontillo, *Daughter of Immigrants* (Cherry Hill, N.J.: the author, c. 2000), 5.

18. *Courier-Post*, October 25, 1952. These organizations included the Salandrese Society, for instance, which traced its ancestral home to Salandra in the Italian

province of Matera, the Third Order of Saint Francis, the Saint Anthony Society, the Saint Francis Cabrini Society, the Saint Gabriel's Women's Society, Saint Lucy's Society of Syragusa, Saint Michael's Society, Saint Rocco's Society, Ordine di Giovane Italia, and, the Devotees of Saint Gaudenzio. *Our Lady of Mount Carmel Parish, 1903–1953: Fiftieth Anniversary* (Camden, 1953).

19. Giuseppe Constantini's obituary, for instance, listed him as both a retired tailor and bandmaster who organized bands for the Italian Knights of Columbus, the Mucci Post, and the old Moose Lodge. *Courier-Post*, April 8, 1954.

20. Interview with Msgr. Michael Argullo, Cherry Hill, December 9. 1997. See also his obituary, *Philadelphia Inquirer*, February 24, 1999. Appropriately enough, Tony Mecca's wife Isabella, according to her obituary, was an active supporter of the effort to raise a bell tower. *Courier-Post*, July 28, 1947.

21. Interview, Louise Gentile Schemanski, Cherry Hill, May 9, 1998.

22. *Courier-Post*, June 24, 1946.

23. Quoted in the *Courier-Post*, July 29, 1997.

24. Letter, Deborah Large-Fox, February 8, 1998.

25. Parishioners would pay five cents a week into the St. Rita beneficial society to support parish activities. The Polish National Alliance enabled members to make small weekly payments to assure long-term insurance. Working from his undertaking business directly across from the church, Stanley Ciechanowski became intimately involved in both the sacred and secular aspects of Whitman Park. He became head of the Polish-American Citizens Club, helping raise funds to build a hall at Warsaw and Lowell Streets, where the community's male population could gather to play cards, shoot pool, and to socialize. Not a week went by there without an event, which could include weddings as well as Friday night bingo. Interviews with Daniel Ciechanowski, Runnemeade, November 13, 1997, and by phone April 18, 2002.

26. Other organizations included a Zionist association; a Council of Jewish Juniors, started in 1932; and the Jewish Welfare Society to handle relief during the Depression. Jewish Federation of Camden County, *With Vision and Compassion: A History of the Jewish Federation in Camden County, 1922–1972* (Cherry Hill: Jewish Community Federation, 1972).

27. *With Vision and Compassion.*

28. Dorwart, *Camden County*, 136.

29. Interview with Ruth Bogutz, Haddonfield, December 15, 1997.

30. Ehrenhalt could well have spoken for older residents not just of Camden but a number of other older urban neighborhoods when he wrote, "A remarkable number of us . . . talk nostalgically of the loyalties and lasting relationships that characterized those days: of the old neighborhoods with mom-and-pop storekeepers who knew us by name; of not having to lock the house at night because no one would think of entering it; of knowing that there would be a neighbor home, whatever the time of day or night, to help us out or take us in if we happened to be in trouble." *The Lost City*, 16.

31. Telephone interview with Natalie Shisler, March 4, 1998.

32. Interview with Judge Joseph Rodriguez, Camden, February 9, 1998.

33. Interview with Luis A. Rodriguez, Camden, June 10, 1998.

34. Luis Rodriguez interview.

35. Judge Joseph Rodriguez interview; obituaries for Mario and Carmen Rodriguez, *Courier-Post*, December 12, 1973, and Roque Longo, May 26, 1998.

36. Dorwart, *Camden County*, 103–4; *Courier-Post*, May 4, 1999.

37. Interview with James Troutman, Pennsauken, November 6, 1997. William Jenkins, who also grew up in Centerville, reported the same experience attending Whittier. Interview, Camden, September 18, 1998. In a February, 1998 letter to me, Dorothy Duncan Fuller wrote that her mother, whose family were the first African Americans to move to the 200 block of Eleventh Street in North Camden, walked from there south to Whittier as well. Although an 1881 New Jersey statute prohibited excluding children from schools on the basis of race, de facto segregation continued in the state at least until expressly prohibited under the state's 1947 constitution. See Peter A. Buchsbaum's essay, "School Desegregation," in Maxine N. Lurie and Marc Mappen, eds., *Encyclopedia of New Jersey* (New Brunswick, N.J.: Rutgers University Press, 2004), 719–20.

38. Interview with Randy Primas, Cherry Hill, August 13, 1997.

39. Interview with Charles Ashley, Pennsauken, March 11, 2002; see also Kevin Riordan's essay, "Separate and Unequal in South Jersey," *Courier-Post*, February 27, 2003.

40. Interview with Doris Nelson, Camden, April 18, 2002.

41. *Courier-Post*, January 15, 1951.

42. Interview with James Troutman, November 6, 1997.

43. Interview with Colandus "Kelly" Francis, Camden, February 8, 2002; see also, Wiggins profile, *Courier-Post*, October 18, 1999.

44. *Courier-Post*, February 27, 2003.

45. Interview with Roseanne Brown and Connie Gland Miller, St. Bartholomew's Church, Camden, April 28, 1998.

46. Ruth Bogutz, "Growing up Jewish in Camden: The War Years and Beyond," in "Fifty Years of Service to the Jewish Community in South Jersey, 1941–1991," *The Voice* (Publication of the Jewish Federation of Camden County), Camden County Historical Society (CCHS).

47. Interview with Odessa Polk-Jones, Camden, August 19, 1998.

48. Harmon told this story twice, the second time, after undergoing a long illness, revealing the continued emotion associated with the event by breaking into tears. Interviews, Camden, January 23, 1998, Pine Hill, May 30, 2002.

49. Telephone interview with Burton Weiser, May 7, 1999.

50. Letter postmarked February 10, 1998.

51. Interviews with Roseanne Brown, April 28, 1998, and Bernice Hackett, June 18, 1999.

52. Edna M. Martin, letter postmarked February 10, 1998.

53. Telephone interviews with Ruth Bogutz, May 30, 2001 and Frank Harrington, April 17, 2002.

54. Telephone interview, September 20, 2002; tape, "Fifty Years of Community Building in Camden" conference, April 20, 2001.

55. Telephone interview with Natalie Shisler, March 14, 1998.

56. *Campbell's People*, October, 1956, Campbell Soup Company Archives.

57. Telephone interview with David Riley, February 10, 2003. According to Riley, Lucius Williams did manage to sustain a good position as one of those rare African Americans who rose to become a foreman for an asphalt company.

58. Interview with Paul Croccia, Camden, March 17, 1998.

59. Unlike other industrial centers, Camden's RCA plant reduced the number of female workers during the war, finding it more cost-effective to shift work previously done in Camden to women working in Bloomington, Indiana and other midwestern facilities. Jefferson Cowie, *Capital Moves: RCA's Seventy-Year Quest for Cheap Labor* (Ithaca, N.Y.: Cornell University Press, 1999), 17, 36.

60. Martha Kozloski, who worked at Consolidated Cigar Company at Liberty and Ninth Streets when she was growing up, hated the work but was part of a generation whose parents expected their children to contribute to the family income. Interview, Camden, November 19, 1998.

61. Interview with Carmela Argentieri, Camden, February 11, 1998.

62. Telephone interview with Marie Laviano Zizzamia, December 1, 1997.

63. *Courier-Post*, June 25, 1998.

64. Telephone interview with Sandra White-Grear, January 18, 2002.

65. Telephone interview with Alex Colalillo, February 21, 2002.

66. Interview, Pennsauken, December 5, 1998.

67. Interview with Jorge and Zoe Mazzoni Rodriguez, Stafford, May 22, 2002.

68. Interview with Joseph Iacovino, Westmont, March 4, 2003.

69. St. Clair Drake and Horace R. Cayton, *Black Metropolis: A Study of Negro Life in a Northern City* (reprint: Chicago: University of Chicago Press, 1993). Originally published in 1945, this revised and enlarged edition includes a foreword by William Julius Wilson comparing the differences between the 1940s, when residents of these Chicago neighborhoods worked, and the more contemporary period of high under- and unemployment. Interviews, Pasquale Giambrone, December 4, 1998 and John Odorisio, March 25, 1998. The *New York Times*, September 5, 1942, reported that a Camden County grand jury indicted seventy-five people on gambling, linking Edward Carroll, a police lieutenant and head of a Camden's 2nd police division, with Reginelli, whom the paper described as a "notorious underworld figure."

70. Telephone interview with Fiore Troncone, December 18, 1997.

71. Interview, May 22, 2002. Verdiglione may have lived in high style in Haddonfield, as Rodriguez put it, but his roots were in Camden, where according to the 1947 city directory he operated a real estate, insurance, and travel agency, living with his wife above his office in the heart of the Italian section at 940–42 South Fifth Street.

Chapter 2. Camden Transformed

Epigraphs: Philip Roth, *American Pastoral* (Boston: Houghton Mifflin, 1997), 364–65; Robert Moore, quoted in the *Philadelphia Inquirer*, April 14, 1970.

1. Telephone interview with Marie Scheffield, February 23, 1998. For her reac-

tion to returning to Camden shortly after this interview, see *Courier-Post*, May 18, 1998.

2. *Courier-Post*, August 26, 1971. Alvarado quoted in the same paper's retrospective commentary on the period, February 27, 1986. *Philadelphia Inquirer*, August 18, 1991.

3. Telephone interview, May 15, 2002.

4. Because of limited funding to produce the play, the several times it was presented in the area readers read from the script, not attempting to dress or act the parts they were representing. As a consequence, the race of the intruders was not specified.

5. Jefferson Cowie, *Capital Moves: RCA's Seventy-Year Quest for Cheap Labor* (Ithaca, N.Y.: Cornell University Press, 1999), 33.

6. The 1947 directory does not indicate the company where workers were employed, but the 1940 directory does. A sample of some three hundred workers from that directory shows that a small portion of workers lived outside the city, notably in Gloucester City, directly adjacent to New York Ship, and a smattering in nearby suburbs Pennsauken, Audubon, and Collingswood. The greatest number of suburban residents appear to have held supervisory positions, as inspectors, foremen, or as clerks. Other shipworkers could be found outside Camden in communities built specifically for the war effort, notably Audubon Park and Bellmawr, both of which were organized as mutual homes associations and which kept membership virtually all-white even to this day. See Gail Greenberg's contributions to Maxine N. Lurie and Marc Mappen, eds., *Encyclopedia of New Jersey* (New Brunswick, N.J.: Rutgers University Press, 2004), 46 and 68 respectively, and Kristin M. Szylvian, "Audubon Park and Labor's Redefinition of the Modern Housing Ideal," paper presented at the Ninth Biennial Conference on Planning History, November 2, 2001. In any case, it can be readily assumed that shortages of war materials, for gasoline as well as for new construction, slowed any outward migration before the end of the war as they did throughout the country.

7. Jon C. Teaford, *The Rough Road to Renaissance: Urban Revitalization in America, 1940–1985* (Baltimore: Johns Hopkins University Press, 1990), 213; Barry Bluestone and Bennett Harrison, *The Deindustrialization of America: Plant Closings, Community Abandonment, and the Dismantling of Basic Industry* (New York: Basic Books, 1982).

8. See the unsigned submission to Laurie and Mappan, *Encyclopedia of New Jersey*, 673.

9. *Courier-Post*, May 25, 1946.

10. *Courier-Post*, June 10, 1945, May 18, 1946.

11. Telephone interview with Marie Zazzamia, December 1, 1997.

12. *Courier-Post*, June 1, 1946. An advertisement for another home in East Camden dated December 8, 1945, offered a "substantial 2 car garage," but also noted its location only a few doors from the bus.

13. A report in the *Courier-Post*, February 12, 1954, asserted that Camden merchants were making $20 million more than they did in 1951 and that retail sales were 34 percent higher than the national average. The average Camden household in-

come, at $5,913 after taxes, was 13 percent above the national average of $5,246. The city's population was reported up 6,500 in less than two years, to 131,800.

14. *Courier-Post*, June 1, 1946, August 6, 1949.

15. Interview with Marc Shuster, Moorestown, N.J., May 25, 1999; see also the retrospective essay, "Cherry Hill Grows into Quintessential American Suburb," *Courier-Post*, May 4, 1999.

16. *Courier-Post*, June 24, 1961.

17. Interview with Ruth Bogutz, Haddon Township, August 26, 2002.

18. *With Vision and Compassion: A History of the Jewish Federation in Camden County, 1922–1972* (Cherry Hill: Jewish Community Federation, 1972); interview with Bernard Dubin, Pennsauken, June 24, 1998.

19. Interview with Louis Skulnick, Pennsauken, January 15, 2002.

20. Interview with Bernard Dubin, June 24, 1998.

21. Lizabeth Cohen, *A Consumer's Republic: The Politics of Mass Consumption in Postwar America* (New York: Knopf, 2003), 199.

22. *Courier-Post*, September 17, 1954.

23. *Courier-Post*, March 20, 1959.

24. *Courier-Post*, June 24, 1961.

25. Quoted in Anne Marie T. Cammarota, *Pavements in the Garden* (Madison, N.J.: Fairleigh Dickinson University Press, 1996), 290.

26. *Courier-Post*, April 2, 1958.

27. Stephanie Dyer, "Markets in the Meadows: Department Stores and Shopping Centers in the Decentralization of Philadelphia, 1920–1980," Ph.D. dissertation, University of Pennsylvania, 2000, 296–301. For the expectations Rouse invested in malls as community centers, see Howard Gillette, Jr., "The Evolution of the Planned Shopping Center in Suburb and City," *APA Journal* (Autumn 1985): 456–57; Joshua Olsen, *Better Places, Better Lives: A Biography of James Rouse* (Washington, D.C.: Urban Land Institute, 2003), 109–11; and Nicholas Dagen Bloom, *Merchant of Illusion: James Rouse, America's Salesman of the Businessman's Utopia* (Columbus: Ohio State University Press, 2004), 114–19.

28. Interview with Gilbert Kerlin, son of long-time Secretary-Treasurer of Camden Forge, Ward Dix Kerlin, Riverdale, N.Y., May 20, 2002.

29. *Courier-Post*, October 1, 1957, April 4, 1959.

30. *Courier-Post*, September 24, 1957.

31. *Courier-Post*, January 19, 1956.

32. "Delaware Valley, U.S.A.," *Philadelphia Inquirer*, October 4, 1963.

33. *Courier-Post*, October 12, 1965.

34. "Delaware Valley, U.S.A.," *Philadelphia Inquirer*, September 25, 1956, 55.

35. Norman Baldwin, *Courier-Post*, October 12, 1965. An accompanying advertisement for the Cherry Hill Industrial Center claimed to have attracted thirty firms in the previous three years, including Esterbrook Pen from Camden.

36. See the review of industrial development in Pennsauken in *Community News*, April 3, 1961, in addition to contemporary industrial directories.

37. Charles Tomlinson, "A Study of the Proposed Waterfront Industrial Highway, Camden, New Jersey," M.A. thesis, Drexel University, June, 1972.

38. *Courier-Post*, May 12, 1942.

39. For example, Collingswood in 1949: *Courier-Post*, August 18, 1949. An effort to pass a zoning ordinance twenty years earlier was defeated when residents overwhelmingly rejected the proposal.

40. *Courier-Post*, February 23, 1954, September 20, 21, 1955.

41. *Courier-Post*, July 26, 1955.

42. *The Suburban*, May 5, June 9, September 29, 1966. Another suburban journal, *Community News*, September 23, 1965, reported restrictions on garden apartments in Haddon Township requiring small units in low-rise structures with the specific goals not just of blending into the landscape but also of excluding families with children, so as not to overburden schools.

43. Robert O. Self, *American Babylon: Race and the Struggle for Postwar Oakland* (Princeton, N.J.: Princeton University Press, 2003), 16.

44. Interview with Edward Burt, Camden, April 16, 2004.

45. Review of sales transactions, Department of Public Works, Camden; interview with Cloie Winston, Camden, March 1, 2002.

46. Telephone interview with Washington Hill, November 7, 2002.

47. See, for instance, advertisements in *Courier-Post*: "COLORED. Princess Ave. 4 bdrm house. $9,400. Small down payment. We have others as low as $4,000," July 16, 1960; "Sacrifice, 1442 Princess," July 8, 1959; or "Owner must sell. Hurry!" June 3, 1961.

48. Interview with Delbert and Doris Langston Nelson, Camden, April 18, 2002.

49. Letter from Edna M. Martin, postmarked February 10, 1998.

50. *Courier-Post*, October 21, 1959.

51. Interview with Peter and Helen McHugh, Williamstown, June 28, 1999.

52. Quote in *Philadelphia Bulletin*, June 10, 1965

53. Interview, Camden, April 6, 1998.

54. Interview, Camden, March 9, 1998.

55. Rev. Roque Longo et al., "Puerto Ricans in Camden." Report of priests and sisters in the churches of Holy Name and Our Lady of Fatima, Camden, June, 1970, Hispanic file, CCHS.

56. See, for instance, *Courier-Post*, May 5, 1962, ads for 1351 Morton, "must sacrifice," and for 1327 Dayton, "must be sold."

57. Interview with Linda Delengowski, Haddonfield, April 5, 2002; *Courier-Post*, January 19, 1970; telephone interview with John Ciechanowski, April 22, 2002.

58. Nine additional properties sold along Jackson, three to Polish buyers, two to Hispanics; seven properties on Sheridan, two to Polish, one to a Hispanic buyer; four properties sold each on Chase, Lowell, and Everett Streets; seven sold on Thurman, one each to Polish and Hispanic buyers. The remaining buyers appear to have been African American.

59. Interview with Jorge Rodriguez, Stratford, May 22, 2002.

60. *Courier-Post*, August 14, 1969. For real estate ads, see for instance, *Courier-Post*, October 8, 1971.

61. Interview with Rosa Ramirez, Camden, November 21, 1997.

62. *Courier-Post*, May 13, 1976.

63. See Thomas J. Sugrue, *The Origins of the Urban Crisis: Race and Inequality*

in Postwar Detroit (Princeton, N.J.: Princeton University Press, 1996), especially Chapter 9, and Arnold Hirsch, *Making the Second Ghetto: Race and Housing in Chicago, 1940–1960* (Cambridge: Cambridge University Press, 1983).

64. Letter from Edna M. Martin, postmarked February 10, 1998.

65. Telephone interview, March 1, 1998; *Courier-Post*, May 18, 1998.

66. Telephone interview, February 23, 1998.

67. Telephone interviews with Marion and Paul Baratz, December 18, 2002, and Brian Baratz, January 13, 2003.

68. Interview, Cherry Hill, March 17, 1996.

69. Telephone interview with Wendy Strang Rooney, February, 2002. See also her letter in the *Courier-Post*, September 6, 2001, defending "Old Fairview" against the suggestion that it had been historically racist.

70. See, for instance, Scott Cummings, *Left Behind in Rosedale: Race Relations and the Collapse of Community Institutions* (Boulder: Westview Press, 1998).

71. Interview with Charles Sharp, Pennsauken, August 18, 1998.

72. Quoted from *Last Rites, Courier-Post*, April 27, 1998.

73. Robert A. Beauregard, *Voices of Decline: The Postwar Fate of U.S. Cities*, 2nd ed. (New York: Routledge, 2003), x, 155.

74. Fred Siegel, *The Future Once Happened Here: New York, D.C., L.A., and the Fate of America's Big Cities* (New York: Free Press, 1997), 9.

Chapter 3. To Save Our City

Epigraph: "Camden Stands at Crossroads," from the eighth in a series on Camden's rebirth as part of election coverage, *Courier-Post*, May 8, 1963.

1. Interviews with William Jenkins, Camden, September 18, 1997, and Joseph Balzano, Camden, November 21, 1997. Both men were active in Camden during the Pierce era.

2. There is an extensive literature on the experience of urban renewal at mid-century as authorized by the national housing acts of 1949 and 1954. For a sense of the contemporary perspective as well as comments on the mayors who took this challenge as part of a reformist mantra at the time, see James Q. Wilson, *Urban Renewal: The Record and the Controversy* (Cambridge, Mass.: MIT Press, 1966) and Jeanne R. Lowe, *Cities in a Race with Time: Progress and Poverty in America's Renewing Cities* (New York: Random House, 1967). The classic historical account of this effort has become Arnold Hirsch, *Making the Second Ghetto: Race and Housing in Chicago, 1940–1960* (New York, Cambridge University Press, 1983).

3. *Courier-Post*, January 27, 1950. See also the effusive Pierce profile, *Courier-Post*, April 17, 1959.

4. *Courier-Post*, May 6, 8, 1959.

5. Advertisement, *Courier-Post*, April 29, 1959.

6. *Courier-Post*, April 28, 1959.

7. *Courier-Post*, May 11, 1959.

8. See, for instance, an August 29, 1959, *Courier-Post* report of his citizen arrest and a December 1, 1959, editorial supporting his actions.

9. *Courier-Post*, June 24, 1960.

10. *Courier-Post*, November 9, 1960.

11. *Courier-Post*, May 5, 1961.

12. Interview with William Jenkins, Camden, September 18, 1997.

13. Interview with Steven Casamassina, Camden, April 22, 1998.

14. Tape, "Community Building in Camden" conference, Rutgers University-Camden, April 20, 2001.

15. *Comprehensive Plan* (City of Camden, 1962), 1.

16. *Rebirth Though Renewal* (Camden: Urban Renewal Division, Housing Authority of the City of Camden, 1969). For a retrospective account of the redevelopment plan and its results, see Kevin Riordan's feature, "Dreams Unrealized in Camden," *Courier-Post*, March 14, 2000.

17. Brochure: "Introduction to the Comprehensive Plan for the City of Camden," 1962, 3; *Comprehensive Plan* (1962), 77, 116, 196; transcript of the hearings on the plan, May 28, 1962, Case 103A, Office of the Municipal Clerk, Camden.

18. Frequently referred to by scholars as the result of progrowth coalitions, such efforts arose with support of federal funds for urban renewal in older industrial cities across the Northeast and Middle West. See John H. Mollenkopf, *The Contested City* (Princeton, N.J.: Princeton University Press, 1983), especially Chapter 1, 12–46.

19. The creation of business advisory groups specifically formed to advance urban redevelopment was a common practice in the 1950s and 1960s. In Pittsburgh, it was the Citizen Committee on City Plan, in New Haven, the Citizens Action Committee, in Washington, D.C., the Federal City Council. See Raymond E. Wolfinger, *The Politics of Progress* (Englewood Cliffs, N.J.: Prentice-Hall, 1974), 228–64; and Howard Gillette, Jr., *Between Justice and Beauty: Race, Planning, and the Failure of Urban Policy in Washington, D.C.* (Baltimore: Johns Hopkins University Press, 1995), 171.

20. Transcript of hearings, February 23, March 16, 1966, Case 111, Office of the Municipal Clerk, City of Camden; *Courier-Post*, March 10, 1966.

21. *Courier-Post*, October 22, 1953.

22. *Courier-Post*, June 2, 1967; interview with Ronald B. Evans, Camden, April 30, 1998.

23. Gail Radford, *Modern Housing for America: Policy Struggles in the New Deal Era* (Chicago: University of Chicago Press, 1997).

24. *Courier-Post*, November 11, 1954, June 8, 1966.

25. *Courier-Post*, June 8, 1966.

26. *Courier-Post*, June 25, 1966.

27. Telephone interview with Donald Greismann, October 14, 1997.

28. Circular, Camden Metropolitan Ministry file, Presbyterian Historical Society (PHS), Philadelphia; Sam Appel, "Finding the Point Again! A Report and Reflections on 25 Years of Urban Ministry in Camden, New Jersey," November, 1988, 11.

29. CMM Newsletter, December, 1966, PHS.

30. Flyer, "What Price Education?" (1966), PHS.

31. *Catholic Star Herald*, June 22, 1962.

32. Interview with Donald Greismann, October 14, 1997.

33. *Courier-Post*, September 16, 23, November 16, 1966.

34. *Courier-Post.*, June 23, 1967.

35. Steven H. Leleiko, *Camden, N.J.: A Report Requested by the U.S. Department of Housing and Urban Development* (Camden, N.J.: Camden Episcopal Community Center, December 1967), 2. In compiling the dramatic loss of cheaper housing in the wake of demolitions from redevelopment and highways, the report pointed specifically to violations of government policy as declared in the 1962 comprehensive plan, that "Clearance cannot proceed at a rate faster than the construction of new dwellings. A surplus of habitable older buildings must be maintained at all times to accommodate the relocation of families displaced by clearance" (33).

36. *Courier-Post*, February 8, 1968; "Camden Task Force Report, Findings and Recommendations," from Warren P. Phelan, Regional Administrator Department of Housing and Urban Development Region II, to Mayor Alfred Pierce, Elizabeth Hawk, and Joseph McComb, July 11, 1968.

37. *Courier-Post*, August 31, 1967; interview with Malik Chaka, Washington, D.C., April 11, 2002.

38. *Courier-Post*, September 1, 2, 1967. Just below the editorial on Brown ran a second editorial expressing relief that Thurgood Marshall, the first African American appointed to the Supreme Court, had finally been confirmed, despite delaying tactics by southern opponents.

39. Stephen Allen, "Who Wants Rap Brown?" *Courier-Post*, September 6, 1967.

40. Sharp quoted in *Courier-Post*, March 14, 1993; Barry Rosenberg, "The Troublemaker," *Philadelphia Magazine* 61 (September 1970); *Philadelphia Inquirer*, "Poppy Sharp Defines Black Militant Goals," May 10, 1970.

41. Interviews with Charles Sharp, Pennsauken, August 18, 1998, and Malik Chaka, Washington, D.C., April 11, 2002.

42. Undated two-page circular, CMM files, PHS, apparently intended for fundraising purposes, as the flyer concluded, "the only ingredient lacking in the support mentioned above is the capital needed to run the programs devised by the BPUM and its supporters."

43. Built in 1962, the twenty-one-story Northgate was an appropriate symbol for the protest, as initially it accommodated the city's elite and appeared to undergird planners' belief that there was still an upscale market in Camden. Pierce had himself made the Northgate a symbol for the city's revitalization in a speech describing the goals of his redevelopment program reported in the *Courier-Post*, January 24, 1961. The building, however, declined along with the area around it.

44. Shortly after the formation of BPUM, Pierce compared Sharp to terrorists, suggesting that the press was contributing to the problem by giving agitators so much publicity. *Courier-Post*, November 14. 1967.

45. *Courier-Post*, May 3, 7, 8, 1968. Whites were involved in all aspects of the Shields demonstrations, though the Camden Metropolitan Ministry newsletter for May 23, 1968, pointed out that BPUM representatives, after complaining about the

futility of letter writing, walked out of the meeting after demanding a more forceful approach.

46. *Courier-Post*, May 21, 1968.

47. *Courier-Post*, May 10, 21, 1968.

48. Minutes, CMM files, March 28, 1968, PHS.

49. Sam Appel, "Finding the Point Again!" 26.

50. Sworn statement submitted as part of a "People's Court of New Jersey: Justice and Truth," June 5, 1969, CMM files, PHS.

51. Interview with Delbert Nelson, Camden, April 18, 2002.

52. *Courier-Post*, May 24, 1968.

53. *Courier-Post*, August 6, 1968.

54. Statement of Charles Sharp, June 27, 1968, CMM files, PHS.

55. Among letters of support for Appel preserved in the CMM Papers was one from Thomas Lindsay, pastor of the First Presbyterian Church in Haddonfield, to Douglas Robinson, Chairman of the Administrative Council of CMM. "If there is any conspiracy in this unfortunate situation, it is not a conspiracy involving Sam to promote violence," he wrote, "for he has worked hard to sell the idea of nonviolence; but rather a conspiracy of ambitious politicians, now frustrated by their loss of control over the political situation in Camden and striking out bitterly at all who have opposed them." Referring to Camden School Board chair Milliken's request of him to get the presbytery to remove Appel from Camden, Lindsay reported that when he refused, "I was informed that one way or another, they would get Sam out of their way."

56. Deposition of Alfred Pierce in the case of the *City of Camden v. Friends of BPUM*, October 3, 1968, CMM files, PHS. Branding civil rights efforts communist was a relatively common tactic in the 1960s. For his part, as he stated in the deposition, Pierce thought he was confirmed in his belief by the presence of John Tisa at the Northgate demonstration. Tisa had been a labor organizer at Campbell's Soup in the late 1930s when he was an acknowledged communist. In his April 11, 2002, interview with me, Malik Chaka indicated there had been a few former communists in the Friends organization, including Tisa, but he denied strongly that BPUM had ever been under communist influence as Pierce charged.

57. Presentment of the Grand Jury, April 21, 1969 and F-BPUM reply, June 5, 1969, CMM files, PHS.

58. *Courier-Post*, September 3,4, 1969

59. *Courier-Post*, September 12, 1967. According to Harvey Johnson, who was hired in 1969 to head the economic arm of BPUM, the clothing factory was started by Haywood Smith, who had lined up contracts, most importantly with J.C. Penny, but the raid killed the effort. Mellaby later settled a suit for damages out of court for $10,000, but Johnson was convinced that police and the FBI subsequently circulated information that no one, especially banks, should have anything to do with BPUM. Interview, Camden, October 21,1997.

60. Interview with Malik Chaka, April 11, 2002. Chaka reported that everyone who knew Sharp realized right away the police had planted the drugs. "Poppy was known to be death on drugs," he reported. "If someone around him was smoking a reefer, he would tell him not to do it because it would get everyone in trouble."

He said a former Camden High basketball star, Calvin Butler, later testified that he had bought ten kilos for the police, was allowed to keep five, and the rest turned up at Sharp's when police raided his home. His account is largely substantiated by reports of Sharp's 1972 trial on the charge, although it was others who accused Butler of participating in the police sting. See *Courier-Post*, April 18, 20, 1972.

61. *Courier-Post*, September 30, 1970; *New York Times*, November 15, 1970.

62. *Camden Civil Rights Ministerium v. Joseph Nardi*, plaintiff's brief, 12.

63. *CCRM v. Nardi*, 4.

64. *Courier-Post*, July 2, 1969.

65. Nardi's father, who migrated to America in 1923, told the classic immigrant story of following his other family members to Camden. He took the *Julius Caesar* out of Naples to New York City, a train to Philadelphia, a ferry to Camden, and a trolley to 522 Royden Street, where he found two sisters playing in the street. Interview with Joseph Nardi, Camden, April 6, 1998.

66. *Courier-Post*, August 20–23, 1971; interview with Yolanda Auguilar DeNeely, Camden, April 6, 1998.

67. *Courier-Post*, May 21, 1968

68. *Courier-Post*, June 23, 24, 30, 1968. According to O'Connor, in a June 3, 2003, interview in Mount Laurel, the unions upheld their end of the bargain. Such efforts only later fell apart as minority contractors, lacking the additional resources to look ahead for other jobs, fell out of the pool.

69. Interview with Peter O'Connor, Camden, September 8, 1997.

70. Interview with Joseph Nardi, February 13, 1998.

71. *Courier-Post*, July 6, 1973. In response to news that Nardi had decided not to seek reelection, the *Courier-Post*, February 22, 1973, had reported that Errichetti had been meeting unobtrusively with members of the Camden Civil Rights Coalition since the riots, using his position as head of an urban renewal task force to develop his own plan for the city's revitalization. See also Joseph Bresler's summary of Errichetti's career, *Courier-Post*, August 30, 1980.

72. Interview with Camden City Comptroller Richard Cinaglia, Camden, March 20, 1996.

73. For the dire fiscal as well as the changing policy climate in the mid-1970s, see Jon C. Teaford, *The Rough Road to Renaissance: Urban Revitalization in America, 1940–1985* (Baltimore: Johns Hopkins University Press, 1990), chapter 6, 200–252.

74. *Courier-Post*, January 3, 1973. Topping the list was Newark, with Trenton listed as eighth, indicating how serious the decline of New Jersey's cities had become. Detroit ranked seventh, and Washington, D.C., which Richard Nixon had dubbed the "crime capital of America," was not even ranked in the top ten.

75. Quoted in Dennis Culnan, "Focus on Camden," *New Jersey Business* 25 (December, 1979): 55.

76. *Courier-Post*, January 18, 1962, January 21, 1966.

77. *Courier-Post*, January 12, 1967. Pierce drew another $300,000 from the same source, to the editorial consternation of the *Courier-Post*, January 14, 1970.

78. *Courier-Post*, January 23, 24, 1970.

79. *Courier-Post*, June 24, 1972, August 30, 1980.

80. According to a March 11, 1975 report in the *Courier-Post*, the $2.5 million

paid for the sewer plant relieved the mayor of the prospect of raising taxes another 60 cents per $100 valuation. See also, *Courier-Post*, December 24, 1975, March 15, 1976.

81. *Courier-Post*, August 30, 1980.

82. *New York Times*, March 10, 1979; *Courier-Post*, November 23, 1979.

83. See Errichetti interview, *Philadelphia Inquirer*, March 20, 1996.

84. *Courier-Post*, May 24, June 28, 1981.

Chapter 4. From City to County: The Rise of the Suburban Power Structure

1. Interview with Charles Sharp, Pennsauken, August 18, 1998.

2. Jon C. Teaford, *City and Suburb: The Political Fragmentation of Metropolitan America, 1850–1970* (Baltimore: Johns Hopkins University Press, 1979); Robert Fogelson, *The Fragmented Metropolis: Los Angeles, 1850–1930* (Cambridge, Mass.: Harvard University Press, 1967); Ann Durkin Keating, *Building Chicago: Suburban Developers and the Creation of a Divided Metropolis* (Urbana: University of Illinois Press, 1988); Carl Abbott, *The New Urban America: Growth and Politics in Sunbelt Cities*, rev. ed. (Chapel Hill: University of North Carolina Press, 1987).

3. *Courier-Post*, editorials January 11, 22, 1968. William Reynolds, the former mayor of Haddonfield, some six miles outside Camden, described conditions in the Cooper River running through the county in a November 13, 2002, telephone interview as horrendous and beyond the capacity of any single suburban jurisdiction to improve upon.

4. *Couier-Post*, December 28, 1967, December 12, 1968.

5. *Courier-Post*, July 12, 1969, *Cherry Hill News*, July 17, 24, 1969. In his November 2002 telephone conversation with me, William Reynolds, described Cherry Hill Mayor John Gilmour as a representative of the established farm families in the area who deeply distrusted county efforts to regionalize the sewer system and preferred to maintain Cherry Hill's independent sewage system, even though it was operating well over capacity. *The Suburban*, October 7, 1965, confirms Reynolds's observation, quoting Gilmour as saying such authorities were like an octopus: "They never want to let go. The regional sewage authority would usurp the authority of township council and reduce the township's taxing ability."

6. *Courier-Post*, August 30, 1970.

7. *Courier-Post*, August 30, 1970, July 7, 21, 25, 1971.

8. *Courier-Post*, March 15, 1972.

9. *Courier-Post*, February 2, June 6, 13, 1973.

10. *Courier-Post*, December 24, 1975.

11. *Courier-Post*, May 10, October 4, 1975.

12. *Courier-Post*, March 16, May 12, June 22, August 10, October 27, December 14–16, 1976, February 1, 1977.

13. Interview, with Frederick Martin, Jr., Camden, November 14, 2002.

14. Martin interview.

15. Assemblyman Kenneth Gewertz, quoted in the *Courier-Post*, May 1, 1979.

16. *Courier-Post*, January 20, February 10, July 27, 1982.

17. *Courier-Post*, February 14, 1984; see Dennis Culnan's analysis as part of a larger series on James Florio, *Courier-Post*, September 30, 1987; *New York Times*, May 27, 1993.

18. *Courier-Post*, December 3, 1981, August 14, 1983. For background on the issue of disposing of solid waste in New Jersey, see Barbara G. Salmore and Stephen A. Salmore, *New Jersey Politics and Government* (Lincoln: University of Nebraska Press, 1993), 283–85.

19. *Courier-Post*, September 30, 1987. Another protege of Errichetti's, Vogelson had gained Florio's friendship and support by backing him for governor in 1977.

20. Interview with Randy Primas, Cherry Hill, August 19, 1996. Quoted in the *New York Times*, July 7, 2002.

21. In addition to evoking Dr. King's memory at the dedication of Wiggins Park the day he was inaugurated, Primas did so again as he departed office in 1990 for a state position. Asked how he wanted to be remembered, Primas replied, "It is not for anything physical, but . . . [the same way] as an individual who had a major impact on my life, and that was Dr. Martin Luther King, Jr. . . . [as] a mayor who tried to make Camden a better place." *Philadelphia Inquirer*, January 18, 1990.

22. Stokely Carmichael and Charles Hamilton, *Black Power: The Politics of Liberation in America* (New York: Vintage, 1967).

23. Interview, Washington, D.C., April 11, 2002.

24. *Courier-Post*, October 16, 1981.

25. *Philadelphia Inquirer*, October 11, 1982.

26. *Philadelphia Inquirer*, May 5, 1981.

27. *Courier-Post*, August 15, 1980.

28. *New York Times*, November 14, 1982. Also important, Primas added in a September 4, 2003, interview with me in Camden, was securing jobs for Camden residents at the prison. Unfortunately, he added, most of those who took the new positions ultimately left the city to live elsewhere.

29. *Courier-Post*, May 24, 1981.

30. Interview with Tom Knoche, Camden, September 17, 1997; *Courier-Post*, September 16, 17, 1987; *Philadelphia Inquirer*, July 15, 1988.

31. Tom Knoche, letter, *Courier-Post*, March 3, 1987.

32. *Philadelphia Inquirer*, February 12, 1987; *Courier-Post*, February 11, 1987.

33. *Courier-Post*, August 29, 1978.

34. *Courier-Post*, March 24, May 16, 1979.

35. *Courier-Post*, October 23, January 26, 1979.

36. *Courier-Post*, December 14, 1983.

37. *Courier-Post*, April 26, 1983.

38. *Courier-Post*, December 16, 1982.

39. Transcript *60 Minutes*, March 20, 1983; *Courier-Post*, March 21, 25, April 1, 1983. According to Msgr. Doyle in a October 24, 2002, interview in Camden, *60 Minutes* offered Primas a minute to reply. Doyle thought it was a wonderful opportunity for the mayor to make a national appeal for help to rebuild the city, but Primas did not accept the offer, Doyle thought, because he had already been so

critical of the program he could not accept the program's premises of extreme distress.

40. The result of a statewide investigation into county sewerage authorities, the new rules were intended to "remove the curtain of secrecy" around their operations. *Bond Buyer*, August 3, 1982; *Courier-Post*, May 16, August 7, 1984.

41. *Courier-Post*, September 17, December 29, 1987.

42. *Courier-Post*, January 13, 1985; *Philadelphia Inquirer*, January 13, 1985.

43. *Courier-Post*, August 15, 1987. Telephone interview with Linda McHugh, August 20, 2002. Activists, McHugh reported, carefully checked signatures on their petitions for accuracy, registering to vote those who were not already on the rolls, but the city aggressively challenged the effort, ultimately defeating it. See *Courier-Post*, November 13, 25, 1987, April 1, 1988. Residents of Rahway, New Jersey, an area similar to Camden in having more than its share of environmentally damaging operations, fought a similar battle against an incinerator. See Michael R. Greenberg, *Restoring America's Neighborhoods: How Local People Made a Difference* (New Brunswick, N.J.: Rutgers University Press, 1999), 83–104.

44. *Courier-Post*, December 18, 1987, April 1, 1988.

45. *Courier-Post*, March 31, 1989.

46. The compromise, dubbed CLEAR (Comprehensive, Long-term, Environment Action Recycling Plan for Camden County) was fashioned by freeholders Michael DiPiero, the leading Republican critic of county environmental policies, and Maria Barnaby Greenwald, the former mayor of Cherry Hill. *Courier-Post*, October 5, 1990, March 26, 1991. The Camden County newsletter announcing the opening of the plant, dated January 1991, indicated the CLEAR plan agreement was in effect. A subsequent *Courier-Post* feature under the title, "The Power to Pollute," September 21–22, 1992, spelled out Camden's weakened position in housing so many environmentally hazardous sites. In an interview with me in his Haddon Heights office February 3, 2003, Congressman Robert Andrews, who helped guide plans for the incinerator through the freeholders while he was director in the late 1980s, reported that after originally supporting the incinerator, he came to have serious concerns. He credited protesters with informing him, but he believed that the county had already invested so much that it would have been liable for years. Although he was no longer a freeholder by the time the CLEAR plan came out, he worked with his former colleagues on it. He thought that Michael DiPiero supported the effort despite his previous criticism because he was not satisfied with just criticizing Democrats and wanted to get something done, which was not likely without bipartisan support as long as Republicans were in a minority on the board.

47. *Courier-Post*, October 11, November 15, 1991; *Philadelphia Inquirer*, October 10, 1990.

48. *Philadelphia Inquirer*, October 6, 1990.

49. *Courier-Post*, January 23, 1995, and letters in the same paper from incinerator critic Joan Leonard from Collingswood and Nancy Kerry from Haddon Heights, February 4, 1995, and from Marks February 24, 1995. Linda McHugh left Fairview for suburban Medford the previous year: interview, August 20, 2002.

50. *Courier-Post*, June 13, 1989; *Philadelphia Inquirer*, August 2, 1989.

51. *Courier-Post*, September 7, 1989; *Philadelphia Inquirer*, September 7, 1989.

52. *Courier-Post* editorial, "Prison Isn't Best Camden Can Do," September 18, 1989.

53. *Catholic Star Herald*, November 3, 1989. See also the detailed and impassioned critique by Richard G. Malloy, associate pastor of North Camden's Holy Name parish, in *Catholic Star Herald*, October 6, 1989, and the letter from James Florio on his campaign letterhead to Msgr. Robert McDermott, October 27, 1989, Prison file, Camden County Historical Society (CCHS).

54. *Philadelphia Inquirer*, January 13, 1990.

55. *Philadelphia Inquirer*, October 14, 1984.

56. New Jersey Election Law Enforcement Commission, Report of Victory 89 Continued Progress with Primas, received January 29, 1990.

57. *New York Times*, May 25, 2003; *Philadelphia Inquirer*, October 30, 2003.

58. *Courier-Post*, March 21, 1993.

59. At issue were fees paid Salema and Rudi's subsidiary company, Armacon Investments, received in connection with the refinancing of New Jersey Turnpike Authority bonds. The SEC investigation uncovered a pattern of payments over time for bond work orchestrated by Robert Jablonski, representing First Fidelity Bank in Newark. Named by John Nero to advise the CCMUA, Jablonski routed fees for work at CCMUA and later the Camden County Pollution Control Authority to First Fidelity, while Consolidated Financial Management served as financial advisor. When Republicans succeeded in reducing those fees, Rudi and Salema requested kickbacks on bond issues routed to Fidelity, which made their way through Jablonski's Meadowlands Security Company. Not surprisingly, Meadowlands, according to October 1986 reports to the New Jersey Election Law Commission, was a contributor to Camden County Democrats. The controversy forcing Salema's resignation even as Governor Florio was running a tough reelection campaign prompted the *Courier-Post* on May 27, 1993, to note "the contradiction that has underlain Florio's entire political career: A reform-minded, issues-oriented politician who has relied on an old-time political machine for support." *New York Times*, May 27, 1993, February 24, 1995, January 4, 1997; *Courier-Post*, March 9, June 26, 1995; *Bond Buyer*, August 15, 1995; *Wall Street Journal*, June 5, 1996.

60. *Courier-Post.*, September 14, 1989, January 12, 1993; Joseph N. DiStefano, "The Local Bank That Could," *Philadelphia Inquirer Magazine*, September 1, 2002.

61. Letter from Vernon W. Hill, III to Kenneth McIlvaine, March 16, 1989, copy Vernon Hill file, CCHS; *Courier-Post*, August 20, 1992.

62. *Courier-Post*, September 18, 1992.

63. Commerce Bankcorp's new role was well reflected in the rise of contributions through its political action committee, from $72,000 in 1996 to $654,000 in 2002. Commerce's expansion paralleled its growing political presence. Between 1997 and 2002 its assets grew from $2.9 billion to $17.7 billion. Government deposits made up a significant portion of that sizeable growth, rising in the same period from $500 million to $2.5 billion. By 2002 the number of government clients at Commerce had grown to five hundred. "No other bank, bond underwriter, or insurance broker operating in New Jersey has doled out more campaign cash, received

more no-bid contracts, or employed more of the state's politically connected figures in the last five years," concluded the *Record* after an eight-month investigation. "Commerce's extraordinary reach allows its executives and board members to bring politicians, lawyers, and developers together for mutual benefit." *Record* (New Jersey), May 5, 2003, May 21, 2003.

64. Interview with Charles Ashley, Pennsauken, March 11, 2002.

65. Delgado press release, 1990 elections file, CCHS; *Courier-Post*, August 8, October 17, November 8, 1990.

66. *Courier-Post*, November 7, 8, 9, 1990. In a letter dated January 19, 1993, to the *Courier-Post*, city activist James Harris charged that Delgado voters were excluded when their signature pages were found missing from the registration books. This document, along with a number of others from the 1990s, was in the back files of *Courier-Post* reporter Kevin Riordan and is now in the James Harris file in the Gillette Camden Collection, CCHS.

67. Interviews with Jose Delgado, Cherry Hill, January 22, 1998, and William Tucker, Haddonfield, April 28, 1998. Tucker served as Delgado's campaign treasurer in 1990 and joined the meeting with Norcross. *Courier-Post*, March 30, April 18, 1991; *Philadelphia Inquirer*, July 16, 2001.

68. *Courier-Post*, May 2, 5, 16, 21, 1991.

69. According to Charles Ashley, in his March 11, 2002, interview, and James Chalmus, in an interview in Camden, March 4, 2002, city council attempted to block Thompson's appointment of Chalmus as director of public works so the job could go to Democratic party chairman Theodore Hinson's wife. Although Thompson managed to prevail in that appointment, Ashley was forced from his job before he could institute a thorough review of departmental procedures. Ashley's active participation in Democrats for the People drew fierce criticism from party regulars. See copies of flyers circulated during the early 1990s in Riordan's political files, CCHS.

70. *Philadelphia Inquirer*, April 4, June 13, 1993.

71. *Courier-Post*, June 9, 10, 1993.

72. For an informed summary of the first seven months of the Webster term, see Kevin Riordan's assessment, "Webster Battling a 'Shadow Government,'" *Courier-Post*, July 24, 1994. Thompson quoted in *Philadelphia Inquirer*, April 12, 1994.

73. *Philadelphia Inquirer*, May 27, 1995; *Courier-Post*, January 11, 1995.

74. *Courier-Post*, June 25, July 2, 1995.

75. *Courier-Post*, November 11, 1996. Comments made to the author by City Councilman Angel Fuentes, the third candidate in the "primary" and believed at the time to be the county organization's candidate, en route from Camden to Trenton, August 12, 1998.

76. *Philadelphia Inquirer*, June 15, 1997. According to Mangaliso Davis, a long-time Camden activist, who stood by Webster during his term in office, Webster alienated his county sponsors early in his administration and was quickly cut loose by the dominant Democratic organization. An informal primary among African Americans would have helped chances of holding the office, he claimed, "but the egos were too big." Interview, Camden, June 22, 1999.

Chapter 5. The Downtown Waterfront: Changing Camden's Image

Epigraphs: *Philadelphia Inquirer*, March 5, 1989; *New York Times*, real estate section, February 2, 2003.

1. John P. Kretzmann and John L. McKnight, *Building Communities from the Inside Out: A Path Toward Finding and Mobilizing a Community's Assets* (Evanston, Ill.: Institute for Policy Research, Northwestern University, 1993).

2. Interview with Thomas H. Kean, Madison, N.J., November 12, 1997. See also his remarks on the opening of the New Jersey State Aquarium, *Philadelphia Inquirer*, March 1, 1992.

3. Dennis R. Judd, "Constructing the Tourist Bubble," in Susan S. Fainstein and Dennis R. Judd, eds., *The Tourist City* (New Haven, Conn.: Yale University Press, 1999), 36. Kean responded according to what historian Jon Teaford labels "the gospel of urban hype" following the opening of Boston's highly successful Quincy Market in 1976: "Older hubs needed to shed their blighted reputations; with a fresh promotional face the expected renaissance would arrive on schedule. Festival marketplaces, waterfront fairs, and big league sports teams were among the flourishes that would brighten the city's image." Jon C. Teaford, *The Rough Road to Renaissance: Urban Revitalization in America, 1940–1985* (Baltimore: Johns Hopkins University Press, 1990), 254.

4. Bernard J. Frieden and Lynn B. Sagalyn, *Downtown, Inc.: How America Rebuilds Cities* (Cambridge, Mass.: MIT Press, 1989), 316. See their Chapter 11, "Privatizing the City," for the policy context for this blending of private with public authority.

5. So argue Michael A. Pagano and Ann O'M. Bowman in their study of redevelopment efforts in ten cities, *Cityscapes and Capital: The Politics of Urban Development* (Baltimore: Johns Hopkins University Press, 1995), Chapter 3, 44–67. For extended essays on efforts to alter particular images in post-industrial circumstances, see John Russo and Sherry Lee Linkon, "Collateral Damage: Deindustrialization and the Uses of Youngstown" and S. Paul O'Hara, "Envisioning the Steel City: The Legend and Legacy of Gary, Indiana," both in Jefferson Cowie and Joseph Heathcott, eds., *Beyond the Ruins: The Meanings of Deindustrialization* (Ithaca, N.Y.: Cornell University Press, 2003), chapters 9 and 10 respectively.

6. *Courier-Post*, June 3, 1961.

7. "Alternative Development Concepts: Central Waterfront Industrial District, Camden, New Jersey." Interim report, Jacknin and Company, Washington, D.C., Ben Dyer Associates, Riverdale, Maryland, January, 1970.

8. "Camden Waterfront: A Prospectus for an Offering of Land," Camden, 1978, 17.

9. Interview with Thomas Corcoran, Camden, January 9, 2003.

10. "Recommended Development Program for Cooper's Ferry, Camden, New Jersey," American City Corporation, October, 1983, 2.

11. "Downtown Camden Riverfront Development: Assessment of Market Support," American City Corporation, Columbia, Maryland, March, 1983, 8, 77. Charles Tomlinson, the designer of Camden's waterfront park, had struck a similar

chord at the dedication ceremony when he said, "Camden has to eliminate the bad stigma. It is something that has to be overcome, and a lot of it is publicity more than anything else." *Courier-Post*, May 18, 1980.

12. "Recommended Development Program for Cooper's Ferry," 28, 29.

13. See Jeffrey M. Dorwart, *Camden County, New Jersey: The Making of a Metropolitan Community, 1626–2000* (New Brunswick, N.J.: Rutgers University Press, 2001), 18–19.

14. *Courier-Post*, February 8, 1984; interview with Thomas Corcoran, January 9, 2003; Thomas Corcoran to Camden Mayor Arnold Webster, April 7, 1994, Cooper Ferry Development Association file, Camden County Historical Society (CCHS).

15. Governor Kean told a somewhat different version of this story in his interview with me November 12, 1997. When I tried to confirm his account in the fall of 2004, he could not recall Musiani's role. It was Thomas Corcoran who confirmed the details by phone December 6, 2004, pointing out that he did not think Kean was aware of the tradeoff Musiani had offered. He remembered being informed in advance of his meeting with Kean by a member of the assembly, which he thought was Wayne Bryant. Corcoran provided other details of the preparations and meeting with Kean in his interview with me, January 9, 2003.

16. *Courier Post*, April 25, 1985. Primas's interest in Baltimore was reported in the same paper January 13, 1984.

17. *Courier-Post*, April 28, 1985.

18. *Philadelphia Inquirer*, April 7, 1986; *Courier-Post*, July 20, 1987.

19. *Philadelphia Inquirer*, July 10, December 6, 23, 1988.

20. *Philadelphia Inquirer*, March 15, 1989; *New Jersey Municipalities*, June, 1989.

21. "City Aquariums Are a Growth Industry," *Philadelphia Inquirer*, April 16, 1990.

22. Corcoran interview, January 9, 2003; *Philadelphia Inquirer*, November 21, 1989; *Courier-Post*, February 9, 1990. Text of remarks by Governor Jim Florio, General Electric Press conference, Camden, March 19, 1991, General Electric file, CCHS.

23. Corcoran interview, January 9, 2003.

24. News Release, Office of the Governor, March 19, 1991, General Electric file, CCHS; *Courier-Post*, March 20, 1991; *New York Times*, January 5, 1992.

25. *Philadelphia Inquirer*, November 2, 1989, March 9, July 15, 1990; *Courier-Post*, December 23, 29, 1993. Subsequently leased to a spin-off corporation, L-3 Communications, worth more than a billion dollars in annual revenue, the facility housed 950, largely highly trained workers in 2003. *Courier-Post*, October 23, 2003.

26. *Philadelphia Inquirer*, March 1, 15, 1992; *Newark Star-Ledger*, March 1, 1992.

27. *Philadelphia Inquirer*, January 28, 1993, January 16, 1994.

28. *Philadelphia Inquirer*, January 9, 1994; *New York Times*, August 27, 1995; David Barringer, "The New Urban Gamble," *American Prospect* (September–October, 1997): 33.

29. Interview with Antoinette Vielehr, Vice President of Development and Membership, New Jersey State Aquarium, Camden, March 21, 2003.

30. *Philadelphia Inquirer*, April 20, 1989, January 31, 1990.

31. "No Heroic Measures," editorial, *Philadelphia Inquirer*, July 6, 1989.

32. *Philadelphia Inquirer*, February 13, 1990; *Courier-Post*, April 16, November 6, 1990.

33. *Philadelphia Inquirer*, October 22, 1993; *Courier-Post*, December 3, 16, 31, 1993.

34. *Courier-Post*, January 9, 1994.

35. *Philadelphia Inquirer*, January 16, 1994.

36. *Courier-Post*, February 2, 1994. According to a report in the *Philadelphia Inquirer*, July 15, 1989, Rendell was an active agent in pursuing negotiations between the city and owners of the sports facility well before he became mayor.

37. The prospect of corporate credit was reported in *Courier-Post*, October 6, 1989. A *Philadelphia Inquirer* report for December 19, 1993, quoted Camden County Freeholder-Director James Beach as saying, "I think most of the jobs ought to go to people from Camden County—not just Camden City." The *Courier-Post* January 9, 1994, cited East Camden activist Dwaine Williams's concern about the availability of decent jobs for Camden residents.

38. *Courier-Post*, November 19, 1992. For an account of the consolidation of Blockbuster, Sony, and Pace's entertainment operations, see Associated Press report November 1, 1993, LexisNexis file, under Pace Entertainment, Camden.

39. *Courier-Post*, December, 17, 1992; Corcoran interview, January 9, 2003.

40. *New York Times*, August 27, 1995.

41. According to a February 14, 1991 press release issued by Cooper's Ferry Development Association, another $1 million in funding came from the New Jersey Department of Transportation. The City of Camden's contribution, listed at $2 million, came in the form of a loan from the Urban Development Corporation of New Jersey.

42. *Washington Post*, March 24, 1992.

43. *Courier-Post*, March 21, December 19, 1991, January 18, 1992, November 17, 1994.

44. Gregory D. Squires, "Public-Private Partnerships: Who Gets What and Why?" in Squires, ed., *Unequal Partnerships: The Political Economy of Urban Redevelopment in Postwar America* (New Brunswick, N.J.: Rutgers University Press, 1989), 7, 9.

45. *Washington Post*, March 14, 1992.

46. *Courier-Post*, March 1, 1992; *Philadelphia Inquirer*, April 5, 1992.

47. Interview with Antoinette Vielehr, March 21, 2003.

48. *Philadelphia Inquirer*, February 23, 1992. A press release dated April 15, 1992, drawn from the files of *Courier Post* reporter Kevin Riordan, suggests that Camden County College was offering a very different kind of training. Funded by Cooper's Ferry, four modules were offered to prepare Camden residents as security personnel. That the work was more basic than technical was suggested by such subjects as "how to interact successfully with people of diverse racial, ethnic, linguistic, and physiological backgrounds," "how to understand human reactions and to manage stress," and basic writing and reporting skills, including how to log daily

activities and write reports about incidents that might become a part of an official record.

49. *Courier-Post*, March 29, 1992, April 10, 1994; *Philadelphia Inquirer*, January 4, 1993. For a full account of Atlantic City's failure to distribute broadly the wealth generated by casinos, see Bryant Simon, *Boardwalk of Dreams: Atlantic City and the Fate of Urban America* (New York: Oxford University Press, 2004).

50. Tom Knoche letter, *Courier-Post*, March, 1991, copy GE file, CCHS.

51. *Courier Post*, October 27, 1977.

52. *Courier-Post*, June 20, 1990; copy letters from architect Greg Winkler to North Camden Land Trust, June 14, 1990, and Tom Knoche to the *Courier-Post*, July 19, 1990, Royal Court file, CCHS.

53. Press release from Royal Court Homebuyers Association and supporting organizations, November 16, 1990, Royal Court file, CCHS. See also report of resident allegations that demolition was planned because they occupied valuable land, *Philadelphia Inquirer*, November 26, 1990.

54. *Courier-Post*, March 26, 1995, March 31, 1999.

55. *Courier-Post*, April 10, 1994.

56. *Courier-Post*, January 1, February 23, 1992.

57. *Philadelphia Inquirer*, April 5, 1992.

58. Thomas P. Corcoran to Everett Landers, April 28, 1992, Cooper's Ferry Development Association file, CCHS.

59. *Courier-Post*, April 11, 1995.

60. "Report of the Camden Waterfront Planning Charrette, September 15–17, 1992." Cooper's Ferry file, CCHS.

61. "Executive Summary, Development Strategy for an Entertainment Destination on the Camden Waterfront," MRA International, June 1999.

62. See reports as New Jersey, the U.S. Congress, and President George H. Bush approved the measure. *Courier-Post*, January 20, October 7, 28, 1992.

63. *Courier-Post*, March 18, 1996. According to MRA's 1999 report, this figure would begin to approach the level of attendance at Baltimore's Inner Harbor of 13 to 15 million a year.

64. *Courier-Post*, March 8, 1996.

65. *Courier-Post*, March 8, August 14, 1998; *Philadelphia Inquirer*, June 19, 1998, March 18, 1999, August 21, 2002.

66. See reports in *Philadelphia Inquirer*, June 25, 1999; *Courier-Post*, July 1, 1999, August 12, 2002.

67. Headline in *Courier-Post*, November 10, 1999, quoting Joseph Azzolina of Bayonne, chairman of the New Jersey Battleship Commission. Youngstown and Gary also had to contend with a similar designation. See Russo and Linkon, "Collateral Damage," 210 and O'Hara, "Envisioning the Steel City," 232, in *Beyond the Ruins*.

68. Among the many news reports on the ship's difficult journey to a berth in Camden, see *Courier-Post*, November 12, 1999, February 12, March 4, 2000, September 24, 27, 2001.

69. Corcoran interview, January 9, 2003.

70. *Courier-Post*, May 6, 2001.

71. *Courier-Post*, May 4, 2001.

72. *Courier-Post*, May 26, 2000; *New York Times* (New Jersey section), June 4, 2000.

73. Quoted from Michael Moore, "Flint and Me," *Money*, July 1996, 86, in O'Hara, "Envisioning the Steel City," 235.

74. See David Harvey, "A View from Federal Hill," in Elizabeth Fee, Linda Shopes, and Linda Zeidman, eds., *The Baltimore Book: New Views of Local History* (Philadelphia: Temple University Press, 1991), 227–49; Marc V. Levine, "Downtown Development as a Growth Strategy: A Critical Appraisal of the Baltimore Renaissance," *Journal of Urban Affairs* 9 (1987): 103–23; Richard C. Hula, "The Two Baltimores," in Dennis Judd and Michael Parkinson, eds., *Leadership and Urban Regeneration* (Newbury Park, Calif.: Sage Publications, 1990), 191–215; and David Rusk, *Baltimore Unbound: A Strategy for Regional Renewal* (Baltimore: Abel Foundation, 1996).

75. M. Christine Boyer, "Cities for Sale: Merchandising History at South Street Seaport," in Michael Sorkin, ed., *Variations on a Theme Park: The New American City and the End of Public Space* (New York: Hill and Wang, 1992), 192.

76. Judd, "Constructing the Tourist Bubble," 36.

Chapter 6. The Neighborhoods: Not by Faith Alone

Epigraph: Robert Halpern, *Rebuilding the Inner City: A History of Neighborhood Initiatives to Address Poverty in the United States* (New York: Columbia University Press, 1995), 5.

1. Paul S. Grogan and Tony Proscio, *Comeback Cities: A Blueprint for Urban Neighborhood Revival* (Boulder, Colo.: Westview Press, 2000), 1.

2. Alexander Von Hoffman, *House by House, Block by Block: The Rebirth of America's Urban Neighborhoods* (New York: Oxford University Press, 2003), 2. See also Neal Peirce's syndicated column, "Inner Cities: New Hope, More Challenges," released October 26, 2003.

3. See, for example, "In Era of Shrinking Budgets, Community Groups Blossom," *New York Times*, February 25, 1996.

4. David Rusk, *Cities Without Suburbs* (Washington, D.C.: Woodrow Wilson Center Press, 1995), 76–77.

5. "Despite some block-by-block victories," Rusk argues, community development corporations and allied community organizations "are losing the war against poverty itself. In effect, CDCs are expected to help a crowd of poor people run up a down escalator, an escalator that is engineered to come down faster and faster than most poor people can run up." *Inside Game/Outside Game: Winning Strategies for Saving Urban America* (Washington, D.C.: Brookings Institution Press, 1999), 18.

6. Kevin Fedarko, "Who Could Live Here?" *Time*, January 20, 1992, 20–23.

7. Rusk, *Inside Game/Outside Game*, chapters 2 and 3; "In Bedford-Stuyvesant,

The Boom Remains a Bust," *New York Times*, May 29, 2000; Grogan and Proscio, *Comeback Cities*, 3, 34.; and reviews of Grogan and Proscio's book by Lisa Krissoff Boehm, H-Urban@H-Net.MSU.Edu, September 3, 2002, and Brad Lander, *Shelterforce* (November/December 2000).

8. Rusk, *Inside Game/Outside Game*, 18.

9. Interview, Camden, January 23, 1998.

10. *Courier-Post*, April 16, 1995.

11. Interview, Pine Hill, May 30, 2002. Harmon received her bachelor's degree from Rowan University in 1999, her son from Hobart and William Smith the same year.

12. Peter Dreier, "Community Empowerment Strategies: The Limits and Potential of Community Organizing in Urban Neighborhoods," *Cityscape* 2 (May 1996): 126, citing Samuel G. Freedman, *Upon This Rock: The Miracles of a Black Church* (New York: HarperCollins, 1993), among other sources.

13. See Norman I. Fainstein and Susan S. Fainstein, "New Haven: The Limits of the Local States," in Susan S. Fainstein, Norman I. Fainstein, Robert Child Hill, Dennis Judd, and Michael Peter Smith, eds., *Restructuring the City: The Political Economy of Urban Development* (rev. ed. New York: Longman, 1986), 27–79.

14. *Courier-Post*, August 8, November 3, 1967, November 12, 1968.

15. *Courier-Post*, March 3, August 1, 1968, July 9, 1971.

16. Joseph Nardi confirmed this picture in a February 13, 1998, interview in Camden, emphasizing that families did not know how to take care of their new homes.

17. BPUM Corporation, certified July 19, 1972, files of Concerned Citizens of North Camden, Camden County Historical Society (CCHS).

18. Robert Halpern, *Rebuilding the Inner City*, 138.

19. *Philadelphia Inquirer*, September 20, 1993.

20. Quoted in *New York Times*, April 3, 1988.

21. North Camden Land Trust brochure, c. 1997. Camden Lutheran Housing Corporation formed in 1986 when CCNC jointed Lutheran Social Ministries of New Jersey, based in Trenton, and Camden Lutheran Parish, a ministry of five parishes under Grace's leadership. It served as the North Camden Land Trust's primary development arm.

22. Interview with North Camden Land Trust Executive Director, Jose Sanchez, who previously initiated this program as land trust administrator. See *Courier-Post*, April 19, 1996, for an account of the process in operation.

23. *Delaware Valley Community Reinvestment News*, Fall 1991; North Camden Land Trust press release, November 19, 1993.

24. *The North Camden Plan*, October 1993, 10. Notices of meetings of the Grassroots Oversight Committee, along with updates on the planning process, were published in the community newspaper, *Moving Forward: La Voz de la Gente (The People's Voice)*.

25. Save Our Waterfront, *People's Plan for the North Camden Waterfront* (Camden, August 1990).

26. *North Camden Plan*, October, 1993. See also coverage in *Courier-Post*, Oc-

tober 16, 1992; *Philadelphia Inquirer*, September 20, 1993; *Delaware Valley Community Reinvestment News*, Summer, 1993.

27. *Philadelphia Inquirer*, July 15, 1993; *Courier-Post*, July 15, 1993. The participating banks were Chemical Bank New Jersey, Commerce Bank, CoreStates New Jersey National Bank, Midlantic Bank, and United Jersey Bank.

28. *Courier-Post*, November 3, 1999.

29. *Courier-Post*, July 20, 1994.

30. Distinctive as it has been in Camden, the North Camden organizing strategy has much in common with other community-based efforts, with Boston's Dudley Square land trust organization, for instance, or the effective use of Community Reinvestment Funds by the Pittsburgh Community Reinvestment Group. See Peter Dedoff and Holly Sklar, *Streets of Hope: The Fall and Rise of an Urban Neighborhood* (Boston: South End Press, 1994) and Elise M. Bright, *Reviving America's Forgotten Neighborhoods: An Investigation of Inner City Revitalization Efforts* (New York: Routledge, 2003), Chapters 4 and 5.

31. See Gerald H. Gamm, *Urban Exodus: Why the Jews Left Boston and the Catholics Stayed Behind* (Cambridge, Mass.: Harvard University Press, 1999).

32. *Courier-Post*, June 21, 1999.

33. *Courier-Post*, July 31, 1997; interview with Brother William Johnson, San Miguel founder and director, April 8, 1998.

34. Much of DeNeely's efforts focused initially around securing safety at a park at Fourth and Clinton Streets near her childhood home, an issue she had been pursuing for several years, as reported in *Courier-Post*, May 31, 2000.

35. This story was retold and, in fact, recreated at an unusual filmed reunion of the event in the building where the break-in took place: *Philadelphia Inquirer*, May 3, 2002; *Courier Post*, May 5, 2002. A commemorative packet put together by the Historical Society of the United States District Court for the District of New Jersey provided further detail.

36. Michael Doyle quoted in *Courier-Post* on the occasion of his thirtieth anniversary in Camden.

37. *Philadelphia Inquirer*, December 24, 1997.

38. "The Sound of Music," Msgr. Doyle's monthly newsletter for May, 2002, reprinted in Michael Doyle, *It's a Terrible Day, Thanks Be to God!* (Camden: Heart of Camden, 2003), 232; *Courier-Post*, May 7, 15, 2000.

39. Interview with Sister Margaret (Peg) Hynes, Camden, March 12, 1998; see also a profile of Sister Peg in the *Philadelphia Inquirer*, November 25, 1999.

40. *Courier-Post*, June 3, 1991.

41. Interview with Monsignor Robert McDermott, Camden, March 19, 1997; *Philadelphia Inquirer*, May 15, 2002.

42. *Delaware Valley Community Reinvestment News*, Fall 1991.

43. Sean Closkey, unpublished paper, "Saint Joseph's Carpenter Society: Development Strategy," c. 1999, Saint Joseph's Carpenter Society file, CCHS.

44. *Courier-Post*, April 6, 1995.

45. *Hope Times*, newsletter of the Saint Joseph's Carpenter Society, Spring 1996.

46. Quoted in the *Philadelphia Inquirer*, September 8, 1996.

47. Sean Closkey, unpublished paper, "Building Assets: Opportunities and Challenges," c. 1999, Saint Joseph's Carpenter Society file, CCHS. For an extended look at the issue of asset accumulation, see Thomas M. Shapiro and Edward N. Wolff, eds., *Assets for the Poor: The Benefits of Spreading Asset Ownership* (New York: Russell Sage Foundation, 2001), especially Chapter 7, Nancy A. Denton, "Housing as a Means of Asset Accumulation: A Good Strategy for the Poor?" 232–66.

48. Interview with Robert McDermott, March 19, 1997; *Courier-Post*, May 24, 1999; *Philadelphia Inquirer*, June 12, 2000, May 15, 2002.

49. *Courier-Post*, June 28, 2000; interview with William Whelan, Camden, September 10, 2002.

50. *East Camden Strategic Investment Plan* (Pittsburgh: Urban Design Associates, 2003), 3–4.

51. *Courier-Post*, June 16, 1993.

52. Interview with Sean Closkey, May 13, 1997. For a description of different national intermediaries, see *Shelterforce* (July/August 1998): 22.

53. The other cities the Ford Foundation supported were Seattle, El Paso, Detroit, and New Orleans. *Courier-Post*, May 25, 1994; interview with H. Ahada Stanford, Camden, April 24, 1997; *Philadelphia Inquirer*, November 27, 1996; *Courier-Post*, May 29, 1998, June 7, 1999.

54. Flyer, "The Camden Development Collaborative: 'A Strategic Partnership for Community Renewal,'" Camden Development Collaborative file, CCHS.

55. *Philadelphia Inquirer*, March 8, April 3, 1988; *Courier-Post*, December 4, 1987, March 29, June 5, 22, July 4, 1998. Interview with Joseph Fleming, Executive Director, CCOP, Camden, October 17, 1997. For a highly sympathetic review of CCOP's origins and its development, see John P. Hogan, "Taking a City off the Cross: CCOP, Camden, New Jersey," in *Credible Signs of Christ Alive: Case Studies from the Catholic Campaign for Human Development* (Boulder, Colo.: Rowman and Littlefield, 2003), 45–63. Hogan's daughter, Pilar, joined the staff of Saint Joseph's Carpenter Society, subsequently marrying its director, Sean Closkey. Another study that chose to emphasize Camden's religious leadership is William H. Hudnut, III, "Filling a Gap with Faith-Based Institutions, Camden, NJ," in *Halfway to Everywhere: A Portrait of America's First-Tier Suburbs* (Washington, D.C.: Urban Land Institute, 2003), 202–14.

56. Mayor August Longo, quoted in the *Philadelphia Inquirer*, April 3, 1988.

57. CCOP memo to Governor Thomas Kean, June 7, 1988, files of CCOP, East Camden. See also Michael Doyle, "City Should Be Paid for Solving Other Towns' Woes," *Courier-Post*, February 19, 1989; *Philadelphia Inquirer* editorial, "Justice and Sewage," April 29, 1989; *New York Times*, June 19, 1991. Assemblymen Bryant and Roberts explained their support for enabling legislation under the title, "Host Community Benefits Are a Matter of Justice," *Courier-Post*, June 7, 1991.

58. Already a problem as far back as 1950, with 1,077 of the city's 35,510 units abandoned, the number soared to 3,510 of 30,130 units in 1990. *Courier-Post*, October 6, 1991.

59. *Courier-Post*, June 23, 1992.

60. *Courier-Post*, April 1, 1993; "CCOP Launches Camden Community Housing Campaign," news release, June 17, 1996; "Impacts of the Camden Community

Housing Campaign on Crime: A Preliminary Report," Center for Social and Community Development, School of Social Work, Rutgers University, 1997, CCOP House Campaign file, CCHS.

61. "Whitman and Kenny Announce Initial Phase of Camden Redevelopment Project," press release, Office of the Governor, June 17, 1996, CCOP House Campaign file, CCHS; interview with Joseph Fleming, Executive Director, CCOP, Camden, October 17, 1997.

62. *Courier-Post*, May 19, 1999, May 31, 2000.

63. Jeannie Appleman, "Evaluation Study of Institution-Based Organizing for the Discount Foundation," paper available at the Discount Foundation's web site dated November 12, 1996, 22–23.

64. Interview with Delbert Nelson, Camden, April 18, 2002.

65. Interview with Carol Dann, Camden Neighborhood Renaissance Executive Director, Camden, November 4, 2002; "Detailed Description of the Holistic Plan for the Camden Neighborhood Renaissance: A Move to Improve," CNR file, CCHS.

66. Dann interview, November 4, 2002; *Courier-Post*, April 21, 1992.

67. Dann interview, November 4, 2002. Dann was drawn into the effort through a chance meeting with City Councilman Angel Fuentes. Previously she had worked as county coordinator for the homeless and as a GED advisor at Camden County Community College in Camden. *Philadelphia Inquirer*, May 16, 2000; *Courier-Post*, May 6, 2000, August 21, 2002.

68. See, for instance, a series of occasional articles by Kevin Riordan, "Building Blocks," *Courier-Post*, May 10, 31, 1992.

69. Leadership conference, "Building Leaders, Building Hope," sponsored by Parkside Business and Community in Partnership, May 4, 2002; "weed and seed" meeting, Fairview, June 17, 2002.

70. *Courier-Post*, May 4, 1999; Michael H. Lang, "The Design of Yorkship Garden Village," in Mary Corbin Sies and Christopher Silver, eds., *Planning the Twentieth-Century American City* (Baltimore: Johns Hopkins University Press, 1996), 120–44.

71. *Courier-Post*, September 19, 23, 1990, September 24, 1992.

72. Interview with Suzanne Marks Brennan, Camden, April 29, 2002; *Philadelphia Inquirer*, December 6, 2001, February 21, 2003; *New York Times*, January 6, 2002.

73. According to figures compiled by CAMConnect, an organization formed to provide data for policy analysis in Camden, the number of properties abandoned in the neighborhood rose from 216, or 11 percent in 1990, to 413 or 21 percent in 2000. By way of contrast, vacancies in the downtown neighborhood dropped by 43 percent over the same period.

74. See, for example, Peter Dreier's summary posed at a symposium revisiting the Kerner Commission report, *North Carolina Law Review* 71 (June 1993): 1394.

75. Only a brief obituary in the *Courier-Post* appeared, October 8, 2003, to note the end of her life. Information about her health in her last year came from the few friends who attended the wake in Parkside October 10.

76. Anthony Downs, "The Challenge of Our Declining Big Cities," *Housing Policy Debate* 8, 2 (1997), 402.

77. *Philadelphia Inquirer* December 22, 23, 25, 2002, *Courier-Post*, December 22, 23, editorial, "Heart and Soul: Camden is Poorer Still for the Death of Sister Peg," December 25, 2002.

Chapter 7. The Courts: Seeking Justice and Fairness

Epigraph: Housing Act of 1949, PL 171, 81st Cong., 1st sess.

1. This was the scene I encountered when Msgr. Michael Doyle gave me my first tour of the area on September 26, 1997, in an old Volkswagen bus, seating us high enough above the action that we might as well have been watching a movie from our perch.

2. Figures compiled on the basis of 1998 census data by Sean Closkey while he was director of the Saint Joseph's Carpenter Society, Camden. Copy in the Affordable Housing file, Camden County Historical Society (CCHS).

3. See Smith's own description of the company's community outreach efforts, "St. Lawrence Cement Has Done Everything It Should," *Courier-Post*, January 24, 2001.

4. *Courier-Post*, November 3, 1999; interview with Gladys Blair, Camden, June 25, 2002.

5. Alexis de Tocqueville, *Democracy in America*, 1: chapters 15 and 16. Originally published in 1833, Tocqueville's classic study has since appeared in many editions.

6. Thomas J. Sugrue, *The Origins of the Urban Crisis: Race and Inequality in Postwar Detroit* (Princeton, N.J.: Princeton University Press, 1996), 58–59.

7. *South Camden Citizens in Action et al. v. N.J. Department of Environmental Protection*, U.S. District Court, District of New Jersey, Docket No: 01-CV-702, 14–15, 27. The primary grounds for action was the contention that the New Jersey Department of Environmental Protection had violated Title VI of the Civil Rights Act, which requires any recipient of federal funding not to discriminate on grounds of race, color, or national origin. Acting also for the plaintiffs were Michael Churchill and Jerome Balter of the Public Interest Law Center of Philadelphia and Luke Cole of the Center on Race, Poverty, and Environment in San Francisco. A twenty-year veteran at Legal Services, Pomar moved from the Trenton to the Camden office in 1994 specifically to do community development work. Marcia Coyle, "Making Pollution a Civil Rights Issue," *National Law Journal* (December 24 2001).

8. *South Camden Citizens in Action*, 4.

9. Msgr. Michael Doyle, quoted in *Courier-Post*, April 2, 2000.

10. Referring to a state standard that requires ballots to be printed in Spanish as well as English in any area where the Spanish-speaking population is 10 percent or more, South Camden Citizens in Action used this omission as evidence of discrimination according to national origin. (19–21)

11. *Philadelphia Inquirer*, April 13, 2001.

12. *Philadelphia Inquirer*, April 20, 23, 2001. The decision was considered important enough to be posted on the Environmental Justice Resource Center's website in Atlanta at www.ejrc.cau.edu, along with an interview by center director Robert Bullard of Phyllis Holmes, one of the individual plaintiffs in the South Camden Citizens in Action suit.

13. *Courier-Post*, April 25, 2001; David Dante Troutt, "Behind the Court's Civil Rights Ruling," *New York Times*, News of the Week in Review, April 29, 2001. *Alexander v. Sandoval*, 121 S. Ct. 1511 (2001) involved the reversal of two lower court decisions challenging Alabama's English-only law. The Spanish-speaking plaintiff filed suit under Title VI, claiming she was discriminated against on the basis of her national origin because the state required her to take her driver's test in English.

14. John F. Gullace, "Conflicting Opinions Add to Haze in Environmental Claims," *Legal Intelligencer* (May 17, 2001): 5.

15. *Philadelphia Inquirer*, May 11, June 5, 2001; *Courier-Post*, May 11, 2001. For a summary of Judge Orlofsky's ruling, see *National Environmental Enforcement Journal* 16, 5 (June 2001): 13. Summarizing the case, Steven C. Russo and Elizabeth A. Read said they expected the Camden decisions to be revisited frequently in the courts "as environmental justice plaintiffs continue to attempt to use federal law as a mechanism to require the analysis of cumulative impacts and disparate impacts from polluting facilities located in minority neighborhoods." *New York Law Journal* (December 17 2001): 9.

16. *Philadelphia Inquirer*, June 19, 2001.

17. *Courier-Post*, July 3, 2001. Lorraine Woellert, "Dumping on the Poor?" *Business Week*, November 19, 2001, 120.

18. Brief of Amici Curiae. . . . *South Camden Citizens in Action, et al. v. New Jersey Department of Environmental Protection, et al.* St. Lawrence Cement file, CCHS.

19. *Philadelphia Inquirer*, September 6, 2001.

20. Shannon P. Duffy, "'Environmental Racism' Suit Against Cement Plant Is Dealt a Mortal Blow," *New Jersey Law Journal*, December 24, 2001.

21. *Courier-Post*, December 18, 2001; *Business Week*, "Polluting Plants Get Built Because People Need Jobs," December 17, 2001, 16. See also St. Lawrence attorneys Brian Montag and Catherine A Trinkle's assessment, "Environmental Justice at a Crossroads," *New Jersey Law Journal* (February 25, 2002), which concluded, "In effect, the *South Camden* decision eliminates the right of private plaintiffs to enforce Title VI disparate impact regulations through an action in federal court." Although clearly sympathetic to the plaintiffs, Lewis Goldshore and Marsha Wolf agreed that only new legislative action could affirm that right. "Environmental Justice: Where Do We Go Now?" *New Jersey Law Journal* (March 18, 2002).

22. *Courier-Post*, January 17, June 26, 2002.

23. *Philadelphia Inquirer*, August 24, 2003

24. *New York Times*, February 28, 1993.

25. Naomi Bailin Wish and Stephen Eisdorfer, "The Impact of *Mount Laurel* Initiatives: An Analysis of the Characteristics of Applicants and Occupants," *Seton Hall Law Review* 77, 4 (1997): 1303.

26. *Courier-Post*, May 4, 1999.

27. Cynthia N. McKee, "Resurrecting *Mount Laurel*: Using Title VIII Litigation to Achieve the Ultimate *Mount Laurel* Goal of Integration," *Seton Hall Law Review* 77, 4 (1997), 1340.

28. David L. Kirp, John P. Dwyer, and Larry A. Rosenthal, *Our Town: Race, Housing, and the Soul of Suburbia* (New Brunswick, N.J.: Rutgers University Press, 1995), 42–43. Interview with Allen Zeller, Cherry Hill, June 26, 2002.

29. *Our Town*, 2. This study provides a detailed account of the *Mount Laurel* decisions, the events leading to the decisions, and their impact. See also the feature in the *New York Times* real estate section, May 1, 1988.

30. Cited in Charles H. Haar, *Suburbs Under Siege: Race, Space, and Audacious Judges* (Princeton, N.J.: Princeton University Press, 1996), 17–18. A professor emeritus at the Harvard Law School, Haar covers in his book some of the same ground as *Our Town*, but with an emphasis on the strengths and weaknesses of the legal case. For a thorough evaluation of Haar's argument and a dissent from its celebration of the effectiveness of the *Mount Laurel* doctrine, see John M. Payne's review, "Lawyers, Judges, and the Public Interest," *Michigan Law Review* 96 (May, 1998): 1685–1714.

31. *Mount Laurel I,* 67 N.J. 179,336 A.2d 728, cited in Haar, *Suburbs Under Siege,* 26.

32. *Suburbs Under Seige,* 77; John Charles Boger, "*Mount Laurel* at 21 Years: Reflections on the Power of Courts and Legislatures to Shape Social Change," *Seton Hall Law Review* 77, 4 (1997): 1452.

33. *Our Town,* 86–87; Payne, "Lawyers, Judges, and the Public Interest," 1685.

34. Peter H. Schuck, *Diversity in America: Keeping Government at a Safe Distance* (Cambridge, Mass.: Belknap Press, 2003), 220.

35. Cited in McKee, "Resurrecting *Mount Laurel*," 1338.

36. Haar, *Suburbs Under Siege,* 146. Peter O'Connor first proposed the idea of a builder's remedy in 1969 to a Mount Laurel developer as a means for settling the original zoning dispute in the township. Kirp et al., *Our Town,* 57.

37. *Courier-Post*, February 14, March 11, 14, 1997; *Burlington County News,* February 16, 1997.

38. *Philadelphia Inquirer*, August 26, 2003.

39. *Courier-Post*, November 25, 1997; *Philadelphia Inquirer*, February 12, December 7, 1997, November 19, 1998.

40. *Courier-Post,* April 12, 1997.

41. See, for instance, the report of objections from township officials over the level of funds to guarantee Fair Share Housing Development's performance bond for the Ethel Lawrence Homes, *Courier-Post*, April 2, 2000, and that of a second successful effort to remove the project announcement sign, *Courier-Post*, August 14, 1998.

42. See the *New York Times*, New Jersey section, November 25, 2001, "The Affordable Housing Complex that Works," and the *Courier-Post*'s extensive report, under the headline, "S.J. Project Shines," May 5, 2002, as well as the reports of the dedication appearing in the *Courier-Post* and *Philadelphia Inquirer*, August 18, 2002.

43. *Courier-Post,* June 27, 1986.

44. *Courier-Post*, December 16, 1986, March 31, December 11, 1987.

45. *Courier-Post*, January 18, 20, 22 (editorial), 1988.

46. *Courier-Post*, April 6, 1989, December 14, 1990, February 2, March 29, 1993. O'Connor's dual role as housing advocate and developer apparently galled Mayor Levin, according to township planning attorney Allen Zeller, and contributed to friction between her and O'Connor despite what appeared to start as a positive relationship: interview June 26, 2002.

47. For the announcement of the sale and history of the Garden State Park and the leisure-time activities it generated , see *Courier-Post*, December 6, 2000, October 16, 2003.

48. *Newark Star-Ledger*, February 11, 2002.

49. Among the properties cited on page 39 of the Zeller, Bryant brief were 79 units of senior housing at the Village at St. Mary's under the sponsorship of the Catholic Diocese of Camden. In order to gain approval for the complex, however, the diocese had to sue the township. See *Courier-Post*, October 16, 1976.

50. Brief and Appendix of Defendant-Respondent, Township of Cherry Hill Planning Board, Supreme Court of New Jersey, Docket No: 52,472, submitted by Allen S. Zeller and Wayne R. Bryant, 42–43.

51. Plaintiffs' Brief in Support of Plaintiffs' Appeal, Supreme Court of New Jersey, Docket No: 52,472, 50–51.

52. *Courier Post*, January 23, March 11, 1998; Plaintiffs' Brief, 61.

53. The 1990 ruling in *Abbott v. Burke*, requiring parity in spending between New Jersey's richest and poorest districts, originated as a class action suit initiated in 1981 by the nonprofit Education Law Center on behalf of eleven-year-old Camden student Raymond Arthur Abbott against Fred Burke, New Jersey Commissioner of Education. For a summary of school equalization law, see Lizabeth Cohen, *A Consumer's Republic: The Politics of Mass Consumption in Postwar America* (New York: Knopf, 2003), 240–51. See also Jonathan Kozol, *Savage Inequalities: Children in America's Schools*, Chapter 4, 133–74.

54. Plaintiff's Brief, 51; Brief in Support of Defendant-Respondent, 7.

55. *Fair Share Housing Center, Inc. v. Township of Cherry Hill et al.* (A-66–01), summarized in *New Jersey Law Journal* (August 12, 2002).

56. *Courier-Post*, August 6–7, 2002. The case that affordable housing advances sprawl has been a favorite of the New Jersey State League of Municipalities, which sided with Cherry Hill against the Fair Share Housing suit. See the report in *New York Times*, "New Jersey's Housing Law Works Too Well, Some Say," March 2, 2001, and the League's amicus brief argued by Edwin W. Schmierer.

57. Jim Crosby, Marlton, *Courier Post*, October 19, 2002. Another writer, responding to an essay by O'Connor's associate on the Garden State case, Kevin Walsh, similarly asserted that good housing should go to those who worked for it and claimed that the neighborhood he grew up in in Cherry Hill recently had been invaded by Camden gangsters. J. Korber, *Courier-Post*, December 18, 2000.

58. Cohen, *A Consumer's Republic*, 228, 240.

59. Schuck, *Diversity in America*, 260. The Chicago *Gautreux* case, requiring the Chicago Housing Authority to disperse a portion of its clients to the city's suburbs is written about more sympathetically in Leonard S. Rubinowitz and James E.

Rosenbaum, *Crossing the Class and Color Lines: From Public Housing to White Suburbia* (Chicago: University of Chicago, 2000).

60. *Courier-Post*, August 13, 2002; interview with Peter O'Connor, Cherry Hill, August 29, 2002; *Newark Star-Ledger*, June 11, 2002.

61. Carl Bisgaier, "An Early Player Assesses Impact," *Housing New Jersey* (January 1993): 9.

62. See O'Connor's essay, "Racial Division Is an Issue N.J. Residents Must Face," *Philadelphia Inquirer*, January 19, 2003, and a complementary story in the *Courier-Post*, January 20, 2003, "Housing Fight Goes On."

Chapter 8. The Politics of Recovery

Epigraph: Letter, *Courier-Post*, June 26, 2002.

1. *Courier-Post*, July 18, 1992.

2. *New York Times*, July 7, October 5, 1999. Clinton's approach to inner-city reinvestment drew on the arguments of Harvard business professor Michael E. Porter, especially "The Competitive Advantage of the Inner City," *Harvard Business Review* (May–June, 1995), 55–71. Porter's approach is throughly critiqued in Thomas D. Boston and Catherine L. Ross, eds., *The Inner City: Urban Poverty and Economic Development in the Next Century* (New Brunswick, N.J.: Transaction Publishers, 1999).

3. *Courier-Post*, September 13, 2000.

4. Entitled the "Municipal Aid Accountability Act," the legislation was approved by the New Jersey Assembly in December, 1992.

5. *Courier-Post*, March 12, 1995. See also the March 2, 1995, editorial, "Someone Must Provide Leadership in Camden," reinforcing the goal of the Crossroads series to "bring a better quality of life for Camden."

6. Interview with Mark Lohbauer, Trenton, September 16, 2002. A former Camden County freeholder, who gained election as a critic of Democratic environmental policies, including planned incinerators in Pennsauken and Camden, Lohbauer was part of a small group of reform-minded Republicans the governor relied on in South Jersey. Another was Lee Solomon, who served on the freeholders with Lohbauer, and whom Whitman appointed Camden County prosecutor over the strong objection of local Democrats.

7. See the report of Governor Whitman's "A Better Camden" initiative, *Courier-Post*, June 18, 1996.

8. Interview with Steven Sasala, Trenton, May 27, 1999; *Courier-Post*, March 12, 1995. The paper had pointed especially to Bryant's lucrative association with the Camden Housing Authority in a detailed article appearing February 2, 1993. His firm had been paid $388,000 over the three preceding years through retainers, which the paper noted were considerably higher than similar-sized housing authorities, including Atlantic City which paid $6,000, Trenton $21,000, and Bayonne $25,000 in 1992. An active member of BPUM while at Rutgers Law School in Camden in the early 1970s, Bryant was recruited by county Democrats as a candidate for

freeholder in 1979. Following three years of service in that body, he was elected to the Assembly in 1982 and the Senate in 1995.

9. *Courier-Post*, April 30, 2000.

10. *Courier-Post*, February 12, 1998.

11. "Statement of Imminent Peril," released as part of the hearings to create the state financial review board, Trenton, August 12, 1998. Two years later, for example, Commissioner of Community Affairs Jane Kenny used the same rationale in defense of special legislation for a complete state takeover of Camden by saying, "We need to restore the climate for private investment in the city. That is the key to long-term recovery. And for that to happen, we need to restore credibility at City Hall." *Courier-Post*, August 22, 2000.

12. *Philadelphia Inquirer*, August 20, 1999. City officials at the time reported that only one or two machines operated daily in the city of 80,000. The issue was significant enough to prompt a resolution of protest from Camden City Council, complaining that the "Fiscal Review Board has crossed the line between fiscal review and operational control by restricting the City's ability to provide its residents with clean streets" and that the board should "deal, once and for all, with the structural deficit in this City's budget." Resolution MC-99: 265, April 22, 1999.

13. George L. Kelling and Catherine M. Coles, *Fixing Broken Windows: Restoring Order and Reducing Crime in Our Communities* (New York: Free Press, 1997). See text of Milan's first state of the city address, February 11, 1998. New York Mayor Rudolph Giuliani made his own proclamation for cleanliness and civility the same month: *New York Times*, February 26, 1998.

14. *Philadelphia Inquirer*, November 21, 1998.

15. *Courier-Post*, July 14, 15, 20–23, 1999; *New York Times* July 21 (New Jersey section), August 1, 1999.

16. *Courier-Post*, July 21, 1999.

17. *Philadelphia Inquirer*, August 5, 27, September 2, 9, 1999; *Courier-Post*, August 27, September 8, 1999.

18. *Philadelphia Inquirer*, *Courier-Post*, September 24, 1999. A copy of Sloan El's resolution, dated September 23, 1999, is in the Milan file, CCHS. For further analysis of the black-Hispanic split in the city, see the *Philadelphia Inquirer*, September 27, 1999.

19. *Philadelphia Inquirer*, March 31, 2000. Both the *Inquirer* and the *Courier-Post* that day posted a copy of he indictment online. A copy is available in the Milan file, Camden County Historical Society (CCHS). For further coverage, see *New York Times*, March 31, 2000, and *Washington Post*, April 11, 2000, which quotes a Milan supporter, Nydia Belfort, attributing Milan's problems to Whitman's wrath: "I guess the governor maybe wants to be president or vice president someday, and I guess Milan embarrassed her. I think maybe how she feels it's the way to get even with the city."

20. *Philadelphia Inquirer*, May 1, 2000; *Courier-Post*, May 6, 2000.

21. *Courier-Post*, *Philadelphia Inquirer*, May 24, 2000.

22. *New York Times*, May 25, 2001; draft copy, "Municipal Rehabilitation and Economic Revitalization Act," supplementing P.L. 1947, Section 5f. Copy in the Camden Recovery file, CCHS.

23. Forum essay signed by Wayne Bryant, Joseph Roberts, and Nilsa Cruz-Perez, *Courier-Post*, August 6, 2000.

24. *Courier-Post*, September 18, 2000.

25. Concerned Black Clergy was a latecomer to the effort to pressure the state into investing new resources in Camden's neighborhoods. Formally known as the Camden Ministerium, the group gave the appearance of broadening CCOP's predominantly Hispanic and white leadership, even though many of the ministers who represented Black Clergy did not live in Camden.

26. *Courier-Post*, June 14, 2000; "A Vision for the Recovery of Camden," State Takeover file, CCHS. In her remarks to conclude the meeting, Commissioner Kenny reported that she had shared the faith-based proposal with the governor and her cabinet and that no one had tampered with the spirit of the document. "The vision for recovery of Camden is now our vision, and we dedicate ourselves to making it a reality," she said.

27. *Philadelphia Inquirer*, September 13, 23, October 16, November 3, 2000. Milan not only named his own appointment but insisted that department heads report only to his choice for the job, leaving the untenable situation of having competing business administrators at work at the same time until the court affirmed the state's right to make the appointment.

28. *Philadelphia Inquirer*, *Courier-Post*, November 22, 2000. The plan was prepared by the Philadelphia-based company Public Financial Management in association with the National Academy of Public Administration. The full text of the Multi-Year Recovery Plan, as it was called, appeared on the New Jersey Department of Community Affairs web site, at www.state.nj/dca/camdensummary.htm. A copy of the report is in the State Takeover file, CCHS.

29. *Courier-Post*, *Philadelphia Inquirer*, November 22, 2000

30. *Philadelphia Inquirer*, September 22, 2000.

31. In a June 24, 2000, *Philadelphia Inquirer* story, Bryant ridiculed the state's offer of $12.5 in additional funds for redevelopment as "almost laughable," charging the effort was a ploy to disenfrancise minorities in urban areas. A proponent of using oversight legislation as a means of bringing new money to the city even before Whitman formed the first review board, Bryant was a constant critic of what he described as Whitman's budget-cutting approach. See *Philadelphia Inquirer*, March 31, 1997, and Bryant's commentary in the same paper July 28, 1997, appearing shortly after the state announced its approach.

32. Office of the Governor News Release, "DiFrancesco Announces Comprehensive Revitalization Plan for Camden—A National Model," May 24, 2001, copy in State Takeover file, CCHS.

33. Facsimile copy, Wayne Bryant to Governor Christine Todd Whitman, May 18, 1994, from the files of *Courier-Post* reporter Kevin Riordan, Wayne Bryant file, CCHS.

34. The innovation of a judicial mediator was introduced by Senator Bryant. In an interview with me in Camden, March 12, 2003, he emphasized his desire to leave a good amount of give and take in the system, believing it would produce better policy outcomes than Whitman's insistence in giving the COO complete control. To assure efficiency as well as accountability, however, he felt it was important

to devise a means of cutting off conflict at some point and that the courts were the place to do that.

35. Interview with Freeholder-Director Jeffrey Nash, Cherry Hill, July 1, 2003.

36. *Philadelphia Inquirer*, May 24, 2001; *Courier-Post*, May 25, 2001.

37. *Philadelphia Inquirer*, May 25, 2001. Mayor Faison's proposed compromise, immediately rejected by the state, was to confine the powers of the appointed COO to those already exercised by the chairman of the Local Finance Board, who had statutory control of all Camden city expenditures in excess of $4,500. Facsimile statement, dated May 31, 2001, in the files of Rutgers-Camden Provost Roger Dennis.

38. *Courier-Post*, June 8, 2001; Jeffrey L. Nash to Wayne R. Bryant, June 12, 2001, copy in the files of Roger Dennis, a central figure in trying to negotiate an early agreement among the interested parties.

39. *Courier-Post*, May 25, 2001, *Philadelphia Inquirer*, June 9, 2001.

40. "Open letter to New Jersey State Senate and General Assembly," November 19, 2001, signed by Ali Sloan El, Sr., copy in State Takeover file, CCHS.

41. *Philadelphia Inquirer*, November 20, December 7, 2001.

42. *Philadelphia Inquirer*, September 29, November 24, December 14, 18, 21, 2001. For McGreevey's position and a summary of the skeptical reaction to it among other policy makers, see *New York Times*, December 23, 2001.

43. "Camden Is Unique and Requires a Different Kind of Response from the State," CCOP/CBC flyer, McGreevey Recovery file, CCHS.

44. The full text of Doyle's closing prayer was reprinted in the Sacred Heart parish newsletter for March 10, 2002. Describing the March 7 meting as part of community organizers "march up Calvary," John P. Hogan stressed the ability to confront not simply structural poverty but what he described as structural sin: *Credible Signs of Christ Alive: Case Studies from the Catholic Campaign for Human Development* (Boulder, Colo.: Rowman and Littlefield, 2003), 56.

45. *Philadelphia Inquirer*, March 8, 2002; *Courier-Post*, March 7, 8, 2002.

46. "A Winning Investment for the City of Camden and New Jersey from the Higher Education and Healthcare Task Force," l; *Philadelphia Inquirer*, April 18, 2002.

47. "Camden Community-Based Recovery Plan Bill," Preliminary Draft, March, 2002, McGreevey Recovery file, CCHS. Funds for this ambitious program were to be drawn from payments from polluters as well as from the Delaware River Port Authority, the state, the county government, and area banks.

48. *Courier-Post*, May 22, June 8, 2002.

49. That Cooper's Ferry was concerned about funding the aquarium's expansion was suggested in a June 12, 2002, editorial in the *Philadelphia Inquirer*—always a sympathetic supporter of the organization—which singled out McGreevey's failure to "follow through on a three-year-old plan for desperately needed private investment" and urged him "to stop stalling on the Delaware River Port Authority's $25 million loan-investment project [for the aquarium]." When McGreevey failed to mention the aquarium during his appearance at Antioch Church in June, William Spearman of Cooper's Ferry was convinced that the governor was determined to kill the project completely by keeping funds out of the recovery bill too. That

was not the case, however, as Senator Bryant put funding for the project back in the recovery package in the following days.

50. *Philadelphia Inquirer*, June 14, 25, 2002.

51. *Newark Star-Ledger*, June 14, 2002; *Philadelphia Inquirer*, June 14, 18, 25, 2002; *Courier-Post*, June 14, 18, 2002.

52. *Philadelphia Inquirer*, June 25, 2002; *Courier-Post*, July 1, 2002. Another Republican, Assemblyman Kevin O'Toole of Essex County, detailed his objections to the bill in a column in the South Jersey commentary section of the *Philadelphia Inquirer*, August 16, 2002. The bill nonetheless passed the Assembly by a vote of 47–32.

53. *Courier-Post*, July 23, 2002.

54. This was the assessment *New York Times* reporter Iver Peterson made, June 24, 2002, that the chief goal of he legislation was to "get the middle class . . . to move into a city that has mostly been given over to the poor."

55. *FutureCamden: Master Plan, City of Camden, New Jersey* (Camden, 2002), I-6.

56. Joseph Roberts essay, "A Boost From the State Means Hope Sets Up Shop in Camden," *Courier-Post*, July 23, 2002. Responsible for introducing the regional impact council concept, Roberts described it as necessary to deal with the regional implications of the legislation: "Consisting of the mayors of Camden's surrounding communities, state planners, and leaders of the region's religious, labor, higher education and business communities, the council will review and coordinate regional issues, such as public safety, economic development, and affordable housing."

57. Jackson's interpretation of the bill, first reported in the *Star-Ledger*'s coverage of McGreevey's proposed recovery program June 14, 2002, became a staple of the protest effort that followed. She reiterated the charge in a telephone interview with me June 14, 2002. It was further reported in the *Courier-Post*, June 19, 2004. For the history of the court-based effort to achieve equalization in school funding in New Jersey and comparisons with other states, see Lizabeth Cohen, *A Consumer's Republic: The Politics of Mass Consumption in Postwar America* (New York: Knopf, 2003), 240–51.

58. P.L. 2002, Chapter 43, "Municipal Rehabilitation and Economic Recovery Act," Section 34.

59. *New York Times*, July 21, 23, 27, August 1, 2, 2000.

60. Doria's loss stemmed directly from a dispute with South Jersey Democrats, who claimed he reneged on a deal that would have had Joseph Roberts succeed him as Assembly leader in 2001. To accommodate South Jersey Democrats, candidate McGreevey secured Roberts's position as party chairman in November 2000 and named Louis Greenwald as one of five Democratic members of the commission responsible for redrawing state legislative districts. That ended a boycott of the South Jersey legislators from the state Democratic caucus and unified the party for McGreevey's election bid in 2001.

61. Interview with Jeffrey Nash, Cherry Hill, July 1, 2003; *New York Times*, April 9, 2003.

62. Although Lynch and Norcross had been rivals for some time, *The Record* (New Jersey), July 3, 2002, reported that both men were lobbying together for the

Newark Arena as part of the Camden recovery legislation. The effort followed, by only a month, Lynch's praise for the opening of a new branch of Commerce Bank in New Brunswick, where he was the former mayor. *Business Wire*, May 22, 2002.

63. Reports of the Greater Camden County Committee made to the New Jersey Election Law Enforcement Committee, April 2, May 1, June 1, July 2, August 6, September 15, October 3, November 9, 2000.

64. *Philadelphia Inquirer*, May 9, 2003.

65. Interview with Todd Poole, Governor McGreevey's chief negotiator on the recovery legislation, Camden, April 22, 2004. According to Jeffrey Nash, no other candidate was considered. Primas, he said, had the necessary business as well as political experience. He knew the city intimately. "The fact that he was black was icing on the cake," he said. Interview, July 1, 2003.

66. *Business Wire*, January 24, 2002; *The Record* (New Jersey), June 9, 2002; *The Bond Buyer*, August 12, October 24, 2002.

67. *Courier-Post*, July 5, 2002; *Philadelphia Inquirer*, June 14, 2002. Responding to a *Courier-Post* series on Norcross's growing influence in the state, nearly half the letters published March 1, 2003, praised Norcross's ability to deliver benefits to South Jersey, including the $175 million revitalization bill, according to Freeholder Riletta Cream. A *New York Times* profile of Norcross dated April 9, 2003, also credited him with helping shape the legislation.

68. Msgr. Robert McDermott, "Camden Needs the Expertise, Resources of State Leadership," *Courier-Post*, October 10, 2000.

69. McGreevey indicated his desire to omit college and hospital funding in a private meeting with Camden clergy, which nonetheless was reported in the *Philadelphia Inquirer*, December 18, 2001. Bryant's response that if that happened "you might as well not do anything," was reported the next day in the *Courier-Post*. One of the few news reports that linked Norcross with the recovery legislation made the connection specifically with Cooper Hospital, reporting, "Norcross concedes he was advocating for the $175 million Camden bailout, which will provide millions of dollars to Cooper Health System to expand its hospital in downtown Camden." *The Record* (New Jersey), July 3, 2002. According to another report, *Asbury Park Press*, September 21, 2003, McGreevey wanted to remove the state aquarium from the bill as well.

70. See the reports of the near-disaster reported in *Courier-Post*, October 15, 16, 1985, and Michael Doyle's newsletter titled, "A Fallen World," February, 1991, reprinted in Michael J. Doyle, *It's a Terrible Day . . . Thanks Be to God* (Camden: Heart of Camden, 2003), 64–65. He confirmed the story in an interview in Camden, October 24, 2002, noting that it was Fair Share Housing attorney Peter O'Connor who intervened with the CCMUA to assure that the damage would be immediately repaired and paid for.

71. Interview, Camden, September 17, 2002. John P. Hogan used the same phrase, apparently drawn from McDermott, in his assessment of CCOP's efforts in Camden. *Credible Signs of Christ Alive*, 60.

72. *Philadelphia Inquirer*, September 5, 2002; *Courier-Post*, November 1, December 6, 2002.

73. Telephone conversation, October 17, 2002. Willis noted that he had of-

fered the city $850,000 three years earlier and that in addition to the tax settlement the city was giving him $200,000 to end a long dispute over city use of his back parking lot. He had blamed the Norcross organization for attempting to take his building in 1999, pointing to Norcross ally Vernon Hill as the head of a committee promoting a clearance plan along Admiral Wilson Boulevard funded primarily by the Delaware River Port Authority. According to Frank Fulbrook, who joined me in a meeting with Willis at the Sears building September 30, 1999, Norcross had previously attempted to buy the building, to put county workers there and to make it a source of patronage. For a summary of the controversy between Willis and Fulbrook and the DRPA, see *Philadelphia Inquirer*, September 30, 1999.

74. *Philadelphia Inquirer*, December 19, 2002.

75. A candidate for mayor both against Primas in 1989 and Milan in 1997, Fulbrook was a Camden anomaly, a white Rutgers dropout who never left the city. Instead, he managed to support himself through rental properties in the Cooper-Grant neighborhood adjacent to the university, where he served for many years as president of the neighborhood association. His presence at practically every public meeting of importance and his ability to file civil suits established his credibility over the years as a public interest gadfly, without, however giving him enough support to win election.

76. Interview with Ali Sloan El, Camden, April 23, 2003.

77. *Philadelphia Inquirer*, March 4, 2003. The original complaint against Jackson was lodged by Philip B. Freeman, the unsuccessful incumbent school board member running on the Norcross ticket in 2003. *Philadelphia Inquirer*, May 15, 2002.

78. *Courier-Post*, February 28, 2003, and March 14, 2003, for Fulbrook's defense.

79. *Courier-Post*, March 19, 2003; *New York Times*, New Jersey section, March 23, 2003. In choosing to focus only on the schools issue, Judge Smithson overlooked entirely the features of the bill that could make it relevant only to Camden, notably the provisions that related to institutions located only in Camden in section 52, covering the Higher Education and Regional Health Care Development Fund. The amended legislation, identified as an act clarifying certain provisions of P:.L. 2002, c 43 (C.52:27BBB-1 et seq.) did not address these features of the original bill. The New Jersey Supreme Court, in a 4–3 decision, authorized public works authorities and other government agencies to borrow money without voter approval: *Philadelphia Inquirer*, April 10, 2003. The issue, as Primas raised it, probably was not relevant to Camden anyway since the New Jersey Economic Development Authority did not require voter approval to issue bonds because they were not viewed as state debt. The issue was more political than anything else since Democrats raised similar concerns about bonding authority when Republicans controlled the governor's office and the DRPA. See *Courier-Post*, February 7, 2001.

80. *Courier-Post*, May 7, 9, 25, 2003. At Rutgers-Camden, Provost Roger Dennis reported that Bryant also logged in 50 hours of work helping obtain a $450,000 grant for the revitalization of the city's Fairview area. Dennis later explained in an October 16, 2003, conversation that hours spent did not necessarily mean direct work on the project but included extended discussions about the funding proposal.

The Gannett news organization renewed its criticism of Bryant as part of a series attacking the mixture of private profit with public service, September 21, 2003, leading with the statement, "State Senator Wayne R. Bryant has always helped the poor—and himself." Bryant's defense of his family's history of public service published in a column in the *Courier-Post*, October 7, 2003, appeared under the telling headline, "A Tradition of Giving Back."

81. *Philadelphia Inquirer*, March 28, November 23, December 20, 2002, April 19, 20, 2003; *Courier-Post*, November 21, 2002. That this was part of an ongoing Camden County Democratic party effort to direct redevelopment in the area was strongly suggested by DRPA sitting executive director Paul Drayton in comments reported in the *Courier-Post*, November 27, 2002, and by the picture in the same issue of Randy Primas seated together with Jeffrey Nash at a meeting described as having the purpose of calling for Drayton's resignation. For his part, Nash, in a July 1, 2003, interview with me, said it was Governor McGreevey who was pressing Drayton to leave office so he could appoint someone loyal to himself. Nash brought charges against Drayton, he said, only after he delayed his departure well beyond a reasonable time after McGreevey's request.

82. *Courier-Post, Philadelphia Inquirer*, April 17, 2003. DRPA press release: "DRPA Oks Aquarium Expansion Funding." Summary Statement, DRPA, Steiner and Associates Renovation and Expansion of the New Jersey State Aquarium, April 16, 2003, Aquarium file, CCHS. *Philadelphia Inquirer*, July 23, 2003.

83. Summary Statement, DRPA board meeting, April 16, 2003.

84. The provision of the bill was never connected publicly to Steiner, but surfaced in association with a report that the Philadelphia-based office of Cigna Corporation, an insurance company considering relocation to Camden, was seeking to extend the provision to cover the state tax on premiums, its major source of revenue. *Courier-Post*, June 3, 2003. The rebate provision was contained in section 55a of the recovery legislation, P.L. 2002, Chapter 43, which clearly had Steiner in mind when it made businesses eligible for the rebate which chose to locate *or expand* (my italics) in a qualified municipality. As further confirmation that this was legislation solely directed at Camden, section 51c authorized $25 million in grants, matching grants or loans to support *the expansion and upgrade of an aquarium in a qualified municipality by a private developer* (my italics), the only terms Cooper's Ferry was promoting at the time.

85. *Courier-Post*, April 16, 2003.

86. Telephone interviews with Thomas Corcoran and Antoinette Vielehr, April 18, 2003; interview with Randy Primas, Camden, September 4, 2003; telephone interviews with Frank Steslow, February 18, December 6, 2004. Although the state was relieved of between $2.5 and $3 million in annual operating costs, it still was responsible, as owner of the facility, for an annual payment in lieu of taxes to the city of $1.5 million, according to a report in the *Courier-Post*, August 17, 2004. Established as an educational institution, the aquarium was expected to rely on the Academy for programming, even after Steiner assumed responsibility for operations. For the Academy CEO's fears about a commercial company's ability to sustain an educational mission and Steiner's own admission of the difficulties, see *Courier-Post*, December 4, 2002, and *Cincinnati Business Courier*, September 2, 2002,

respectively. Beyond the educational nature of the exhibits themselves, the Academy administered several important programs directed at underserved families. The Camden Aquarium Urban Science Enrichment Program, started in 1993 to attract minorities to the science workforce and to provide quality science education to K-12 youth, trained students in marine science and biology in preparation for appointment as junior staff members in jobs as exhibit interpreters. In the first eight years of the program, every one of the fifty-five trainees graduated from high school and 88 percent continued to college. With the assistance of a grant from the National Science Foundation, the aquarium launched an additional program to increase parental involvement in science education among minorities. It was expected to reach up to twelve hundred African-American, Latino, and Asian-American families according to information supplied by Antoinette Vielehr, April 18, 2003. See also the column by Kevin Riordan, "Aquarium Hopes New Operators Will Keep Aquarium's Outreach Programs," *Courier-Post*, April 20, 2003.

87. *Philadelphia Inquirer*, May 24, 2001; P.L. 2001, Chapter 266, approved December 11, 2001, "An Act Authorizing Municipalities to Contract for Property Tax Lien Management Services Under Certain Circumstances"; P.L. 2002, Chapter 43, "Municipal Rehabilitation and Economic Recovery Act," C.52, section 43.

88. The nonbid contract before City Council was reported in the *Courier-Post*, March 27, 2001, and passed June 28. The *Courier-Post* ran an extensive story on Roberts's role in getting the bill through the legislature on September 22, 2003. Roberts's contention that he was unaware of Florio's involvement with the legislation was disputed by one of the two legislators who voted against it, who said, "I don't believe that. . . . If Republican staffers knew, it is inconceivable that the sponsor of the legislation was unaware of the fact." Tax collection in Camden brought Xspand about $1.97 million in fees by the end of 2004, not a huge profit given the difficulties the firm faced sorting out a bad system. Potentially more profitable, offering to bring the firm an additional $2 million, was authorization for Xspand's parent company, Plymouth Financial, to loan $12 million to the city to balance its budget, with repayment secured through anticipated future collections. The loan was backed by 5,800 delinquent Camden properties. Such a practice was authorized by the establishment of a state tax lien financing corporation, which like the municipal recovery bill, was written to cover the entire state but was directed specially at Camden. The *Courier-Post* reported the loan authorization May 28, 2004, and its association with Florio, December 14, 15, 2004.

89. The abject nature of the city's tax collection process was detailed by the state's Local Finance Board in a report dated May 6, 2002, and handed out by Mark Willis at a Camden City Council meeting May 8, 2003, at which Willis questioned Xspand's ability to be fair when the records were so poor. That council meeting was not reported in the press. For other coverage, see *Philadelphia Inquirer*, November 2, 2002, April 4, May 1, 2, 2003.

90. *Philadelphia Inquirer*, April 4, 2003. In an interview with me in Camden, September 4, 2003, Primas was equally unsympathetic to those behind in their taxes, saying only that everyone has an obligation to pay or face the consequences.

91. *Philadelphia Inquirer*, May 2, 2003; town meeting, Parkside, May 29, 2003.

92. Records of the New Jersey Election Law Enforcement Commission. A report in *Philadelphia Inquirer*, May 8, 2003, not picked up by the *Courier-Post*, which had frequently criticized Fulbrook's opposition to the Bryant recovery legislation, noted that a glossy Fuentes circular pictured Fulbrook standing menacingly nearby as a drug addict shot a needle into his veins and accused Fulbrook of using drugs himself. Although Fulbrook had long advocated needle exchange and the legalizing of drugs as a means of controlling them, he was not a known drug user, and he and other independent activists, including Tom Knoche, denounced the attack on him.

93. Pittsburgh's experience with fiscal oversight coinciding with the changes in Camden represents a more typical direction in recovery efforts, where layoffs, rollbacks in benefits to public employees, and reductions in service have been employed in place of new public investments. See reports *Philadelphia Inquirer* October 16, November 7, 2003, December 6, 2004. In their assessment of failing cities, Helen F. Ladd and John Yinger dismiss management efforts alone, concluding that "Poor fiscal health is not caused by poor management, corruption, or profligate spending, and [thus] a city government's ability to alter the city's fiscal health is severely limited." *America's Ailing Cities: Fiscal Health and the Design of Urban Policy*, updated ed. (Baltimore: Johns Hopkins University Press, 1991), 291.

Chapter 9.   Future Camden: Reinventing the City, Engaging the Region

Epigraph: *Philadelphia Inquirer*, April 5, 1992.

1. *Courier-Post*, April 15, 2003. Formed through the joint effort of the Catholic bishop of the Camden diocese, Nicholas DiMarzio, and Lewis Katz, who provided the funding, the makeup of the board, as its predecessor entities had been, was almost exclusively white men. A few activists known to the church, including Msgr. Michael Doyle and Peter O'Connor, stood out from a business and political elite that included former Florio Chief-of-Staff Joseph Salema, listed initially inaccurately as a lawyer and later as a representative of the Katz Foundation. The Reverend James C. Jones, the chair of the Concerned Black Clergy, was asked to join the board just in time for the April 14 announcement. Walking out of the meeting, he remarked that he believed the organization had decided belatedly to add a little local color.

2. *Center City Camden: The Economic Engine of Camden's Revitalization* (Camden: Greater Camden Partnership, April 2003), 27. At the end of the year, the Partnership updated its estimate of new investment to $1 billion in presenting its strategic plan for the downtown: *Philadelphia Inquirer*, December 17, 2003.

3. The $60 million in funding was completed when the Casino Reinvestment Development Authority made a $8.7 million loan. The remaining funding came from a $30 million loan from Fleet Bank, a $3 million loan and an additional $5 million clean-up grant from the Delaware River Port Authority, and a $11.3 million equity investment from Related Capital of New York City: *Courier-Post*, November 7, 2002. In addition, Camden City Council, at Thomas Corcoran's request, granted the project a $200,000 tax abatement. *Philadelphia Inquirer*, August 22, 2001.

4. *Courier-Post*, April 18, 2003; *Philadelphia Inquirer*, August 30, 2003. Headlines alone revealed the cachet attached to the new building when it first opened for inspection: "Renters Lap Up Camden Luxury; Old Nipper Building Draws Raves, Deposits," *Philadelphia Inquirer*, June 2, 2003; "The Victor Attracts Tenants Who Could Revitalize Camden," *Courier-Post*, May 28, 2003; "The Nipper Building is Attracting a Crowd," *New York Times* (New Jersey Section), June 1, 2003. A further column by Monica Yant Kinney in the June 5 *Inquirer* opened, "This is what cool has come to: I've been priced out of Camden." Dranoff renamed the Nipper Building the Victor so as to avoid any possible copyright infringement on RCA's signature trademark.

5. *Philadelphia Inquirer*, May 30, 31, 2003; *Courier-Post*, June 10, 2003. The *Inquirer* reported Equity's decision to make good its promise to bring another 100 jobs to Camden January 24, 2004, a decision that the paper noted "was hailed as another forward step in Camden's rebirth."

6. *Philadelphia Inquirer*, May 19, 2003; *Courier-Post*, June 19, October 1, 24, 2003.

7. Builders League of South Jersey Camden Action Committee, "Camden Action Report: Building a Plan for the Ages," May, 2003; *Philadelphia Inquirer*, June 6, 2003. The League described itself as a housing trade association of 550 member firms, including builders, developers, engineers, architects, planners, suppliers, landscapers, contractors, and other consulting professionals: in short, just the constituency the Camden County Democratic organization had been so successful in tapping to build its campaign finances.

8. The recovery legislation, P.L. 2002, Chapter 43, section 38a, stated that "The revitalization plan shall incorporate a blueprint for the economic, social, and cultural revitalization of the municipality through the promotion of development and redevelopment in both the downtown business district and residential neighborhoods." Among the specific charges were to promote diversification of land uses, including housing, strategic land assembly, and a transportation system that "capitalizes on high density settlement patterns by encouraging the use of public transit, walking, and alternative modes of transportation." The plan was commissioned even before the legislation cleared the courts, so as not to lose more time. The contract offered under competitive bidding went to the Silver Spring, Maryland, firm of Hammer Siler George Associates. As the chief consultant for the plan, Clifton Henry stated privately that he believed that the selection of his firm was itself a sign of an independent process. In preparing the document, he conducted a large number of interviews in and around Camden, touching base with a number of neighborhood activists—notably those associated with CCOP and Concerned Black Clergy—as well as those in city and state government. None of those he spoke to, however, had actively opposed the final recovery legislation, and the report he rendered reflected that omission. Interview with Clifton Henry, Camden, February 6, 2003. The list of interviewees for the revitalization report appears in *Camden Strategic Revitalization Plan*, draft dated April 10, 2003, and made available on the Economic Recovery Board website, at www.camdenerb.com, as Appendix B. The *Philadelphia Inquirer*, November 2, 2002, reported the appointment of the planning consultants.

9. *Camden Strategic Revitalization Plan*, 37.

10. *Camden Strategic Revitalization Plan*, 45–46. Such an emphasis on attract-ing middle class residents to the city should not have been surprising. Even as Gov-ernor McGreevey first addressed Camden's recovery, the *Philadelphia Inquirer* con-cluded in a May 24, 2001, editorial praising the effort, "Overall, the plan shows a welcome understanding that any city revival depends on making it economically rational for the middle class and businesses to invest in Camden—a goal which re-quires special incentives that only the state, not a nearly bankrupt city, can offer." The concept of providing employees incentives to reside nearby had been intro-duced successfully at a number of academic institutions, including Yale and the University of Pennsylvania. A similar short-lived program for Rutgers employees was abandoned for budgetary reasons before the recovery legislation passed and was not cited in the planning report.

11. *Camden Strategic Revitalization Plan*, 6. In its opening section, on regional context, the plan stated, "The reinforcement of Camden as the urban center for South Jersey can be accomplished by building on local and regional assets, and by encouraging regional and multi-jurisdictional cooperation to address common challenges." In this, the plan echoed the city's 2001 master plan which listed "Seek-ing regional solutions to common issues" as the first of four guiding principles and devoted a whole section of its summary report to a section titled "Reinforcing Cam-den's Role in the Philadelphia-South Jersey Region." *FutureCamden: Master Plan Summary Report* (City of Camden, 2001), 13, 18–20.

12. *Courier-Post*, April 16, 2003; *Philadelphia Inquirer*, April 16, 2003.

13. Although Clifton Henry made the effort to meet with a number of stake-holders, his only contact with North Camden was a telephone call to Camden Lu-theran Housing Director Betsy Russell, whom he asked for suggestions for redevel-opment sites. When Russell learned that her own organization would not be considered as the developer for any of these sites, she concluded that the recovery board was not interested in working directly with local nonprofit organizations. Telephone interview with Betsy Russell, May 22, 2003; conversation with Christo-pher Auth, Camden, May 6, 2003.

14. Memorandum to the Camden Recovery Board on changes to the Strategic Revitalization Plan and the Capital Improvement and Infrastructure Master Plan, circulated at the June 20 meeting, copy deposited in the Camden Recovery Board file, CCHS. Stating the negative effect of Tier II designation, twelve of the thirteen member organizations of the Camden Non-Profit Housing Association submitted a letter for the record June 20 endorsing the 10 percent set-aside and urging the board to consider its own submission of principles to guide the allocation of the funds: copy, Economic Recovery Board file, CCHS; *Courier-Post*, June 21, 2003.

15. Peter O'Connor, undated letter to State Treasurer John McCormac and Caren Franzini, Executive Director, New Jersey Economic Development Authority: copy, Economic Recovery Board file, CCHS. Quotation from Myron Orfield, *Amer-ican Metropolitics: The New Suburban Reality* (Washington, D.C.: Brookings Institu-tion Press, 2002), 72.

16. See the copy of my letter to Clifton Henry, copied to the ERB, May 9,

2003, Camden Recovery Board file, CCHS, and my column "Board Isn't Fully Resolving Camden's Problems," *Philadelphia Inquirer*, June 30, 2003.

17. Interview with Jeremy Nowak, Philadelphia, April 22, 2003.

18. Edward W. Hill and Jeremy Nowak, "Nothing Left to Lose: Only Radical Strategies can Help America's Most Distressed Cities," *Brookings Review* (Summer, 2000): 25–28; Jeremy Nowak and Edward W. Hill, "New Regime, New Strategy for Camden," *Philadelphia Inquirer*, January 27, 2001; Nowak's speech at Cooper Hospital in Camden, *Courier-Post*, May 11, 2001.

19. "Urban Development Testimony," submitted June 14, 2003, and included as Appendix VII to the New Jersey Housing and Mortgage Finance Agency response to Comments of Fair Share Housing Center, Inc. et al. on 2003 Amendments to the Qualified Allocation Plan for Low Income Housing Tax Credits, June 19, 2003.

20. Nowak's own plan was to work with a nationally recognized training organization based on the West Coast, MDRC, but that effort as of early 2004 lagged behind other efforts in the city, which included a few other initiatives. See, for instance, the report of Edward J. Gorman III, president of the Washington-based American Community Partnerships, *Philadelphia Inquirer*, September 2, 2003, and a summary of work directed by the Rev. Floyd White out of Woodland Avenue Presbyterian Church in Camden, *Philadelphia Inquirer*, April 21, 2004. The city subsequently announced a modest $350,000 two-year program funded by the U.S. Environmental Protection Agency, the New Jersey Enterprise Zone Authority, and the Camden Empowerment Zone to train fifty Camden residents as environmental workers: *Courier-Post*, August 12, 2004.

21. "The Camden Project: A Framework for Investment," proposal submitted by MDRC and the Reinvestment Fund to the Ford Foundation, February 28, 2003, 24–25.

22. The significant passage of the bill, section 2g, read "While State aid dollars which have been directed toward such municipalities have served to address their structural deficits, they have not, and cannot, function as an economic impetus towards the rebuilding of those municipalities." Section 20 added that "it is incumbent upon the State to take exceptional measures, on an interim basis, to rectify certain governance issues faced by such municipalities and to strategically invest those sums of money necessary in order to assure the long-term financial viability of these municipalities."

23. "The Camden Project," 39.

24. Discussion with Carl Anthony, Program Officer, Community and Resource Development, Ford Foundation, New York City, June 16, 2003.

25. Myron Orfield and Thomas Luce, Foreword, *New Jersey Metropatterns: A Regional Agenda for Community and Stability in New Jersey* (Minneapolis: Ameregis: April 2003).

26. For a summary of the plan's origins and intent, see Barbara G. Salmore and Stephen A. Salmore, *New Jersey Politics and Government* (Lincoln: University of Nebraska Press, 1993), 298–300. It was an early version of this plan that the New Jersey Supreme Court drew on to justify the regional allocation of affordable housing opportunities in the *Mount Laurel II* decision, as described in Chapter 7. Guidelines for its final adoption included balancing development and conservation and

integrating the concerns of the poor, minorities, and the *Mount Laurel* decisions. The final version, adopted in 1992, embraced the concept, often referred to popularly as "smart growth," of directing state capital construction funds to cities and already developed areas.

27. *New Jersey Metropatterns*, 1, 3, 39.

28. *New Jersey Metropatterns*, 42. In this conclusion, the New Jersey study reflected Orfield's comments, cited in the Preface, in *American Metropolitics: The New Suburban Reality* (Washington, D.C.: Brookings Institution Press, 2002), 153.

29. Interview with Harold Adams, Pennsauken, September 13, 2002, *Philadelphia Inquirer*, May 22, 2000.

30. Interview with Louise Bonifacio, Cherry Hill, May 9, 1998.

31. *Courier-Post*, April 16, 1989.

32. Jane M. Madara, letter in the *Courier-Post*, June 13, 2001. For the larger context of suburban change in the area, based on thorough examination of shifting property values, see Paul David Caris, "Declining Suburbs: Disinvestment in the Inner Suburbs of Camden County, N.J.," Ph.D. dissertation, Rutgers University, 1996.

33. Bryant quoted in *Courier-Post*, November 29, 2001; Levin quoted in a *Philadelphia Inquirer* editorial, "Camden Waits," December 17, 2001 and reported in *Courier-Post*, December 12, 2001; Maley's essay in *Philadelphia Inquirer*, December 5, 2001, "The Region's Welfare Rests on Camden Recovery Bill." Perceptions that suburban change was closely connected to outmigration from Camden were reinforced by newspaper accounts of the 2000 U.S. Census, such as the March 12, 2001, report in the *Philadelphia Inquirer* under the headline, "Camden Feeds Towns' Diversity."

34. Myron Orfield, *Metropolitics: A Regional Agenda for Community and Stability* (Washington, D.C.: Brookings Institution Press, 1997), especially chapter 7.

35. *Courier-Post*, July 7, 12, 26, 1994.

36. See *Courier-Post*, September 8, 1999, for the township decision to redevelop the Eldridge Garden Apartments occupied mostly by African Americans and Kevin Riordan's column, *Courier-Post*, September 13, 1999, linking that action to the demolition of the Denby Hall apartments and the conversion of Sutton Towers to luxury status. Collingswood Mayor James Maley dated Collingswood's resurgence from 1996 when the Sutton Towers project was undertaken: *Philadelphia Inquirer*, May 17, 2002.

37. *Philadelphia Inquirer*, April 23, 1997, April 17, 2000. The *Inquirer* printed two extensive articles on the spread of poverty to the suburbs July 31 and August 25, 2002.

38. *Philadelphia Inquirer*, May 7, 2000.

39. *Philadelphia Inquirer*, May 22, 2000; telephone interview with Lynn Cummings, September 18, 2002. See also her essay in the New Jersey "Community Voices" section, *Philadelphia Inquirer*, December 5, 2004, which appeared beside a complementary essay by Don and Loretta DeMarco, representing the Fund for an Open Society.

40. Interview with Harold Adams, Pennsauken, September 13, 2002. Acutely aware of the implications of racial concentration in a neighborhood, Adams had

chosen to locate in a section of Pennsauken that had a significant black presence when he bought there in 1987, choosing the level of comfort he and his wife expected to find there rather than becoming the first black family to move into a newer development further east.

41. *Philadelphia Inquirer*, December 22, 1997; *Courier-Post*, March 25, 1999.

42. See David Rusk, *Inside Game/Outside Game: Winning Strategies for Saving Urban America* (Washington, D.C.: Brookings Institution Press, 1999), chapter 13.

43. Rev. Robert J. Vitillo, "Address to Priests and Diocesan Leaders of Camden Diocese," St. Stephen's Church, Pennsauken, May 12, 2003, copy in Inner Ring Suburbs file, CCHS.

44. john a. powell, "Addressing Regional Dilemmas for Minority Communities," in Bruce Katz, ed., *Reflections on Regionalism* (Washington, D.C.: Brookings Institution Press, 2000), 129.

45. john a. powell, "Racism and Metropolitan Dynamics: The Civil Rights Challenge of the Twenty-first Century," April 2002, posted at the Institute on Race and Poverty, University of Minnesota, at www.umn.edu/irp.

46. For the origin and relative effectiveness of this program, see Jean L. Cummings and Denise DiPasquale, "The Low-Income Housing Tax Credit: An Analysis of the First Ten Years," *Housing Policy Debate* 10, 2 (1999): 251–307.

47. Comments dated June 4, 2002 of Southern Burlington County Branch of the NAACP, Camden County Branch of the NAACP, and Fair Share Housing Center, Inc., on the New Jersey Housing and Mortgage Finance Agency Low Income Housing Tax Credit Program 2002 Qualified Allocation Plan Proposed May 6, 2002, 2–3.

48. Response dated June 19, 2003, to the comments of Fair Share Housing Center, Inc., the Southern Burlington County Branch of the NAACP, the Camden County Branch of the NAACP, and the Camden City Taxpayers Association on 2003 Amendments to the Qualified Allocation Plan for Low Income Housing Tax Credits.

49. "Comments," June 4, 2002, 8–10. Drawing also from the New Jersey Governor's Select Commission on Civil Disorders, released in February 1968, O'Connor drew on the associated statement that "As development proceeds in the city core, planning must go ahead in the metropolitan context for a more deliberate approach to integrated housing throughout the area."

50. Interview with Peter O'Connor, Cherry Hill, August 29, 2002. See also O'Connor's comment, *Star-Ledger*, November 9, 2003, "The major deterrent in Camden is the presence of 80,000 poor people and all the social ills that accompany them. With no regional strategy for the elimination of poverty, it just won't work."

51. *Star-Ledger*, May 24, 2003. Francis further defended his position in a column prepared for the King holiday, *Philadelphia Inquirer*, January 19, 2004.

52. Edward G. Goetz, *Clearing the Way: Deconcentrating the Poor in Urban America* (Washington, D.C.: Urban Institute Press, 2003), 255.

53. "Comment on Scott A. Bollens's 'In Through the Back Door: Social Equity and Regional Governance,'" *Housing Policy Debate* 13, 4 (2003): 659–68. In an email to me August 11, 2004, Orfield described Goetz's book as "too pessimistic about what was accomplished and particularly on the possibility of progress."

54. Tim Evans, "Realistic Opportunity? The Distribution of Affordable Housing and Jobs in New Jersey," July, 2003, 7, 11, 12, available at www.njfuture.org; *Courier-Post*, July 16, 2003.

55. John M. Payne, "Remedies for Affordable Housing: From Fair Share to Growth Share," *Land Use Law & Zoning Digest* 49 (June 1997): 3–9. While sympathetic to the goals of the *Mount Laurel* decisions, Payne has detailed in a series of articles the limits the court faced in what was at heart a political process. See especially his review of Charles Haar's *Suburbs Under Siege* in *Michigan Law Review* 96 (May 1998): 1695–98, and "Tribute to Chief Justice Robert N. Wilentz: Politics, Exclusionary Zoning, and Robert Wilentz," *Rutgers Law Review* 49 (Spring 1997): 689–712.

56. Walsh quoted in the *Philadelphia Inquirer*, August 26, 2003. See also his essay with Peter O'Connor, *Philadelphia Inquirer*, September 12, 2003, and further news reports on the COAH decision in *Courier-Post*, August 26, 2003, and *New York Times*, August 27, 2003.

57. Email to the author, August 26, 2003.

58. *Philadelphia Inquirer*, August 26, 2003. In an interview with me April 29, 2002, in Camden, Suzanne Marks Brennan described an aggressive effort among speculators to buy up properties in the Fairview area, often taking listings from the Department of Housing and Urban Development webpage and making purchases before they were offered at public auction.

59. According to a report in the *Philadelphia Inquirer*, April 27, 2004, Pennsylvania provided Cigna $4.5 million in grants and a $5 million low interest loan. Seeking not to weaken its hand in negotiating with other companies whose leases were soon to expire, Philadelphia officials refused to reveal the nature of the city's support. For critical views of the bidding wars to retain business in downtown Philadelphia, see the columns by Andrew Cassel and Joseph Gyourko, of the University of Pennsylvania's Wharton School, *Philadelphia Inquirer*, February 1, 2004. To New Jersey's additional offer of a $90 million new produce facility in Camden, Pennsylvania responded with a $150 million facility and the waiver of state business taxes through 2015: *Philadelphia Inquirer*, May 19, 2004.

60. *Courier-Post*, March 18, April 9, 14, 2004.

61. *Philadelphia Inquirer*, December 17, 2003.

62. *Cramer Hill Tomorrow: A Strategic Plan for Neighborhood Development*, prepared by Kaufman Consulting, Philadelphia, January, 2000; interview with Thomas Holmes II, Camden, January 28, 2002.

63. *Courier-Post*, December 4, 2001.

64. *Cramer Hill Commercial Corridor: Streetscape Improvement Guidelines* (Philadelphia: Hillier Urban Design, 2002); interview with Thomas Holmes II, Camden, December 10, 2002.

65. The proposal came from the North Carolina firm known for its work in large-scale environmental remediation for residential development, Cherokee Investment Partners. Formed in 1990 and credited in 2003 with $1 billion in assets, Cherokee already had a powerful presence in the state with major projects in East Rutherford, Elizabeth, Bayonne, and most notably in the conversion of the Meadowlands sports complex into a mixed use development, including a hotel, a confer-

ence center, retail, and two golf courses. *Philadelphia Inquirer*, December 14, 18, 19, 2003, *Raleigh News and Observer*, December 23, 2003.

66. Governor McGreevey, quoted in *Courier-Post*, December 18, 2003. An associated *Courier-Post* headline December 17, 2003, read, "Mega Projects Bring New Hope to Camden." An *Inquirer* headline December 18, 2003 read, "American Dream Is Camden's Vision." A *Courier-Post* editorial appearing December 17 under the headline "Reinvest in Camden and Its People," concluded, "It really is starting to look as though Camden has turned the corner on recovery. . . . The building boom certainly benefits everyone who lives or works in Camden, but we shouldn't forget that a successful Camden is likely to be far more self-sufficient when it comes to the need for state aid. In other words, a stronger Camden benefits everyone in South Jersey and across the state." Under the headline, "A Comeback in Camden?" an *Inquirer* editorial, December 22, 2003, printed an insert in bold, "This serious, exciting plan for a struggling area shows how public investment can lure private capital."

67. *Cramer Hill Redevelopment Project: Proposal and Statement of Qualifications*, Cherokee Camden, Submitted to the Camden Redevelopment Agency, September 30, 2003.

68. *Philadelphia Inquirer*, March 17, 2004.

69. *Philadelphia Inquirer*, March 14, 2004.

70. Letter from Geneva Sanders, *Courier-Post*, February 6, 2004. See also letter from Gerald F. White, Pennsauken, January 20, 2004.

71. In a telephone conversation October 29, 2003, Heart of Camden director Christopher Auth reported that COO Primas, in telling Msgr. Doyle that the city would not sign off on funds that could be made available for further rehabilitation work in Waterfront South, suggested that the church pick up and move its facilities to operate elsewhere. Part of this story was further reported in a column by Kevin Riordan, *Courier-Post*, January 11, 2004, and in Msgr. Doyle's February 2004 newsletter, which was marked "urgent" in boldface on the top. See also Doyle's column, "Enclave Deserves a Clean Start," in the *Philadelphia Inquirer*, April 20, 2004.

72. *Philadelphia Inquirer*, March 14, 2004.

73. *Philadelphia Inquirer*, March 16, April 1, 7, 2004; *Courier-Post*, March 16, April 2, 9, 2004.

74. Interview, Camden, April 22, 2004.

75. See the commentary from Angel Cordero, "Camden Is Victimized Again," *Philadelphia Inquirer*, January 7, 2004, and news report, *Philadelphia Inquirer*, 4, 2004; *Courier-Post*, February 16, April 16, 2004.

76. Interview with Graciela Cavicchia, Camden, April 17, 2004; *Philadelphia Inquirer*, May 7, 2004.

77. State law authorized municipalities to designate areas "in need of redevelopment" and certified as enterprise zones to offer tax exemptions and tax abatements. The law further stated, in a section omitted from the planning report, that designation of a larger area for eminent domain was not authorized until approved by the municipal governing body and the planning board. It was impossible, therefore, to cite the law as a justification for a process that had yet to be completed. The planning department's justification for citing Cramer Hill's designation as an

enterprise zone appears on page 3 of the Cramer Hill Study Area Redevelopment Plan, submitted by the City of Camden Department of Development and Planning, April 19, 2004. The full text of the state enterprise regulation in question appears on page 3 of the critique submitted to the planning board by staff members of South Jersey Legal Services, May 11, 2004. Both documents are located in the Cramer Hill file, CCHS.

78. Interview with Thomas Holmes, II, Camden, December 10, 2002.

79. Cramer Hill Area Redevelopment Plan, 12–13. These figures were presented at the Cramer Hill meeting in the form of a power point presentation, which remained on the city's web site afterward.

80. Quotes from *Philadelphia Inquirer*, May 19, 2004; other information from observation and discussions at the Cramer Hill meeting.

81. Thomas Darden, letter in *Courier-Post*, May 20, 2004, quoted in *Philadelphia Inquirer*, May 20, 2004.

82. *Courier-Post, Philadelphia Inquirer*, July 1, 2004. The meeting was held at the Rutgers-Camden campus at 5 p.m. Despite the availability of buses to bring residents from Cramer Hill, the early hour and distant location clearly reduced attendance from the six hundred who attended the planning board meeting in Cramer Hill. Still, at least 150 people attended the final hearing, virtually all of them hostile to the plan with the exception of public officials and their staffs. A good summary of public reaction to the plan can be found in *New York Times* (New Jersey section), June 27, 2004.

83. Memo submitted to City of Camden Planning Board, May 11, 2004, by staff members of South Jersey Legal Services, Olga Pomar, David Podell, and David Rammler, Cramer Hill file, CCHS. The Cramer Hill proposal required new zoning, the critique pointed out, and its plan was inconsistent with the provisions of the *Mount Laurel* decisions "because the widespread use of eminent domain, resulting in the forcible taking and demolition of affordable homes, the displacement of residents from their community, and the failure to ensure the creation of replacement units that are truly affordable to persons with all ranges of income, including very low-income current residents, is contrary to the general welfare."

84. *Courier-Post*, March 9, 23, 24, 25, 30, June 1, 2004.

85. *Courier-Post*, August 5, 2004. According to this report, African Americans represented 27 percent of Lindenwold's population, but 35 percent of those in the redevelopment area. Hispanics constituted 8 percent of the population but 22 percent of the target area.

86. *Philadelphia Inquirer*, January 20, 2004.

87. *In re Adoption of the 2003 Low Income Housing Tax Credit Qualified Allocation Plan*, Superior Court of New Jersey Appellate Division, Docket No. A-0109–03T3, 41, 14.

88. With Philip Freeman, newly appointed and elected as chair despite his loss on the Norcross backed ticket in 2002, the board immediately signaled its shift to county control by replacing the lucrative insurance contract taken from Norcross by an independent board in the early 1990s with one assigned to a company with long ties to the county boss. Asked why contracts for the $500 million in new school funding in the city had yet to be let, the displaced holder of the contract answered,

"They will be now." Named as the new insurer was the same agency, McCollum, that Norcross supporters selected in 1991 when they took control of the school board and canceled a contract with Calif's firm. The premium at that time, according to the *Courier-Post*, May 16, 1991, was $800,000. Additionally, the board named a new labor attorney from a firm, Brown and Connery, which had been a major giver to county Democrats, and approved new banks as depositors, including Commerce. *Philadelphia Inquirer*, April 27, 2004; telephone conversation with insurance broker Benjamin Calif, April 29, 2004; *Courier-Post*, September 10, 2004. Once again, Other politicians proved central to evolving projects. Former U.S. Senator Robert Torricelli, whose trips to Camden to consider redevelopment opportunities were widely reported after he dropped out of his 2002 campaign for reelection, was hired by the developer seeking a favorable land deal in Camden for Cigna. State Senator Wayne Bryant provided the legislation the company sought to extend the 75 percent break on corporate taxes offered to companies relocating to Camden under the recovery legislation to premiums earned by banks and insurance companies. Bryant acted while a member of Equity Bank's board of directors. *Philadelphia Inquirer*, May 30, 31, June 6, 2003; *Courier-Post*, June 10, 2003. Cherokee too worked a political connection to enter Camden. Governor McGreevey's chief counsel, Michael R. DeCotiis's father, Robert, represented Cherokee in the company's two South Jersey projects. To the dismay of environmentalists, the younger DeCotiis added a fast-track approval process in "smart growth" areas as a concession to developers like Cherokee after the governor had set tight restrictions on development in the Highlands area of the state. This was first reported in the *Courier-Post*, October 22, 2004, as part of an assessment of environmental objections to Cherokee's plans to develop Petty's Island across from Pennsauken.

89. Primas had succeeded in reorganizing city government to consolidate all redevelopment functions in one office under the direction of his longtime ally Arijit De. By having City Council appoint himself to the Redevelopment Agency, which De also headed, Primas signaled clearly that proposals for reinvestment would be acted on swiftly and effectively in what would be a reversal of years of ineptitude in that function in the city. For De's appointment see *Courier-Post*, November 28, 2002.

90. The first steps in this process were taken at the Camden City Council meeting June 26, 2003, when resolutions were submitted for conducting the required determination of need study and to prepare a redevelopment plan for the North Camden Industrial Park, the Gateway neighborhood, Lanning Square, Cooper Plaza, the Central Waterfront, and Bergen Square (U.S. census tracts 6002-5 and 6007-8).

91. Referring to an earlier conflict over control of Governor James Florio's Camden Initiative, the *Courier-Post* editorialized on July 12, 1993, "Rescuing Camden, many people have come to recognize, is not just a question of doing the right thing. It's a question of enlightened self-interest. Leave the city isolated and in despair and it will continue to be a drag on the region. Revitalize it and the towns around it will benefit too. Camden residents have to be assured, however, that when the bulldozers arrive they will not be driven out to make way for other people. Camden's courageous and determined church and civic organizations—the ones

that have been rehabilitating houses and helping people all along—have to be assured that they will continue to be key players in the city's rebirth."

92. Jeffrey Nash column, "Revitalization Will Answer Prayers for Many Residents," *Courier-Post*, April 25, 2004.

93. Peter H. Schuck, *Diversity in America: Keeping Government at a Safe Distance* (Cambridge, Mass.: Belknap Press, 2003), 208–9. Because of that continued resistance to court-mandated integration, Schuck argues for greater use of housing vouchers which offer the advantage both of lower costs and less intrusive changes. In addition to his discussion of this issue in Chapter 6 in the above book, see his essay in *New York Times*, August 8, 2002, reacting to the New Jersey Supreme Court's decision upholding the builder's remedy in *Toll Brothers, Inc. v. Township of West Windsor* (A-103/104-00), discussed here in Chapter 7. The rising costs of those vouchers and their record of reconcentrating poor in marginal suburban locations such as Lindenwold, make Shuck's argument problematic, however.

94. Note: "Making Mixed-Income Communities Possible: Tax Base Sharing and Class Desegregation," *Harvard Law Review* 114 (March 2001): 1575. Marc Shuster, former solicitor for the Cherry Hill planning board, made the same point in a 2003 telephone conversation with me.

Conclusion

1. *Courier-Post* editorial, "City Within City, Great!" February 26, 1966.

2. See, for example, Jonetta Rose Barras, *The Last of the Black Emperors: The Hollow Comeback of Marion Barry in the Age of New Black Leaders* (Baltimore: Bancroft, 1998).

3. Robert Halpern, *Rebuilding the Inner City: A History of Neighborhood Initiatives to Address Poverty in the United States* (New York: Columbia University Press, 1995), 127–28.

4. David C. Perry, "The Politics of Dependency in Deindustrializing America: The Case of Buffalo, New York," in Michael Peter Smith and Joe R. Feagin, eds., *The Capitalist City: Global Restructuring and Community Politics* (Oxford: Basil Blackwell, 1987), 129.

5. *Philadelphia Inquirer*, November 7, 2004.

6. *Courier-Post*, November 17, December 1, 2004.

7. On the resistance to regional governance in particular, see Jon C. Teaford, *Post-Suburbia: Government and Politics in the Edge Cities* (Baltimore: Johns Hopkins University Press, 1997).

8. In this observation, this book affirms conclusions drawn by Robert Self, *American Babylon: Race and the Struggle for Postwar Oakland* (Princeton, N.J.: Princeton University Press, 2003); Lizabeth Cohen, *A Consumer's Republic: The Politics of Mass Consumption in Postwar America* (New York: Knopf, 2003); and David L. Kirp, John P. Dwyer, and Larry A. Rosenthal, *Race, Housing, and the Soul of Suburbia* (New Brunswick, N.J.: Rutgers University Press, 1995).

9. Interview with Charles Lyons, Camden, May 29, 2003. The *Courier-Post* reported elements of this plan on December 17, 2003.

10. David Rusk, *Inside Game/Outside Game: Winning Strategies for Saving Urban America* (Washington, D.C.: Brookings Institution Press, 1999), 324, 334.

11. Although the meeting assumed a form much like the faith-based conventions that generated extensive coverage in Camden, this suburban gathering was so lacking in precedent that it generated only a single column well after the fact, *Courier-Post*, November 4, 2004.

12. *Philadelphia Inquirer*, November 11, 2004. Neither the meeting nor the selection of Maley could be considered official, as the public members of the council had yet to be selected under the terms of the recovery legislation. The Camden Hub Smart Growth Plan was prepared by the Senator Walter Rand Institute for Public Affairs at Rutgers-Camden with the assistance of a state grant passed through Camden County. The draft plan was released in the spring of 2004, where it was aired at a few poorly attended meetings in the area, including a meeting in Camden June 30, the same night Camden City Council approved the Cramer Hill Redevelopment plan. The New Jersey Department of Community Affairs made a preliminary ruling as the plan circulated that the mayors serving in that planning process would serve on the regional impact council. As of the first meeting of the council, public members were yet to be appointed by the governor and the heads of each legislative branch.

13. *Courier-Post*, July 30, August 5, 2004. *Cramer Hill Residents Association et al. v. State of New Jersey, Melvin R. Primas, City of Camden, City of Camden Planning Board, Camden City Council, and Camden Redevelopment Agency*, Superior Court of New Jersey, Docket No. L 08135 04. Among the preemptive actions cited in the complaint were decisions by the planning board and city council to accept a redevelopment plan without considering the complaints submitted in writing or orally at public meetings. Votes were taken immediately after public comment in both instances. Although such actions may not have formed the most compelling legal portion of the complaint, there was precedent, in Washington, D.C., among other places, for halting redevelopment for lack of adequate public hearings. See Howard Gillette, Jr., *Between Justice and Beauty: Race, Planning, and the Failure of Urban Policy in Washington, D.C.* (Baltimore: Johns Hopkins University Press, 1995), 168.

Index

Acknowledgments

In completing this work, I have incurred more than the usual share of debts, none greater than to the many current and former residents of Camden who generously gave me their time and interest. In acknowledging in the text but a small portion of those I have talked to, I have not intended to slight anyone. Whether I have acknowledged their contributions directly in the text or not, I have benefitted immeasurably from the assistance I received from many different interested parties. Equally important has been the support I received from George Washington University, where a sabbatical leave helped me launch this effort during the 1997–98 academic year. A research grant from the National Endowment for the Humanities, added to a semester's leave from Rutgers-Camden, was crucial in helping me complete the work.

In Camden, I received early and considerable encouragement as well as information from Randy Primas, Tom Knoche, Peter O'Connor, Yolanda Auguilar DeNeeley, William Jenkins, Carmen Marinez, Ruth Bogutz, Jamie Reynolds, Judge Joseph Rodriguez, and Kevin Riordan, whose coverage of Camden for the *Courier-Post* during the 1990s was a major foundation for my understanding of the contemporary city. Over time many others assisted, most notably Tom Corcoran, Frank Fulbrook, Kelly Francis, Kevin Walsh, Olga Pomar, Roy Jones, Sue Brennan, Jeremy Nowak, Msgr. Robert McDermott, and the always quotable and passionate Msgr. Michael Doyle. Dwight Ott's continued coverage of Camden for the *Philadelphia Inquirer* into the new century proved another foundation for my own analysis.

I am grateful as well to Eric Schneider, fellow urbanist and friend, at the University of Pennsylvania, for reading an early draft of this manuscript and for providing insight and advice on earlier papers on the subject. Ed Fox, Tom Knoche, and Olga Pomar read complete drafts of the manuscript and provided many helpful suggestions. Ruth Bogutz, Paul Schopp, Kevin Walsh, and Camilo Jose Vergara also read and commented on parts of the draft. Steven Conn and especially an anonymous reader for the University of Pennsylvania Press provided thorough and compelling criticisms. Bob

Lockhart remained encouraging and patient throughout the two years this manuscript was before him at the University of Pennsylvania Press. Lauren Osborne's wonderful editing suggestions helped bring the manuscript to completion.

A number of people I met in the course of this work have died in recent years. I especially regret the losses of Carmela Argenteiri, who not only informed but fed me on a number of occasions, and Donza Harmon, who dared to share her dreams as well as the formidable challenges facing her life. Missed too will be Joseph Carroll, Jim Harris, and especially Poppy Sharp, whose dedication to civic well-being motivated them to the end of their lives. Though I knew them less well, I share with many others the sense of great loss, of Sister Peg Hynes, Gloria Lyons, and Odessa Polk-Jones, all of whom have left powerful legacies to their Camden communities.

I am especially grateful as well to Skip Hidlay, former executive editor of the *Courier-Post,* both for bringing my research interest to the attention of his readers and for granting me access to news clips in the paper's back files. Pat Straub was a wonderful guide to those materials and a cheerful companion during long hours of research. Thanks too to the paper's current executive editor, Derek Osenenko, for the use of photographs from the *Courier*'s files, without which much of this could not be animated. I have had the pleasure of working closely with photographer Camilo José Vergara, on the next Camden project, and I am grateful both for the photograph that graces the front page of this book and for the assistance of the Ford Foundation for underwriting his continued work in Camden. Thanks too to Bernice Gouch for sharing her extensive collection of Camden photographs.

From the start, staff members at the Camden County Historical Society have been tremendously helpful and supportive, including Joanne Seitter and Jean Crensczi and former directors Paul Schoop and John Seitter. Professor Robert Beauregard of the New School, generously shared notes and clippings he had gathered some years earlier for a study of Camden. My former colleague Robert Fishman, now at the University of Michigan, wrote letters endorsing this project well before the National Endowment provided support. Tom Sugrue must have made the difference, for with his added support, the National Endowment responded with assistance. I have greatly valued Tom's insights, not just in his writing but also through his comments in a twentieth century American history reading group we have belonged to. Finally, I want to thank my provost, Roger Dennis, for the occasional opportunity to discuss Camden's recovery process but most of all for standing fully behind the academic freedom to explore this topic wherever it took me. Neither he nor any others who have been so generous with their time or insight are responsible for my conclusions.

Earlier versions of portions of Chapters 3, 4, and 8 were published as "The Wages of Disinvestment: How Money and Politics Aided the Decline of Camden, New Jersey," in Jefferson Cowie and Joseph Heathcott, eds., *Beyond the Ruins: The Meanings of Deindustrialization* (Ithaca, N.Y.: Cornell University Press, 2003). Reprinted by permission of Cornell University Press.